QUANTITATIVE SOCIAL SCIENCE DATA WITH R

Sara Miller McCune founded SAGE Publishing in 1965 to support the dissemination of usable knowledge and educate a global community. SAGE publishes more than 1000 journals and over 800 new books each year, spanning a wide range of subject areas. Our growing selection of library products includes archives, data, case studies and video. SAGE remains majority owned by our founder and after her lifetime will become owned by a charitable trust that secures the company's continued independence.

Los Angeles | London | New Delhi | Singapore | Washington DC | Melbourne

2nd Edition

QUANTITATIVE SOCIAL SCIENCE DATA WITH R

An introduction

BRIAN J. FOGARTY

Los Angeles | London | New Delhi
Singapore | Washington DC | Melbourne

Los Angeles | London | New Delhi
Singapore | Washington DC | Melbourne

SAGE Publications Ltd
1 Oliver's Yard
55 City Road
London EC1Y 1SP

SAGE Publications Inc.
2455 Teller Road
Thousand Oaks, California 91320

SAGE Publications India Pvt Ltd
B 1/I 1 Mohan Cooperative Industrial Area
Mathura Road
New Delhi 110 044

SAGE Publications Asia-Pacific Pte Ltd
3 Church Street
#10-04 Samsung Hub
Singapore 049483

Editor: Jai Seaman
Editorial assistant: Rhiannon Holt
Assistant editor, digital:
Production editor: Ian Antcliff
Copyeditor: Richard Leigh
Proofreader: Richard Walshe
Marketing manager: Ben Griffin-Sherwood
Cover design: Shaun Mercier
Typeset by: C&M Digitals (P) Ltd, Chennai, India

Library of Congress Control Number: 2022944907

British Library Cataloguing in Publication data

A catalogue record for this book is available from the British Library

ISBN 978-1-5297-9046-7
ISBN 978-1-5297-9045-0 (pbk)

TABLE OF CONTENTS

PREFACE

INTRODUCTION

There continues to be little need for another statistics textbook. Last I checked, the equations for the standard error and linear regression have not changed and the mathematical details of introductory statistics can be found in hundreds of texts and other resources. However, there is still a need for books that take students and practitioners through step-by-step procedures for hands-on analysis of quantitative social science (QSS) data.

One common reason students choose to study social sciences at university is that they were not good at or interested in STEM subjects in secondary school. If someone excelled in mathematics and wanted to work with data, they probably would be studying statistics or a similar subject. However, students in social science subjects often need to work with and analyse quantitative data for courses, theses, and dissertations. This is particularly the case for students pursuing graduate degrees in the social sciences. As data increasingly dominates our world, people already in the workforce may also feel unprepared to work with data and perform statistical analysis, and are pursuing self-learning to increase their skill set. It is not uncommon for people in these situations to experience anxiety when approaching the material for the first time. Here's the thing though: *data analysis really does not require mathematics*. It requires an interest in using quantitative data to make sense of the social world. It may be a different way of thinking about the world, but it should not be scary or make you see ghosts.

I use myself as an example of learning quantitative social science. I have taught undergraduate and graduate quantitative methods (QM) for over 15 years, have published QM articles, and now I am writing the second edition of a QM book. However, as an undergraduate I studied Political Science, History, and Medieval Studies. To be sure, studying Dante and Cicero did not prepare me for writing R code and running regression models. It was not until graduate school that I fully understood and appreciated the importance and value of working with quantitative social science data.

Students in quantitative social science courses often ask how what they are learning is different from what their friends are learning in statistics? In reality, it is not. The difference is that we are working with social science data, focusing on applications to the social world, and not, for example, trying to compare samples of the widths of fruit fly wings. In many quantitative social science courses and in this book, we are also not getting bogged down with the mathematics behind statistics. Greek letters and equations do exist in this book, but they should not activate our fight or flight response. They should be thought of as symbolic representations of ideas and concepts. Just as the Union Jack represents the nations of England, Scotland, Wales, and Northern Ireland or the 50 stars on the American flag represents the 50 states of the U.S., we use, for example, the Greek letter μ to represent the average and the Greek letter β to represent a regression coefficient. We use symbols and equations to represent and convey sometimes complicated ideas in a short amount of space.

Students also often ask why an employer might prefer someone with a quantitative social science background than a traditional statistics background? Quantitative social science focuses not only on the methods, but also emphasizes the importance of interpreting and discussing statistical results in a way the average person can understand. We are able to bring social science theory and context to help make sense of data and statistical results. Statistics undergraduates are taught the mathematics and methods with typically minimal attention to the substance. QSS students know why certain variables exist in models and the broader societal, political, economic, etc., implications of the results. For statistics students, it is all about the data and methods. This is not to put down statisticians – I am a big fan of statisticians – but QSS teaches us how to bring the context to the data. To answer the question that started this paragraph: it depends on the job. Some employers may want a technically skilled statistician for a specific position – here, quantitative social scientists can't compete. Other employers want people who have and can combine substantive knowledge with data and statistical skills: this is quantitative social scientists' bread-and-butter.

WHAT DOES THIS BOOK COVER?

This book covers content and materials commonly taught in multidisciplinary/interdisciplinary introductory QSS courses at the undergraduate and graduate levels. The materials are pitched as multidisciplinary/interdisciplinary as a means of breaking down disciplinary silos that are increasingly irrelevant for contemporary QSS. A consequence of this approach is that the book does not cover all the topics, methods, and techniques that every social science field thinks is critical. However, this book should provide a strong foundation to allow easy mastery of more discipline-specific methods and applications in R.

The core feature of the book is that it takes you step-by-step through all the material in R. We get into the nitty-gritty of R and try to address common questions, errors, and sticking points commonly encountered by students and new R users. Working with data and performing data analysis is often messy, dirty, and, at times, frustrating. R is something that can only be learned by putting in the time; and not simply reading, watching, and listening. The text should provide the support needed to make this all a less Herculean journey.

CHANGES IN THE SECOND EDITION

Since the first edition, the world has substantially changed in good and bad ways, as tends to happen. Foremost, we have collectively been hit by a global pandemic, which has flipped many people's lives upside down. A silver lining of the pandemic lockdowns is that (some) people had the time to advance R's and RStudio's functionality through a wave of new and updated packages. While keeping up-to-date on everything new in R can feel like Sisyphus pushing the boulder up a hill, some of the new-new in R is stickier than others. Specifically, the **tidyverse** suite of packages, and its ever expanding universe of extensions and modifications, has come to dominate how we work with and visualise data in R. The establishment and growth of **tidymodels** packages has further extended `tidyverse` principals into data modelling, machine learning, and natural language processing.

This edition incorporates core **tidyverse**'s functions and packages throughout all of the chapters and content. This is most drastically seen in how we manage data and manipulate variables. At first glance `tidyverse` functions can appear daunting, particularly when we link functions together using *piping*. However, once we get used to `tidyverse`, its intuitiveness, functionality, and flexibility becomes clearly evident.

This edition also provides brief treatments of utilising **tidymodels** for different statistical analysis techniques. We don't go all-in on using `tidymodels` since its functions and packages are primarily designed for machine learning applications in R. Therefore, performing simple analyses with `tidymodels` can be laborious and circuitous. Instead, we'll use many of the same R functions and packages to conduct statistical analysis that appeared in the first edition.

There are two new chapters on **generalised linear models (GLMs)** as a next step beyond linear regression. Although GLMs can encompass a wide variety of different regression techniques, our focus is on using GLMs for analysing categorical outcome variables (i.e., non-continuous outcome variables). Categorical variables make up the majority of social science datasets and often there is nary a continuous outcome variable in sight (e.g., survey data) to use in a linear regression model. Therefore, it is important to at least have a cursory understanding of how to analyse categorical outcome variables. After a brief discussion of maximum likelihood estimation, Chapter 13 provides an introduction to binary outcome, ordered outcome, and nominal outcome regression models in R. Chapter 14 addresses humans' love for counting things by covering count regression models in R. Both chapters may be advanced for some readers, but the material is presented in a very user-friendly, applied manner.

Finally, most of the messages and warnings that R throws our way are removed from this edition's text. They were purposefully included in the first edition to demonstrate the messiness of working with real data in R. In retrospect, they may have come across more as sloppiness than managed chaos. Just realise that working with R will likely be dirtier and more frustrating than what is found in this book.

WHO IS THIS BOOK FOR?

As with the first edition, this book is designed for people starting to learn quantitative social science and R in undergraduate or graduate courses and programmes. Individuals performing self-learning and those coming to R after years (or decades) of using other statistical programs like Stata and SPSS should also find great value and benefit in the book's content.

ACKNOWLEDGMENTS

First and foremost I want to acknowledge my wife and kids for their infinite support while working on both editions of this book.

I want to acknowledge and thank Jai Seaman and the people at SAGE for the opportunity to write this second edition. I also want to thank the reviewers, lecturers, professors, students, and readers who have provided valuable feedback on the first edition and comments and suggestions for this edition. This includes the insight and contributions from members of the Q-Step community. Finally, I want to acknowledge colleagues at Glasgow and Notre Dame for their support and assistance.

ABOUT THE AUTHOR

Brian Fogarty is Director of the Center for Social Science Research, and Associate Director and Associate Professor of the Practice in the Lucy Family Institute for Data & Society at the University of Notre Dame, USA. He is also a concurrent Associate Professor of the Practice in the Department of Political Science at Notre Dame. Brian has taught undergraduate and graduate quantitative methods courses in political and social science for more than 15 years at universities in the USA and UK. His research interests include political communication, quantitative methodology, and voting and elections.

ONLINE RESOURCES

Quantitative Social Science Data with R is supported by a wealth of online resources for lecturers to aid study and support teaching, which are available at https://study.sagepub.com/Fogarty2e.

FOR LECTURERS

- **Lecturer's guide** provides you with suggested exercises and solutions to use in class or for assignments and directs you towards further resources such as datasets, code, weblinks and video screencasts.
- **PowerPoint decks** with additional chapter guidance that can be downloaded and customised for use in your own lectures and presentations.

1

INTRODUCTION

Chapter contents

WHAT IS QUANTITATIVE SOCIAL SCIENCE?

What is quantitative social science (QSS)? Although it is a mouthful to say, it is probably the most accurate term to describe what we will be doing in this book. *Quantitative* simply means we are working with numbers, specifically data, and *social science* is, well, the broad subject that we are studying. Hence, QSS can be considered to be *studying social science using numeric data and analysis*. QSS is a more generic term for studying social science with data than something like *social science statistics* because the latter communicates certain connotations; in particular, it is 'statistics' that makes the public and students shiver in their boots. Different social science subjects and fields use different labels for quantitative social scientists – such as *political methodologist*, *methodologist*, or *social statistician*, and a bit more specific to the type of analysis such as *psychometrician* or *econometrician*. But all of these different scientists can be considered to be quantitative social scientists.

More importantly, social science 'methodologists' increasingly understand the need to embrace techniques and methods from all branches of social science and certain STEM fields (e.g., statistics, computer science). It is not possible for researchers to only use and focus on methods of their particular field and become tunnel-visioned. Political scientists are not the only ones who use survey research, psychologists are not the only ones who conduct experiments, and geographers are not the only ones who work with spatial data. Therefore, possibly more than ever, these researchers really need to be *quantitative social scientists*.

Quantitative social science is not statistics, not mathematics, and not computer science. The critical, and obvious, difference is that QSS is interested in social science questions first and foremost. QSS is about using, and developing, the best techniques to answer social, economic, and political phenomena of interest. Although statisticians, for instance, often work with social science data, their interests more often lie with applying new techniques and methods to different datasets; and not necessarily answering substantive questions with statistics. Computer scientists are more concerned with the computational and prediction metrics of algorithms than whether the algorithms provide substantive insight into, for example, opinion diffusion of a particular policy on Twitter.

Data scientist is a trendy term to refer to people who blend computer science and statistics techniques and approaches, often involving machine learning and artificial intelligence, in data analysis. Although the term is at risk of losing its meaning, like 'big data' has, we can think of data science as using techniques beyond traditional applied statistics. Most quantitative social scientists are not data scientists. Probably a better term for quantitative social scientists who use data science techniques (e.g., machine learning, natural language processing) is *computational social scientist*. This semantic difference stems from the application and motivation of computational methods to answer substantively interesting social science questions. This book does not cover data science techniques. However, the skills we learn in this book (particularly the R skills) provide a foundation for pursuing data science.

Important for students learning QSS is that not knowing advanced mathematics really does not matter.[1] Knowing maths can help flatten the learning curve, but in this book we are not going to worry about how to find the area under a curve or find the maximum of a function. As noted in the preface, what is required for QSS is an interest in using quantitative data to answer social science questions and phenomena; you only need to 'like' numbers in the most general sense.

---

[1]However, the emphasis on mathematics varies depending on who is teaching the course.

Contemporary QSS and this book are not about mathematics and formulae, but about analysing data using computers. There is no way around this. If you do not feel comfortable with using a computer, you may feel overwhelmed trying to learn this material. You do not need to have vast coding experience, but knowing the ins and outs of basic computing, specifically how to download and install software, is critical. If you frequently use computers and/or are a digital native, there should be nothing mystifying in this book as regards computing skills. If you only know how to turn on the computer, this book may seem like drinking water from a fire hydrant.

What QSS is not about is qualitative data, methods, and analysis. It does not deal with conducting interviews, focus groups, carrying out case studies, discourse analysis, etc. Qualitative analysis has its time, place, and usage. But QSS concerns what we do when we have quantitative data; and/or how to find quantitative data. People have strong opinions and, frankly, existential debates on quantitative versus qualitative research and analysis. There is little need to laboriously rehash or summarise this divide here. But there are a few things to consider regarding the difference between quantitative and qualitative analysis.

First, quantitative analysis can be more objective than most qualitative analysis. Good qualitative researchers understand that it is impossible to be objective regarding their subject and smartly integrate their bias into their discussion and conclusions. Bad qualitative researchers probably know they cannot be objective, but pretend they are merely holding up a mirror to reality. To be fair, all research involves some sort of non-objectivity in that the choices made by researchers can affect findings and conclusions. Probably the least objective part of quantitative analysis involves creating new datasets; for example, crafting survey questions can easily introduce bias (consciously or not). However, particularly with secondary data analysis, in quantitative analysis I can tell you what data and specific methods were used, and provide the code that was used to produce the results.

This leads to the second point: quantitative analysis allows for easy replication and thus greater transparency. Replication involves other researchers using the same data, methods, and code being able to identically reproduce the original findings.[2] This assures that researchers are not 'making things up' or are being biased – intentionally or not. If researchers know their work is subject to replication and scrutiny, they are less likely to intentional create falsehoods. In the long run, this creates good science. Qualitative research, on the other hand, is unreplicable in the sense that it would be impossible for multiple researchers to come to identical findings. Even if researchers were provided all the original primary research materials (e.g., interview transcripts and notes), their findings and conclusions would not be identical.

Finally, quantitative analysis allows us to generalise our findings to some extent; again, something that is impossible to do in qualitative analysis. To generalise means to take our results from sample data, for instance, and make an informed statement about the population from which the sample originates. For example, if we had a well-constructed and well-implemented survey of the Kenyan public's political attitudes, we would be able to make informed statements about the political attitudes of all Kenyans – of course, subject to some error. But we would not be able to only interview people in Nairobi and then generalise the results to people in Mombasa.

Qualitative analysis is most useful and valuable in circumstances where it is impossible to carry out quantitative analysis. It might be that the topic of interest is impossible to measure or that

---

[2]Some refer to this process as *duplication* rather than *replication* (see Gayle and Lambert, 2017).

obtaining the data is impractically arduous, and in these situations qualitative analysis is the way to go. But, frankly, if we can use quantitative analysis to study some topic than we should.

When quantitative social scientists carry out data analysis they all do so in their own unique ways. What data to use, how to get the data, the type of statistical program, the particular coding syntax, the choice of R functions, the type of analysis, and how to understand the results are always different. Therefore, how we do things in this book may well differ from how your instructor does things, how you will eventually do things, and how other researchers carry out QSS.

LAYOUT OF THIS BOOK

In the next 14 chapters, we will cover the basics of R, how to get data and manipulate variables, and learn introductory to intermediate data analysis (i.e., statistical analysis) all in R.

In *Chapter 2* we will discuss how to find and install R and RStudio, how to download and load R packages, and go through the basics of the RStudio interface and its functionality. In *Chapter 3* we will discuss the differences between primary and secondary data, and how to find and download secondary data from a variety of sources. In *Chapter 4* we will examine how to get data into R and RStudio, how to wrangle datasets in the aggregate, and how to save our datasets. This chapter provides our first adventure in how to wrangle and work with data and variables. We will continue the wrangling in *Chapter 5* by considering various ways to recode and manipulate variables in R.

Chapter 6 takes a brief break from using R to discuss how to create good empirical hypotheses. Though potentially a pedantic and dull exercise, we will try to have some fun with the examples.

Chapter 7 provides our first proper taste of data analysis in R by looking at univariate and descriptive statistics. We will examine measures of central tendency and dispersion, and simple ways they can be used to create interesting narratives about race and segregation in the USA. In *Chapter 8* we will begin to consider how to visualise data and quantitative relationships. Though we will only touch on the basics, the chapter provides a strong foundation for *data visualisation* using the `ggplot2` R package.

In *Chapter 9* we will discuss the foundations and origins of hypothesis testing and the tricky notion of *statistical significance*. We end the chapter by conducting hypothesis testing through using difference-in-means tests and nonparametric analysis in R. *Chapter 10* extends hypothesis testing to analysing bivariate relationships. We will consider measures of association, chi-square analysis, and correlation analysis in R.

Chapters 11 and 12 provide our first introduction to multivariate analysis by examining the ins and outs of linear regression. Chapter 11 lays out the foundation of linear regression, ordinary least squares (OLS) estimation, and its implementation in R. A critical aspect of this chapter is learning how to understand the results from R and convert them into plain language that normal humans can understand. In Chapter 12 we intricately go through the assumptions of OLS, how to test the assumptions, and possible solutions to violations.

In *Chapters 13 and 14* we move beyond linear regression and expand our skill set through a hands-on introduction to generalised linear models (GLMs). GLMs provide regression-based analytical techniques for when the outcome variable does not meet the requirements for linear regression. In Chapter 13 we will examine binary outcome (logit and probit models), ordered outcome (ordered logit and ordered probit models), and unordered outcome (multinomial logit and multinomial probit models) regression models. Chapter 14 extends GLMs for analysing count data where we will work through common count (Poisson and negative binomial models) regression models. GLMs can be a rather advanced topic in an introductory book. Therefore, our focus will be on the application of these models in R.

We conclude the book in *Chapter 15* by bringing together the material we learned through the chapters by analysing Kenyans' satisfaction with their political system and support for an authoritarian government using data from the World Values Survey. This final chapter of the book provides a solid run-down of (almost) everything it takes to carry out successful QSS projects.

2

INTRODUCTION TO R AND RSTUDIO

Chapter contents

R can be difficult to use, has a steep learning curve, and can be a temperamental teammate in our data analysis pursuits. So, why do we use it? First, it is *free*! Since academics and students usually have little or no money, free is something to be valued. Second, and most importantly, we can perform almost any type of statistical analysis in R – from the simplest to the most advanced – and every day there are more and more techniques and methods being added to the R toolkit. Third, recent advances have made R one of the best statistical programs for producing aesthetically appealing data visualisations. Fourth, learning R and its code-based approach to data analysis will make using other commonly used statistical programs in the social sciences (e.g., Stata and SPSS) much easier. Fifth, learning the R programming language will allow you to more easily learn other programming languages such Python and Ruby, if you so choose. If, like me, you are coming to R through a social science pathway, you probably are not experienced in programming languages; do not worry, almost no social scientists began university with programming experience. Sixth, and potentially most importantly for university students, R will make you considerably more employable and more competitive in applying to graduate programmes. Odds are that you want to get a job (or to go to graduate school) after your undergraduate studies, and learning R will put you ahead of most other social science graduates.

R was originally developed in the mid-1990s, but it was not until the turn of the millennium that quantitative social scientists begin to use the program over rivals like Stata, SPSS, and SAS. The initial users of R liked the open-source format which allowed them to write and execute their own statistical methods and applications. For those of us who had no background in programming, the original R interface left much to be desired. In fact, R's interface really has not changed much over the past two decades.

```
R RGui (64-bit)
File  Edit  View  Misc  Packages  Windows  Help

R Console

R version 4.1.2 (2021-11-01) -- "Bird Hippie"
Copyright (C) 2021 The R Foundation for Statistical Computing
Platform: x86_64-w64-mingw32/x64 (64-bit)

R is free software and comes with ABSOLUTELY NO WARRANTY.
You are welcome to redistribute it under certain conditions.
Type 'license()' or 'licence()' for distribution details.

  Natural language support but running in an English locale

R is a collaborative project with many contributors.
Type 'contributors()' for more information and
'citation()' on how to cite R or R packages in publications.

Type 'demo()' for some demos, 'help()' for on-line help, or
'help.start()' for an HTML browser interface to help.
Type 'q()' to quit R.

>
```

The non-user-friendliness of R added to the lack of uptake by quantitative social scientists, and using R became a status symbol in some social science fields, signalling that the researcher was hardcore. This all changed around 10 years ago with the introduction of RStudio as an integrated development environment (IDE) for working in R. In essence, RStudio took all the disparate, opaque parts of R and developed a considerably more user-friendly way to use R. Now quantitative researchers view R not as a mountain to climb but a hill. Since its initial release, RStudio has continued to make significant advances in usability and operationalisation of R through inclusion of various options, extensions, and interoperatility tools. For example, R Markdown has revolutionised how researchers write papers, books, and reports; Shiny has revolutionised how data analysis can be taught on the internet and has provided an open-source solution for building data dashboards; and more recent developments have focused on interoperatility such as the ability to leverage the functionality of Spark and TensorFlow for machine learning applications in R.

This chapter serves as an introduction to R and RStudio, and provides the basics of getting the software set up and a run-down of the basic syntax and output. The only way we learn programs like R and RStudio is to get our hands dirty and simply do the work. This book will help you in that process by providing a gentle introduction to conducting data analysis in R through using real-world social science data and a conversational narrative. There are also copious R books, R websites, and R discussion boards to find all sorts of information, help, and advice. The large and growing R community essentially ensures you'll always be able to find a solution to your problem.

One final comment on coming to R without previous programming or statistical software knowledge: learning R programming and performing analysis in R can easily feel massively overwhelming. We all want to sprint to complete our analysis and move on to the next thing on our to-do list (e.g., other data analysis, writing a paper, going to bed). When we get stuck on something in R, we can easily become frustrated, annoyed, or despondent. When this happens, and as a general approach to learning R, remember to take things *bird by bird*. Originating with the writer Anne Lamott in her 1994 book *Bird by Bird* and more recently referenced in the television show *Ted Lasso*, the phrase means to take things step by step, complete one small task, go to the next small task, and not to let the magnitude of something paralyse you. Terrific advice!

By the end of this chapter, you should be able to:

- Find and install R and RStudio
- Understand the layout of RStudio
- Understand R scripts and R Markdown documents
- Know how to set up working directories
- Know how to write basic R syntax
- Find, install, and load R packages

FINDING AND INSTALLING R AND RSTUDIO

Wait, I thought this book uses R? What's the deal with RStudio? This book uses the R programming language, but we use the RStudio IDE to actually work in R. As mentioned previously, RStudio is an extremely user-friendly interface for working with R. Therefore, we need to download software for R and RStudio.

OK, where do we find R and RStudio, and how do we install them? Finding and installing R is not difficult, particularly if you have experience downloading and installing software. We need to have R installed before we can use RStudio, so let's start with downloading and installing R. R can be downloaded from the Comprehensive R Archive Network (CRAN) by either googling R or going directly to this URL: https://cran.r-project.org/.

On the homepage, click on the download option that applies to you – likely Mac or Windows. The instructions are slightly different depending on whether you are using a Mac or PC. For the Mac version, you are directly taken to a page that has an installation package (with the suffix .pkg) that you download and follow the instructions. For the PC version, you are directed to a page with a few options, but most importantly there is a link called install R for the first time. After you click on that link, you are taken to a page where at the top in large letters there is a link for downloading R. R frequently comes out with updated versions, hence the version numbers, but we do not need to frequently update our version. The reason is that the new versions of R are usually not fundamentally different. Additionally, when we update R, we often will need to reinstall or update all of R packages, which can be laborious. The main time that we do update our version of R is when it comes out with a substantially different version (e.g., the release of R 4.0 in 2020) and when packages become out of date and are no longer supported by our version of R. After you save the execute file, simply follow the installation instructions.

Now that R is installed on our computer, we want to install RStudio. To do so, either google RStudio or go directly to this URL: https://posit.co/.[1] On Posit's main page, hover on the Products tab at the top of the page and click on the RStudio IDE option. Over the years, Posit has added and continually adds commercial versions and additional products to its base RStudio software. This can make navigating through Posit's webpage a little tricky and it's easy to become distracted by the bling. Just remember that we want the *free* version, which is the Open Source Edition IDE option.

---

[1]In Autumn 2022, RStudio, the company, changed its name to Posit. However, RStudio, the product, is still named RStudio.

Detailed Product
Comparison

	Professional
Open Source Edition	RStudio Desktop Pro
The Premier IDE for R	The RStudio IDE, superpowered for your professional workflow
Pricing	
Free	**$995** per year
DOWNLOAD RSTUDIO DESKTOP	BUY NOW
✓ Access the RStudio IDE locally	ALL OF THE FEATURES OF OPEN

Scroll down the page and click on the button that says DOWNLOAD RSTUDIO DESKTOP. We are now directed to a new page with two RStudio download options. We want the first option titled RStudio Desktop with the Open Source License (the free desktop one); click on DOWNLOAD. (Posit's website makes it sound like you get awesome additional things with the paid version. Yet I do not know anyone in academia who has a paid version.)

Step 2: Install RStudio
Desktop

DOWNLOAD RSTUDIO DESKTOP FOR WINDOWS

Size: 202.76MB | SHA-256: FC8F64B4 | Version: 2022.12.0+353 |
Released: 2022-12-15

All Installers and Tarballs

We now find and click on the installer that matches our computer's operating system – again, likely Mac or Windows – and then save and run the executable file. Simply follow the instructions for installing RStudio on your computer and everything should be good to go.

After we have installed R and RStudio there should be icons on the desktop and/or the programs listed in the Start menu (for PC) or Applications folder (for Mac). We can double-click on the R icon to take a look at the raw ugliness, but instead let's double-click on the RStudio icon and begin our adventure.

ENVIRONMENT AND LAYOUT OF RSTUDIO

Let's a take a few minutes to go through the layout of RStudio and look at a few critical aspects. As mentioned, the best way to learn R and RStudio is through using and playing around with the software. Since R and RStudio are free and we can easily download and install the software on our own computer, we should have more freedom to play around and get our bearings than we would if we were stuck in a computer lab using statistical software that costs money like Stata and SPSS.

Every RStudio user has their own preferences and ways to do things. Some of these differences are quirks and pet peeves, and some are larger ways of operating. In this book, we will make use of the RStudio environment, but we will not use all the various point-and-click options that exist.[2] Instead, we will do most things using R code. There are several reasons for this. First, if we become reliant on current point-and-click options and those options change or disappear in the future, we may struggle to figure out how to do something. Second, using code forces us to gain a deeper understanding of the R programming language than we would from relying on point-and-click options. Third, writing and saving R code allows us to more easily share our work in R and simplifies replication tasks for other R users.

The following screen is what you see when you open RStudio:

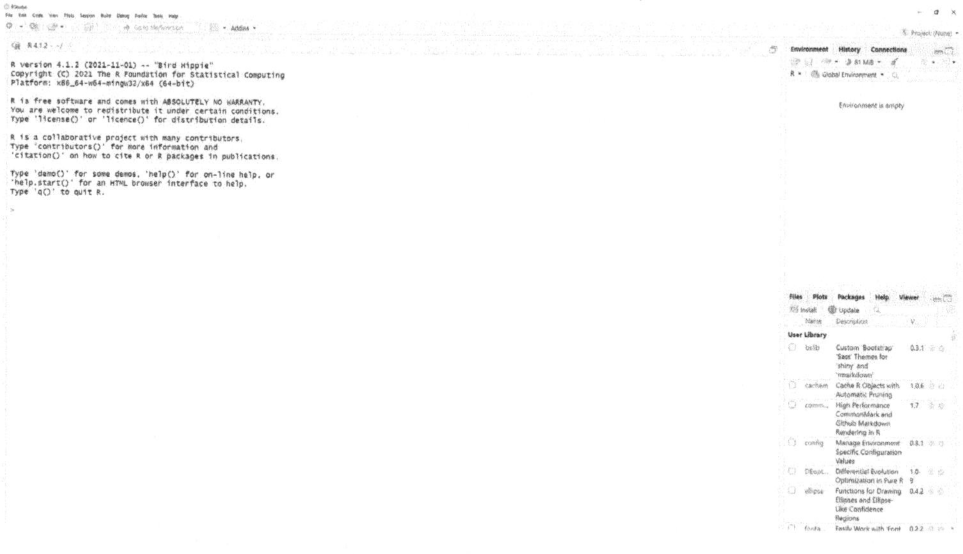

Each time we open R or RStudio, we start what is called a new *session*. The main large window on the left-hand side, titled `Console`, is where we can type in R commands and where the main output is displayed. On the right-hand side, there are two windows with several tabs – generally referred to as the `Workspace Browser` – which are customisable via drop-down menus (`Tools >`

---

[2]In truth, RStudio is not full of drop-down menus with point-and-click options, particularly compared to programs like SPSS.

Global Options). The top window traditionally has two main tabs: Environment where the different datasets, values, and functions we have loaded in and created during our RStudio session will be listed, and History where a list of all the code we have ever typed into the Console window is kept. We can include additional tabs such as Connections which lists any external database connections we have launched (e.g., Spark). The Environment information is available if we save our workspace on exiting RStudio and load it when launching it again. We will not focus on saving and loading workspaces in this book, because we will make use of R scripts and it is not necessary to deal with workspaces; also it is nice to start with a clean slate so that we are less likely to make errors. However, many researchers do save and load their workspaces. It is something to consider if we do not want to repeat any code or analyses when starting a new session of RStudio.

The bottom window on the right-hand side includes six different tabs: Files, Plots, Packages, Help, Viewer, and Presentation. The Files tab gives us a list of all the files in the current directory. The Plots tab shows us any plots we have created, while the Packages tab gives us a list of all the R packages installed in our R library folder. We will discuss packages more below, but we can think of packages as folders of different kinds of R functions. We can think of functions as instructions that tell R to do different things. For example, the function mean() tells R to give us the mean (or average) value of a certain variable or object. In order to use different techniques and methods in R, we need to have those functions installed in our R library and loaded in our current session. There is a basic set of packages that are automatically installed when we first download R and allow us to use basic functions. R classifies these default packages as either base or recommended. We will see the default set of packages listed in the Packages tab or by running installed.packages(). As we progress and need different R functions, we will need to install additional R packages, and thus slowly grow our library. Next is the Help tab that, unsurprisingly, provides R documentation for any R function. We can type in the relevant R code that we want more information on and RStudio will provide basic documentation on the function. The documentation is not always the most illuminating as it is derived from the information in the reference manual on CRAN. Some developers provide clear explanations of the functions, while other developers provide bare-bones information. We can also type ? followed by the function name in the Console window and the documentation will appear in the Help tab window. We may prefer to just google the function to find more information, documentation, and tutorials than what is included in the help tab, though obviously this does not work if you are not connected to the internet. The Viewer tab allows us to view or locate web content; I never use this window. The final tab is Presentation, which displays HTML slides from a Quarto file; I have never used this window.[3]

If we wanted to, we could type code directly into the Console window, hit Enter on our keyboard, and see the output. Our code would be saved in the History tab or we could use an external code editor such as Emacs or Notepad++. However, there is a much better way to use R in RStudio. In the top-left corner of RStudio is a menu item titled File, similar to Word. If we do not have a pre-existing file, we want to click on New File, which opens a menu to the right, and then we want to click on the first option, R Script.

---

[3]Quatro is a new publishing system that has been integrated into RStudio. Quatro is very similar to R Markdown, but is more flexible since it allows R, Python, JavaScript, and Julia programming languages.

When we do this a new window opens at the top of the left-hand side and pushes the `Console` window down. We can write code and notes in this new window, and save them for future use; this is the same thing as a Stata do-file.

We want to save the file to some place that we can locate again and the file will save with the suffix .R, which stands for R script. This is what we will use for the rest of this book to write all our code and do all of our analysis. Not only can we save a script file and reopen it at a later date, but also using a script file allows us to easily make corrections to errors in our code. To *run* the code in the `Console` window, we can highlight the code either using our mouse or clicking on the line numbers, and then click on the option `Run` on the window's toolbar. Alternatively, after we highlight the code, we can run the code using `Ctrl + Enter (for Windows)` or `Cmd + Return (for Mac)`.

An alternative to using an R script is to use an R Markdown file (which has a .Rmd file suffix). R Markdown allows a seamless integration of plain text, code, and output into a single document – specifically a Word, pdf, or HTML document. So, instead of writing up a Word document, for example, and then copying and pasting in R code and output, R Markdown does it all simultaneously. Not only does R Markdown make it easier to write up results, but it also looks much better.

We start an R Markdown file by clicking `File > New File > R Markdown`. To include R code, which will be automatically run by R Markdown, we place the code a shaded section (known as a *chunk*) by typing three quotation marks (```` ```{r} ````), include our R code, and then end the section with three quotation marks (```` ``` ````). Any text we type outside of the code chunk is treated as plain text. When we are ready to create our document (e.g., a Word document), we click on the `Knit` icon in the top toolbar. There are many options and formatting tricks for R Markdown, but even creating a basic version is an improvement over copying and pasting.[4]

WORKING DIRECTORIES

Each time a new R session is started a default *working directory* is opened; normally, this is the user's home directory. A working directory is a folder on our computer where all the files from an R session are saved and read in. Specifically, we use working directories to read in and save data, keep our R scripts, and save plots. We do not have to use a working directory for R and RStudio, but it can make our lives and data management much easier. Further, a working directory is always active, whether we want to use it or not, and so we might as well use it. To do so, we first check where the working directory is currently located by using the `getwd()` function; which stands for 'get working directory'.

```
getwd()
[1] "C:/Users/bfoga/Documents"
```

Currently my working directory is set to my default user profile. This is a probably a bad place to set the working directory because it is easy for files to get lost in the user profile. Instead, I'll change the working directory to a different folder in my C drive using the `setwd()` function and specifying a path to our chosen folder. The exact path will depend on whether you are using a PC or Mac. Below I set the working directory to a folder I'm using for this chapter.

```
setwd("C:/QSSD/Chapter 2 - Introduction to R and RStudio/")
```

We can double-check whether we have the correctly set the working directory by rerunning `getwd()`.

```
getwd()
[1] "C:/QSSD/Chapter 2 - Introduction to R and RStudio"
```

---

[4]More details at http://rmarkdown.rstudio.com.

If we set the path to a non-existent folder or the syntax is not correct in the `setwd()` function, R will give us an error message and not change the working directory. It is fairly common to mess up the path on our first attempt since the path needs to be exactly correct. For example, if I had specified `RStudio` as `R Studio` it would not have worked.

Although we have already saved our R script, it is a good idea to resave our R script in our working directory so that we have the code and data in the same place. We can work with our working directory folders outside of R and RStudio in the same manner as for any folder on your computer, where we might add, rename, delete, copy, and paste different files.

R BASICS

Arithmetic and Objects

In this section we will go through the basics of R syntax by starting with R as a *fancy calculator*. R is what is known as an *object-oriented* programming language, which means that all data, variables, models, output, etc., are stored as *objects*. When we read in a dataset or create a new variable, it is stored in the R session as an object; this should become clearer as we go through some examples.

We want to use R for more than arithmetic, but it is an easy way to introduce R syntax. Each line in an R script is considered to be a new command or operation, unless we link it together using something like a comma; more on this later in the book.

Let's go through some simple arithmetic examples.

```
3+3
[1] 6
3-3
[1] 0
3*3
[1] 9
3/3
[1] 1
```

For each line of code, R gave us the numerical answer. To demonstrate how R uses objects, let's consider this example:

```
a <- 3+3
a
[1] 6
```

What we did was to have the operation `3 + 3` stored in the object a by using the assignment operator `<-` (we could use = instead of `<-`, but `<-` is the standard syntax to create objects in R). Note that when we created the object a, R did not give us the answer to `3 + 3` and instead we need to include another line with just the object name a. If we wrap parentheses around the code, R will print the answer.

```
(a <- 3+3)
[1] 6
```

R syntax is also *case-sensitive*, where lower-case or upper-case letters matter.

```
A
Error: object 'A' not found
```

It is also possible to do arithmetic on objects, depending on whether it makes sense to do so. For example, let's create a new object called b that is composed of the operation 3 * 3 and perform some arithmetic with the object a.

```
b <- 3*3
b
[1] 9
a+b
[1] 15
a*b
[1] 54
a/b
[1] 0.6666667
```

We can also create a new object out of other objects.

```
c <- a+b
c
[1] 15
d <- a*b
d
[1] 54
e <- a/b
e
[1] 0.6666667
```

These are basic examples of creating objects in R, but we will use objects throughout the entirety of this book for creating variables and models, reading in data, and a ton of other things.

Vectors, Matrices, and Data Frames

Let's spend a bit of time looking at vectors, matrices, and data frames in R, which are all considered different classes of objects in R. Vectors, matrices, and data frames make up datasets in R. A *vector* is a one-dimensional collection of information or data, usually numbers, stored in some specific order. A *matrix* is a combination of columns and rows with numeric values; so, where a vector is a row or column, a matrix contains at least one row and one column. Finally, a *data frame* is a matrix that R treats as a dataset. We can think of a data frame as a spreadsheet, where all the columns (whether one, two, or many columns) have an equal number of rows.

For our purposes, we can refer to the columns in our data frame as *variables*. We will discuss variables more in later chapters, but generally a variable is a collection of elements which assigns an alpha-numerical value to each observation (each row in a data frame).[5] We can refer to the rows in our data frame as *observations* (the individual elements). Lastly, a tibble, which sounds like something silly, is the data frame equivalent for `tidyverse`. We'll discuss `tidyverse` in much greater detail starting in Chapter 4.

Let's look at a simple example of creating vectors, matrices, and data frames. First, we'll create a vector called `v1` composed of five numbers, using the `c()` function. The function `c()` stands for *concatenate*, which tells R to glue or paste numbers, values, or objects together to create a new vector (or list) object.

```
v1 <- c(1,2,3,4,5)
v1
[1] 1 2 3 4 5
```

Now let's create a new vector called `v2` and then combine it with `v1` to create the vector `v3`.

```
v2 <- c(6,7,8,9,10)
v2
[1]  6  7  8  9 10
v3 <- c(v1,v2)
v3
 [1]  1  2  3  4  5  6  7  8  9 10
```

We can turn the vector `v3` into a data frame by using the `as.data.frame()` function and creating a new object that we will call `df1`.

```
df1 <- as.data.frame(v3)
df1
   v3
1   1
2   2
3   3
4   4
5   5
6   6
7   7
8   8
9   9
10 10
```

We see that R has converted `v3` into a data frame where there are 10 observations with their corresponding values. In this data frame, we can consider `v3` to be a variable (the column `v3`) that has 10 observations (the rows).

---

[5]The definition of 'variable' in R is actually broader than how we will be talking about variables in this book. For example, in R, the simple objects we created in the previous section (a, b) are considered variables.

INSTALLING PACKAGES IN R

When we downloaded and installed R for the first time, a base set of packages were also installed. The base packages provide the basics we need for using R. If we want to use different functions not in the base packages – that is, certain methods, techniques, and procedures – we need to download and install additional packages. In essence, installing additional R packages allows us to expand and customise the functionality of R. This provides substantial flexibility in R since the open-source user-written packages allow us to carry out cutting-edge data analysis without needing to wait for commercial software developers to decide whether something is important enough to include in the next version of their statistical program (e.g., Stata and SPSS – though they do allow some external packages to be installed). We will be using a variety of packages throughout the book, though it will only be a tiny subset of the existent R packages (follow this link to view the universe of packages: https://cran.r-project.org/web/packages/).

There are two things we need to do in order to use the functions from packages: install and activate/load. We install packages using the `install.packages()` function, where we put the name of the package in quotes in the parentheses; this requires us to know the exact name of the package. One package that we will make frequent use of throughout this book is `tidyverse`; the `tidyverse` package is actually a collection of eight different packages. Let's practise installing packages by installing `tidyverse`.

```
install.packages("tidyverse")
```

The first time we install packages, RStudio may pop open a window that asks us which package depository (known as a CRAN mirror) we want to download the package from. The convention is to choose the one physically closest to us in order to ensure faster installation. R will then proceed to install the packages while giving us information on the progress of the installation. Normally, we can ignore the progress of the installation, but we should check the last message to make sure there were no errors. After a package has been successfully installed, it will appear in our list of packages in the `Packages` tab in the lower right-hand window. We only need to install a package once, although we might need or want to update the package by reinstalling.

Once we have installed a package, we need to *load* (i.e., activate) the package to use its functions each time we start a new R session. We do this by using the `library()` or `require()` functions, where we include the name, without quotes, of the package we want to load. Though both functions do the same thing, a main difference is that `library()` gives an error message when a package has not been installed, while `require()` just gives you a warning. Hence, it may be better practise to use the `library()` function, but different R users have different preferences. Another way to load a package in RStudio is just to click the little box for the package in the `Packages` tab list.

Let's load `tidyverse`.

```
library(tidyverse)
-- Attaching packages ------------------------------- tidyverse 1.3.1 --
✓ ggplot2 3.3.5      ✓ purrr   0.3.4
✓ tibble  3.1.6      ✓ dplyr   1.0.7
✓ tidyr   1.1.4      ✓ stringr 1.4.0
✓ readr   2.1.0      ✓ forcats 0.5.1
-- Conflicts ---------------------------------- tidyverse_conflicts() --
✗ dplyr::filter() masks stats::filter()
✗ dplyr::lag()    masks stats::lag()
```

Now that we have loaded the package, all of the functions that are part of the package(s) can be used. The output shows the eight packages that `tidyverse` loads and also what functions have conflicts with currently loaded functions. We see conflicts when packages have functions with the same name. When this occurs, R is unable to reconcile the two different versions and will use the versions from the most recently loaded package. Here, we see that the `filter()` and `lag()` functions from the `dplyr` package conflict with the `filter()` and `lag()` functions from the `stats` package (which is part of base R).

If we wanted to use a certain function but we didn't want to load the package we could do the following: `tidyverse::filter()`. This calls the `filter()` function without loading `tidyverse`.

As we progress through this book, and as you engage in your own work, we will install more and more packages and your list of packages in the `Packages` tab will get longer and longer. We can scroll down the window to see all the installed packages, but we can also use the `library()` function with nothing in the parentheses to get a full list of installed packages.

CONCLUSION

This chapter provides an introduction to R and RStudio – how to get the programs, the layout of RStudio, basic R syntax, and how to install and load R packages. We have only touched on R and RStudio's functionality in this chapter. As we progress through the book we'll utilise more and more of the programs' functionality. Instead of having a separate chapter listing a ton of R functions, it is much more effective and efficient to learn R and statistical functions as needed.

R Packages Used in This Chapter

- `tidyverse`

R Functions Used in This Chapter

- `as.data.frame()` - create new data frame
- `c()` - concatenate
- `getwd()` - provide working directory location
- `install.packages()` - install R packages
- `library()` - load R package
- `setwd()` - set working directory

Additional Resources

Books

- Harris, J. K. (2020) *Statistics with R: Solving Problems Using Real-World Data*. Sage.
- Long, J. D. and Teetor, P. (2019) *R Cookbook*, 2nd edition. O'Reilly Media.

Online

- R-bloggers: https://www.r-bloggers.com/

3

FINDING DATA

Chapter contents

As individuals and collectively, we produce enormous daily amounts of data through web activity, mobile phones, Spotify, Netflix, Amazon, Facebook, Twitter, TikTok, etc. Average people don't usually think about how they are filling their data lakes except to know that data is continually shaping our lives. Hence, when we begin searching for data for our research, there is a tendency to believe the data will be easy to find, use, and will solve our problems. However, there is a critical difference between usable data and data that only highly skilled programmers at the NSA, GCHQ, Google, etc. can decipher. If you are reading this book to learn quantitative social science using R, it is unlikely that you can gain access to and make sense of the data from the 'internet of things', although learning R begins to open pathways to further training in programming and computational methods.

Instead, in QSS, we want data that is usable, manageable, and decipherable. So, while 'data is everywhere', there are not necessarily swarms of social science data we can easily obtain and/or utilise for our research. There is no doubt that with every year that passes there are more and more available social science datasets, but do not expect that we can find data on every topic of interest.

This being said, there is a difference between neatly constructed, available secondary datasets and data that is available for us to create primary datasets. More and more data sources are now electronically available which only a couple of decades ago only existed on paper; to gather this data it is no longer necessary to physically go to some office or library and plough through lots of pieces of paper. This is most dramatically evident in news media data, such as newspapers, and government data including election results, economic statistics, and legislative voting. This move to electronic data sources has substantially increased the speed with which social science research can be accomplished and has created a substantial leap in knowledge.

The focus in this book is using secondary social science datasets. Why? Because these datasets allow us not to worry about the process of collecting, validating, and a million other things – in essence, other people have already done the work for us. Instead of concerning ourselves with how data is created, we can concentrate on learning the foundations of QSS through using R. Therefore, our challenge is finding secondary datasets that fit our purpose.

In this chapter, we will get a taste of how one would construct a primary dataset using secondary data sources. The focus of our discussion, though, is on locating and downloading secondary datasets from data depositories such as the UK Data Service, ICPSR, and Harvard Dataverse, and other open data sources such as the World Bank, World Health Organization, and Google. We will also briefly consider how to use application programming interfaces (APIs) to access data.

By the end of this chapter, you should be able to:

- Understand the difference between primary and secondary data
- Understand how we construct 'contemporary' primary datasets
- Locate secondary data from data depositories
- Locate secondary data from governments and organisations
- Appreciate the relevance of the 'open data' movement
- Understand what APIs are

PRIMARY DATA

Traditionally, we are taught that primary data involves conducting interviews, reading diaries and speeches, conducting focus groups, among other practices; essentially, things we can consider qualitative data. Primary data, though, can more generally be defined as *data that we collect ourselves* – data that does not come from an existing, ready-to-use dataset. Quantitative social scientists frequently engage in primary data collection through gathering data to create different variables and then constructing their own datasets; when others use these datasets they can be considered secondary data. Conducting surveys and experiments, common in QSS, is another form of primary data collection. Although we frequently engage in primary data collection, many feel squeamish, likely due to our intuitive understanding of primary data, in saying we are using 'primary data'. Instead, quantitative social scientists often use terms like 'novel' or 'new' to describe datasets they created. Depending on the area of research, researchers may need to create new datasets for each project (e.g., in communication research) or they may be lucky enough to use pre-existing, off-the-shelf data (e.g., in public opinion research).

In this section, we will discuss why students first learning QSS should *not* collect their own data and then go through an example of the process of researchers creating a new dataset.

Students and Primary Data

At its most elemental level, students learning how to conduct QSS, particularly through statistical programs like R, do not have the time to gather primary data in an adequate or sufficient manner. It can be tough enough to keep all the various data analysis techniques straight, and adding the task of primary data collection is infeasible. I have seen this both while teaching QSS courses and serving as an undergraduate- and master's-level thesis/dissertation supervisor.[1] Many students at the dissertation stage of their degree have a notion of using primary data and performing data analysis, but lack the knowledge of how to conduct rigorous data analysis. In these circumstances, I advise students to try to find secondary data sources that address their research questions instead of trying to gather their own. If secondary data sources do not exist then students do need to do primary data collection, which may necessitate a very basic data analysis approach (e.g., percentages). It is much wiser to check secondary data sources prior to finalising research questions and theories, in order to uncover what is feasible within the degree's time span.

Initially, when teaching QSS courses that had a research paper assessment, I would allow students to use any dataset they wanted. This approach seemed to offer the most flexibility to students and allowed them to research any topic of interest. However, I quickly realised this was a terrible idea. Too many students were overconfident in their ability to gather primary data and create datasets, while simultaneously learning the data analysis techniques. These students would nearly always panic at the end of the semester and throw together papers using one of the datasets from the course, papers that were obviously undeveloped. I changed the research paper assessment so that students had to use one of a handful of predefined, secondary datasets. This restricted the breadth of potential topics, but students did not need to worry about finding data and could concentrate on the *how* of data analysis and QSS. This is not to say that students should never collect primary data, but simply that working with pre-existing datasets will make the challenge of learning QSS and data analysis using programs like R much easier.

---

[1] At the PhD level, students commonly must collect their own data and build their own datasets.

24 | QUANTITATIVE SOCIAL SCIENCE DATA WITH R

An Example of Constructing a 'Primary' Dataset

Although I advise against students creating their own datasets, it is instructive to see the process that QSS researchers go through to develop new datasets for their projects. In this section, we will go through the process of collecting data and creating a dataset for the article 'News Attention to Voter Fraud in the 2008 and 2012 US Elections' in the journal *Research & Politics* (Fogarty et al. 2015).

For this project, my co-authors and I wanted to examine how US newspapers covered voter fraud during the 2008 and 2012 US elections. Voter fraud has been and continues to be a hot topic in US politics, with Republicans and conservatives claiming extensive and rampant fraud even in the face of scant evidence. Therefore, we were interested in what the media was reporting since most people receive their political information through the media. In this article, we simply wanted to know what propelled newspapers to publish more or fewer voter fraud articles during election seasons.

Our first challenge was to figure out what US media to study. We decided to use newspapers since it is easier to locate electronic copies of articles than tracking down television or radio broadcasts. Further, though readership of physical newspapers has declined, readership of newspapers' websites is still robust. Having settled on newspapers, the next question was what newspapers to study. Since US presidential elections are fought by state, we decided to look at state-level newspapers. We used two newspaper databases, *Lexis-Nexis* and *Newsbank*, along with newspapers' own websites to collect news coverage on voter fraud from the major and/or largest newspaper in each state that we could get access to. Getting access to data can be tricky. There may be certain data sources that we want access to that are either impossible or prohibitively costly to obtain. In these circumstances, we make do with what we can get. *Lexis-Nexis* and *Newsbank* do not have all newspapers and not all newspapers online are free to read, and therefore we used the best available news sources.

Once we figured out which newspapers, we gathered news articles using the search term 'voter fraud' for the traditional primary US election season (from the first Monday of September to the first Tuesday of November) for the 2008 and 2012 elections.[2] Once we downloaded all the news articles, we made a simple count of how many articles existed for each newspaper and entered this data into an Excel spreadsheet.

Then we needed to collect data on the variables we thought might explain why certain newspapers would devote different amounts of attention to voter fraud. We decided to use eight variables to explain variations in news coverage: whether a state was a battleground state for the US presidential election, whether a state had passed a restrictive voting law in the past year, the number of voter fraud cases in a state in the past year, the percentage of state legislators by state who were members of the conservative American Legislative Exchange Council (ALEC), the 2004 presidential vote difference in the newspaper's media market, the percentage of black and Hispanic residents in the newspaper's media market, and the circulation size of the newspapers we examined; the article provides the rationale and justification for including this set of variables. We needed to find data for these eight variables and match it up with the newspaper coverage data in an Excel spreadsheet. Therefore, we had to collect essentially 'primary' data from an array of different sources to create a new dataset.

---

[2]It should already be evident from this discussion that, although I argued in Chapter 1 that quantitative analysis is more objective than qualitative research, all research involves making choices.

We used *CNN*, the *New York Times*, and *Politico* to construct our battleground state variable and data from the *Brennan Center for Justice* for whether a state had passed a restrictive voting law. We used data from *News21* for the number of voter fraud cases in each state. The percentage of state legislators who were ALEC members was gathered from the *Center for Media and Democracy*, a non-profit organisation studying corruption in government. Presidential vote difference in media markets data came from academics Karol and Miguel (2007), while percentages of black and Hispanic residents in media markets were gathered from the *Nielsen Company*. Finally, data on newspaper circulation was cobbled together from a variety of sources, including the newspapers' own websites and the *Media Intelligence Center*.

In summary, creating the dataset for this one research article involved primary data collection of news stories on voter fraud and primary/secondary data collection from media sources, non-profit and for-profit organisations, policy centres, and academics. Hopefully, this discussion illustrates the laborious process of creating new datasets for QSS research and why as a student first learning the methods and techniques you should avoid this task. Whether we can call this primary or secondary data collection is debatable, but it certainly was more involved than the secondary datasets we will use in this book.

SECONDARY DATA

How do we find secondary data? More specifically, how do we find secondary datasets that are ready to use and easily available? As discussed in the introduction, this is not as simple as we may expect, though it is becoming easier and easier with each passing year. When looking for secondary data we inevitably spend a lot of time googling, poking around, and trying to avoid going down rabbit holes that waste our time. Sometimes this will lead to the sources we discuss below and other times we may discover new sources of secondary data.

Library Resources

You may be shocked to read that university libraries are a great place to start searching for secondary data. Indeed, many university libraries have curated websites with annotated information on secondary data sources. Although these sites typically focus on major secondary data sources, their organisation and information can be useful when we are just starting out.

If you are at a university it is best to start with your university library's website. Some secondary data sources are not open, and we may only be able to access the data through our university credentials. Further, some universities have research librarians who may be able to assist us in locating data pertinent for our research. If you are not at a university or your university is lacking actionable information on secondary data, you can simply google something like 'research libraries secondary data sources' and a bunch of useful resources are returned.

Data Depositories

One of the best places to first look for secondary datasets is in what are known as *data depositories*. These are websites where researchers have uploaded their data, code, and data information for others to use. We will look at three such depositories: the UK Data Service, ICPSR, and the

Harvard Dataverse.[3] Even in these depositories, there is great variation in the quality of data and information provided, but they are often our best bets in locating relevant secondary social science data for our research topics.

UK Data Service

The UK Data Service (UKDS) has been through a few variations, but it is now settled as one of the best data depositories in the world (https://www.ukdataservice.ac.uk/). Exceptionally, researchers who have received an Economic and Social Research Council (UK) grant must make their data open and publicly available, and most deposit their data and background information with the UKDS; other researchers make their data publicly available and open on their own or their university websites. However, not all data at the UKDS is publicly available due to data restrictions placed by the researchers, typically on sensitive data such as surveys with participant-identifying information. We also must register with the UKDS to download most of the datasets on the site.

ICPSR

The ICPSR, which stands for the long-winded 'Inter-university Consortium for Political and Social Research', is also a major social science data depository and is situated at the University of Michigan (https://www.icpsr.umich.edu/web/pages/ICPSR/index.html). Just as the UKDS focuses mostly on the UK and Europe, the ICPSR focuses mostly on the USA. Since, unlike the UK, the USA does not have a requirement to make data publicly available when it comes from government-supported research, the ICPSR depository can be a bit hit-and-miss. You may find exactly what you are looking for, but personal experience suggests the ICPSR is rather thin on recent academically focused datasets. For example, we may find data on our topic of interest, but it is from five or ten years ago. If we do find data, there are generally fewer restrictions and permissions than exist with the UKDS. To download the data, we still need to register and sign in; however, this can be done in easier ways such as through Gmail and Facebook. Additionally, there are some data that only individuals affiliated with member institutions can download; many USA research universities are members, but outside the USA there are far fewer members.

Harvard Dataverse

Harvard Dataverse, part of the broader Dataverse Project, is a key part of the open data movement (https://dataverse.harvard.edu/dataverse/harvard). The open data movement is based on the concept that data and code should be publicly available in order to promote transparency and replication in research. Science and social science continue to experience a 'replication crisis', where published findings, including field-defining findings, have proved impossible to replicate and thus impossible to confirm as correct. There are dramatic examples of data fraud, but often replication problems are down to unconscious decisions and errors in data collection and analysis by researchers that lead to incorrect results.[4] If researchers cannot *check* or *double-check* results, there is no way to determine whether quantitative results are accurate or not.

---

[3]In this edition, I avoid discussing many of the detailed aspects of data depositories sites. The reason is that sites often undergo change and thus such information can quickly become stale and irrelevant.

[4]The website *Retraction Watch* (https://retractionwatch.com/) monitors research that has been retracted from journals due to fraud, errors, etc.

It may seem obvious that there should be some type of check on research. Yet, at least in the social sciences, the tradition in peer-reviewed research is for scholars to review papers, chapters, and books only with the information provided in the text. Experts in academic fields can normally tell whether the analysis appears correct and whether the results are supported by the data. Further, reviewers are normally not paid to do academic journal reviews and replicating all of the analysis can be extremely time-consuming. Therefore, it is not feasible for reviewers to replicate all the data analysis for all submissions at the review stage.

The compromise solution journal editors have come to is to require that, following publication of an article in their journal, the researchers *must* make the data and code publicly available for others.[5] This means putting all materials needed for replication on a publicly available website. This can be researchers' own websites, their universities' data sites, or the journal's website, but increasingly journals and researchers have decided to deposit materials in centralised locations such as the Harvard Dataverse. This allows other researchers to replicate published results and allows students to learn data analysis techniques through replication of published articles. One intended consequence of demanding that authors make their data and code publicly available is that there will be less conscious academic fraud.

This sounds terrific, right? Well, not all social science fields or journals have moved towards publicly available replication materials. Economics, political science, and psychology have been at the forefront of the open data movement in the social sciences, but only some journals in these fields have taken this step; though an increasing number of journals have moved in this direction. Other social science fields, specifically sociology, have dropped the ball on having publicly available replication materials. Some sociology journals require that authors make their data available on request from researchers. However, this leaves it up to scholars to actually respond and provide the materials to individual requests (i.e., via email). If you do not want your data to be examined and replicated, it is very easy to 'miss' an email, say you cannot find a specific file, or only send part of the files; for example, the requirement is often just to provide the data and not any of the code.

Some journals, particularly economics and political science journals, have their own separate depositories (e.g., *Quarterly Journal of Economics, American Journal of Political Science*) on the Harvard Dataverse, but typically researchers post their replication materials on their own dataverses. On the main page, we just need to type in whatever we want to search for – an author, journal, article title, topic, etc. The files we find will depend on the journal's requirements and researchers' own preferences; at minimum, there should be the main datasets, but often there is also the code used for the analysis. Quantitative researchers sometimes deposit their data in one location (e.g., the Harvard Dataverse) and post their code somewhere else (e.g., GitHub). Posting code to GitHub is commonly done to allow users to flag bugs, suggest improvements, and ask questions of implementations of new methods in programs like R and Python.

It is difficult to argue against the merits of the open data movement. To be fair, there are legitimate reasons why researchers are not willing to make replication materials publicly available. First, researchers may have spent hundreds of thousands (or more) of dollars in acquiring the data, creating datasets, and performing data analysis. In these cases, there is a legitimate claim to a 'data embargo' that allows the original researchers exclusive access for a couple of years. Second, researchers sometimes work with highly sensitive data. This may be surveys, experiments, interviews, web browsing behaviour, etc., on sensitive topics, or classified government data where

---

[5]Some journals also verify statistical results between the acceptance and publication stages.

researchers are not ethically or legally able to make the data available. In one example, Boston College researchers working on the *Boston Project* had interviews with Irish Republican Army members discussing activities in Northern Ireland. As an extremely sensitive (and criminal) topic, the researchers did not make these interviews publicly available; however, the US courts forced the researchers to hand over the interviews on request by British authorities for criminal investigations in Northern Ireland. In another example, researchers may publish an article using terrorist cell network data to demonstrate new social network analysis methods. The researchers clearly cannot make this data publicly available, though they can make the code available. Other times, researchers may have used proprietary data in their analyses and data-sharing agreements restrict what can be made public.

Excluding these two main legitimate reasons for not making replication materials publicly available, we should be suspicious of researchers not willing to disclose their materials. Further, social science journals should all move to having open data depositories. Not only will this help increase transparency and integrity in research, it also helps students to learn data analysis methods and techniques, and develop good research practices.

Other Secondary Data Sources

In addition to these established data depositories there are numerous other places where we can find secondary data. As mentioned, researchers often have replication materials on their websites in addition to or instead of putting the data in a depository. Another source of secondary data is governments, international and national organisations, think tanks, and policy research centres. Often data from these other sources do not come in nice, clean pre-packaged dataset formats with accompanying code. But if you are interested in building your own dataset by compiling data from various secondary sources, these sources can be quite useful. Let's briefly discuss a few places where we can find such data.

Government Sources

Depending on the country and the topic we are interested in, we can find enormous amounts of data on government websites. The availability, quality, and accessibility of government data often depend on the openness and economic wealth of the country. We generally find the best data on government sites in the USA, UK, Canada, European Union, and similar countries. These countries tend to view government data as a public good and have the resources to create and make high-quality data publicly available. For example, the USA has made great strides in developing open data platforms where researchers and the public can find relevant data (https://www.data.gov/). The availability of this data can vary based on existing data privacy laws (e.g., GDPR in Europe) and the continuing evolving landscape of data legislation. However, quality government data does not exclusively come from wealthy Western countries. For example, the South African government provides a number of excellent data resources.

We can also find quality government data at the subnational level in many countries. The prominence and availability of this data will vary based on a country's government systems and structure. Less centralised government systems (i.e., more devolved systems) tend to have more data available at the subnational level. For example, the Scottish government controls policy for many areas (e.g., education, health) due to devolved powers from the UK government. Therefore, we can find data specific to Scotland on Scottish government sites for some of those areas. In the

USA, we often can find data on state, county, and city government websites. Again, the quality and availability will vary based on resources and an interest in creating and providing the data.

We can also gain access to data not publicly posted on websites through a data request with the government department or agency. The ease, speed, and costs of data access will vary widely based on every reason imaginable. However, it is definitely something to investigate if certain data may be critical to answering our research questions.[6]

Governmental and Non-Governmental Organisations

Many international organisations have their own data related to their field or topic of interest. As can be gathered from the previous subsection, governmental organisations may have their data centralised on an open government data site. We can find non-governmental data on the organisations' websites. Some of the most commonly used in social science come from the Central Intelligence Agency's World Factbook, the World Bank, the World Health Organization, the United Nations, and similar organisations. As with government data websites, the ease of use and helpfulness vary by organisation and the topic we are studying.

Survey Research Firms

There are a number of survey research firms around the world that study social science questions. Most are purely commercial enterprises, where businesses, governments, and researchers commission surveys to be conducted by the firms. In those situations, the raw data is proprietary and is not publicly available; however, the survey firm might include a brief, general report on the findings on their website. Depending on our research topics, this might serve our purposes well – for example, if we are studying aggregate trends, such as approval of the US president and Congress, we only need the overall numbers and we do not need the raw data that the firm collected to produce the numbers. If we want access to the raw data collected by survey research firms we are mostly out of luck. However, if the researchers commissioned the firms to conduct the surveys using government funding, we should be able to access the data at some point in the future.

The one notable exception is the *Pew Research Center* in the USA (http://www.pewresearch.org/). Pew is a non-partisan think tank funded by charitable contributions, and thus does not rely on outside customers to keep it afloat. Pew conducts research, mainly survey-based, on a wide range of social and political topics, though normally pertaining to the USA, and publishes reports based on its findings. Most importantly, we can download the raw data from most of Pew's surveys typically after a six-month or one-year data embargo. To download the data, we do need to fill out a basic information sheet and agree to some conditions, but this is just a formality.

Google Public Data

One last place of note for obtaining secondary data is *Google Public Data* (https://www.google.com/publicdata/directory). Google Public Data is basically more about playing around with data on their website, but the site does list different data sources from governmental and non-governmental organisations.

---

[6]Pursuing data requests is not advisable for anyone on a tight timeline as acquiring the data always takes longer than expected.

Ask Someone

Last, but not least, we can ask someone (e.g., faculty, researchers, students) about secondary data sources. This may be in person, by email, or even on social media (something Twitter is great for). Depending on our personality, we might do this first instead of last. We should avoid burdening the person with extra work, but they may know the perfect source, be able to recommend another person to talk to, or even have the data we are looking for. This is a very common practice. For example, academics who are creating their own datasets frequently will ask colleagues about data sources for specific variables they want to use in their research. Asking others can save us an enormous amount of time in our quest for secondary data.

COLLECTING DATA FASTER

Our discussion has thus far been framed around collecting data 'by hand' – going to websites, downloading data and documents, or copying and pasting information from other documents. Over the past couple of decades, researchers have increasingly gathered data using automated techniques and processes in R, Python, and similar programs. Depending on the data, this can cut data collection time from weeks or months to hours or days. Such techniques include webscraping and APIs. The mechanics of how to do this are beyond this book, particularly webscraping, but let's briefly discuss APIs as their use is increasingly common in the social sciences.

Although there are many uses of APIs specific to app developers, quantitative social scientists mainly use websites' APIs to automatically collect and import data using R (or other programming languages). Many organisations, institutions, and companies have APIs, and government organisations and agencies are increasingly creating APIs to share data more efficiently. For example, the US Census Bureau allows us to manually search, browse, and download data on its website. However, the Census Bureau also provides an API to access the same data without needing to play around on its website. We could try to write our own code to access and import data from APIs, but it is generally better to piggyback on others' efforts. For example, the R package `tidycensus` has functions to automatically collect and import data from the Census's API (Walker 2022). The specific data we can collect is based on APIs' *end-points*. We can think of API end-points as the different types of variables we are able to collect from a database. For example, the Census has end-points for geographical unit, size of the population, age of the population, etc.

Among the most prominent uses of APIs in social science research is accessing and collecting Twitter data. Twitter is one of the few social media companies that still allows relatively open access to its data, through APIs and in general. Before beginning there are many details, rules, and restrictions for working with Twitter's API and using Twitter data, particularly as Twitter frequently changes its data policies and API end-points. We can easily collect Twitter data by utilising R functions from the `rtweet` package (Kearney 2019). This package makes extracting Twitter data and importing it into R very simple and user-friendly.

Although we will not work with APIs, this book provides the necessary foundation for advancing to collecting data quickly and efficiently using R.

CONCLUSION

In this chapter, we discussed the differences between primary (and 'contemporary' primary) data and secondary data, how to find secondary data, and some data depositories and organisations with commonly used data.

The most important thing to take away from this chapter for students is the strong recommendation to avoid engaging in primary data collection as much as possible. Students' time should be focused on correctly analysing secondary data and working to deliver clear verbal and written discussions of results. Let researchers with more experience, time, and money to do the heavy lifting of data collection. As the open data movement progresses, the number and quality of open data and replication materials should increase exponentially, offering more resources for secondary datasets.[7]

In the next chapter, we explore how to open data in R and perform basic data cleaning and processing.

━━━━━━━ Additional Resources ━━━━━━━

Books and Articles

- Gandrud, C. (2020) *Reproducible Research with R and RStudio*. Chapman and Hall/CRC.
- Kearney, M. W. (2019) 'rtweet: Collecting and analyzing Twitter data', *Journal of Open Source Software*, 42(4): 18-29.
- Walker, K. (2022) *Analyzing US Census Data: Methods, Maps, and Models in R*. Chapman and Hall/CRC.

Online

- Gary King on Replication in Social Sciences: http://methods.sagepub.com/video/gary-king-discusses-replication-in-the-social-sciences

---

[7]However, students pursuing a PhD in a social science field often need to create new datasets.

4

DATA MANAGEMENT

Chapter contents

Now that we have found datasets, the next challenge is reading in (i.e., opening) the datasets in RStudio and cleaning the data. This is generally known as data management or data wrangling (the cool kid verbiage which also encompasses variable recoding/manipulation). RStudio has increasingly made data management easier in R, particularly with the inclusion of the point-and-click option for opening data. However, data management in R can be a bit trickier than in programs like Stata or SPSS. One reason for this is that R can accommodate nearly every type of data file, while proprietary programs like Stata, SPSS, and SAS traditionally require the data to be in a specific data format. R's flexibility means there is not a single one-size-fits-all approach to data management, which can sometimes be frustrating.

In this chapter, we begin by introducing the world of and discuss the relevant packages in `tidyverse`. Then we take on the seemingly simple process of reading data into the RStudio (and R) environment. Once we have read in the data, we will examine the datasets and variables. This is followed by how to clean the data and variables, and how to subset data and variables. We will also look at merging multiple datasets and pivoting datasets – increasingly necessary components of QSS. The chapter concludes with how to save data in R. As with many aspects of this book, this chapter does not have an exhaustive list of all data management situations, but it should provide a solid foundation which you can adapt for your own needs.

By the end of the chapter, you should be able to:

- Understand the world of `tidyverse`
- Understand different data suffixes
- Read in different types of data files
- Understand how to examine whole datasets
- Understand how to examine specific variables
- Manage missing values
- Merge different datasets
- Pivot datasets
- Save new datasets

THE WORLD OF TIDYVERSE

As noted in Chapter 2, `tidyverse` is a set of R packages that use a common approach to comprehensively deal with data management, wrangling, and visualisation (Wickham et al. 2019). The goal of `tidyverse` is to develop more elegant and efficient R code, and to provide solutions to new problems that emerge in the rapidly evolving field of data science. The `tidyverse` package proper includes a suite of packages, but there are other packages which are part of the `tidyverse` universe but not formally in the package. Although the focus of `tidyverse` to date has been on data wrangling and visualisation, the creators and developers have branched out into statistical modelling and machine learning with the `tidymodels` packages.

The first edition of this book extensively used one of `tidyverse`'s core packages, `ggplot2`, for data visualisation as well as functions from the `haven`, `readxl`, and `tibble` packages. In this edition, we will use all of `tidyverse`'s core packages (except for the `purrr` package, which is designed for advanced programming) and the `haven`, `readxl`, and `lubridate` packages.

The main benefit of `tidyverse` for average R users is that we can use and connect the numerous functions for all aspects of data management, wrangling, visualisation, and analysis. Even if the code sometimes looks a bit beastly, working from a common starting point and language makes our lives much easier. In this chapter, we will get our first true taste of `tidyverse`, but the benefit will be clearly evident in the next chapter on the manipulation of variables.

HOW TO READ IN DATA

Reading in data should not be a challenge or hurdle for us to overcome. However, the process is not as straightforward as we would like in R, particularly when we first encounter the task. There are a variety of different ways of getting data into R, and every researcher has their preferred way. We will consider two different ways: reading in from our working directory and using RStudio's built-in option. My personal preference is to read in data from a working directory so I know that everything is located in the same folder, particularly since we often need to create and save graphics into a specific folder.

Reading in Data from a Working Directory

In Chapter 2, we discussed how to set our working directory.

```
setwd("C:/QSSD/Chapter 4 - Data Management/")
getwd()
[1] "C:/QSSD/Chapter 4 - Data Management"
```

With our working directory set, we need to know the name of the dataset and the data file type. There are a number of different data file types that exist, but in social science we commonly encounter comma-separated values files (.csv), text files (.txt), table files (.tab), Excel files (.xlsx), and files saved in other statistical program formats including Stata (.dta), SPSS (.sav or .por), and SAS (.sas7bdat). R also has its own data file format, .RData, but researchers sometimes prefer to save data in a commonly used data format such as .csv. Personal experience has shown that .csv, .dta, and .sav are the most common secondary data formats we come across in the social sciences.

Generally, the code for reading in data using `tidyverse` takes the form `read_<filetype>` `("file name")`, where `<filetype>` is the data format suffix and `"file name"` is the name of the data; the name of the file must be in quotes.[1] The file name must match the data name in our working directory or it will not work. We also typically create a new object for the data we read in, so that we do not make any permanent changes to the original dataset. Lastly, all of the `read_` functions include options to help correctly read in data. Below, we go through how to read in a variety of different data file types.

---

[1]Standard R code for reading in data uses . instead of _ in read_<filetype>. For example, read. csv() instead of read_csv().

Reading in .csv Files

Let's first read in a dataset called `simd2020.csv`, which is the 2020 Scottish Index of Multiple Deprivation (SIMD) for all Scottish datazones.[2]

We will use the `read_csv()` function that is part of the `readr` package – which is automatically activated with `library(tidyverse)`. The `readr` package provides a ton of options for delimited files (e.g., .csv, .txt). The immediate benefit of using `read_csv()` instead of `read.csv()` is that the data is read in as a `tibble`, which is the equivalent of a data frame in `tidyverse`. Many `tidyverse` functions require that our data be classified as a `tibble`. Also, `read_csv()` provides a number of different options for reading in .csv files and guesses the variable formats (i.e., the variable classes).

In the `read_csv()` function, we include the name of the file (`"simd2020.csv"`) and we also specify how the missing values are characterised in the .csv file. Missing values are said to occur when, for whatever reason, observations are 'missing' responses or values for variables. In surveys, missing values typically arise because the respondent refused to answer a question, could not answer a question, or the survey was designed to ask only certain questions of certain sets of respondents (often due to survey experiments). In non-survey data, missing values generally occur when the researcher(s) who created the data could not find a value for an observation for certain variables or the value was 'suppressed' to prevent individuals from potentially being identified. The latter is common in observational government data where the unit of analysis is a geographical unit and there are only a few observations for a given variable. For example, Covid-19 daily case data is routinely suppressed for geographical units (e.g., US counties) if the total cases in the geographical units are below a certain threshold value (e.g., 10 cases). If these values are not suppressed, people may be able to identify individuals who tested positive for Covid-19 on a given day. The former is common for datasets that rely on reports from the unit of analysis to build the data and variables. For example, not all countries report complete economic statistics, such as unemployment percentages, and so those countries would have missing values on those variables. Although frequently observed in datasets on developing countries, this is also a problem for data on sensitive subjects in developed countries. For example, the majority of US police departments do not share data on use of force by officers and thus these departments would be coded as missing data.[3]

We will deal more explicitly with missing values later in this chapter, but for now we include the option `na = "*"`, where `na` means 'not available' and `*` is how missing values are represented in the raw SIMD data. This ensures that missing values from the .csv data file are coded in the way that R recognises missing values (i.e., `"NA"`). If we do not specify the missing values, the data will still be read in, but we will get a warning message about the cells with `*`.[4] Let's name this dataset `csvdata`.

---

[2]A datazone is a small geographical area, here of Scotland. The datazones in the SIMD are nested in council areas, are roughly equal in size (500–1000 people), and are constructed to maintain physical and natural communities (www.gov.scot/Topics/Statistics/SIMD/FAQUsingSIMD).

[3]https://www.washingtonpost.com/nation/2021/06/09/police-use-of-force-data/

[4]Sometimes we come across values that R designates as `NaN`. This stands for 'not a number' and is commonly seen for undefined values such as 0/0. `NaN` is not the same thing as `NA`. We will also see that `tidyverse` uses several different versions of `NA`, which can cause problems when recoding variables.

```
library(tidyverse)
csvdata <- read_csv("simd2020.csv", na = "*")
```

In the upper right-hand `Environment` window in RStudio a new line should appear under `Data` with the name of our new dataset (`csvdata`), the number of observations (6976), and number of variables (38).

We read in the data only using the missing-value option, which for the `simd2020.csv` data is not a problem. If we type `?read_csv` into the `Console` window we will get a help file in the lower right-hand `Help` window with the various options for the `read_csv()` function. Two options for `read_csv()` that I have found useful are the `n_max` and `name_repair` options. The `n_max =` option allows you to limit the number of observations that are read in. We might use this when working with datasets that are too large to open on our machines and we just want to see the data structure. The `name_repair =` option corrects problematic column names (i.e., variable names) when the data is first read in. For example, `name_repair = "universal"` ensures each variable is unique and removes syntax incompatible with `tidyverse` functions.

Reading in Excel Files

We often encounter Excel data files – particularly when downloading public data from government, non-profit, and similar organisations' websites. Although Excel files mostly operate the same as .csv files, the additional metadata and functionality of Excel require the `readxl` package to read the files into R. The `readxl` package offers three functions to read in Excel files: `read_xls()` for older Excel files, `read_xlsx()` for newer Excel files, and `read_excel()` if you do not know the Excel version and want the function to figure it out.

The `readxl` package is not loaded when we load the `tidyverse` package and thus we need to first activate it with `library(readxl)`. We will read in the file `simd2020.xlsx` using the `read_xlsx()` function and again specify the missing values. Let's name this dataset `xlsxdata`.

```
library(readxl)
xlsxdata <- read_xlsx("simd2020.xlsx", na = "*")
```

We see that we have the same number of observations and variables as the .csv file – which is what we want.

The `read_xlsx()` function has many of the same options as the `read_csv()` function. However, one important option that `read_xlsx()` has that `read_csv()` does not is the `sheet =` option. This option allows you to specify the Excel file sheet to read in the data when the file has multiple sheets. We commonly find secondary data Excel files that include a sheet describing the variables and a sheet with the raw data, as well as files that have different data in different sheets.

Reading in .txt Files

We also encounter data files stored as text files (.txt). For standard datasets, the data columns are separated by tabs within the .txt file. We are not looking at .txt files that contain actual text (e.g., newspaper articles) that are used for automated text analysis. Let's open a .txt version of the SIMD file and name it `txtdata`. We use the `read_delim()` function and include the option `delim = "\t"`, which tells R that our data is 'tab-delimited'; if you include `delim = ","` it means the data is 'comma-separated', and if you include `delim = ""` it means the data is separated by white space (which is the default). Generally, to figure out which separator needs to be used we need to check the data documentation.

```
txtdata <- read_delim("simd2020.txt", delim = "\t")
```

Once again in the `Environment` window we see that our data object `txtdata` has 6976 observations and 38 variables.

Reading in .tab Files

We may also encounter data files stored as tab-separated files (.tab). To read them into R, we use the same code as we did for the .txt file, except now the file suffix is .tab.

```
tabdata <- read_delim("simd2020.tab", delim = "\t")
```

Check the `Environment` window to see if our new data object is present.

Reading in Stata Files

Datasets that are saved as proprietary statistical software files are commonly referred to as 'foreign' data formats in R: commonly Stata, SPSS, and SAS formats. There are a variety of packages to read in data from these software into R (e.g., the `foreign` package), but the `haven` package in `tidyverse` allows us to read in data saved as Stata, SPSS, and SAS files. More importantly, the functions in `haven` are frequently updated to reflect changes and updates in the proprietary software, and the data is read in as `tidyverse`-friendly.

Let's first look at a dataset from Stata, which has the suffix .dta. We will use the `read_dta()` function to read in a Stata version of the 2020 SIMD data.

```
library(haven)
dtadata <- read_dta("simd2020.dta")
```

We see in the `Environment` window that we have the same number of observations and variables as before.

Reading in SPSS Files

Let's quickly look at reading in a SPSS data file using the `haven` package's function `read_sav()`. SPSS data files have the suffix .sav or .por.

```
savdata <- read_sav("simd2020.sav")
```

Reading in SAS Files

Finally, let's read in a SAS data file by using the `haven` package's function `read_sas()`. SAS data files have the suffix .sas7bdat.

```
sasdata <- read_sas("simd2020.sas7bdat")
```

Reading in Data Using RStudio

Another option for reading data into R is to use RStudio's `Import Dataset` function/option in the `Environment` window. When we click on the little spreadsheet icon a tab opens that allows us to select datasets in five different formats. After we click on a data format type, a new window pops open that guides us through finding and reading in the data. We are also provided with the code that is used to read in the data. Before clicking on the `Import` button, we should check that the data is correctly separated in the `Data Preview` window. I'm not a big fan of point-and-click functionality as it distracts users from learning code and reduces replicability. However, the `Import Dataset` option can be valuable when you are starting to learn R and when you are unsure of the formatting of a dataset.

EXAMINING DATASETS

Thus far, we have not actually looked at the data; we have just checked in the `Environment` window that each data format version had the same number of observations and variables. In this section, we will take a look at the overall dataset; in the next section, we will look at individual variables. We look at datasets to familiarise ourselves with the data and as a check that there are no data entry errors. Additionally, if we encounter problems when performing analysis, we may go back and look at the overall dataset to find any errors.

For simplicity, let's work with the .csv version of the SIMD data. Let's read in this file again.

```
csvdata <- read_csv("simd2020.csv", na = "*")
Rows: 6976 Columns: 38
-- Column specification ---------------------------------------------
---------
Delimiter: ","
chr  (3): Data_Zone, Intermediate_Zone, Council_area
dbl (35): Total_population, Working_age_population, Income_rate,
Income_coun...

i Use `spec()` to retrieve the full column specification for this data.
i Specify the column types or set `show_col_types = FALSE` to quiet this
message.
```

There are a few different ways using base R and `tidyverse` to look at the dataset.

The first option is to 'view' the dataset using the `view()` function from the `tibble` package. We put the name of the dataset object into the parentheses of `view()`.

```
view(csvdata)
```

This opens up a new tab in RStudio where we can see all the variables and observations. The view() function is the lower-case version of the View() function in base R; I assume that the tidyverse folks were annoyed with the upper-case 'V'. In fact, if we click on the spreadsheet icon in the Environment window for csvdata, the same tab opens; notice that clicking on the spreadsheet icon has R run the line View(csvdata) in the Console window.

Another way to take a quick look at the variables in our data is using the names() function. This function provides the names of all the variables in our dataset, and is particularly useful when performing analysis and we cannot remember the particular name of a certain variable.

```
names(csvdata)
 [1] "Data_Zone"            "Intermediate_Zone"       "Council_area"
 [4] "Total_population"     "Working_age_population"   "Income_rate"
 [7] "Income_count"         "Employment_rate"         "Employment_count"
[10] "CIF"                  "ALCOHOL"                 "DRUG"
[13] "SMR"                  "DEPRESS"                 "LBWT"
[16] "EMERG"                "Attendance"              "Attainment"
[19] "no_qualifications"    "not_participating"       "University"
[22] "drive_petrol"         "drive_GP"                "drive_post"
[25] "drive_primary"        "drive_retail"            "drive_secondary"
[28] "PT_GP"                "PT_post"                 "PT_retail"
[31] "Broadband"            "crime_count"             "crime_rate"
[34] "overcrowded_count"    "nocentralheat_count"     "overcrowded_rate"
[37] "nocentralheat_rate"   "urban"
```

We can also look at the *class* of the dataset using the class() function. This is important as R functions require that data are specified as certain classes.

```
class(csvdata)
[1] "spec_tbl_df" "tbl_df"      "tbl"          "data.frame"
```

This shows four different classes; here tbl stands for tibble. Note that the data is also classified as a data.frame, which is the standard data frame class and would be the only class listed if we used read.csv(). Therefore, our dataset will work for tidyverse and non-tidyverse functions.

EXAMINING VARIABLES

Now that we have correctly read in and taken a quick look at our data, we want to examine the contents of our variables. There are a number of things we might want to look at in our variables, but we are usually most interested in the *variable type*. At the most basic level, we want to know whether our variables are *numeric* or *string/character*. Numeric variables are composed of numbers, while string or character variables are composed of letters or symbols. We likely already know whether our variables are numeric or string/character, but sometimes when we read data into R, variables will be misclassified. For example, numeric variables wind up mischaracterised as string/character variables. Since our data analysis is, usually, dependent on numbers, we will not be able to perform statistical analysis with string/character variables. That is why it is always good practice to make sure that our variables are of the correct variable type from the start.

The next thing we are concerned about is whether our numeric variables are being treated as *numeric* (the values imply some order), *integer* (numeric variables that only include integers), or whether they are treated as *factor* (variables whose numeric values do not have order). As with numeric and string/character variables, we probably know whether the variables should be numeric or factor. With factor variables, we are restricted from doing certain types of statistical analysis, something that will become more apparent later in this book.

When classifying variable types `tidyverse` follows base R, but it uses slightly different terminology in places. When we read in data using `tidyverse` functions, the numeric variables are specified as `col_double()`, integer variables are specified as `col_integer()`, string/character variables are specified as `col_character()`, and factor variables are specified as `col_factor()`. The prefix `col_` simply refers to 'column', where 'column' is the generalised term for what we are calling 'variables'. We can see the specifications (i.e., classifications) by using the `spec()` function from the `readr` package.

```
spec(csvdata)
cols(
  Data_Zone = col_character(),
  Intermediate_Zone = col_character(),
  Council_area = col_character(),
  Total_population = col_double(),
  Working_age_population = col_double(),
  Income_rate = col_double(),
  Income_count = col_double(),
  Employment_rate = col_double(),
  Employment_count = col_double(),
  CIF = col_double(),
  ALCOHOL = col_double(),
  DRUG = col_double(),
  SMR = col_double(),
  DEPRESS = col_double(),
  LBWT = col_double(),
  EMERG = col_double(),
  Attendance = col_double(),
  Attainment = col_double(),
  no_qualifications = col_double(),
  not_participating = col_double(),
  University = col_double(),
  drive_petrol = col_double(),
  drive_GP = col_double(),
  drive_post = col_double(),
  drive_primary = col_double(),
  drive_retail = col_double(),
  drive_secondary = col_double(),
```

```
    PT_GP = col_double(),
    PT_post = col_double(),
    PT_retail = col_double(),
    Broadband = col_double(),
    crime_count = col_double(),
    crime_rate = col_double(),
    overcrowded_count = col_double(),
    nocentralheat_count = col_double(),
    overcrowded_rate = col_double(),
    nocentralheat_rate = col_double(),
    urban = col_double()
)
```

This shows we have three variables specified as `character` and the rest are classified as `double`. We actually saw a summary of this information when we used the `read_csv()` function, but here it is provided for each variable.

To get a quick look at our variables, we can use the `glimpse()` function from the `pillar` package; `pillar` is not part of `tidyverse`, but `tidyverse` automatically imports `pillar` functions when loaded. The `glimpse()` function is the tibble-friendly version of the `str()` function from base R.

```
glimpse(csvdata)
Rows: 6,976
Columns: 38
$ Data_Zone              <chr> "S01006506", "S01006507", "S01006508",
"S010065~
$ Intermediate_Zone      <chr> "Culter", "Culter", "Culter", "Culter",
"Culter~
$ Council_area           <chr> "Aberdeen City", "Aberdeen City",
"Aberdeen Cit~
$ Total_population       <dbl> 894, 793, 624, 537, 663, 759, 539, 788,
1123, 8~
$ Working_age_population <dbl> 580, 470, 461, 307, 415, 453, 345, 406,
709, 52~
$ Income_rate            <dbl> 0.08, 0.05, 0.06, 0.10, 0.10, 0.04, 0.02,
0.02,~
$ Income_count           <dbl> 71, 43, 40, 52, 68, 30, 13, 14, 17, 5,
14, 24, ~
$ Employment_rate        <dbl> 0.08, 0.05, 0.04, 0.08, 0.08, 0.04, 0.02,
0.03,~
$ Employment_count       <dbl> 49, 25, 19, 26, 32, 17, 8, 13, 12, 7, 14,
24, 4~
$ CIF                    <dbl> 65, 45, 45, 80, 95, 50, 40, 40, 25, 25,
35, 40,~
$ ALCOHOL                <dbl> 28.728183, 129.921017, 71.021154,
80.473293, 89~
```

```
$ DRUG              <dbl> 30.36573, 126.43368, 18.26983, 28.48559,
44.290~
$ SMR               <dbl> 69.55405, 80.57479, 41.14113, 103.48468,
138.64~
$ DEPRESS           <dbl> 0.13154961, 0.14250310, 0.12812500,
0.16396396,~
$ LBWT              <dbl> 0.00000000, 0.00000000, 0.03703704,
0.04761905,~
$ EMERG             <dbl> 74.21743, 86.08168, 69.31582, 88.17561,
88.7019~
$ Attendance        <dbl> 0.85207, 0.84746, 0.90476, 0.94268,
0.79739, 0.~
$ Attainment        <dbl> 5.882353, 5.961538, 5.750000, 6.200000,
5.86666~
$ no_qualifications <dbl> 52.758631, 95.854081, 38.559683, 80.060071,
77.~
$ not_participating <dbl> 0.000000000, 0.017699115, 0.014925373,
0.000000~
$ University        <dbl> 0.297297, 0.117188, 0.185185, 0.250000,
0.16494~
$ drive_petrol      <dbl> 2.540103, 3.915072, 3.323025, 2.622991,
2.11500~
$ drive_GP          <dbl> 3.074295, 4.309812, 3.784549, 2.778026,
2.35833~
$ drive_post        <dbl> 1.616239, 2.555858, 1.440991, 2.620681,
2.40841~
$ drive_primary     <dbl> 2.615747, 3.646697, 3.247325, 1.936908,
1.84567~
$ drive_retail      <dbl> 1.544260, 2.849656, 2.062255, 2.160142,
1.78463~
$ drive_secondary   <dbl> 9.930833, 11.042816, 10.616768,
10.036471, 9.65~
$ PT_GP             <dbl> 8.863589, 9.978272, 8.620700, 7.935112,
5.56896~
$ PT_post           <dbl> 5.856135, 7.515000, 4.321493, 8.433328,
6.96642~
$ PT_retail         <dbl> 6.023406, 7.926029, 5.770910, 8.329819,
6.63260~
$ Broadband         <dbl> 0.105050505, 0.013586957, 0.005633803,
0.113074~
$ crime_count       <dbl> 11.139188, 10.126535, 8.101228, 4.050614,
11.13~
$ crime_rate        <dbl> 124.59942, 127.69905, 129.82737, 75.43043,
168.~
$ overcrowded_count <dbl> 87, 85, 31, 42, 50, 27, 27, 15, 10, 29,
12, 39,~
$ nocentralheat_count <dbl> 10, 4, 8, 6, 7, 8, 9, 4, 3, 1, 1, 9, 0,
0, 0, 0~
```

```
$ overcrowded_rate    <dbl> 0.102112676, 0.101674641, 0.048211509,
0.072413~
$ nocentralheat_rate  <dbl> 0.011737089, 0.004784689, 0.012441680,
0.010344~
$ urban               <dbl> 0, 0, 0, 0, 0, 0, 0, 0, 0, 0, 0, 1, 1, 1,
1, 1,~
```

The output provides a summary of the number of rows and columns (which is the same information as in the Environment window), the variable names, the classification type of each variable, and the first few values of each variable. This output is most useful for checking the variable classifications and whether any wonky values are present. For example, we see that a number of variables (e.g., ALCOHOL) have many numbers to the right of the decimal point. Depending on our analysis goals, we likely will want to round these variables to have only two or three decimal places. Also, notice that the specification types are abbreviations – here, we have <chr> for a character variable and <dbl> for a double variable. The meaning of the abbreviations should be obvious, but we will also note new ones as we progress in the book.

If we are only interested in a single variable's classification, we can use the class() function. Unless we create a separate object for the variable, we need to tell R what dataset the variable belongs to. We do this by specifying the name of the dataset, then include a dollar sign ($), followed by the name of the variable. Let's look at the Council_area variable:

```
class(csvdata$Council_area)
[1] "character"
```

We see that its variable type is character. We can do the same for any variable in our dataset. If we want to look at the first few rows of a variable, we can use the head() function.

```
head(csvdata$Council_area)
[1] "Aberdeen City" "Aberdeen City" "Aberdeen City" "Aberdeen City"
[5] "Aberdeen City" "Aberdeen City"
```

This shows that the first few observations are 'Aberdeen City'.

If we want to look at the last few rows of a variable, we can use the tail() function.

```
tail(csvdata$Council_area)
[1] "West Lothian" "West Lothian" "West Lothian" "West Lothian" "West
Lothian"
[6] "West Lothian"
```

This shows that the last few observations are 'West Lothian'.

We can also get basic statistical summaries of our variables by using the summary() function. Depending on the variable type, we will get different statistical summaries. First, let's look at Total_population, which is a double variable.

```
summary(csvdata$Total_population)
   Min. 1st Qu.  Median    Mean 3rd Qu.    Max.
    0.0   635.0   755.0   777.6   886.0  3847.0
```

This provides the minimum, maximum, median, mean, and first and third quartiles; we will look extensively at summary statistics in Chapter 7.

Now, let's look at Council_area, which is a character variable.

```
summary(csvdata$Council_area)
  Length      Class      Mode
    6976 character character
```

Since Council_area is a character variable, R only gives us the total number of observations, the class, and a mode of character. For examining Council_area, this output is not useful.

Instead of using the summary() function, we can use two different options to see the values for character and factor variables. First, let's use the table() function to see all the council areas and the number of observations.

```
table(csvdata$Council_area)
```

Aberdeen City	Aberdeenshire	Angus
283	340	155
Argyll and Bute	City of Edinburgh	Clackmannanshire
125	597	72
Dumfries and Galloway	Dundee City	East Ayrshire
201	188	163
East Dunbartonshire	East Lothian	East Renfrewshire
130	132	122
Falkirk	Fife	Glasgow City
214	494	746
Highland	Inverclyde	Midlothian
312	114	115
Moray	Na h-Eileanan an Iar	North Ayrshire
126	36	186
North Lanarkshire	Orkney Islands	Perth and Kinross
447	29	186
Renfrewshire	Scottish Borders	Shetland Islands
225	143	30
South Ayrshire	South Lanarkshire	Stirling
153	431	121
West Dunbartonshire	West Lothian	
121	239	

This shows the number of observations for all 32 council areas.

Second, let's use the count() function from the dplyr package. The count() function literally counts the number of observations and is commonly used when we are grouping the data by multiple observations. To use count(), we need to introduce a new coding concept and syntax. Tidyverse utilises **pipes**, which allows us to link multiple functions together in one block of code. While this is a more elegant coding approach, it also makes tidyverse easier to work with and allows us to manipulate multiple aspects of the data simultaneously.[5]

We start using pipes with the %>% pipe operator. This is one of several pipe operators and is the most extensively used. We can think of %>% as telling R to continue to and combine the next line of code with the previous line. Although though not strictly correct, I tend to think of %>% as adding together lines of code. Let's use the count() function to see the number of observations (which are datazones) per council area.

```
csvdata %>%
  count(Council_area)
# A tibble: 32 x 2
   Council_area                 n
   <chr>                    <int>
 1 Aberdeen City              283
 2 Aberdeenshire              340
 3 Angus                      155
 4 Argyll and Bute            125
 5 City of Edinburgh          597
 6 Clackmannanshire            72
 7 Dumfries and Galloway      201
 8 Dundee City                188
 9 East Ayrshire              163
10 East Dunbartonshire        130
# ... with 22 more rows
```

The output shows the first 10 council areas alphabetically and that there are an additional 22 council areas not shown. Depending on our goal, this might not be very useful. Instead, we might want to sort variables by the number of observations. If we add the option sort = TRUE into the count() function specification, Council_area will be sorted in descending order.

```
csvdata %>%
  count(Council_area, sort = TRUE)
# A tibble: 32 x 2
   Council_area             n
   <chr>                <int>
 1 Glasgow City           746
 2 City of Edinburgh      597
 3 Fife                   494
 4 North Lanarkshire      447
```

---

[5]For more information on pipes, see https://r4ds.had.co.nz/pipes.html.

```
 5 South Lanarkshire    431
 6 Aberdeenshire        340
 7 Highland             312
 8 Aberdeen City        283
 9 West Lothian         239
10 Renfrewshire         225
# ... with 22 more rows
```

This shows that Glasgow City and City of Edinburgh have the most observations in the data, which makes sense since they are the two largest cities in Scotland.

MANAGING MISSING VALUES

When reading in data and before we perform statistical analysis, we often need to deal with the missing values in some way. In the next chapter, we will look at recoding variables, where we specify certain variable values as missing, but here we will look at dealing with missing values in the aggregate.

Many statistical analysis functions in R allow us to remove missing values from the particular analysis, 'on the fly' as it were, instead of having a dataset that has no missing values. For many statistical functions, the typical default is for R to automatically delete any observations with missing values for the variables we are using (known as listwise deletion). For other statistical functions, we need to specify how missing values are treated. Possible options we commonly come across to do this include:

- na.rm = TRUE or na.rm = FALSE, where na.rm stands for 'remove missing value'.
- na.action = na.omit or na.action = na.exclude, where na.action stands for the 'action' to be taken with missing values. Both na.omit and na.exclude perform the same job of simply removing the missing values from the analysis.

Below is an example of how we would use na.rm = TRUE for the mean() function.

```
mean(csvdata$Total_population, na.rm = TRUE)
[1] 777.6376
```

While we could remove all observations with missing values for any variable in a dataset, this approach often removes more observations than is needed. An alternative approach is to remove observations with missing values only for the specific variables we are using. We can do this with the filter() function from the dplyr package. The filter() function acts just as you imagine: it filters the data based on a set of conditions. Below, we use the is.na() function in the filter() function to remove missing values from the variable Attendance. Since is.na() means 'is missing', we actually need to specify that we want to keep observations that are 'not missing'. To do this, we include ! before is.na(), where ! means 'not'.

```
csvdata %>%
  filter(!is.na(Attendance))
# A tibble: 6,409 x 38
   Data_Zone Intermediate_Zone    Council_area  Total_population Working_
age_pop~
   <chr>     <chr>                <chr>                    <dbl>    <dbl>
 1 S01006506 Culter               Aberdeen City              894      580
 2 S01006507 Culter               Aberdeen City              793      470
 3 S01006508 Culter               Aberdeen City              624      461
 4 S01006509 Culter               Aberdeen City              537      307
 5 S01006510 Culter               Aberdeen City              663      415
 6 S01006511 Culter               Aberdeen City              759      453
 7 S01006512 Culter               Aberdeen City              539      345
 8 S01006513 Cults, Bieldside a~  Aberdeen City              788      406
 9 S01006514 Cults, Bieldside a~  Aberdeen City             1123      709
10 S01006515 Cults, Bieldside a~  Aberdeen City              816      529
# ... with 6,399 more rows, and 33 more variables: Income_rate <dbl>,
#   Income_count <dbl>, Employment_rate <dbl>, Employment_count <dbl>,
#   CIF <dbl>, ALCOHOL <dbl>, DRUG <dbl>, SMR <dbl>, DEPRESS <dbl>, LBWT <dbl>,
#   EMERG <dbl>, Attendance <dbl>, Attainment <dbl>, no_qualifications <dbl>,
#   not_participating <dbl>, University <dbl>, drive_petrol <dbl>,
#   drive_GP <dbl>, drive_post <dbl>, drive_primary <dbl>, drive_retail <dbl>,
#   drive_secondary <dbl>, PT_GP <dbl>, PT_post <dbl>, PT_retail <dbl>, ...
```

The output shows there are 6409 datazones that *do not* have missing values for Attendance. For completeness, let's see what happens when we do not include !.

```
csvdata %>%
  filter(is.na(Attendance))
# A tibble: 567 x 38
   Data_Zone Intermediate_Zone      Council_area Total_population Working_
age_pop~
   <chr>     <chr>                  <chr>                   <dbl>    <dbl>
 1 S01006516 Cults, Bieldside an~   Aberdeen Ci~              629      419
 2 S01006518 Cults, Bieldside an~   Aberdeen Ci~              664      370
 3 S01006522 Cults, Bieldside an~   Aberdeen Ci~              675      412
 4 S01006524 Cults, Bieldside an~   Aberdeen Ci~             1056      629
 5 S01006532 Braeside, Mannofiel~   Aberdeen Ci~              793      445
 6 S01006537 Braeside, Mannofiel~   Aberdeen Ci~              920      497
 7 S01006538 Braeside, Mannofiel~   Aberdeen Ci~              548      335
 8 S01006539 Braeside, Mannofiel~   Aberdeen Ci~              781      462
 9 S01006541 Braeside, Mannofiel~   Aberdeen Ci~              864      468
10 S01006542 Braeside, Mannofiel~   Aberdeen Ci~             1131      664
# ... with 557 more rows, and 33 more variables: Income_rate <dbl>,
#   Income_count <dbl>, Employment_rate <dbl>, Employment_count <dbl>,
```

```
#   CIF <dbl>, ALCOHOL <dbl>, DRUG <dbl>, SMR <dbl>, DEPRESS <dbl>, LBWT <dbl>,
#   EMERG <dbl>, Attendance <dbl>, Attainment <dbl>, no_qualifications <dbl>,
#   not_participating <dbl>, University <dbl>, drive_petrol <dbl>,
#   drive_GP <dbl>, drive_post <dbl>, drive_primary <dbl>, drive_retail <dbl>,
#   drive_secondary <dbl>, PT_GP <dbl>, PT_post <dbl>, PT_retail <dbl>, ...
```

This time the output shows there are 567 datazones that *do* have missing values for Attendance.

SUBSETTING DATA

There are many reasons why we might want to subset data. Particularly when we download public data, we often want to get rid of irrelevant variables. Or, we may only want to work with a handful of variables instead of hundreds or thousands of variables.

While we could use the common subset() function, subsetting in tidyverse is a terrific introduction to the data-wrangling approach of tidyverse. We make use of the select() function from the dplyr package, where we specify the variables we want to subset. We will create a new object for each new tibble in order to take a closer look.

First, we will subset the data to keep a single variable, Council_area.

```
simd1 <- csvdata %>%
    select(Council_area)
```

To select an additional variable, we just include a comma and then the variable name.

```
simd2 <- csvdata %>%
    select(Council_area, Total_population)
```

If we want to subset for a range of variables, we can include a colon.

```
simd3 <- csvdata %>%
    select(Council_area:Income_rate)
```

Often, especially when we are just exploring the data, we want to drill down to specific observations or variable values. We can do this by using the filter() function with the select() function. We will first subset the data to only look at datazones in Glasgow City. Note, we need to specify == and not = in the code. Also, if we are using the select() function, the variable we are filtering needs to be included in the selected variables.

```
simd4 <- csvdata %>%
    select(Intermediate_Zone:Income_rate) %>%
    filter(Council_area=="Glasgow City")
```

We see in the `Environment` window that there are 746 datazones in Glasgow City.

We can drill further down by adding new conditions. Below we ask for the Hillhead intermediate zone of Glasgow City; we can think of an intermediate zone as a neighbourhood. We do this by including `& Intermediate_Zone=="Hillhead"`, where, as you might guess, `&` is for 'and'. Our `filter()` function specification tells R to only keep observations that are in Glasgow City *and* are in the Hillhead intermediate zone.

```
simd5 <- csvdata %>%
    select(Intermediate_Zone:Income_rate) %>%
    filter(Council_area=="Glasgow City" & Intermediate_Zone=="Hillhead")
```

This subsets the data down to seven datazones. (Although it might appear that specifying the `Council_area` is redundant, if we do not include it we will actually get datazones in a suburb of Glasgow.)

Sometimes we want to subset data by a certain variable value. This might be a string (or character) or numeric value. First, let's look at how to do this with a string/character value. Let's subset the data to only include intermediate zones in cities' downtowns, which are commonly referred to as 'city centres' in the UK. We will use the `str_detect()` function from the `stringr` package, wrapped by the `filter()` function, which literally detects the string value we specify – here `"Centre"`.

```
simd6 <- csvdata %>%
    select(Intermediate_Zone:Income_rate) %>%
    filter(str_detect(Intermediate_Zone, "Centre"))
```

Looking at the observations in `simd6`, we see this actually does a poor job, as a number of small town centres are included and Edinburgh is completely missing.

Second, let's subset the data by a specific numeric value. Here, we'll do a simple version where we filter for datazones that have 25% or more of their residents classified as employment deprived (which includes people receiving unemployment support, disability or incapacity support, etc.). We specify the variable (`Employment_rate`), the greater than or equals condition (>=), and the numeric value (.25 for 25%).

```
simd7 <- csvdata %>%
    select(Intermediate_Zone:Income_rate, Employment_rate) %>%
    filter(Employment_rate >= .25)
```

We see this includes 293 datazones.

Let's further drill down to see how many of these datazones are in Glasgow by adding `Council_area=="Glasgow City"` to the `filter()` function.

```
simd8 <- csvdata %>%
    select(Intermediate_Zone:Income_rate, Employment_rate) %>%
    filter(Employment_rate >= .25 & Council_area=="Glasgow City")
```

We see that Glasgow has 113 of the 293 datazones where 25% or more residents are employment deprived. (Glasgow is generally considered to be the most deprived city in the UK.)

MERGING DIFFERENT DATASETS

Tidyverse provides a number of ways to merge data through the use of join() functions from the dplyr package. The *key* – pun intended – to all the join() functions is that there needs to be a variable (a *key*) in each dataset we are merging that can individually identify the cases/observations. Without this key we are unable to merge the data. We specify the key using the by = option in the join() functions.

We start with the inner_join() function, which we use when the datasets all have the same number of observations; otherwise, all unmatched observations will be deleted. We will merge the 2020 SIMD data with a dataset that has the NHS Scotland health boards by datazone. We need to first read in the health board data (titled scottish health boards by datazone.xlsx) using the read_xlsx() function.

```
healthboard <- read_xlsx("scottish health boards by datazone.xlsx")

glimpse(healthboard)
Rows: 6,976
Columns: 4
$ data_zone          <chr>      "S01006506", "S01006507", "S01006508",
"S01006509", ~
$ intermediate_zone  <chr> "Culter", "Culter", "Culter", "Culter",
"Culter", "C~
$ council_area       <chr> "Aberdeen City", "Aberdeen City", "Aberdeen
City", "~
$ health_board       <chr> "Grampian", "Grampian", "Grampian",
"Grampian", "Gra~

table(healthboard$council_area)
```

Aberdeen City	Aberdeenshire	Angus
283	340	155
Argyll and Bute	City of Edinburgh	Clackmannanshire
125	597	72
Dumfries and Galloway	Dundee City	East Ayrshire
201	188	163
East Dunbartonshire	East Lothian	East Renfrewshire
130	132	122
Falkirk	Fife	Glasgow City
214	494	746

Highland	Inverclyde	Midlothian
312	114	115
Moray	Na h-Eileanan an Iar	North Ayrshire
126	36	186
North Lanarkshire	Orkney Islands	Perth and Kinross
447	29	186
Renfrewshire	Scottish Borders	Shetland Islands
225	143	30
South Ayrshire	South Lanarkshire	Stirling
153	431	121
West Dunbartonshire	West Lothian	
121	239	

We see there are the same number of observations as in the 2020 SIMD data.

Because the *keys* have different variable names, we need to specify the keys for each dataset. We specify the *key* (Data_Zone) from our first dataset (csvdata) first and then the *key* (data_zone) from the dataset we are merging (healthboard) second.

```
merged_simd1 <- csvdata %>%
    inner_join(healthboard, by = c("Data_Zone" = "data_zone"))


glimpse(merged_simd1)
Rows: 6,976
Columns: 41
$ Data_Zone               <chr> "S01006506", "S01006507", "S01006508",
"S010065~
$ Intermediate_Zone       <chr> "Culter", "Culter", "Culter", "Culter",
"Culter~
$ Council_area            <chr> "Aberdeen City", "Aberdeen City", "Aberdeen
Cit~
$ Total_population        <dbl> 894, 793, 624, 537, 663, 759, 539, 788,
1123, 8~
$ Working_age_population  <dbl> 580, 470, 461, 307, 415, 453, 345, 406,
709, 52~
$ Income_rate             <dbl> 0.08, 0.05, 0.06, 0.10, 0.10, 0.04,
0.02, 0.02,~
$ Income_count            <dbl> 71, 43, 40, 52, 68, 30, 13, 14, 17, 5,
14, 24, ~
$ Employment_rate         <dbl> 0.08, 0.05, 0.04, 0.08, 0.08, 0.04,
0.02, 0.03,~
$ Employment_count        <dbl> 49, 25, 19, 26, 32, 17, 8, 13, 12, 7,
14, 24, 4~
$ CIF                     <dbl> 65, 45, 45, 80, 95, 50, 40, 40, 25, 25,
35, 40,~
$ ALCOHOL                 <dbl> 28.728183, 129.921017, 71.021154, 80.473293,
89~
$ DRUG                    <dbl> 30.36573, 126.43368, 18.26983, 28.48559,
44.290~
```

```
$ SMR                   <dbl> 69.55405, 80.57479, 41.14113, 103.48468,
138.64~
$ DEPRESS               <dbl> 0.13154961, 0.14250310, 0.12812500,
0.16396396,~
$ LBWT                  <dbl> 0.00000000, 0.00000000, 0.03703704,
0.04761905,~
$ EMERG                 <dbl> 74.21743, 86.08168, 69.31582, 88.17561,
88.7019~
$ Attendance            <dbl> 0.85207, 0.84746, 0.90476, 0.94268,
0.79739, 0.~
$ Attainment            <dbl> 5.882353, 5.961538, 5.750000, 6.200000,
5.86666~
$ no_qualifications     <dbl> 52.758631, 95.854081, 38.559683, 80.060071,
77.~
$ not_participating     <dbl> 0.000000000, 0.017699115, 0.014925373,
0.000000~
$ University            <dbl> 0.297297, 0.117188, 0.185185, 0.250000,
0.16494~
$ drive_petrol          <dbl> 2.540103, 3.915072, 3.323025, 2.622991,
2.11500~
$ drive_GP              <dbl> 3.074295, 4.309812, 3.784549, 2.778026,
2.35833~
$ drive_post            <dbl> 1.616239, 2.555858, 1.440991, 2.620681,
2.40841~
$ drive_primary         <dbl> 2.615747, 3.646697, 3.247325, 1.936908,
1.84567~
$ drive_retail          <dbl> 1.544260, 2.849656, 2.062255, 2.160142,
1.78463~
$ drive_secondary       <dbl> 9.930833, 11.042816, 10.616768, 10.036471,
9.65~
$ PT_GP                 <dbl> 8.863589, 9.978272, 8.620700, 7.935112,
5.56896~
$ PT_post               <dbl> 5.856135, 7.515000, 4.321493, 8.433328,
6.96642~
$ PT_retail             <dbl> 6.023406, 7.926029, 5.770910, 8.329819,
6.63260~
$ Broadband             <dbl> 0.105050505, 0.013586957, 0.005633803,
0.113074~
$ crime_count           <dbl> 11.139188, 10.126535, 8.101228, 4.050614,
11.13~
$ crime_rate            <dbl> 124.59942, 127.69905, 129.82737, 75.43043,
168.~
$ overcrowded_count     <dbl> 87, 85, 31, 42, 50, 27, 27, 15, 10, 29,
12, 39,~
$ nocentralheat_count   <dbl> 10, 4, 8, 6, 7, 8, 9, 4, 3, 1, 1, 9, 0,
0, 0, 0~
$ overcrowded_rate      <dbl> 0.102112676, 0.101674641, 0.048211509,
0.072413~
```

```
$ nocentralheat_rate        <dbl> 0.011737089, 0.004784689, 0.012441680,
0.010344~
$ urban                     <dbl> 0, 0, 0, 0, 0, 0, 0, 0, 0, 0, 0, 1, 1,
1, 1, 1,~
$ intermediate_zone         <chr> "Culter", "Culter", "Culter", "Culter",
"Culter~
$ council_area              <chr> "Aberdeen City", "Aberdeen City",
"Aberdeen Cit~
$ health_board              <chr> "Grampian", "Grampian", "Grampian",
"Grampian",~
```

Viewing the merged data, we see that we have just pasted three variables from the health boards data (`intermediate_zone`, `council_area`, and `health_board`) to the end of the SIMD data. The `data_zone` variable is removed since we told R that it had the same information as `Data_Zone`. If we had identical variable names in the merged datasets, then suffixes are automatically added to the duplicate variable names; with just two datasets, `.x` and `.y` will automatically be added to the duplicate variable names. Even though the SIMD data already has variables for the intermediate zone and council area, the variable names are not identical (because of the use of upper- and lower-case letters) and thus suffixes are not added.

If we know there are duplicate variables, we can remove them when we do the merge by adding the `select()` function and specifying which variables to remove by including `-c()`. Doing this clearly demonstrates the benefit of using `tidyverse`: we are able to merge and subset the data in a single code chunk. Below we repeat the merge and remove `intermediate_zone` and `council_area` that were in the `healthboard` data.

```
merged_simd1 <- csvdata %>%
    inner_join(healthboard, by = c("Data_Zone" = "data_zone")) %>%
    select(-c(intermediate_zone, council_area))

glimpse(merged_simd1)
Rows: 6,976
Columns: 39
$ Data_Zone                 <chr> "S01006506", "S01006507", "S01006508",
"S010065~
$ Intermediate_Zone         <chr> "Culter", "Culter", "Culter", "Culter",
"Culter~
$ Council_area              <chr> "Aberdeen City", "Aberdeen City",
"Aberdeen Cit~
$ Total_population          <dbl> 894, 793, 624, 537, 663, 759, 539, 788,
1123, 8~
$ Working_age_population    <dbl> 580, 470, 461, 307, 415, 453, 345, 406,
709, 52~
$ Income_rate               <dbl> 0.08, 0.05, 0.06, 0.10, 0.10, 0.04,
0.02, 0.02,~
$ Income_count              <dbl> 71, 43, 40, 52, 68, 30, 13, 14, 17,
5, 14, 24, ~
```

```
$ Employment_rate    <dbl> 0.08, 0.05, 0.04, 0.08, 0.08, 0.04,
0.02, 0.03,~
$ Employment_count   <dbl> 49, 25, 19, 26, 32, 17, 8, 13, 12, 7,
14, 24, 4~
$ CIF                <dbl> 65, 45, 45, 80, 95, 50, 40, 40, 25, 25,
35, 40,~
$ ALCOHOL            <dbl> 28.728183, 129.921017, 71.021154,
80.473293, 89~
$ DRUG               <dbl> 30.36573, 126.43368, 18.26983, 28.48559,
44.290~
$ SMR                <dbl> 69.55405, 80.57479, 41.14113, 103.48468,
138.64~
$ DEPRESS            <dbl> 0.13154961, 0.14250310, 0.12812500,
0.16396396,~
$ LBWT               <dbl> 0.00000000, 0.00000000, 0.03703704,
0.04761905,~
$ EMERG              <dbl> 74.21743, 86.08168, 69.31582, 88.17561,
88.7019~
$ Attendance         <dbl> 0.85207, 0.84746, 0.90476, 0.94268,
0.79739, 0.~
$ Attainment         <dbl> 5.882353, 5.961538, 5.750000, 6.200000,
5.86666~
$ no_qualifications  <dbl> 52.758631, 95.854081, 38.559683, 80.060071,
77.~
$ not_participating  <dbl> 0.000000000, 0.017699115, 0.014925373,
0.000000~
$ University         <dbl> 0.297297, 0.117188, 0.185185, 0.250000,
0.16494~
$ drive_petrol       <dbl> 2.540103, 3.915072, 3.323025, 2.622991,
2.11500~
$ drive_GP           <dbl> 3.074295, 4.309812, 3.784549, 2.778026,
2.35833~
$ drive_post         <dbl> 1.616239, 2.555858, 1.440991, 2.620681,
2.40841~
$ drive_primary      <dbl> 2.615747, 3.646697, 3.247325, 1.936908,
1.84567~
$ drive_retail       <dbl> 1.544260, 2.849656, 2.062255, 2.160142,
1.78463~
$ drive_secondary    <dbl> 9.930833, 11.042816, 10.616768, 10.036471,
9.65~
$ PT_GP              <dbl> 8.863589, 9.978272, 8.620700, 7.935112,
5.56896~
$ PT_post            <dbl> 5.856135, 7.515000, 4.321493, 8.433328,
6.96642~
$ PT_retail          <dbl> 6.023406, 7.926029, 5.770910, 8.329819,
6.63260~
$ Broadband          <dbl> 0.105050505, 0.013586957, 0.005633803,
0.113074~
```

```
$ crime_count          <dbl> 11.139188, 10.126535, 8.101228, 4.050614,
11.13~
$ crime_rate           <dbl> 124.59942, 127.69905, 129.82737, 75.43043,
168.~
$ overcrowded_count    <dbl> 87, 85, 31, 42, 50, 27, 27, 15, 10, 29,
12, 39,~
$ nocentralheat_count  <dbl> 10, 4, 8, 6, 7, 8, 9, 4, 3, 1, 1, 9, 0,
0, 0, 0~
$ overcrowded_rate     <dbl> 0.102112676, 0.101674641, 0.048211509,
0.072413~
$ nocentralheat_rate   <dbl> 0.011737089, 0.004784689, 0.012441680,
0.010344~
$ urban                <dbl> 0, 0, 0, 0, 0, 0, 0, 0, 0, 0, 0, 1, 1,
1, 1, 1,~
$ health_board         <chr> "Grampian", "Grampian", "Grampian",
"Grampian",~
```

We now see that `intermediate_zone` and `council_area` have been removed.

If we do not want to delete unmatched observations, there are several alternatives to the `inner_join()` function. Commonly, we want to preserve the observations in one main dataset when merging additional datasets. In this case, we can use the `left_join()` function, which keeps all the observations that appear in the first dataset (the left or *X* dataset) and deletes all the unmatched observations that appear in the second dataset (the right or *Y* dataset). Any observations in the first dataset that are not matched to the second dataset will have `"NA"` included for the variable values of the second dataset.

```
merged_simd2 <- csvdata %>%
    left_join(healthboard, by = c("Data_Zone" = "data_zone")) %>%
    select(-c(intermediate_zone, council_area))

glimpse(merged_simd2)
Rows: 6,976
Columns: 39
$ Data_Zone               <chr> "S01006506", "S01006507", "S01006508",
"S010065~
$ Intermediate_Zone       <chr> "Culter", "Culter", "Culter", "Culter",
"Culter~
$ Council_area            <chr> "Aberdeen City", "Aberdeen City", "Aberdeen
Cit~
$ Total_population        <dbl> 894, 793, 624, 537, 663, 759, 539, 788,
1123, 8~
$ Working_age_population  <dbl> 580, 470, 461, 307, 415, 453, 345, 406,
709, 52~
$ Income_rate             <dbl> 0.08, 0.05, 0.06, 0.10, 0.10, 0.04,
0.02, 0.02,~
$ Income_count            <dbl> 71, 43, 40, 52, 68, 30, 13, 14, 17, 5,
14, 24, ~
```

```
$ Employment_rate      <dbl> 0.08, 0.05, 0.04, 0.08, 0.08, 0.04, 0.02,
0.03,~
$ Employment_count     <dbl> 49, 25, 19, 26, 32, 17, 8, 13, 12, 7, 14,
24, 4~
$ CIF                  <dbl> 65, 45, 45, 80, 95, 50, 40, 40, 25, 25,
35, 40,~
$ ALCOHOL              <dbl> 28.728183, 129.921017, 71.021154, 80.473293,
89~
$ DRUG                 <dbl> 30.36573, 126.43368, 18.26983, 28.48559,
44.290~
$ SMR                  <dbl> 69.55405, 80.57479, 41.14113, 103.48468,
138.64~
$ DEPRESS              <dbl> 0.13154961, 0.14250310, 0.12812500,
0.16396396,~
$ LBWT                 <dbl> 0.00000000, 0.00000000, 0.03703704,
0.04761905,~
$ EMERG                <dbl> 74.21743, 86.08168, 69.31582, 88.17561,
88.7019~
$ Attendance           <dbl> 0.85207, 0.84746, 0.90476, 0.94268,
0.79739, 0.~
$ Attainment           <dbl> 5.882353, 5.961538, 5.750000, 6.200000,
5.86666~
$ no_qualifications    <dbl> 52.758631, 95.854081, 38.559683, 80.060071,
77.~
$ not_participating    <dbl> 0.000000000, 0.017699115, 0.014925373,
0.000000~
$ University           <dbl> 0.297297, 0.117188, 0.185185, 0.250000,
0.16494~
$ drive_petrol         <dbl> 2.540103, 3.915072, 3.323025, 2.622991,
2.11500~
$ drive_GP             <dbl> 3.074295, 4.309812, 3.784549, 2.778026,
2.35833~
$ drive_post           <dbl> 1.616239, 2.555858, 1.440991, 2.620681,
2.40841~
$ drive_primary        <dbl> 2.615747, 3.646697, 3.247325, 1.936908,
1.84567~
$ drive_retail         <dbl> 1.544260, 2.849656, 2.062255, 2.160142,
1.78463~
$ drive_secondary      <dbl> 9.930833, 11.042816, 10.616768, 10.036471,
9.65~
$ PT_GP                <dbl> 8.863589, 9.978272, 8.620700, 7.935112,
5.56896~
$ PT_post              <dbl> 5.856135, 7.515000, 4.321493, 8.433328,
6.96642~
$ PT_retail            <dbl> 6.023406, 7.926029, 5.770910, 8.329819,
6.63260~
$ Broadband            <dbl> 0.105050505, 0.013586957, 0.005633803,
0.113074~
```

```
$ crime_count          <dbl> 11.139188, 10.126535, 8.101228, 4.050614,
11.13~
$ crime_rate           <dbl> 124.59942, 127.69905, 129.82737, 75.43043,
168.~
$ overcrowded_count    <dbl> 87, 85, 31, 42, 50, 27, 27, 15, 10, 29,
12, 39,~
$ nocentralheat_count  <dbl> 10, 4, 8, 6, 7, 8, 9, 4, 3, 1, 1, 9, 0,
0, 0, 0~
$ overcrowded_rate     <dbl> 0.102112676, 0.101674641, 0.048211509,
0.072413~
$ nocentralheat_rate   <dbl> 0.011737089, 0.004784689, 0.012441680,
0.010344~
$ urban                <dbl> 0, 0, 0, 0, 0, 0, 0, 0, 0, 0, 0, 1, 1,
1, 1, 1,~
$ health_board         <chr> "Grampian", "Grampian", "Grampian",
"Grampian",~
```

In this case, the `merged_simd2` dataset is the same as the `merged_simd1` dataset because they have the same observations.

There are other join functions, including `right_join()`, `full_join()`, `semi_join()`, and `anti_join()`. The `right_join()` function keeps all the observations in the second dataset (the right or *Y* dataset), the `full_join()` function keeps all the observations from both datasets, the `semi_join()` function keeps all the observations in the first dataset *with* a match in the second dataset, and the `anti_join()` function keeps all the observations in the first dataset *without* a match in the second dataset. Lastly, the `join()` functions allow us to merge more than two datasets at the same time as long as each dataset has a key to link the observations.

The `join()` functions provide an easy and effective way to merge different datasets in R. However, it is very easy to use the wrong `join()` function for what we want to accomplish. Therefore, it is important to closely examine our merged data before moving on to any analysis.

PIVOTING DATASETS

We can perform an array of different data-pivoting operations using the `tidyr` package. If you have done table pivoting in Excel, then you are already familiar with the concept of data pivoting. Pivoting simply involves simultaneously transforming columns to rows or rows to columns. We commonly pivot data for specific types of data visualisations and statistical analysis techniques. Let's read in a new dataset on the number of Covid-19 cases by NHS Scotland health board to demonstrate data pivoting. The file is called `covid total by health board.xlsx` and we'll use the `read_xlsx()` function.

```
covid <- read_xlsx("covid total by health board.xlsx")
covid
# A tibble: 14 x 3
  health_board          `2020` `2021`
   <chr>                 <dbl>  <dbl>
```

```
 1 Ayrshire and Arran          9388  36168
 2 Borders                     1586   7569
 3 Dumfries and Galloway       1705  11108
 4 Fife                        6278  34551
 5 Forth Valley                5622  30073
 6 Grampian                    7870  39166
 7 Greater Glasgow and Clyde  41341 134789
 8 Highland                    2172  20279
 9 Lanarkshire                24351  77406
10 Lothian                    18577  85890
11 Orkney                        39    502
12 Shetland                     128    630
13 Tayside                     8300  37099
14 Western Isles                 96    949
```

This data is wide or what the `tidyverse` folks would call *untidy* data.

To *tidy* the data, we will move each year's Covid total to a new row for each health board. To do this, we will use the `pivot_longer()` function from the `tidyr` package, where we first specify the variables to pivot, then the name of a new variable with the original variable names (here, `year`), and finally the name of a new variable with the original variables' values (here, `cases`).

```
covid1 <- covid %>%
    pivot_longer(c(`2020`,`2021`), names_to = "year", values_to = "cases")
covid1
# A tibble: 28 x 3
   health_board           year  cases
   <chr>                  <chr> <dbl>
 1 Ayrshire and Arran     2020   9388
 2 Ayrshire and Arran     2021  36168
 3 Borders                2020   1586
 4 Borders                2021   7569
 5 Dumfries and Galloway  2020   1705
 6 Dumfries and Galloway  2021  11108
 7 Fife                   2020   6278
 8 Fife                   2021  34551
 9 Forth Valley           2020   5622
10 Forth Valley           2021  30073
# ... with 18 more rows
```

We see that the new dataset `covid1` now has 28 observations (14 observations × 2 variables). This data is now considered *tidied*.

We can do the reverse with the `pivot_wider()` function from the `tidyr` package.

```
covid2 <- covid1 %>%
    pivot_wider(names_from = "year", values_from = "cases")
covid2
```

```
# A tibble: 14 x 3
   health_board                `2020` `2021`
   <chr>                        <dbl>  <dbl>
 1 Ayrshire and Arran            9388  36168
 2 Borders                       1586   7569
 3 Dumfries and Galloway         1705  11108
 4 Fife                          6278  34551
 5 Forth Valley                  5622  30073
 6 Grampian                      7870  39166
 7 Greater Glasgow and Clyde    41341 134789
 8 Highland                      2172  20279
 9 Lanarkshire                  24351  77406
10 Lothian                      18577  85890
11 Orkney                          39    502
12 Shetland                       128    630
13 Tayside                       8300  37099
14 Western Isles                   96    949
```

SAVING DATA

Now that we have done all this work of reading in data, dealing with missing values, and subsetting data, we probably want to save the work we have done. In truth, it is not critical to save everything we did, because by having a saved R script or R Markdown file of all the code we can easily re-create our work during a different R session. However, let's consider several ways of saving our data.

Saving data in R is slightly different from many statistical programs. Many programs like Stata allow you to simply save the data like you might in Word. In R, we generally use a `write()` function where we 'write' our data in a specific format, which creates a new data file that we save (usually in our working directory). As we saw with reading in different types of data formats, we can write to different types of data formats. We should also make sure that the data is correctly saved in the file type. For example, .csv files can struggle with text characters and, possibly obviously, commas in the data. If this occurs, we might want to save the data as a .xlsx file. Saving data to proprietary statistical program file types like Stata also can cause problems. For example, Stata does not allow certain characters to be used in variable names and thus may refuse to open the data. Since we are mostly using .csv, .xlsx, and .dta files in this book, let's just look at how to write to those formats.

Let's first write our dataset `csvdata` to a .csv file using the `write_csv()` function from the readr function. In the parentheses of `write_csv()`, we include the name of the dataset in R that we want to save (`csvdata`) and what we want the name of the dataset to be saved as (`csvdata.csv`).

```
write_csv(csvdata, "csvdata.csv")
```

We simply need to look in our working directory to see whether the file saved (in my case it saved successfully).

Now let's write `csvdata` to a .xlsx file using the `write_xlsx()` function from the `writexl` package, which we need to load first.

```
library(writexl)
write_xlsx(csvdata, "csvdata.xlsx")
```

Next, let's write `csvdata` to a .dta file using the `write_dta()` function from the haven package.

```
write_dta(csvdata, "csvdata.dta")
```

Frequently R (and other statistical programs) gets grumpy when we switch data formats. Even if you do not get an error message in R, do not forget to check the newly created dataset in the other statistical program (e.g., Stata, SPSS) to make sure it is correct.

Another option we have is to save our workspace, which includes all the objects we have created during our session in RStudio. These objects routinely include variables and data frames/tibbles (which we have been referring to as datasets), and they are all listed in the `Environment` window. To save our workspace, we can click on the file icon in the `Environment` window, click on `Save Workspace As` under `Session` in the menu bar at the top of RStudio, or use the `save.image()` function as below. Regardless of how you save the workspace, you need to use the file extension .RData.

```
save.image("C:/QSSD/Chapter 4 - Data Management/example.RData")
```

If we do not want to save the whole workspace, but only specific objects, we can use the `save()` function. Let's save the `csvdata` dataset as a .RData file. We need to specify the object name (`csvdata`) and the name under which we want the object saved (`csvdata.RData`). The new file will then be saved to our working directory.

```
save(csvdata, file="csvdata.RData")
```

Any of the objects we saved with the .RData file extension can be loaded into our session using the `load()` function.

```
load("csvdata.RData")
```

Different users have different preferences as to whether to save the workspace and/or the objects we created. Generally, it is advised not to save our whole workspace since it might create confusion in our next R session (Imai 2017). It makes sense to save certain objects such as data visualisations or objects that took a long time to create, such as objects created from simulations. Even in these cases, however, we have different options instead of saving the entire workspace.[6]

---

[6]Note that when we quit an R session we will be asked whether we want to save the workspace.

CONCLUSION

Although we have gone through a great deal of material on data management, in truth we have just scratched the surface. This chapter provides the basics to get us going, but there is not space here to cover all different scenarios and problems dealing with data management. You can usually find the answer or at least a suggestion by searching the internet; the nitty-gritty of coding is where the internet is quite excellent. Data management is not the most exciting aspect of doing QSS, but it is critical for doing any type of data analysis. In the next chapter, we expand on an important aspect of data management by examining variable recoding and manipulation.

R Packages Used in This Chapter

- `dplyr` (loaded with `tidyverse`)
- `haven`
- `pillar` (loaded with `tidyverse`)
- `readr` (loaded with `tidyverse`)
- `readxl`
- `stringr` (loaded with `tidyverse`)
- `tidyr` (loaded with `tidyverse`)
- `tidyverse`
- `writexl`

R Functions Used in This Chapter

- `c()` - concatenate
- `class()` - class of object
- `count()` - counts the number of unique values of a variable or variables using the `dplyr` package
- `filter()` - subset data based on variables' values using `dplyr` package
- `glimpse()` - quick view of data using `pillar` package
- `head()` - provides first few observations' values for dataset
- `inner_join()` - joins (or merges) datasets using `dplyr` package
- `is.na()` - checks for missing values (NAs) in variables
- `left_join()` - joins (or merges) datasets using `dplyr` package
- `load()` - load objects saved as .RData file
- `mean()` - mean/average
- `names()` - provides names of saved values of object
- `pivot_longer()` - pivot data from wide to long format using `tidyr` package
- `pivot_wider()` - pivot data from long to wide format using `tidyr` package
- `read_csv()` - read in .csv data file using `readr` package
- `read_delim()` - read in delimited files including .tab and .txt files using `readr` package
- `read_dta()` - read in .dta data file using `haven` package
- `read_sas()` - read in .sas data file using `haven` package

- `read_sav()` - read in .sav data file using `haven` package
- `read_xlsx()` - read in an Excel data file using `readxl` package
- `save.image()` - save R workspace as .RData file
- `save()` - save data as .RData file
- `select()` - subset data based on variables using `dplyr` package
- `spec()` - view variables' specifications (classifications) using `readr` package
- `str_detect()` - detects pattern in a string variable using `stringr` package
- `summary()` - summarises object
- `table()` - basic frequency table
- `tail()` - provide last few observations' values for dataset
- `view()` - view data sheet in RStudio
- `write_csv()` - save data as .csv file using `readr` package
- `write_dta()` - save data as .dta file using `haven` package
- `write_xlsx()` - save data as .xlsx files using `writexl` package

Additional Resources

Books and Articles

- Long, J.D. and Teetor, P. (2019) *R Cookbook*, 2nd edition. O'Reilly Media.
- Wickham, H. and Grolemund, G. (2017) *R for Data Science*. O'Reilly Media.
- Wickham, H., Averick, M., Bryan, J., Chang, W., McGowan, L., François, R., Grolemund, G. et al. (2019) 'Welcome to the Tidyverse', *Journal of Open Source Software*, 4(43): 1686. https://doi.org/10.21105/joss.01686.

Online

- R-bloggers: https://www.r-bloggers.com/
- RStudio Blog: https://www.rstudio.com/blog/
- Tidyverse: https://www.tidyverse.org/.

5

VARIABLES AND MANIPULATION

Chapter contents

Working with data is often a messy business. Even when we have rather 'clean' secondary data, such as from the UK Data Service, we will likely need to make changes in one way or another. We have seen ways to clean data and variables, but it is also critical to understand how to manipulate data and variables to suit our purposes. Generally, this is all discussed under the heading of recoding variables or data wrangling. In this chapter, we will look at common variable recoding tasks and techniques.

We will also discuss the levels of measurement of variables. This topic may seem pedantic and dull, but in fact is critical for knowing the types of statistical analysis we are able to perform. Misunderstanding levels of measurement can lead to using incorrect techniques and thus obtaining incorrect results. Levels of measurement and analysis do not necessarily live by hard-and-fast rules, and often we employ rule-of-thumb decisions, but understanding the 'textbook' version helps inform our choices.

By the end of this chapter, you should be able to:

- Understand the four levels of measurement
- Assess the level of measurement of any variable
- Convert variable types
- Remove unwanted symbols and responses in variables
- Understand *why* and *when* we recode and manipulate variables
- Implement recoding procedures using `tidyverse`

LEVELS OF MEASUREMENT

There are four different levels of measurement for variables – nominal, ordinal, interval, and ratio. It is critical to understand the level of measurement of our variables, particularly our outcome variable, in order to choose the most appropriate statistical techniques and data analysis options. Often the level of measurement is quite obvious, but sometimes it can be a judgement call. Fortunately, in situations where it may be a judgement call, either choice often leads to similar decisions about the type of data analysis to perform. We will be discussing the relevance of levels of measurement throughout the rest of this book – particularly when using univariate, bivariate, and multivariate statistics.

Nominal Variables

Nominal-level variables are the simplest and most basic variables. Nominal variables have no order to their values and each value is a distinct category or classification. Nominal variables may have as little as two values or may have many values. If at any time we need to rationalise whether a variable has an order to its values, it is likely a nominal variable.

The most basic nominal variable is one that only has two values. In fact, *if a variable has two values it can only be a nominal variable.* Can you think of any variables like that? In survey data the most common is someone's sex. Nominal variables with only two values are known as binary variables. Commonly, binary variables are coded as 1 and 0, where the '1' category tells you the attribute is present and the '0' tells you it is not present. These variables are known as dummy variables or indicator variables. For example, instead of a variable called *sex*, we may have a variable called *female*, where the value 1 indicates female and 0 indicates male. We often recode nominal variables to create dummy variables. This is particularly the case when we want to use nominal variables in regression analysis (see Chapter 11). In US data, we often create dummy variables for race and ethnicity, such as *white*, where 1 indicates the person is white and 0 is either a specific race or all other races, or *black*, where the 1 indicates the person is black and 0 is either a specific race or all other races. Another common dummy variable social science researchers use in the USA is *south*, where 1 indicates a person lives in the South and 0 indicates the person lives somewhere else.[1]

Nominal variables can also take on many values. In the race dummy variable example above, the original variable would typically have values of white, black, Hispanic, Asian, and other. The south dummy is created out of a US region variable which typically has values of Northeast, South, Midwest, Mountains, and West. Religion is normally a nominal variable where you might have values of Protestant, Catholic, Jewish, Muslim, etc. In all of these examples, the key is that there is *no order* to the values. The values of these variables are arbitrary in that changing them has no effect on the variable. To assess whether a variable has order, we ask ourselves whether this statement makes sense: *as the variable X increases, ….* Does the statement *as race increases* make sense? Obviously not. Does the statement *as region increases* make sense? Nope.

In summary, to figure out whether a variable is at the nominal level we ask *is there a meaningful order to the values* or *if I move the values does it affect the variable in any substantial way*? If the answer is no, we can have high confidence that the variable is nominal.

Ordinal Variables

Clearly, ordinal-level variables are variables that have order to the values. This means that an increase or decrease in the values provides meaningful information. Ordinal variables, then, have more or less of some attribute. An additional key aspect of an ordinal variable is that the distance between two (or more) values is not meaningful. Consider an education variable that has the following four values: 1 = 'no high school diploma', 2 = 'high school diploma', 3 = 'undergraduate degree', and 4 = 'graduate degree'. Do this variable's values have an order? Yes, the values tell us increasing levels of education attainment. Do the differences between the variable's values provide any meaningful information? No, not really. The difference between having no high school diploma and having a high school diploma is not the same as the difference between having an undergraduate degree and a graduate degree, even though the numbers we assigned both say the difference is 1. Therefore, the numbers assigned to values in ordinal variables are arbitrary. If instead we had an education variable that had the number of formal years of schooling, then the values would not be arbitrary and thus the variable would also not be an ordinal variable.

Ordinal variables, along with nominal variables, make up the majority of types of variables we have in social science data, conditional on your field of study. This is particularly true about survey data. Social science surveys often ask questions about how much the respondent approves or disapproves and whether something should be increased or decreased. You have

---

[1] In US quantitative social science research the south dummy stands in for the social and cultural differences of Southern residents that cannot be measured by conventional economic, social, and political measures.

likely common across survey questions such as *How much do you approve or disapprove of the job of the president/prime minister?*, where the values are 1 = 'strongly disapprove', 2 = 'disapprove', 3 = 'neither approve or disapprove', 4 = 'approve', and 5 = 'strongly approve'. And questions such as *Should the Canadian government increase or decrease the amount of immigration from the Middle East?*, where the values are 1 = 'greatly decrease', 2 = 'decrease', 3 = 'remain the same', 4 = 'increase', 5 = 'greatly increase'. All variables like these are ordinal variables.

In summary, a variable is an ordinal variable when there is a meaningful order to the values, but the differences between the values are meaningless.

Interval Variables

Interval-level variables have order, the difference between values has meaning, but the 0 value is arbitrary. Huh? Let's unpack this a bit. We know what it means for a variable to have order. If the difference between the values is meaningful, that implies the difference between 1 and 2 provides the same meaning as the difference between 2 and 3. The last part is that the value 0 does *not* mean the attribute does not exist. The most common example of an interval variable is temperature, measured in either Celsius or Fahrenheit. If the temperature outside is 0 degrees Fahrenheit, does it mean that temperature does not exist? No, it just means it is really cold outside.

There are not many interval-level variables in social science data. One of the common situations where we encounter interval variables in social science data are with what are known as *feeling thermometer* survey questions. These questions ask respondents how they feel towards certain public figures (e.g., politicians), certain organisations (e.g., political parties), and certain groups of people (e.g., immigrants). The American National Election Study has been using feeling thermometer questions for decades. These questions are along the lines of *On a scale from 0 to 100, where 0 means 'cold' and 100 means 'hot', how do you feel about President Biden?* Here, 0 does not mean the respondent has no feelings towards Biden; it means the respondent really, really does not like him.

Ratio Variables

The only difference between ratio- and interval-level variables is that with ratio-level variables the 0 value actually means the attribute does not exist. For example, if we have a variable of people's salaries and someone has a value of 0, it means the person has no salary. If we have a variable of countries' unemployment percentage and a country has a value of 0, it means the country has no unemployment. If we have a variable of the number of murders in different cities and a city has a value of 0, it means the city had no murders. You get the idea.

Commonly, we will have variables that are in fact ratio-level, but the data does not have 0s. For example, no country has a 0% unemployment rate. In this case, you need to ask yourself, if such a value did exist in this data, would it mean the attribute does or does not exist? If it does not exist, then the variable is ratio and if it does, then it is interval.

The good thing for us is that whether a variable is interval- or ratio-level does not usually affect the type of data analysis and statistics we can use. There may be an effect on substantive interpretations of the variables – for example, there can be negative temperatures, but not negative unemployment percentages – but the statistical techniques we use will be the same. An additional determinant of interval- and ratio-level variables is that they are normally assumed to have a lot of values. How many values is part of the art of QSS, but a rule of thumb is at least 10 values.

A final note on both interval- and ratio-level variables is that we can always recode them to make them ordinal or nominal. For example, we might group individuals' salaries instead of using raw salaries. Or we may group countries together by whether they have low, medium, or high unemployment. As researchers, we normally do not want to do this since we lose variation in our data, but there are times when it may be expedient.

Determining Levels of Measurement

Now, let's take a look at some data and figure out the variables' level of measurement. We will use a 2019 survey about perceptions of voter fraud in England. The name of the data is VF England. csv, and we will read it in using the read_csv() function.

```
setwd("C:/QSSD/Chapter 5 - Variables & Manipulation/")
getwd()
[1] "C:/QSSD/Chapter 5 - Variables & Manipulation"

library(tidyverse)
vf_england <- read_csv("VF England.csv")

glimpse(vf_england)
Rows: 2,034
Columns: 8
$ vfalter       <chr> "Slightly agree", "Disagree", "Neither agree nor
disagree~
$ vfproblem     <chr> "Slightly agree", "Disagree", "Neither agree nor
disagree~
$ age           <dbl> 66, 59, 54, 68, 58, 67, 51, 59, 59, 65, 69, 71,
61, 70, 6~
$ sex           <chr> "Female", "Male", "Male", "Female", "Male",
"Male", "Male~
$ education     <dbl> 1, 2, 1, 2, 2, 3, 3, 3, 3, 3, 1, 2, 2, 2, 2, 1,
2, 3, 2, ~
$ brexit_vote   <chr> "2. Leave", "2. Leave", "2. Leave", "1. Remain", "2.
Leav~
$ vote2017_dum  <chr> "Winner", "Winner", NA, "Winner", "Winner",
"Winner", "Wi~
$ pid           <chr> "UKIP Brexit", "Conservative", "Other",
"Conservative", "~
```

Let's use the count() function to determine the level of measurement of a few variables. We may also need to look at the data codebook to be certain we understand the variables' labels.

First, let's examine the variable brexit_vote, which is how the respondents voted in the 2016 Brexit referendum.

```
vf_england %>%
  count(brexit_vote)
# A tibble: 3 x 2
  brexit_vote      n
  <chr>        <int>
1 1. Remain      864
2 2. Leave       875
3 <NA>           295
```

We see that the values are 1. Remain (in the EU), 2. Leave (the EU), and missing values. Since brexit_vote only has two values, we know that it is *nominal*.

Now let's look at pid, which is a recoded version of respondents' political party identification.

```
vf_england %>%
  count(pid)
# A tibble: 3 x 2
  pid               n
  <chr>         <int>
1 Conservative    550
2 Other          1351
3 UKIP Brexit     133
```

This variable has three values, but there is no rational order to the values. Therefore, we know that pid is *nominal*.

Now let's turn to education, which is the respondent's education level.

```
vf_england %>%
  count(education)
# A tibble: 3 x 2
  education      n
      <dbl> <int>
1         1   586
2         2   889
3         3   559
```

The three values do not have labels and thus it is difficult to know whether this is a nominal or ordinal variable. Typically, education variables in survey data are coded so that higher values imply a higher level of education. To be sure, we should check the codebook, which tells us that 1 = Low, 2 = Medium, and 3 = High in education. Therefore, we know that education is an *ordinal* variable.

Lastly, let's look at the variable vfproblem which asked respondents how much they agree or disagree that voter fraud is a big problem in British elections.

```
vf_england %>%
  count(vfproblem)
# A tibble: 7 x 2
  vfproblem                   n
  <chr>                   <int>
1 Agree                     167
2 Disagree                  245
3 Neither agree nor disagree 670
4 Slightly agree            398
5 Slightly disagree         302
6 Strongly agree            140
7 Strongly disagree         112
```

What is the level of measurement of `vfproblem`? This question is a tricky one! The value labels indicate this is a classic seven-point Likert-type agree/disagree question. However, the values are all out of order. This is due to the variable labels being alphabetically ordered when the data is read into R. Therefore, in this current version, `vfproblem` is a *nominal* variable. If we recoded `vfproblem` to make the values go from 'Strongly disagree' to 'Strongly agree', or vice versa, the variable would then be *ordinal*.

RECODING AND MANIPULATING VARIABLES

We will now examine a few common variable manipulation techniques using `tidyverse`. This includes renaming variables, creating new variables (e.g., dummy variables, collapsing categorical and numerical variables), labelling variable values, dealing with missing values, and numeric variable transformations. We will primarily use functions from the `dplyr` and `forcats` packages.

While variable manipulation with `tidyverse` really is not any easier than using other approaches in R, one of the main benefits is that we can use and connect the various `tidyverse` functions for the data visualisation and analysis we will do later in the book. More than anywhere else in R, variable manipulation is an area where there are a slew of different approaches that get the job done. Even within `tidyverse`, there are multiple variable manipulation functions that do the same job. Hence, it is impossible to cover all the possibilities here (or indeed in a book of anything less than *Infinite Jest* length). The types of recoding and manipulating for your data needs will likely differ from what we do here. By covering some common variable manipulation techniques, this section should provide you a solid foundation.

Renaming

We will start with the simplest (but often critical) task of renaming variables. We will use the `rename()` function from the `dplyr` package. The `rename()` function replaces the existing variable names with new ones.

If you remember from the previous chapter, the 2020 SIMD data used capital letters for a number of the variables. Generally, it is best practice to use lower-case variable names. Let's read in the data and name it `simd`.

```
simd <- read_csv("simd2020.csv", na = "*")
```

If we want to rename a single variable, we can easily do so with the `rename()` function. In the function, we first specify the new variable name, then =, and then the old variable name. Let's rename `Data_Zone` as `data_zone`.

```
simd %>%
  rename(data_zone = Data_Zone)
# A tibble: 6,976 x 38
    data_zone Intermediate_Zone   Council_area  Total_population Working_
age_pop~
    <chr>       <chr>               <chr>                 <dbl>          <dbl>
 1 S01006506 Culter              Aberdeen City          894            580
 2 S01006507 Culter              Aberdeen City          793            470
 3 S01006508 Culter              Aberdeen City          624            461
 4 S01006509 Culter              Aberdeen City          537            307
 5 S01006510 Culter              Aberdeen City          663            415
 6 S01006511 Culter              Aberdeen City          759            453
 7 S01006512 Culter              Aberdeen City          539            345
 8 S01006513 Cults, Bieldside a~ Aberdeen City          788            406
 9 S01006514 Cults, Bieldside a~ Aberdeen City         1123            709
10 S01006515 Cults, Bieldside a~ Aberdeen City          816            529
# ... with 6,966 more rows, and 33 more variables: Income_rate <dbl>,
#    Income_count <dbl>, Employment_rate <dbl>, Employment_count <dbl>,
#    CIF <dbl>, ALCOHOL <dbl>, DRUG <dbl>, SMR <dbl>, DEPRESS <dbl>,
LBWT <dbl>,
#   EMERG <dbl>, Attendance <dbl>, Attainment <dbl>, no_qualifications <dbl>,
#   not_participating <dbl>, University <dbl>, drive_petrol <dbl>,
#   drive_GP <dbl>, drive_post <dbl>, drive_primary <dbl>, drive_retail <dbl>,
#   drive_secondary <dbl>, PT_GP <dbl>, PT_post <dbl>, PT_retail <dbl>, ...
```

We can rename additional variables by adding a comma and then other variables. Below, we rename `Intermediate_Zone` as `intermediate_zone`.

```
simd %>%
  rename(data_zone = Data_Zone, intermediate_zone = Intermediate_Zone)
# A tibble: 6,976 x 38
    data_zone intermediate_zone   Council_area  Total_population Working_
age_pop~
    <chr>       <chr>               <chr>                 <dbl>          <dbl>
 1 S01006506 Culter              Aberdeen City          894            580
 2 S01006507 Culter              Aberdeen City          793            470
 3 S01006508 Culter              Aberdeen City          624            461
 4 S01006509 Culter              Aberdeen City          537            307
 5 S01006510 Culter              Aberdeen City          663            415
```

```
 6 S01006511 Culter              Aberdeen City           759          453
 7 S01006512 Culter              Aberdeen City           539          345
 8 S01006513 Cults, Bieldside a~ Aberdeen City           788          406
 9 S01006514 Cults, Bieldside a~ Aberdeen City          1123          709
10 S01006515 Cults, Bieldside a~ Aberdeen City           816          529
# ... with 6,966 more rows, and 33 more variables: Income_rate <dbl>,
#   Income_count <dbl>, Employment_rate <dbl>, Employment_count <dbl>,
#   CIF <dbl>, ALCOHOL <dbl>, DRUG <dbl>, SMR <dbl>, DEPRESS <dbl>,
LBWT <dbl>,
#   EMERG <dbl>, Attendance <dbl>, Attainment <dbl>, no_qualifications <dbl>,
#   not_participating <dbl>, University <dbl>, drive_petrol <dbl>,
#   drive_GP <dbl>, drive_post <dbl>, drive_primary <dbl>, drive_retail <dbl>,
#   drive_secondary <dbl>, PT_GP <dbl>, PT_post <dbl>, PT_retail <dbl>, ...
```

If we want to rename all the variables in the dataset at once, we can use the `rename_with()` function from the `dplyr` package. The `rename_with()` function requires specifying a function for renaming all the variables. Here, we use the `tolower` function, part of base R, to convert all the variable names to lower-case names.

```
simd_lc <- simd %>%
  rename_with(tolower)
```

Notice that we saved the renamed variables as a data object named `simd_lc` (for the lower-case version of simd).

Changing Variables' Classifications

As we discussed in Chapter 4, each variable is classified (or specified) as some type (e.g., double/ numeric, factor, character). There are situations when R reads in variables with the wrong variable type or we want to change the variable type to conduct a certain statistical analysis or data visualisation. There are a number of different conversions we can make to variables, but the most common are: `as.numeric()`, `as.double()`, `as.character()`, and `as.factor()`. All of the `as.()` functions coerce a variable to be a certain type. Tidyverse uses `as.numeric()`, `as.double()`, `as_character()`, and `as_factor()`.[2] There are subtle differences between `as_factor` and `as.factor`, but the main takeaway is that `as_factor()` allows greater control over variables' value labels. It is good practice when converting the variable type to create a new variable. Let's look at the variable `council_area` from the renamed `simd_lc` dataset. Remember, `council_area` is currently considered a character variable. R will throw a fit if we try to convert a character variable to a numeric or double variable. So, first, let's convert it to a factor variable

---

[2]Tidyverse actually has two versions of `as_factor()`: one from the `haven` package and one from the `forcats` package.

using the as.factor() function and name the new variable council_area_fac. For simplicity, we will create these variables using the base R approach.

```
simd_lc$council_area_fac <- as.factor(simd_lc$council_area)
class(simd_lc$council_area_fac)
[1] "factor"
```

We see that our new variable council_area_fac is now a factor variable.

Next, let's convert council_area_fac to a numeric variable using the as.numeric() function. We will name this new variable council_area_num.

```
simd_lc$council_area_num <- as.numeric(simd_lc$council_area_fac)
class(simd_lc$council_area_num)
[1] "numeric"
```

We see that our new variable council_area_num is now a numeric variable.

Let's now convert council_area_fac to a double variable using the as.double() function. We will name this new variable council_area_dbl.

```
simd_lc$council_area_dbl <- as.double(simd_lc$council_area_fac)
class(simd_lc$council_area_dbl)
[1] "numeric"
```

Although we used the as.double() function, the output here says that council_area_dbl is a numeric variable. Huh? Again, numeric and double variables are essentially the same thing. If we look at how tidyverse treats council_area_dbl, we see that it is classified as a double (<dbl>).

One important thing to note is that the as.numeric() and as.double() functions will strip out any value labels in the original variable. This is another reason why we create a new variable when we perform any variable type conversions.

The mutate() Function

The core function in dplyr (and tidyverse) for recoding variables is the mutate() function. For a quick look at mutate(), we will simply reclassify urban as a factor. For mutate(), we name the new variable first, then =, and then the old variable. We do not have to create a new variable, but it is good practice when recoding – so, if/when we screw up, we do not need to reread in the data, etc.

Let's first take a look at urban.

```
simd_lc %>%
  count(urban)
# A tibble: 2 x 2
```

```
  urban     n
  <dbl> <int>
1     0  2139
2     1  4837
```

We see that `urban` is classified as `double`.

Now let's reclassify `urban` as a factor variable using the `as_factor()` function and create a new variable called `urban_fct`.

```
simd_lc <- simd_lc %>%
           mutate(urban_fct = as_factor(urban))

simd_lc %>%
    count(urban_fct)
# A tibble: 2 x 2
  urban_fct     n
  <fct>     <int>
1 0          2139
2 1          4837
```

In the `count()` output, we see that `urban_fct` is now a factor variable instead of a double variable.

Removing Characters in Variables

Sometimes we have datasets that include non-numeric values (e.g., `$` or `@`), which we need to remove in order to perform statistical analysis. We may also want to change the characters and symbols that were used by the original dataset creators. We could do this by hand in, for example, an Excel file, but it could take forever and it reduces replicability.

As an example of how to remove certain characters, let's look at a Federal Bureau of Investigation dataset on the number, type, and location of hate crimes in the USA during 2020. The dataset is saved as an Excel file named `2020_HateCrime_Location.xlsx`. To demonstrate 'real-world' data cleaning in action, I have only done minimal prior cleaning of this file. The first problem we will have reading in the file is that the first five rows are header information about the data table. We can easily deal with this problem by including the `skip = 5` option in the `read_xlsx()` function – this tells R to skip the first five rows when reading in the data.

```
library(readxl)
hcrime <- read_xlsx("2020_HateCrime_Location.xlsx", skip = 5)

glimpse(hcrime)
Rows: 47
Columns: 9
$ Location                 <chr> "Total", "Abandoned/condemned
struct~
$ `Total\r\nincidents`     <dbl> 8263, 10, 118, 4, 9, 11, 25,
82, 12,~
```

```
$ `Race/\r\nethnicity/\r\nancestry` <dbl> 5227, 6, 77, 3, 6, 6, 21, 43,
6, 50,~
$ Religion                          <dbl> 1244, 0, 9, 0, 3, 2, 1, 4,
6, 218, 3~
$ `Sexual\r\norientation`           <dbl> 1110, 0, 20, 1, 0, 0, 0, 25,
0, 10, ~
$ Disability                        <dbl> 130, 0, 2, 0, 0, 0, 0, 2, 0,
0, 2, 0~
$ Gender                            <dbl> 75, 0, 0, 0, 0, 0, 1, 1, 0,
0, 5, 0,~
$ `Gender\r\nidentity`              <dbl> 266, 2, 6, 0, 0, 3, 2, 4, 0,
0, 1, 0~
$ `Multiple-\r\nbias\r\nincidents`  <dbl> 211, 2, 4, 0, 0, 0, 0, 3, 0,
7, 4, 1~
```

We immediately see another problem – several variables have \r\n in their names, which indicates a 'new line' in a Microsoft Office document. We could remove these characters after we read in the data, but an easier solution is to use the option .name_repair = "universal" in the read_xlsx() function.

```
hcrime <- read_xlsx("2020_HateCrime_Location.xlsx", skip = 5,
                    .name_repair = "universal")
New names:
* `Total\r\nincidents` -> Total..incidents
* `Race/\r\nethnicity/\r\nancestry` -> Race...ethnicity...ancestry
* `Sexual\r\norientation` -> Sexual..orientation
* `Gender\r\nidentity` -> Gender..identity
* `Multiple-\r\nbias\r\nincidents` -> Multiple...bias..incidents

glimpse(hcrime)
Rows: 47
Columns: 9
$ Location                    <chr> "Total", "Abandoned/condemned
structure", ~
$ Total..incidents            <dbl> 8263, 10, 118, 4, 9, 11, 25, 82,
12, 285, ~
$ Race...ethnicity...ancestry <dbl> 5227, 6, 77, 3, 6, 6, 21, 43, 6,
50, 114, ~
$ Religion                    <dbl> 1244, 0, 9, 0, 3, 2, 1, 4, 6, 218,
36, 5, ~
$ Sexual..orientation         <dbl> 1110, 0, 20, 1, 0, 0, 0, 25, 0,
10, 21, 3,~
$ Disability                  <dbl> 130, 0, 2, 0, 0, 0, 0, 2, 0, 0,
2, 0, 0, 2~
$ Gender                      <dbl> 75, 0, 0, 0, 0, 0, 1, 1, 0, 0, 5,
0, 0, 0,~
$ Gender..identity            <dbl> 266, 2, 6, 0, 0, 3, 2, 4, 0, 0,
1, 0, 0, 5~
```

```
$ Multiple...bias..incidents  <dbl> 211, 2, 4, 0, 0, 0, 0, 3, 0, 7, 4,
1, 1, 4~
```

Following the `read_xlsx()` function, we see that the problematic names were automatically repaired by replacing \r\n and / with .. and .... Although the variable names will now work for `tidyverse` functions, they are pretty ugly. So, let's change the names of the variables with .. and ... using the `rename()` function.

Before we rename the variables, let's convert all the letters to lower case using the `rename_with()` function. Let's also create a new tibble called `hcrime1`.

```
hcrime1 <- hcrime %>%
           rename_with(tolower) %>%
           rename(total_incidents = total..incidents,
               race_ethnicity_ancestry = race...ethnicity...ancestry,
               sexual_orientation = sexual..orientation,
               gender_identity = gender..identity,
               multiple_bias_incidents = multiple...bias..incidents)
```

```
glimpse(hcrime1)
Rows: 47
Columns: 9
$ location                  <chr> "Total",  "Abandoned/condemned
structure", "Air~
$ total_incidents           <dbl> 8263, 10, 118, 4, 9, 11, 25, 82,
12, 285, 183,~
$ race_ethnicity_ancestry   <dbl> 5227, 6, 77, 3, 6, 6, 21, 43, 6,
50, 114, 22, ~
$ religion                  <dbl> 1244, 0, 9, 0, 3, 2, 1, 4, 6, 218,
36, 5, 8, 1~
$ sexual_orientation        <dbl> 1110, 0, 20, 1, 0, 0, 0, 25, 0,
10, 21, 3, 0, ~
$ disability                <dbl> 130, 0, 2, 0, 0, 0, 0, 2, 0, 0, 2,
0, 0, 2, 3,~
$ gender                    <dbl> 75, 0, 0, 0, 0, 0, 1, 1, 0, 0, 5,
0, 0, 0, 2, ~
$ gender_identity           <dbl> 266, 2, 6, 0, 0, 3, 2, 4, 0, 0,
1, 0, 0, 5, 5,~
$ multiple_bias_incidents   <dbl> 211, 2, 4, 0, 0, 0, 0, 3, 0, 7, 4,
1, 1, 4, 7,~
```

That looks much better.

Although the /s in the values for `location` are not problematic, let's replace them with commas for demonstration purposes. To do so, we use the `str_replace_all()` function from the `stringr` package. In the `str_replace_all()` function, we specify the variable we are manipulating (`location`), what we want to replace (/), and what we want to replace it with (,). In order to remove all instances of / in the values, we need to use the `str_replace_all()` function instead of the `str_replace()`, which will only remove the first occurrence. Let's wrap the `mutate()` function around the `str_replace_all()` function and create a new variable called `location1` in case we mess up. Note that we include a space in `", "` to make the values print better.

```
hcrime1 <- hcrime1 %>%
          mutate(location1 = str_replace_all(location, "/", ","))

glimpse(hcrime1)
Rows: 47
Columns: 10
$ location                 <chr> "Total", "Abandoned/condemned
structure", "Air~
$ total_incidents          <dbl> 8263, 10, 118, 4, 9, 11, 25, 82,
12, 285, 183,~
$ race_ethnicity_ancestry  <dbl> 5227, 6, 77, 3, 6, 6, 21, 43, 6,
50, 114, 22, ~
$ religion                 <dbl> 1244, 0, 9, 0, 3, 2, 1, 4, 6, 218,
36, 5, 8, 1~
$ sexual_orientation       <dbl> 1110, 0, 20, 1, 0, 0, 0, 25, 0,
10, 21, 3, 0, ~
$ disability               <dbl> 130, 0, 2, 0, 0, 0, 0, 2, 0, 0, 2,
0, 0, 2, 3,~
$ gender                   <dbl> 75, 0, 0, 0, 0, 0, 1, 1, 0, 0, 5,
0, 0, 0, 2, ~
$ gender_identity          <dbl> 266, 2, 6, 0, 0, 3, 2, 4, 0,
0, 1, 0, 0, 5, 5,~
$ multiple_bias_incidents  <dbl> 211, 2, 4, 0, 0, 0, 0, 3, 0, 7,
4, 1, 1, 4, 7,~
$ location1                <chr> "Total", "Abandoned, condemned
structure", "Ai~
```

We see that the values in the new variable `location1` include a comma instead of /.

Now that we know the above code works, we could redo all of it a single code chunk. Although not necessary here, it is good practice for data analysis replication files, course assignments, beauty purposes, etc. Let's create a new tibble named `hcrime_clean` and overwrite the `location` variable.

```
hcrime_clean <- hcrime %>%
          rename_with(tolower) %>%
          rename(total_incidents = total..incidents,
             race_ethnicity_ancestry = race...ethnicity...ancestry,
             sexual_orientation = sexual..orientation,
             gender_identity = gender..identity,
           multiple_bias_incidents = multiple...bias..incidents) %>%
          mutate(location = str_replace_all(location, "\\.+", "_"))
```

```
glimpse(hcrime_clean)
Rows: 47
Columns: 9
$ location              <chr> "Total", "Abandoned, condemned
structure", "Ai~
$ total_incidents       <dbl> 8263, 10, 118, 4, 9, 11, 25, 82,
12, 285, 183,~
$ race_ethnicity_ancestry <dbl> 5227, 6, 77, 3, 6, 6, 21, 43, 6, 50,
114, 22, ~
$ religion              <dbl> 1244, 0, 9, 0, 3, 2, 1, 4, 6, 218,
36, 5, 8, 1~
$ sexual_orientation    <dbl> 1110, 0, 20, 1, 0, 0, 0, 25, 0, 10,
21, 3, 0, ~
$ disability            <dbl> 130, 0, 2, 0, 0, 0, 0, 2, 0, 0, 2,
0, 0, 2, 3,~
$ gender                <dbl> 75, 0, 0, 0, 0, 0, 1, 1, 0, 0, 5,
0, 0, 0, 2, ~
$ gender_identity       <dbl> 266, 2, 6, 0, 0, 3, 2, 4, 0, 0, 1,
0, 0, 5, 5,~
$ multiple_bias_incidents <dbl> 211, 2, 4, 0, 0, 0, 0, 3, 0, 7, 4,
1, 1, 4, 7,~
```

We can also use the column parser functions from readr to automatically remove certain characters and also change the variable classifications. To demonstrate, we will use data on the outcomes of local school referendums in Indiana from 2010 to 2019. This data has spaces between some of the variable names, so we'll include the name_repair = "universal" option in the read_csv() function.

```
school <- read_csv("indiana school referendum data.csv",
                   name_repair = "universal")
New names:
* `Date of Referendum` -> Date.of.Referendum
* `Type of Referendum` -> Type.of.Referendum
* `School Corp. Locale` -> School.Corp..Locale
* `School Corporation` -> School.Corporation
* `Percent For` -> Percent.For
* ...
Rows: 172 Columns: 12
-- Column specification -------------------------------------------
-----------
Delimiter: ","
chr (11): Date.of.Referendum, Month, Type.of.Referendum, School.Corp..
Locale...
dbl  (1): Corp_num

i Use `spec()` to retrieve the full column specification for this data.
i Specify the column types or set `show_col_types = FALSE` to quiet
this message.

glimpse(school)
```

We see that a few variables have % in their values and are classified as <chr>. We could remove % with the `str_replace_all()` function and convert the variables to double or numeric with one of the `as.()` functions. Instead we will use the `parse_number()` function to simultaneously remove % and convert to a double. What's cool about this function is that we do not need to specify anything except for the variable name. Let's clean up `Percent.For`, `Percent.Against`, and `Margin.For.Against`.

```
school1 <- school %>%
            mutate(pct_for = parse_number(Percent.For),
                   pct_against = parse_number(Percent.Against),
                   margin = parse_number(Margin.For.Against))
```

```
glimpse(school1)
Rows: 172
Columns: 15
$ Date.of.Referendum    <chr>  "5/4/2010",  "5/4/2010",  "5/4/2010",
"5/4/2010", "5~
$ Month                 <chr> "May", "May", "May", "May", "May", "May",
"May", "~
$ Type.of.Referendum    <chr> "General Fund", "General Fund", "Construction",
"C~
$ School.Corp..Locale   <chr>  "Rural",  "Suburb",  "Rural",  "Rural",
"Rural", "Sub~
$ School.Corporation    <chr> "Western Boone County Community School
District", ~
$ Corp_num              <dbl> 615, 1000, 1180, 1655, 1655, 3070, 3060,
3070, 314~
$ City                  <chr> "Thornetown", "Clarksville", "Rossville",
"Greensb~
$ County                <chr> "Boone", "Clark", "Clinton", "Decatur",
"Decatur",~
$ Outcome               <chr> "Failed", "Failed", "Failed", "Failed",
"Failed", ~
$ Percent.For           <chr>  "31.00%", "45.00%", "40.00%", "43.00%",
"37.00%", ~
$ Percent.Against       <chr>  "69.00%", "55.00%", "60.00%", "57.00%",
"63.00%", ~
$ Margin.For.Against    <chr> "-38.00%", "-10.00%", "-20.00%", "-14.00%",
"-26.0~
$ pct_for               <dbl> 31.0, 45.0, 40.0, 43.0, 37.0, 60.0, 58.0,
63.0, 32~
$ pct_against           <dbl> 69.0, 55.0, 60.0, 57.0, 63.0, 40.0, 42.0,
37.0, 68~
$ margin                <dbl> -38.0, -10.0, -20.0, -14.0, -26.0, 20.0,
16.0, 26.~
```

We see that our new variables have the % removed and are now classified as double.

We also probably want to clean up other variables in this dataset. First, let's use the `parse_date()` function to classify `Date.of.Referendum` as a `<date>` variable. Unlike the `parse_number()` function, we need to specify the date formatting in the `parse_date()` function. The `Date.of.Referendum` follows the American date convention of month–day–year. In the `parse_date()` function, we specify the variable and then include `"%m%d%Y"` where the upper-case `Y` is for the four-digit year.

Second, we'll also deal with the upper-case first letter and full stops between the variables. We use the `str_replace_all()` function and specify . to identify that we are applying this to all of the variables, then what we want to replace (`"[\\.+]"` where `\\.` is any full stop and `+` means 1 or more full stops), and finally what we want to replace it with (`"_"`). We wrap the `str_to_lower()` function around this, which is wrapped by the `rename_with()` function and `~` to specify it's all of the variables.

Finally, we let's remove the old versions of the variables we change using the `select()` function.

```
school2 <- school %>%
           mutate(pct_for = parse_number(Percent.For),
               pct_against = parse_number(Percent.Against),
               margin = parse_number(Margin.For.Against),
               date = parse_date(Date.of.Referendum, "%m/%d/%Y")
           ) %>%
         rename_with(~ str_to_lower(str_replace_all(., "\\.+","_"))
           ) %>%
        select(-c(date_of_referendum, percent_for, percent_against,
               margin_for_against))

glimpse(school2)
Rows: 172
Columns: 12
$ month              <chr> "May", "May", "May", "May", "May", "May",
"May", "M~
$ type_of_referendum <chr> "General Fund", "General Fund", "Construction",
"Co~
$ school_corp_locale <chr> "Rural", "Suburb", "Rural", "Rural", "Rural",
"Subu~
$ school_corporation <chr> "Western Boone County Community School
District", "~
$ corp_num           <dbl> 615, 1000, 1180, 1655, 1655, 3070, 3060,
3070, 3145~
$ city               <chr> "Thornetown", "Clarksville", "Rossville",
"Greensbu~
$ county             <chr> "Boone", "Clark", "Clinton", "Decatur",
"Decatur", ~
$ outcome            <chr> "Failed", "Failed", "Failed", "Failed",
"Failed", "~
$ pct_for            <dbl> 31.0, 45.0, 40.0, 43.0, 37.0, 60.0, 58.0,
63.0, 32.~
$ pct_against        <dbl> 69.0, 55.0, 60.0, 57.0, 63.0, 40.0, 42.0,
37.0, 68.~
```

```
$ margin                  <dbl> -38.0, -10.0, -20.0, -14.0, -26.0, 20.0,
16.0, 26.0~
$ date                    <date> 2010-05-04, 2010-05-04, 2010-05-04,
2010-05-04, 20~
```

This looks awesome now.

Labelling and Relabelling

We often need to label and relabel variable values, especially after we read in data for the first time. Using the `recode()` function from the `dplyr` package, let's label the `urban_fct` variable from the `simd_lc` data.[3]

Above we saw that `urban_fct` is currently labelled as 0 and 1. A reasonable guess is that 1 = 'urban', but let's add labels to these values so it is clearer. In the `recode()` function, we first specify the variable we are recoding and then the labels we are applying to the values. For the labels, we first specify the old value, =, then the new label. One quirk for relabelling numbers is that we need to put tick marks around the numbers.

```
simd_lc <- simd_lc %>%
            mutate(urban_fct = recode(urban_fct,
                              `1` = "urban", `0` = "rural"))


simd_lc %>%
    count(urban_fct)
# A tibble: 2 x 2
  urban_fct       n
  <fct>       <int>
1 rural        2139
2 urban        4837
```

That looks better.

If we want to change existing labels using the `recode()` function, we just specify the existing labels in quotes followed by the new labels in quotes. Here, let's change 'urban' to 'city' and 'rural' to 'boonies', and save this new version as `urban_fct1`.

```
simd_lc <- simd_lc %>%
            mutate(urban_fct1 = recode(urban_fct,
                              "urban" = "city", "rural" = "boonies"))
```

---

[3]Note that the `car` package, which we used in the first edition of the book, also has a `recode()` function. If we have both `car` and `dplyr` loaded at the same time there will be conflicts. If this occurs, we just need to unload/deactivate the package we are not currently using. This can be done using the `detach()` function or simply by unchecking the package in the `Packages` tab.

```
simd_lc %>%
    count(urban_fct1)
# A tibble: 2 x 2
  urban_fct1      n
  <fct>        <int>
1 boonies       2139
2 city          4837
```

Rearranging Values

We often want to rearrange a variable's values. This is especially the case when we have a variable that is substantively ordinal, but is currently coded as unordered. If we put the unordered version in a regression, R will treat it as an ordered variable instead of a nominal variable – R is not that smart (yet). Note that R will treat any `factor` variable as nominal and will automatically 'dummy it out' in a regression.

Let's look again at the variable `vfproblem` from the `vf_england` data using the `count()` function.

```
vf_england %>%
  count(vfproblem)
# A tibble: 7 x 2
  vfproblem                       n
  <chr>                        <int>
1 Agree                         167
2 Disagree                      245
3 Neither agree nor disagree    670
4 Slightly agree                398
5 Slightly disagree             302
6 Strongly agree                140
7 Strongly disagree             112
```

We see that the agree/disagree values are ordered alphabetically, which is what R does automatically when reading in character and factor variables.

Let's rearrange the values of `vfproblem` to make them ordered from 'Strongly disagree' to 'Strongly agree'. We do this using the `factor()` function from the `forcats` package and using the `levels` = option to order the labels. Let's create a new variable titled `vfproblem1` by wrapping everything with the `mutate()` function.

```
vf_england <- vf_england %>%
                mutate(vfproblem1 = factor(vfproblem,
                  levels = c("Strongly disagree","Disagree",
                    "Slightly disagree","Neither agree nor disagree",
                    "Slightly agree","Agree","Strongly agree")))

vf_england %>%
  count(vfproblem1)
```

```
# A tibble: 7 x 2
  vfproblem1                    n
  <fct>                     <int>
1 Strongly disagree           112
2 Disagree                    245
3 Slightly disagree           302
4 Neither agree nor disagree  670
5 Slightly agree              398
6 Agree                       167
7 Strongly agree              140
```

This is nice and ordered. Further, with the rearranged value labels, `vfproblem1` is now an ordinal variable.

If we have a number of variables where we need to rearrange the same set of values, we could set the levels prior to rearranging the values. Although we still need to type out the levels (once), we might do this to save time and space if we reuse the same levels multiple times in our recoding.

To do this, we just create an object that contains our levels. Let's name this object `agree_levels`.

```
agree_levels <- c("Strongly disagree","Disagree",
                  "Slightly disagree","Neither agree nor disagree",
                  "Slightly agree","Agree","Strongly agree")
```

Now, instead of writing out the levels in our `factor()` function, we just specify `levels = agree_levels`. Let's also create a new variable titled `vfproblem2`.

```
vf_england <- vf_england %>%
                mutate(vfproblem2 = factor(vfproblem,
                       levels = agree_levels))

vf_england %>%
  count(vfproblem2)
# A tibble: 7 x 2
  vfproblem2                    n
  <fct>                     <int>
1 Strongly disagree           112
2 Disagree                    245
3 Slightly disagree           302
4 Neither agree nor disagree  670
5 Slightly agree              398
6 Agree                       167
7 Strongly agree              140
```

Sometimes we have variables where we want to flip the values so that the higher value is more intuitive for interpretations; for example, in a regression analysis. Let's do this for `vfproblems2` using the `fct_rev()` function from the `forcats` package. The `fct_rev()` function automatically and symmetrically reverses the values for a factor variable.

```
vf_england <- vf_england %>%
              mutate(vfproblem3 = fct_rev(vfproblem2))

vf_england %>%
  count(vfproblem3)
# A tibble: 7 x 2
  vfproblem3                        n
  <fct>                         <int>
1 Strongly agree                  140
2 Agree                           167
3 Slightly agree                  398
4 Neither agree nor disagree      670
5 Slightly disagree               302
6 Disagree                        245
7 Strongly disagree               112
```

That was super easy!

Collapsing Variables

There are times when we take a variable with many values and recode it so that it only has a few categories. This is commonly known as *collapsing variables*. As a general rule, we prefer to have variables with as many values as possible and so collapsing a variable can be a bad idea. However, we typically collapse variables that have many values when we want to present the variable in tabular form. It is easier to read and understand a variable with five values than a variable with 50 values in a table.

Collapsing Categorical Variables

Let's first look at how to collapse categorical variables. To do this, we will use the `fct_collapse()` function from the `forcats` package. The nice thing with `fct_collapse()` is that we can combine multiple categories within a single line.

Let's use the `vfproblem1` variable and collapse all the 'disagree' categories into one category and all the 'agree' categories into one category; we will leave the 'neither' category alone. We will create a new variable called `vfproblem4`.

```
vf_england <- vf_england %>%
              mutate(vfproblem4 = fct_collapse(vfproblem1,
                      "Disagree" = c("Strongly disagree","Disagree",
                              "Slightly disagree"),
                          "Agree" = c("Strongly agree","Agree",
                              "Slightly agree")))

vf_england %>%
  count(vfproblem4)
# A tibble: 3 x 2
```

```
   vfproblem4                     n
   <fct>                      <int>
1  Disagree                     659
2  Neither agree nor disagree   670
3  Agree                        705
```

We see that vfproblem4 has three categories instead of the original seven.

Collapsing Numeric Variables

Although it is best practice to not collapse numeric variables (double variables in tidyverse terminology) when performing analysis, we commonly do it for tabular data presentations and certain data visualisations. Below, we will use the cut_interval() function from the ggplot2 package to collapse the variable age from vf_england into three categories. The cut_interval() function automatically creates equal-sized categories based on the requested number of categories – below, we ask for three categories by including the option n = 3.

```
vf_england <- vf_england %>%
            mutate(age_cat = cut_interval(age, n = 3))

vf_england %>%
  count(age_cat)
# A tibble: 3 x 2
  age_cat        n
  <fct>      <int>
1 [18,41.3]    719
2 (41.3,64.7]  785
3 (64.7,88]    530
```

We can add labels to the categories using the labels = option in the cut_interval() function. Let's label our categories as 'Young', 'Middle Age', and 'Old', and create a new variable called age_cat1.

```
vf_england <- vf_england %>%
            mutate(age_cat1 = cut_interval(age, n = 3,
                      labels = c("Young","Middle Age","Old")))

vf_england %>%
  count(age_cat1)
# A tibble: 3 x 2
  age_cat1       n
  <fct>      <int>
1 Young        719
2 Middle Age   785
3 Old          530
```

Although the cut_interval() function automatically collapses the data with equal-sized categories, sometimes we want to manually control the breaks and category sizes. We can manually set the breaks and labels using the `cut()` function which is part of base R.[4] Let's set the categories as 18 to 40, 41 to 65, and 66 to 88.

To specify the cut points, we use the `breaks =` option, where you need to specify the lower bound (here 17, so that the category starts with 18) and the upper bound (here 88, so that the category ends at 88), and then where we want the other cut points to be (here 40 and 65). The `breaks =` option is a bit strange because the lower bound number is not included in the category, but the upper bound number is included in the category. Let's first do the recoding without labels, so we can check the cut points.

```
vf_england <- vf_england %>%
              mutate(age_cat2 = cut(age, breaks = c(17,40,65,88)))

vf_england %>%
  count(age_cat2)
# A tibble: 3 x 2
  age_cat2      n
  <fct>     <int>
1 (17,40]     675
2 (40,65]     862
3 (65,88]     497
```

This looks correct.

Now, let's add in the labels with the `labels =` option.

```
vf_england <- vf_england %>%
              mutate(age_cat3 = cut(age, breaks = c(17,40,65,88),
                     labels = c("Young","Middle Age","Old")))

vf_england %>%
  count(age_cat3)
# A tibble: 3 x 2
  age_cat3         n
  <fct>        <int>
1 Young          675
2 Middle Age     862
3 Old            497
```

Dummying Nominal Variables

As quantitative social scientists, we often have variables that are nominal, but have multiple categories; that is, not just binary variables. Earlier we discussed several common ones that appear in survey data – race, religion affiliation, and region of residence. Many statistical techniques assume that variables with multiple values have an order, regardless of whether they are ordinal, interval, or ratio. This is particularly the case with multiple linear regression – which we will

---

[4]The `cut_interval()` function actually passes all the options to the `cut()` function.

examine starting in Chapter 11 – and other types of regression models. Computers and statistical programs are smart, but they do not catch every dumb thing we do. If we include a nominal variable with multiple categories into a method where the assumption is that the variable has order, R is not going to catch it and will provide results assuming the variable is ordered. For example, if we included a race variable with multiple categories into a linear regression, our interpretation of the coefficient would start with 'as we increase on race …'. Obviously, this makes no sense.

However, students who are first learning data analysis frequently make this mistake. This occurs because they are not considering the level of measurement of their variables and how R has classified the variable. As dull and pedantic as learning levels of measurement may be, this is another situation where not knowing the correct level bites you.

We will create a sequence of dummy variables using the variable `pid`, short for 'partisan identification'. Before we do that, let's take another look at `pid`.

```
vf_england %>%
  count(pid)
# A tibble: 3 x 2
  pid                n
  <chr>          <int>
1 Conservative     550
2 Other           1351
3 UKIP Brexit      133
```

We see there are three categories ('Conservative', 'Other', and 'UKIP Brexit') and a number of missing values. We also see that `pid` is classified as a character variable.

Let's first create a dummy variable for Conservative Party identifiers. We do this using the `fct_collapse()` function. We also want to change `pid` to a `factor` variable and then use the `filter()` function to remove the NAs. Since pipes work sequentially, we need to first change `pid` to a factor, then filter out the NAs, and then recode the variable. Because we are filtering out the NAs in `pid`, thus reducing our *N*, we will create a new tibble named `vf_england1`. If possible it is also good practice to name the dummy variable whatever the higher value equals. We name this dummy variable `conservative`.

```
vf_england1 <- vf_england %>%
               mutate(pid1 = as_factor(pid)) %>%
               filter(!is.na(pid1)) %>%
               mutate(conservative = fct_collapse(pid1,
                        "Conservative" = "Conservative",
                        "Other" = c("UKIP Brexit","Other")))

vf_england1 %>%
  count(conservative)
# A tibble: 2 x 2
  conservative       n
  <fct>          <int>
1 Other           1484
2 Conservative     550
```

This dummy variable looks good. But, we see that the values 1 and 2 are attached and not the standard dummy variable values of 0 and 1. *Is that problem?* Usually it is not a problem as long as the values are just separated by one unit. For regression modelling, a dummy variable that has values of 1 and 2 (instead of 0 and 1) simply shifts the constant/intercept, but the variable's coefficient will be the same. Hence, this only matters if we are using the constant/intercept for interpretation purposes.

Now, let's create a dummy variable for 'UKIP Brexit', which is a combined category of UKIP and Brexit Party identifiers. Since we created the `pid1` variable previously, we do not need to include the first `mutate()` and the `filter()` lines again. In order for 'UKIP Brexit' to be the higher category, we need to use the `fct_rev()` function on an additional line. We name this dummy variable `ukip_brexit`.

```
vf_england1 <- vf_england1 %>%
               mutate(ukip_brexit = fct_collapse(pid1,
                     "UKIP Brexit" = "UKIP Brexit",
                     "Other" = c("Conservative","Other"))) %>%
               mutate(ukip_brexit = fct_rev(ukip_brexit))


vf_england1 %>%
  count(ukip_brexit)
# A tibble: 2 x 2
  ukip_brexit       n
  <fct>         <int>
1 Other          1901
2 UKIP Brexit     133
```

We have now created two dummy variables from the `pid` variable.

In fact, we have done something known as *dummying out* a variable. This is where we take all of the values from a multi-category nominal variable and make them dummy variables. We need to specify that one of the original values is 0 in all of the dummy variables (which is the `Other` respondents without Conservative and UKIP/Brexit identifiers). If we do not and we use all of the dummy variables at the same time, we have what is known as *collinearity* among predictors, which means that the dummy variables explain one another. In this case, R, and other statistical programs, will not be able to perform the analysis. Hence, the one value that is kept out is considered the base or reference category. When we want to make dummy variables of all the values, we create $J - 1$ dummy variables, where J is the number of categories or values of the original nominal variable.

A common question is which category we decide to leave out as the reference category. There are a few different ways to decide this, but the two most common are to use the category with the most observations as the reference or use a category that we have a substantive interest in as the reference. For example, when dummying out race, we may decide that we want all the categories to be compared to white respondents and so we keep whites as the reference group.

In some analyses in R, we can also use the `as_factor()` function to automatically dummy out a nominal variable. For example, instead of creating the two dummy variables above, we could use `as_factor(pid)` within another R function. This is particularly useful in regression analysis where we want to include all of the values of a nominal variable.

Dealing with Missing Values

In Chapter 4, we discussed how to manage missing values at the aggregate dataset level. In this section, we discuss how to deal with missing values for individual variables. How we deal with NAs will depend on our data and analysis plans. Although we often exclude or filter out NAs, sometimes we want to change NAs to a certain value or set certain values to be missing. Below we explore a few different options.

Let's look at the variable vote2017_dum from the vf_england data. This is a dummy variable where respondents who voted for the Conservative Party in the 2017 UK general election are coded as a 'Winner' and respondents who did *not* vote for the Conservative Party are coded as a 'Loser'.

```
vf_england %>%
  count(vote2017_dum)
# A tibble: 3 x 2
  vote2017_dum      n
  <chr>         <int>
1 Loser           919
2 Winner          757
3 <NA>            358
```

We see the 'Loser' and 'Winner' values as well as 358 missing values. Although respondents may have refused to answer the question or could not remember who they voted for, let's imagine the missing values represent respondents who did not vote in the 2017 UK election. Let's recode these missing values to be considered 'Did not vote'.

There are a few different ways we can do this recoding, but let's use the aptly named replace_na() function from the tidyr package. This function replaces NA values with some value that we specify. In the replace_na() function, we specify the variable we are recoding (vote2017_dum) and then the value to replace the NAs ("Did not vote"). We will also wrap the mutate() function around the replace_na() function to create a new variable called vote2017, because it is not a dummy variable now.

```
vf_england <- vf_england %>%
              mutate(vote2017 = replace_na(vote2017_dum, "Did not vote"))

vf_england %>%
  count(vote2017)
# A tibble: 3 x 2
  vote2017          n
  <chr>         <int>
1 Did not vote    358
2 Loser           919
3 Winner          757
```

We see that the NA values are now coded as 'Did not vote'.

Now let's look at how we take an existing variable value and recode it as missing. Let's look again at vfproblem1 from the vf_england data; this is the correctly ordered version.

```
vf_england %>%
  count(vfproblem1)
# A tibble: 7 x 2
  vfproblem1                      n
  <fct>                       <int>
1 Strongly disagree             112
2 Disagree                      245
3 Slightly disagree             302
4 Neither agree nor disagree    670
5 Slightly agree                398
6 Agree                         167
7 Strongly agree                140
```

There are many respondents who said 'Neither agree nor disagree' to whether voter fraud is a big problem in British elections. Let's imagine we want to recode these respondents as NAs.

Again, there are a variety of ways we can do this with `tidyverse` functions. Below we use the `na_if()` function from the `dplyr` package. This function is useful when we want to make a certain value missing without any other recoding. We just need to specify the variable we are recoding (vfproblem1) and then the value we want recoded as NA ("Neither agree or disagree"). Again, we wrap the `mutate()` function around the `na_if()` function to create a new variable, which we name as vfproblem1a.

```
vf_england <- vf_england %>%
              mutate(vfproblem1a = na_if(vfproblem1,
                  "Neither agree nor disagree"))

vf_england %>%
  count(vfproblem1a)
# A tibble: 7 x 2
  vfproblem1a            n
  <fct>             <int>
1 Strongly disagree   112
2 Disagree            245
3 Slightly disagree   302
4 Slightly agree      398
5 Agree               167
6 Strongly agree      140
7 <NA>                670
```

All of the 'Neither agree nor disagree' responses are now recoded as NA.

Variable Functional Form Transformations

Let's look at how to do arithmetic transformations of variables in R. We typically transform variables in this way for statistical reasons (as we will see in Chapter 12) or for substantive reasons (e.g., we believe a predictor does not have a linear relationship with an outcome variable). We will consider two different ways of going about this – first, by creating new variables; and second, by using the `I()` function in R. There are many types of transformations we could do, but we will just briefly look at how to square, cube, and take the log of a variable; these are the three most common transformations we are likely to do in QSS.

Transformations by Creating New Variables

There are no special functions to do functional form transformations in `tidyverse`. Below, we use the `mutate()` function to create logged, squared, and cubed versions of the `age` variable in the `vf_england` data. Among variables in QSS analysis, age is often considered to have a nonlinear relationship with other variables, and thus researchers often transform the variable.

```
summary(vf_england$age)
  Min. 1st Qu.  Median    Mean 3rd Qu.    Max.
 18.00   36.00   49.00   49.53   65.00   88.00

vf_england <- vf_england %>%
           mutate(age_sq = (age)^2)
summary(vf_england$age_sq)
  Min. 1st Qu.  Median    Mean 3rd Qu.    Max.
   324    1296    2401    2735    4225    7744

vf_england <- vf_england %>%
           mutate(age_cd = (age)^3)
summary(vf_england$age_cd)
  Min. 1st Qu.  Median    Mean 3rd Qu.    Max.
  5832   46656  117649  162644  274625  681472

vf_england <- vf_england %>%
           mutate(log_age = log(age))
summary(vf_england$log_age)
  Min. 1st Qu.  Median    Mean 3rd Qu.    Max.
 2.890   3.584   3.892   3.835   4.174   4.477
```

Transformations Using the `I()` Function

There are times when we do not want to transform a variable by creating a new variable. We simply want to do a quick manipulation and be done with it. We can accomplish this by using the `I()` function in base R. The `I()` function tells R to treat a variable or value 'as is', which allows us to do an arithmetical operation without creating a new variable. Let's go through how to square, cube, and take the log of age using the `I()` function. We wrap the `summary()` function around the operation, so the results print nicely.

```
summary(I(vf_england$age^2))
  Min. 1st Qu.  Median    Mean 3rd Qu.    Max.
   324    1296    2401    2735    4225    7744
summary(I(vf_england$age^3))
  Min. 1st Qu.  Median    Mean 3rd Qu.    Max.
  5832   46656  117649  162644  274625  681472
```

```
summary(I(log(vf_england$age)))
   Min. 1st Qu.  Median    Mean 3rd Qu.    Max.
  2.890   3.584   3.892   3.835   4.174   4.477
```

Using the `I()` function, we obtained the same results as in the previous section, but we did not need to create new variables. However, if we are going to make repeated use of a transformed variable, it is probably wise to actually create a new variable that has the transformation.

Creating New Variables from Existing Variables

Up to now we have focused our attention on manipulating and recoding individual variables, but often researchers need to create a new variable that uses multiple existing variables. For example, we might be interested in a variable that tells us whether a person voted for the winning party across several elections. Or, we might want to create a dummy variable where the '1' category is cities that are all above certain thresholds on different environmental policy measures.

Using the `vf_england` data, let's create a new variable that tells us whether a respondent voted for the winning side in the Brexit referendum and the 2017 UK general election. If we want a variable that contains all the possible combinations, we can use the `unite()` function from the `tidyr` package. The `unite()` function allows us to combine variables without carrying out more involved recoding. In the `unite()` argument, we need to first include the new variable name, the first existing variable, the second existing variable, and then how we want the values separated. Note that in the `sep =` argument we include a space after the comma in order for the new variable's values to appear more natural. We also want to specify the option `remove = FALSE`, so that our existing variables are not removed from the tibble; the default is `remove = TRUE`.

```
vf_england <- vf_england %>%
              unite(both_elections, brexit_vote, vote2017_dum,
                    sep = ", ", remove = FALSE)

vf_england %>%
  count(both_elections)
# A tibble: 9 x 2
  both_elections        n
  <chr>             <int>
1 1. Remain, Loser    578
2 1. Remain, NA        69
3 1. Remain, Winner   217
4 2. Leave, Loser     270
5 2. Leave, NA         87
6 2. Leave, Winner    518
7 NA, Loser            71
8 NA, NA              202
9 NA, Winner           22
```

Instead of a variable with every possible combination, let's now create a variable that has three values – 'Double Winner', 'Single Winner', and 'Double Loser' – using `brexit_vote` and `vote2017_dum`. To do this, we'll use the `case_when()` function from `dplyr`. The `case_when()` function allows us to create new variables using complicated combinations of existing variables. In the `case_when()` argument we first specify that people who voted to leave the EU *and* (using the `&` operator) who voted for the winner of the 2017 election be labelled `"Double Winner"`; `~` separates the condition from the label. Second, we specify that people who voted to leave the EU *or* (using the `|` operator) who voted for the winner of the 2017 election be labelled `"Single Winner"`. Finally, we specify that people who voted to remain in the EU *and* (using the `&` operator) who voted for the loser of the 2017 election be labelled `"Double Loser"`. All respondents who do not meet these conditions are automatically labelled as `NA` by the function.

```
vf_england <- vf_england %>%
   mutate(vote_win = case_when(
     brexit_vote=="2. Leave" & vote2017_dum=="Winner" ~ "Double Winner",
     brexit_vote=="2. Leave" | vote2017_dum=="Winner" ~ "Single Winner",
     brexit_vote=="1. Remain" & vote2017_dum=="Loser" ~ "Double Loser"
   ))

vf_england %>%
   count(vote_win)
# A tibble: 4 x 2
   vote_win          n
   <chr>          <int>
1 Double Loser    578
2 Double Winner   518
3 Single Winner   596
4 <NA>            342
```

We see there are slightly more 'Single Winners' than any other category.

If we wanted a simpler version to emphasize the 'Double Winners', we can use the `if_else()` function from `dplyr` to create a binary variable. The logic of the `if_else()` function is that if a variable meets a condition that we specify, then it is coded as a specific value (e.g., 1). If the variable does not meet the condition that we specify, then it is coded as a different value (e.g., 0). Therefore, variables that we create with `if_else()` can only have two values. Let's create a new variable called `vote_win_dum` that is either 'Double Winner' or 'Not Double Winner'. In the `if_else()` function, we specify the variables and the conditions, the value if an observation meets the condition, then the value if an observation does not meet the condition.

```
vf_england <- vf_england %>%
               mutate(vote_win_dum = if_else((
                      brexit_vote=="2. Leave" & vote2017_dum=="Winner"),
                      "Double Winner","Not Double Winner"))

vf_england %>%
   count(vote_win_dum)
```

```
# A tibble: 3 x 2
  vote_win_dum         n
  <chr>            <int>
1 Double Winner      518
2 Not Double Winner 1205
3 <NA>               311
```

CONCLUSION

Although we have examined a wide range of variable recoding and manipulation techniques, we have only scratched the surface. What you need will depend on your data, variables, and specific analysis techniques. As we move throughout the rest of the book, this will become increasingly evident.

R Packages Used in This Chapter

- `dplyr` (loaded with `tidyverse`)
- `forcats` (loaded with `tidyverse`)
- `ggplot2` (loaded with `tidyverse`)
- `haven`
- `pillar` (loaded with `tidyverse`)
- `readr` (loaded with `tidyverse`)
- `readxl`
- `stringr` (loaded with `tidyverse`)
- `tibble` (loaded with `tidyverse`)
- `tidyr` (loaded with `tidyverse`)
- `tidyverse`

R Functions Used in This Chapter

- `as.double()` - convert variable to double
- `as.factor()` - convert variable to factor
- `as_factor()` - convert variable to factor using `haven` or `forcats` package
- `as.numeric()` - convert variable to numeric
- `c()` - concatenate
- `case_when()` - vectorised if statement using `dplyr` package
- `class()` - class of object
- `count()` - count the number of unique values of a variable or variables using `dplyr` package
- `cut()` - recode variable into categories
- `cut_interval()` - recodes variable into equal categories using `ggplot2` package
- `factor()` - specify variable as a factor

(Continued)

- `fct_collapse()` – collapse values of a factor variable using `forcats` package
- `fct_rev()` – reverse values of a factor variable using `forcats` package
- `filter()` – subset data based on variables' values using `dplyr` package
- `glimpse()` – quick view of data using `pillar` package
- `I()` – transform variable without creating a new variable
- `if_else()` – recode variable based on condition using `dplyr` function
- `is.na()` – check for missing values (NAs) in variables
- `log()` – natural log of variable
- `mutate()` – recode variables using `dplyr` package
- `na_if()` – specify value as missing (NA) using `dplyr` package
- `names()` – provide names of saved values of object
- `parse_date()` – parse (convert) variable to date classification using `readr` package
- `parse_number()` – parse (convert) variable to number classification using `readr` package
- `read_csv()` – read in .csv data file using `readr` package
- `read_xlsx()` – read in an Excel data file using `readxl` package
- `recode()` – recode variable using `dplyr` package
- `replace_na()` – replace missing values (NAs) with different value using `tidyr` package
- `rename()` – rename variable using `dplyr` package
- `rename_with()` – rename variable using a function using `dplyr` package
- `select()` – subset data based on variables using `dplyr` package
- `str_replace_all()` – replace characters in string (character) variable using `stringr` package
- `str_to_lower()` – convert all characters to lower case in a variable using `stringr` package
- `summary()` – summarise object
- `table()` – basic frequency table
- `unite()` – combine string (character) variables into one variable using `tidyr` package
- `view()` – view data sheet in RStudio using `tibble` package

Additional Resources

Books

- Harris, J. K. (2020) *Statistics with R: Solving Problems Using Real-World Data*. Sage.
- Ismay, C. and Kim, A. Y. (2019) *Statistical Inference via Data Science*. Chapman and Hall/CRC.
- Long, J. D. and Teetor, P. (2019) *R Cookbook*, 2nd edition. O'Reilly Media.
- Wickham, H. and Grolemund, G. (2017) *R for Data Science*. O'Reilly Media.

Online

- RStudio Blog: https://www.rstudio.com/blog/
- Tidymodels: https://www.tidymodels.org/
- Tidyverse: https://www.tidyverse.org/

6

DEVELOPING HYPOTHESES

Chapter contents

Quantitative social science seeks to explain phenomena and determine relationships in an empirically rigorous manner. Critical to this endeavour is developing clear empirical hypotheses that a researcher can test using data and statistical methods. We could spend considerable time navel-gazing about the philosophy of empirical research, indulging in extraneous existential discussions, but instead, in this chapter, we discuss and work on creating 'good' empirical hypotheses from a practical standpoint. We will first define what makes a good hypothesis and then go through a number of examples. In the last section of the chapter, we will look at how visualising relationships helps our hypothesis building. This is one of the few chapters in the book where R code is not integrated into the discussion.

By the end of this chapter, you should be able to:

- Understand what makes a good empirical and quantitative hypothesis
- Understand how to make hypotheses empirically clear
- Be able to write your own good hypotheses
- Examine data to help develop hypotheses

WHAT MAKES A GOOD HYPOTHESIS?

There is not one answer to what makes a good hypothesis. However, we can perhaps all agree that a good empirical hypothesis provides a clear expectation of a relationship that one can actually empirically test. You would be surprised how often people develop 'hypotheses' that they cannot test given their data. Sometimes this is due to a simple misunderstanding, such as misidentifying the unit of analysis (e.g., developing a hypothesis for individuals, but the data is actually only about cities). Or the hypotheses are nearing tautologies (e.g., 'the candidate who received the most votes won the election') and/or are blindingly obvious (e.g., 'Americans who strongly identified with the Democratic Party were more likely to vote for Biden than Trump in the 2020 election'). Other times, researchers may develop hypotheses that require logical leaps from their data and methods to adequately test.

In this chapter, given a dataset and variables, our main focus is on how we develop good hypotheses (or at least not bad hypotheses) that have a clear empirical test. In particular, our hypothesis needs to be an explicit statement of how a predictor variable is expected to affect an outcome variable. A hypothesis puts your empirical theory into action through a testable empirical and quantitative form.

While there is not one way to write a good hypothesis, there are two main components that good hypotheses should have. First, a good hypothesis should provide an expected direction of the relationship between the predictor and outcome variables. Direction means including whether something is *increasing or decreasing*, *more or less*, *greater or smaller*, *higher or lower*, etc. In essence, what is the expected effect that the predictor variable will have on the outcome variable? Notice the term *expected*. When we develop hypotheses, we are creating something that is testable, and thus falsifiable, and therefore it is something we *expect*, but do not know for certain until we actually test it.

Second, a hypothesis should provide some type of comparison. At the simplest level, we can do this by breaking our predictor variable in half and comparing expected relationships of the high and low values on the outcome variable. We do this by including terms like *compared to* or *than*.

There are other times when we do not need an explicit comparison, because we are describing the expected relationship in a more continuous manner – such as *increasing* or *decreasing*.

If these two recommendations are not clear, they should be by the end of this chapter. We will look at examples *ad nauseam*, because developing a good hypothesis is an essential element of QSS. Understanding the expected relationship between predictor and outcome variables allows us to quickly take statistical analysis results and convert them into 'plain language'. Again, being able to explain statistical results in plain language is one of the key aspect that separates QSS from applied statistics.

There are three final things to note about developing hypotheses. First, a good hypothesis is structured as the effect of the predictor variable on the outcome variable (i.e., $x \rightarrow y$). The predictor variable always comes first in a hypothesis, followed by the expected effect on the outcome variable. Second, we need to have a different hypothesis for each predictor variable; we cannot just clump a bunch of them together. So, if we have three predictors, we need to develop three different hypotheses. This may become clearer when we move to hypothesis testing and more advanced statistical analysis. Third, a well-written and well-formed hypothesis does not have to fit intuition. While some hypotheses make more sense to us *a priori*, we can create good hypotheses that may intuitively sound ridiculous. These are hypotheses that are correct in form, but may strike us as likely to be wrong. But the point of QSS is to take *any* hypothesis and be able to tell whether there is any statistical merit to it. There are times when you may hear a hypothesis and think it sounds completely wrong, only to discover that it has statistical merit. A classic example comes from *Freakonomics* by Steven Levitt and Stephen Dubner (2006), which, if you have not read it, is a reader-friendly version of quirky empirical and quantitative economics articles by Levitt and co-authors. One chapter in the book presents this hypothesis: higher abortion rates are expected to lead to lower crime rates. What the analysis showed was that US states that legalised abortion saw drops in crime before states that only legalised abortion after the US Supreme Court case *Roe* v. *Wade*. *A priori* this is a hypothesis that may sound completely wrong, but turns out to have statistical merit.

Now that we have reviewed critical elements of good hypotheses and related concerns, let's move on to actually developing good hypotheses by walking through a set of examples.

CRAFTING GOOD HYPOTHESES

Example I: Smart People Are All about Covid-19 Vaccines?

Let's think about the relationship between a person's education level and Covid-19 vaccination status. Suppose you encounter the following hypothesis:

People who have college degrees are more likely to be vaccinated against Covid-19.

This hypothesis looks pretty good. However, based on the discussion in the previous section, what is the problem with it? The hypothesis tells us the *direction* of the relationship, but we do not know who people with college degrees are being *compared* to. Is it people with only high school diplomas? People without high school diplomas? How about this correction to the hypothesis?

People who have college degrees are more likely to be vaccinated against Covid-19 compared to people who only have high school diplomas.

The inclusion of the comparison (*compared to*) makes this a better empirical hypothesis as it satisfies our two main components. Are there any other problems? If we think about *how* we would empirically test this hypothesis (i.e., the logistics of data manipulation and analysis), we probably realise we want more clarification on a couple of aspects. First, is it any type of college degree? Are we referring to people with just bachelor's degrees? What about people with master's, doctorate, and/or professional degrees (e.g., law, business, or medical degrees)? Second, what does it mean to be 'vaccinated'? Does it mean 'fully vaccinated' based on the definition provided by the vaccine manufacturers and/or government? Does it include Covid-19 booster shots? Some of this might seem like splitting hairs and we probably do not need to specify every contingency, but we want to be as clear as possible when developing hypotheses. Let's revise the hypothesis to provide greater clarity:

People who have at least a bachelor's degree are more likely to be fully vaccinated against Covid-19 than people who only have a high school diploma.

Additionally, what is the predictor variable and what is the outcome variable? The predictor variable is *education level* and the outcome variable is *Covid-19 vaccination status*. What about the unit of analysis? The unit of analysis is individuals/people.

Example II: Smart People Are *Really* All about Covid-19 Vaccines?

Let's consider a follow-up to the first example. For people with children, how should we craft a good hypothesis to test the relationship between education level and whether they choose to have their kids vaccinated against Covid-19? Would we just use the last hypothesis in the previous example? Are there any changes we should make?

Clearly, we would not use the same hypothesis as above because we are now discussing people with children. Let's have a go at one:

People who have at least a bachelor's degree are more likely to have their children fully vaccinated against Covid-19 compared to people who only have a high school diploma.

We can make the hypothesis clearer by changing a single word – replace 'people' with 'parents'.

Parents who have at least a bachelor's degree are more likely to have their children fully vaccinated against Covid-19 compared to parents who only have a high school diploma.

This is now a solid empirical hypothesis. What is the predictor variable, outcome variable, and unit of analysis? The predictor variable is still *education level*, but the outcome variable is now *Covid-19 vaccination status of children*. The unit of analysis is now parents instead of simply individuals/people.

Example III: Curing Covid-19 with Political Ideology?

Perhaps unsurprisingly, large divides along political ideology lines quickly emerged in many countries on how (and sometimes whether) to manage the Covid-19 pandemic. While much of the scuttlebutt swirled (and continues to swirl) around wearing masks and vaccinations, let's consider the following hypothesis:

> There is a relationship between political ideology and the use of homeopathic medicine to cure Covid-19 infections.

This is a bad hypothesis. Yet, we often encounter hypotheses that take this form. This hypothesis might work for brainstorming chit-chat, but otherwise it is a non-starter. It provides no expectations regarding the relationship between political ideology and using homeopathic medicine to cure Covid-19. Specifically, there is nothing on the expected direction of the relationship between the two variables and we don't know anything about the comparison.

There are many ways to make this hypothesis better and provide a clearer link to an empirical test. We might rewrite it as:

> Politically conservative individuals are more likely to use homeopathic medicine to try to cure Covid-19 infections than politically liberal individuals.

Or we can flip it around to say:

> Politically liberal individuals are less likely to use homeopathic medicine to try to cure Covid-19 infections than politically conservative individuals.

Or we might write it as:

> As people become more politically conservative, they are more likely to use homeopathic medicine to try to cure Covid-19 infections.

All three of these examples provide direction and a comparison. All three provide a clear link to an empirical test.

Finally, what is the predictor variable, outcome variable, and unit of analysis? The predictor variable is *political ideology*, the outcome variable is *homeopathic medicine to try to cure Covid-19 infections*, and the unit of analysis is individuals/people.

Example IV: Negative Effects of Online Learning?

When the Covid-19 pandemic hit in early 2020, many countries moved primary and secondary education completely to online learning for the rest of the school year. For the 2020–2021 school year, US states and school districts substantially differed on whether and how to continue to offer online learning along with traditional in-person education. A prominent argument against continuing online learning was that students' learning would be negatively impacted and these effects could be long-lasting. The variation in education offerings across the USA offers a unique opportunity to test the efficacy of online learning. To test the argument against continuing online learning, let's consider this hypothesis:

Online learning is bad for children.

By now, we know that this is not a great hypothesis. Although *bad* suggests a direction, it is not clear what *bad* is referring to? Does it refer only to their academic progress? What about kids' social maturation? Or kids' mental and physical health? The hypothesis also does not include a comparison. While we assume the comparison is to in-person learning, the hypothesis should make the comparison specific and clear. Let's revise the hypothesis:

Online learning negatively impacts a child's academic progress compared to in-person learning.

This version can now be considered a good hypothesis – it has direction (*negatively*) and includes a comparison (*online versus in-person learning*).

As quantitative researchers, we also need to think about operationalisation – how do we measure these concepts and what is the research design? Our hypothesis does not make this clear. For example, how is *academic progress* measured? Are we comparing schools who only offered online learning to schools who only offered in-person learning? What about schools who offered both options? What is the unit of analysis? Is it at the state level, school district level, and/or student level? Are we considering primary or secondary students (or both)? Since some school districts offered online learning or hybrid options for only a couple of months, how are we accounting for variation in time? There are further clarifications and questions we could make, and collectively these might require multiple hypotheses. Let's create a few hypotheses to address some of these questions. We'll start with a hypothesis on the US state level:

States that allowed online learning for secondary education are expected to have lower graduation rates than states that did not allow online learning during the 2020–2021 school year.

This hypothesis has direction (*lower*), makes a comparison (*allowed online learning* versus *did not allow online learning*), specifies the 'academic measure' (*graduation rates*), includes the unit of analysis (*states*), and specifies the time period (*2020–2021 school year*).

Here's one for the school district level:

School districts that offered online and in-person learning are expected to perform worse on state tests for primary school students than school districts that only offered in-person learning during the 2020–2021 school year.

This hypothesis has direction (*worse*), makes a comparison (*offered online and in-person learning* versus *only offered in-person learning*), specifies the 'academic measure' (*state tests for primary school students*), includes the unit of analysis (*school districts*), and specifies the time period (*2020–2021 school year*).

Example V: Gaining Weight by the Day in Lockdown?

Aside from the direct negative health effects of contracting Covid, health professionals and researchers are also concerned with how the pandemic has affected other aspects of people's health. One broad concern is that people in lockdown will not be able to exercise, will gain excess weight, and consequentially will become more susceptible to the negative health effects of obesity. Let's consider the following hypothesis for this:

Covid-19 lockdowns cause people to gain weight.

Are there any problems with this hypothesis? Although we may assume that the comparison being made is to times not under lockdown due to Covid-19, the hypothesis should make it explicit. Let's add a comparison:

Covid-19 lockdowns cause people to gain weight compared to people who are not under lockdown.

This hypothesis now has a comparison and the word *gain* suggests direction, but we can make both clearer. Additionally, the hypothesis uses the word *cause*, which implies *cause and effect*. In the social sciences, we generally stay clear of using language that explicitly or implicitly implies cause and effect. The reason is that our data rarely provides us the evidence to establish cause and effect. Let's revise the hypothesis:

People in lockdowns due to Covid-19 are more likely to gain weight than people who are not in lockdown.

We replaced *cause* with *more likely*, which improves the direction and also fixes the cause-and-effect issue. We also moved *people* to the start of the sentence to make the comparison clearer.

Finally, what is the predictor variable, outcome variable, and unit of analysis? The predictor variable is *Covid-19 lockdowns*, the outcome variable is *weight gain*, and the unit of analysis is individuals/people.

DEVELOPING HYPOTHESES FROM DATA VISUALISATIONS

We will perform and examine a host of data visualisations in Chapter 8, but in this section we will develop hypotheses from viewing data visualisations. Understanding what data visualisations are showing (and not showing) and being able to derive expectations and hypotheses from visualisations are important skills for everyone. We are not talking about using data-mining approaches to uncover patterns in data. Instead, we can use visualisations to add to our theoretical understanding and expectations about social phenomena. We may see patterns that suggest relationships between variables that we had not considered before, but that is not the goal.

We will look at a few scatterplots using the 2020 Scottish Index of Multiple Deprivation data and try to develop good hypotheses. For our outcome variable, our *y*-axis variable, we will use the percentage of psychiatric medication prescriptions by datazone. For the first scatterplot, we will use as our predictor variable (on the *x*-axis) the percentage of people in a datazone who are employment deprived. This variable measures the percentage of people in a datazone receiving incapacity benefits, employment and support allowance, or severe disablement allowance – essentially, financial support from the government due to being unable to work.

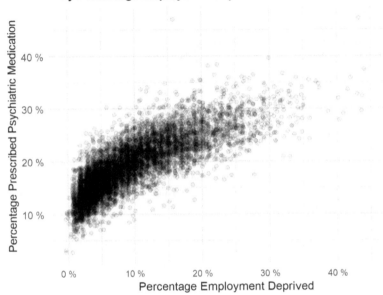

Based on the scatterplot, what might be a good hypothesis? We see that psychiatric medication prescriptions increase as employment deprivation increases. Therefore, one good hypothesis might be:

> *Datazones with a high percentage of employment deprivation are expected to have a higher percentage of psychiatric medication prescriptions than datazones with a low percentage of employment deprivation.*

This hypothesis splits employment deprivation into high and low, thus providing a comparison through *than*. We also have direction provided by *higher percentage of psychiatric medication prescriptions*.

We could flip the employment deprivation order and thus the direction of effect:

> *Datazones with a low percentage of employment deprivation are expected to have a lower percentage of psychiatric medication prescriptions than datazones with a high percentage of employment deprivation.*

We could rephrase the hypothesis to take account of the apparent trend in the scatterplot:

> *As the percentage of employment deprivation increases, the percentage of psychiatric medication prescriptions is expected to increase in datazones.*

Let's look at the same scatterplot, but now the datazones are coloured by whether they are urban or rural.

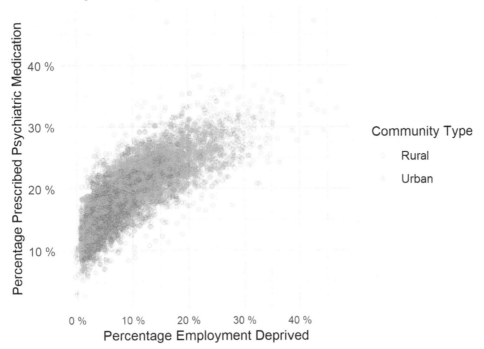

What is a good hypothesis for this scatterplot? For the most part, urban and rural datazones have similar levels of employment deprivation and psychiatric medication prescriptions. However, it appears that datazones with the highest levels of employment deprivation and psychiatric medication prescriptions are all urban datazones. Since the relationship is more complicated than in the first scatterplot, there are a few different ways to incorporate urban and rural datazones into hypotheses. We could craft a hypothesis only for urban datazones, such as:

Urban datazones with a high percentage of employment deprivation are expected to have a higher percentage of psychiatric medication prescriptions than urban datazones with a low percentage of employment deprivation.

We could create a similar hypothesis only for rural datazones:

Rural datazones with a high percentage of employment deprivation are expected to have a higher percentage of psychiatric medication prescriptions than rural datazones with a low percentage of employment deprivation.

However, if we expect the same relationship between employment deprivation and psychiatric medication prescriptions, we probably should use the hypothesis from earlier that did not include urban and rural.

To contrast urban and rural datazones, we might have a hypothesis like the following:

Urban datazones with a high percentage of employment deprivation are expected to have a higher percentage of psychiatric medication prescriptions than rural datazones with a high percentage of employment deprivation.

Lastly, let's look at a scatterplot where the predictor variable (the *x*-axis variable) is the percentage of 17–21-year-olds entering university in a datazone.

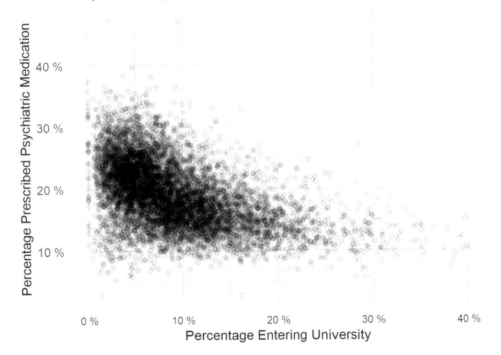

What do we see with this scatterplot? It appears that as university attendance increases, psychiatric medication prescriptions decrease. However, the relationship does not appear as strong as what we saw with employment deprivation on the *x*-axis. A good hypothesis for this relationship might be:

Datazones with a high percentage of 17–21-year-olds entering university are expected to have a lower percentage of psychiatric medication prescriptions than datazones with a low percentage of 17–21-year-olds entering university.

We could also phrase this as:

As the percentage of 17–21-year-olds entering university increases, the percentage psychiatric medication prescriptions is expected to increase in datazones.

There are times when looking at data visualisations provides us with very clear expectations between predictor and outcome variables. Other times, data visualisations are less useful for developing expectations between variables. In the latter cases, it is best practice to use our intuition and substantive knowledge to develop hypotheses. In later chapters, we will move beyond visualisations and learn more rigorous statistical techniques for testing relationships. However, the point of this section was to get practice at looking at data and developing good hypotheses that describe the expected relationship between predictor and outcome variables.

CONCLUSION

This chapter presented and discussed what makes *good* empirical hypotheses – hypotheses that are clear and empirically and quantitatively testable. Much of the material may seem pedantic and dull, but understanding how to assemble and develop good hypotheses is critical for aiding your data analysis and being able to interpret and discuss the results you find. Hopefully, this chapter will set you on the right path and the examples have provided you a foundation to build confidence in your hypothesis-writing ability.

Additional Resource

- King, G., Keohane, R. O. and Verba, S. (1994) *Designing Social Inquiry*. Princeton University Press.

7

UNIVARIATE AND DESCRIPTIVE STATISTICS

Chapter contents

When encountering a dataset for the first time, we ordinarily like to perform some univariate and descriptive statistics on our variables of interest. As is obvious from the name, univariate statistics simply means statistics for *one* variable and descriptive statistics means information that *describes* the attributes of a variable. We look at univariate and descriptive statistics to get a sense of the data and variables, problems that we may face, and methods we may choose. Ordinarily we do not conclude our analysis with univariate and descriptive statistics, and often we may not even include the information in a paper or report; we instead perform bivariate and multivariate analysis. These statistics are, in essence, for our information and something that the reader might not really care about.

We will begin this chapter by considering frequency distributions and tables, and then move onto measures of central tendency, measures of dispersion, and *z*-scores. The chapter concludes with two examples of applying univariate and descriptive statistics to understand the racial composition of locations in the USA.

Understanding levels of measurement of variables is critical at this stage. The level of measurement of a variable tells us what type of descriptive statistics we can consider and provide. Sometimes this will be quite obvious, other times it may be a bit tricky, and there are times when it is a grey area. Though univariate and descriptive statistics might not be the most exciting analysis, they are critical for more advanced analysis; not looking at them is akin to trying to drive a car without a steering wheel.

By the end of this chapter, you should be able to:

- Understand frequency distributions and tables
- Know how to create more appealing frequency tables
- Understand measures of central tendency and dispersion
- Understand the appropriate uses of univariate and descriptive statistics
- Implement univariate and descriptive statistics in R
- Understand the normal distribution
- Understand how to calculate and interpret *z*-scores in R

FREQUENCY DISTRIBUTIONS AND TABLES

Often the first thing we do when we encounter a new variable is to look at the variable's frequency distribution. Some students recoil at the phrase *distribution* as it sounds statistically scary. Here, though, a frequency distribution simply tells us how many observations there are at different values of a variable. If we were sadists, or did not have a computer, we could look at a datasheet and count them up by hand. Instead we look at frequency distributions by using a frequency table – here, for one variable. This table provides a summary of a variable's values in a condensed and easy-to-understand presentation. We can use frequency tables to look at any variable from any dataset.

To start, let's look at the average life expectancy by Scottish council area for the years 2018 to 2020. Since the data is in an Excel file, we use the `read_xlsx()` function to open the file called `Scottish_LE_Council_2018_2020.xlsx` and name the data `le`.

```
setwd("C:/QSSD/Chapter 7 - Univariate & Descriptive Statistics/")
getwd()
[1] "C:/QSSD/Chapter 7 - Univariate & Descriptive Statistics"

library(tidyverse)
library(readxl)

le <- read_xlsx("Scottish_LE_Council_2018_2020.xlsx")
glimpse(le)
Rows: 32
Columns: 3
$ council_area <chr> "Aberdeen City", "Aberdeenshire", "Angus", "Argyll and Bu~
$ female       <dbl> 81.26, 82.44, 82.27, 81.57, 82.36, 80.62, 81.47, 79.38, 7~
$ male         <dbl> 76.93, 78.94, 78.45, 78.01, 78.15, 76.17, 78.03, 73.80, 7~
```

Let's look at a frequency table for female life expectancy. Here we will keep it simple and use the base R function table().

```
table(le$female)

78.28 78.59 78.83 79.21 79.38 79.81  80.1 80.36  80.4 80.47 80.48 80.62 81.14
    1     1     1     1     1     1     1     1     1     1     1     1     1
81.17 81.26 81.41 81.47 81.57 81.82 81.86 81.92  82.1 82.27 82.36 82.44 82.86
    1     1     1     1     1     1     1     1     1     1     1     1     1
82.88 83.03 83.21 83.43 83.49 83.96
    1     1     1     1     1     1
```

This output is not really informative as each value is unique. Let's round the values for both female and male, so we can get a better idea of how the observations are clustered.

We use the round() function from base R, where we first specify the variable and then the number of decimals to round. To make it easier to use the values later, we create new variables with the rounded values using the mutate() function.

```
le <- le %>%
    mutate(female_rd = round(female,0),
           male_rd = round(male,0))
```

Now let's look at the rounded values for female life expectancy.

```
table(le$female_rd)

78 79 80 81 82 83 84
 1  4  6  6  8  6  1
```

We see that most of the values are centred around 80–83 years.

Let's look at male life expectancy.

```
table(le$male_rd)

73 74 75 76 77 78 79 80 81
 1  3  3  3  5  7  6  3  1
```

We see that male life expectancy is more spread out, but there are a number of council areas between 77 and 79 years.

We often want to know the frequency percentages of the different values of a variable. These are simply the value's frequencies divided by the total number of observations and then multiplied by 100. The `table()` function does not make this easy, so we will use the `freq()` function from the `descr` package. We include `plot = FALSE` in the specification in order to suppress an automatically generated bar plot. Let's first look at female life expectancy.

```
library(descr)
freq(le$female_rd, plot = FALSE)
le$female_rd
          Frequency Percent
78             1     3.125
79             4    12.500
80             6    18.750
81             6    18.750
82             8    25.000
83             6    18.750
84             1     3.125
Total         32   100.000
```

The frequency percentages appear in the right-hand column conveniently under the heading `Percent`. We see that 3.125% of council areas have a female life expectancy of 78 years, 12.5% of council areas have a female life expectancy of 79 years, etc. Notice at the bottom of the table, there is a row titled `Total` that includes the total number of observations and the combined percentage (which should always be 100%).

Now let's look at male life expectancy.

```
freq(le$male_rd, plot = FALSE)
le$male_rd
          Frequency Percent
73             1     3.125
74             3     9.375
75             3     9.375
76             3     9.375
77             5    15.625
78             7    21.875
79             6    18.750
80             3     9.375
81             1     3.125
Total         32   100.000
```

We interpret this output the same as we did before.

MEASURES OF CENTRAL TENDENCY

Measures of central tendency convey what the *typical case* looks like for a variable. These measures are generally referred to as *descriptive statistics*. There are a number of different of measures we can look at, but we will focus on three: mode, median, and mean.

Mode

The mode is simply the value of a variable that occurs most frequently. The mode does not need to be near the centre of a distribution, it can take on multiple values, and we can use it with all levels of measurement. Although we can use it for all levels of measurement, if we have nominal-level variables, we can *only* use the mode.

To find the mode of a variable, we just look at what value of a variable has the most observations. Let's find the mode for `female_rd` and `male_rd`.

```
freq(le$female_rd, plot = FALSE)
le$female_rd
      Frequency Percent
78            1   3.125
79            4  12.500
80            6  18.750
81            6  18.750
82            8  25.000
83            6  18.750
84            1   3.125
Total        32 100.000

freq(le$male_rd, plot = FALSE)
le$male_rd
      Frequency Percent
73            1   3.125
74            3   9.375
75            3   9.375
76            3   9.375
77            5  15.625
78            7  21.875
79            6  18.750
80            3   9.375
81            1   3.125
Total        32 100.000
```

The mode for female life expectancy is 82 years and the mode for male life expectancy is 78 years. We can phrase this as *the modal category for female life expectancy is 82 years and for male life expectancy is 78 years*.

We can also locate the mode from a graphical display of a variable. Below, we remove the option `plot = FALSE` from the `freq()` argument for `female_rd` and `male_rd`. Can you find the mode?

```
freq(le$female_rd)
```

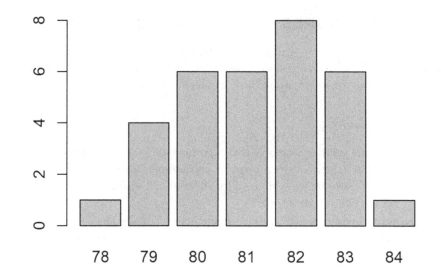

```
le$female_rd
        Frequency Percent
78              1   3.125
79              4  12.500
80              6  18.750
81              6  18.750
82              8  25.000
83              6  18.750
84              1   3.125
Total          32 100.000

freq(le$male_rd)
```

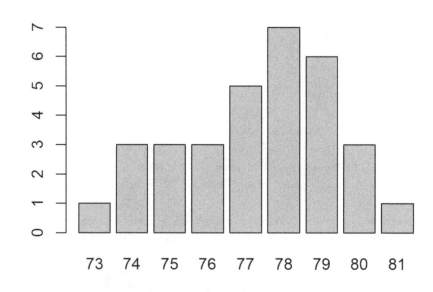

```
le$male_rd
         Frequency Percent
73              1    3.125
74              3    9.375
75              3    9.375
76              3    9.375
77              5   15.625
78              7   21.875
79              6   18.750
80              3    9.375
81              1    3.125
Total          32  100.000
```

Simply, the mode is the value that has the largest bar for each variable.

We do not spend much time on the mode, because it is often not that informative, particularly in comparison to other descriptive statistics (e.g., the median and mean). Two final things to remember regarding the mode: first, it tells us which value of a variable occurs most frequently; and, second, if we have a nominal-level variable we can only look at the mode.

Median

The median is the middle value in a variable's distribution, where an equal number of observations lie below and above. Another way of saying this is that the median is the 50th percentile of a variable. The median is not affected by extreme values of a variable, though it is not too useful for distributions where the observations do not cluster near the middle. For example, the median is informative when a distribution appears like a normal distribution, but it is not informative when a distribution is U-shaped (with most observations at the minimum and maximum). The median can only be used when a variable has order to the values; for ordinal, interval, and ratio-level variables we can use the median, but not for nominal-level variables.

You have probably heard of the median used to describe economic figures like the median house price in New York City or the median income in India. The median is used in these situations because outliers will not affect the median value as they would the mean. For example, if we looked at the mean house price in New York City it will be unnaturally high due to homes that are tens or hundreds of millions of dollars.

To find the median of a variable, all the values need to be ordered from lowest to highest (or highest to lowest). Consider this exercise: find the median among these values?

15, 3, 8, 12, 9, 17, 1, 7, 11

First, we need to order them.

1, 3, 7, 8, 9, 11, 12, 15, 17

Then we pick the value in the middle – here the median is 9. What if there are an even number of values? We simply pick the number that splits the two middle values. For example, suppose the values are:

3, 4, 5, 7, 8, 9, 10, 11, 14, 79

The two middle values are 8 and 9, thus the median is 8.5.

If we have many observations, we can use the following formula to locate the middle value:

$$Middle = \frac{N+1}{2}$$

where N is the number of observations. For example, if we have 1533 observations, we calculate:

$$Middle = \frac{1533+1}{2} = 767$$

So, the median is the value of observation 767.

In a frequency table, we can find the median by finding which value of the variable includes the 50th percentile (which you find using the cumulative frequency). We use the `freq()` function and wrap the `ordered()` function around our variable (here, `le$female_rd`) in order to get the cumulative frequency percentage.

```
freq(ordered(le$female_rd), plot = FALSE)
ordered(le$female_rd)
      Frequency Percent Cum Percent
78            1   3.125       3.125
79            4  12.500      15.625
80            6  18.750      34.375
81            6  18.750      53.125
82            8  25.000      78.125
83            6  18.750      96.875
84            1   3.125     100.000
Total        32 100.000
```

We see that the median is 81 years since the 50th percentile lies in that category; 80 years includes the 34th percentile and 81 years includes the 53th percentile, thus the 50th percentile is in the 81 years category.

Let's find the median of `male_rd`.

```
freq(ordered(le$male_rd), plot = FALSE)
ordered(le$male_rd)
      Frequency Percent Cum Percent
73            1   3.125       3.125
74            3   9.375      12.500
75            3   9.375      21.875
76            3   9.375      31.250
77            5  15.625      46.875
78            7  21.875      68.750
79            6  18.750      87.500
80            3   9.375      96.875
81            1   3.125     100.000
Total        32 100.000
```

Here we see that the median is 78 years.

We can also get the median of a variable by using the `median()` function.

```
median(le$female_rd)
[1] 81
median(le$male_rd)
[1] 78
```

Mean

The **mean**, as mentioned above, is simply the average. By this point in your career as a student (and/or a person), you have undoubtedly calculated a mean. To do so, we just add all the values up and divide by the total number of observations. A few things to note about the mean: there can only be one mean for a variable, sometimes the mean is not realistic due to outliers, and the mean can only be used with interval- and ratio-level variables. Though the *textbook* definition is that the mean can only be used with interval- and ratio-level variables, in fact we often look at means for ordinal-level variables as well. A rule of thumb is if an ordinal variable has seven categories or more, then we can use the mean.[1] Similar to the median, the mean is most informative when a variable's values are clustered around the middle of the distribution.

We could calculate the mean by hand, but let's use the `mean()` function instead.

```
mean(le$female_rd)
[1] 81.1875
mean(le$male_rd)
[1] 77.3125
```

We see that the mean female life expectancy is 81.19 years and the mean male life expectancy is 77.31.

Let's also look at the means for the non-rounded versions.

```
mean(le$female)
[1] 81.31812
mean(le$male)
[1] 77.26406
```

As we should expect, these values are roughly the same.

Note that like other statistical programs, R will often let us use certain statistics in situations where we probably should not. Specifically, R will provide the mean for variables classified as numeric, double, and integer. Since we can coerce a variable to another type, we should not rely on R to tell us whether we should or should not use the mean (or any statistic) for a given variable. For example, let's force R to tell us the mean of `council_area`.

---

[1] Some researchers even use the mean for dummy variables that are coded 0 and 1. For example, if a variable is coded 1 = 'female', 0 = 'male', and the mean is 0.52, then 52% of the observations are female.

```
mean(as.numeric(as.factor(le$council_area)))
 [1] 16.5
```

We see that the mean for `council_area` is 16.5, which means nothing. Again, we need to be mindful of which statistics we can and cannot use, depending on the level of measurement of a variable and the variable's values.

Although `tidyverse` is not really focused on statistical analysis functions, we can use it to wrangle data and variables to easily calculate descriptive statistics for combinations of variables. Let's use the `VF England.csv` dataset to demonstrate a few examples.

```
vf_england <- read_csv("VF England.csv")
glimpse(vf_england)
Rows: 2,034
Columns: 8
$ vfalter     <chr> "Slightly agree", "Disagree", "Neither agree nor disagree~
$ vfproblem   <chr> "Slightly agree", "Disagree", "Neither agree nor disagree~
$ age         <dbl> 66, 59, 54, 68, 58, 67, 51, 59, 59, 65, 69, 71, 61, 70, 6~
$ sex         <chr> "Female", "Male", "Male", "Female", "Male", "Male", "Male~
$ education   <dbl> 1, 2, 1, 2, 2, 3, 3, 3, 3, 3, 1, 2, 2, 2, 2, 1, 2, 3, 2, ~
$ brexit_vote <chr> "2. Leave", "2. Leave", "2. Leave", "1. Remain", "2. Leav~
$ vote2017_dum <chr> "Winner", "Winner", NA, "Winner", "Winner", "Winner", "Wi~
$ pid         <chr> "UKIP Brexit", "Conservative", "Other", "Conservative", "~
```

Let's first look at the mean of `age` using the `mean()` function.

```
mean(vf_england$age)
 [1] 49.53441
```

We see the mean age of respondents is 49.5.

If wanted to calculate the means of certain groups or under certain conditions, we could still use base R. But, `dplyr` functions can make this much easier. Let's calculate the mean age of respondents based on their Brexit vote. We first use the `filter()` function to remove the missing values in `brexit_vote`. Next, we use the `group_by()` function to group the observations based on the values of `brexit_vote` (Remain and Leave) and the `summarise()` function to calculate the mean for `age`.

```
vf_england %>%
  filter(!is.na(brexit_vote)) %>%
  group_by(brexit_vote) %>%
  summarise(mean(age))
# A tibble: 2 x 2
  brexit_vote `mean(age)`
  <chr>            <dbl>
1 1. Remain         47.7
2 2. Leave          55.9
```

This shows that the mean age of Remain voters is 47.7 and the mean age of Leave voters is 55.9. So, Leave voters were much older on average than Remain voters.

The `summarise()` function actually creates a new data frame based on the grouping and the operations specified in the `summarise()` function. To see this, let's save the object as `df`.

```
df <- vf_england %>%
   filter(!is.na(brexit_vote)) %>%
   group_by(brexit_vote) %>%
   summarise(mean(age))
```

We see in the `Environment` window that `df` has two observations and two variables.

When to Use the Mode, Median, and Mean

We can summarise when to use the mode, median, and mean as follows:

- Nominal-level variable: mode
- Ordinal-level variable: mode, median
- 'High' ordinal-level variable (7+ categories): mode, median, mean
- Interval- or ratio-level variable: mode, median, mean

MEASURES OF DISPERSION

Measures of dispersion convey information about the variability in our data. These measures basically tell us how the observations in our variables are spread out. Often these measures are more important and informative than measures of central tendency. The best practice is to combine measures of central tendency with measures of dispersion to gain a complete picture of our data and variables. In this section, we will focus on three measures of dispersion: the minimum/maximum (range), variance, and standard deviation.

Minimum/Maximum (Range)

The range is simply the maximum value minus the minimum value of a variable. I do not find knowing the *value* of a variable's range very informative, but knowing the minimum and maximum values can be. The minimum and maximum provide the boundaries of a variable and together are informative when considering other statistics such as the median and mean. Additionally, in more advanced analysis, we might want to know the effect of some variable at its minimum and maximum values.

There is nothing mysterious or difficult in finding this information. Simply, what is the lowest value of the variable (minimum) and what is the highest value of the variable (maximum)? For the variable `female_rd`, from above, the minimum is 78 and the maximum is 84. For `male_rd`, the minimum is 73 and the maximum is 81.

Standard Deviation and Variance

While we can get the minimum and maximum for any variable, we can only look at the standard deviation and variance if we can look at the mean of a variable – so, only with interval-, ratio-, or 'high' ordinal-level variables. Let's discuss the standard deviation and variance at the same time.

The standard deviation is defined as a measure of dispersion around the mean, while the variance is defined as a measure of dispersion around the mean. Wait, what? The standard deviation and the variance provide the same information about the spread of observations in a variable with the only difference being the units of measurement. The variance is simply the standard deviation squared (or the standard deviation is just the square root of the variance). We have generally avoided equations in this book, but here they are useful to demonstrate the difference between standard deviation and variance.

Before we take a look at the equations, we need to briefly discuss populations and samples. A *population* is the entire universe of observations of something; for example, all voters in Brazil or all Canadian newspapers. A *sample* is a small proportion of the population; for example, 2000 Brazilian voters or 25% of Canadian newspapers. Samples are created using various collection procedures, particularly the use of *randomness*, in selecting the elements of the sample. Randomness helps mitigate bias and limited representativeness in samples.

The equation for the sample variance is as follows:

$$s^2 = \frac{\sum (x_i - \bar{x})^2}{N - 1}$$

where x_i is the value of each individual observation i, $\bar{x}$ is the sample mean, N is the total number of observations, and s^2 represents the variance. $\sum$ (affectionately known as *the giant E of death*) simply says add up everything in the parentheses – so for each i, the squared value of x minus the mean. Then divide that sum by $N - 1$. Notice that if every observation has the same value as the mean, then the variance equals 0. The more observations that are far away from the mean, the larger the variance gets.

Now the equation for the standard deviation:

$$s = \sqrt{\frac{\sum (x_i - \bar{x})^2}{N - 1}}$$

or

$$s = \sqrt{s^2}$$

where s represents the standard deviation. Again, the standard deviation is just the square root of the variance.

We usually prefer using the standard deviation instead of the variance because of the awkwardness in the interpretation of the variance. Let's do an example using `female_rd`. The function for the variance is `var()` and the function for the standard deviation is `sd()`.

```
var(le$female_rd)
[1] 2.28629
sd(le$female_rd)
[1] 1.512048
```

We find that the variance is 2.29 and the standard deviation is 1.51. We can double-check that the variance is the standard deviation squared.

```
1.51*1.51
[1] 2.2801
```

It is close enough (due to rounding).

Let's add a bit of love to these numbers by including the unit of measurement. The standard deviation is 1.51 years and the variance is 2.29 years squared. What does 2.29 years squared mean? It is not obvious, thus we prefer to use the standard deviation since it is easier to understand 'years' than 'years squared'.

Let's also look at the variance and standard deviation for male_rd.

```
var(le$male_rd)
[1] 4.157258
sd(le$male_rd)
[1] 2.038936
```

We find that the variance is 4.16 years squared and the standard deviation is 2.04 years. Again, we prefer to use the standard deviation instead of the variance.

At this point, you might be wondering what exactly the standard deviation exactly tells us. To understand the standard deviation, we need to consider the **normal distribution**.

Normal Distribution

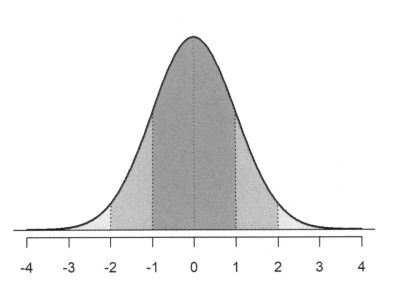

The normal distribution is commonly referred to as the bell curve and less commonly, though not for statisticians and econometricians, the Gaussian distribution. You have probably seen and/or heard of the normal distribution previously. Let's take a look at it.

With the mean at 0, the darker blue is ±1 standard deviations (away from the mean), the blue is ±2 standard deviations, and the light blue is ±3 standard deviations. Based on the normal distribution, approximately 68% of the observations are expected to fall between one standard deviation above and one standard deviation below the mean, 95% of the observations are expected to fall between two standard deviations above and two standard deviations below the mean, and 99.7% of the observations are expected to fall between three standard deviations above and three standard deviations below the mean.

Two things to note about the normal distribution. First, the mode, median, and mean are the same value in a perfect normal distribution. Second, the meaning of the standard deviation is only true asymptotically (as the number of observations gets very large ($N \to \infty$)). With real-world data, the standard deviation rarely fits the description of a perfect normal distribution.

With this information, let's interpret the values of `male_rd`. Again, the mean was 77.31 years and the standard deviation was 2.04 years. So, we conclude that 68% of the observations are expected to lie between 75.27 years (77.31 – 2.04) and 79.35 years (77.31 + 2.04). Similarly, 95% of the observations are expected to lie between 73.23 years (77.31 – (2.04 × 2)) and 81.39 years (77.31 + (2.04 × 2)). Finally, 99.7% of the observations are expected to lie between 71.19 years (77.31 – (2.04 × 3)) and 83.43 years (77.31 + (2.04 × 3))

Often with real data, the lower and upper bounds of 2 or 3 standard deviations will not be realistic. This is particularly common when we have small Ns and/or a large range of values. This problem speaks directly to the point raised above: the relationship between the mean and standard deviation is only true asymptotically. Although there are only 32 observations in the `le` data, the values are relatively close together and the range is fairly small.[2]

If we cannot often directly interpret the standard deviation, what should we be looking for? Simply if the standard deviation is large *relative* to the mean, then our observations are well spread out (which we might use the minimum and maximum to understand). If the standard deviation is small *relative* to the mean, then our observations are close to the mean.

When to Use Certain Measures of Central Tendency and Dispersion

We can update our summary of when to use certain measures of central tendency and dispersion as follows:

- Nominal-level variable: mode, minimum and maximum
- Ordinal-level variable: mode, median, minimum and maximum
- 'High' ordinal-level variable (7+ categories): mode, median, mean, minimum and maximum, variance, and standard deviation
- Interval- or ratio-level variable: mode, median, mean, minimum and maximum, variance, and standard deviation

---

[2]There is a whole branch of statistics dedicated to corrections to equations for small Ns.

Remember that if we cannot look at a variable's mean, then we cannot look at a variable's variance and standard deviation.

Z-Scores

Now that we have seen measures of central tendency and dispersion, and the normal distribution, let's take a look at something called z-scores, also known as standardised scores. Assuming a standard normal distribution (where $\mu = 0$ and $\sigma = 1$), z-scores do two things for us.[3] First, z-scores tell us the probability of a score (or value) occurring within a standard normal distribution. Second, z-scores allow us to compare two scores from different variable distributions.

We calculate z-scores using the following equation:

$$z = \frac{x - \mu}{\sigma}$$

where x is our value of interest, μ is the population mean, and σ is the population standard deviation; note that this assumes we know the population values and if we do not then we should use a t distribution (Lynch 2013).

Once we calculate the z-score, we look up the value in a z-distribution table and locate the probability associated with the score.[4] The probability that we find tells us the *probability of the value being greater than or equal to* other values in a given distribution. For example, if we find a probability of 0.651, then x is greater than or equal to 65.1% of the other values in the distribution.

Z-score tables often only show negative or positive values, and not both. This is a bit annoying, but understanding the general range of values helps alleviate the problem. A z-score of 0 corresponds to a probability of 50%, right in the middle of a normal distribution. A negative z-score, then, corresponds to a probability below 50% and a positive z-score corresponds to a probability above 50%. For example, if we get a z-score of 1.5 we know the probability must be above 50% and if we have another z-score of –1 we know the probability must be below 50%. If the table just has negative values and we have a positive z-score, we just find the value with the same absolute value and then subtract the probability from 1. For example, if our z-score is 1, we locate the probability for –1, which is 0.159. Then we subtract 0.159 from 1 (1 – 0.159) and we get a probability of 0.841 (or 84.1%). If the table just has positive values and we have a negative z-score, we just go through the same process: a z-score of 1 has a probability of 0.841, then we subtract from 1 and we are left with 0.159 (the probability for a z-score of –1).

Let's look at an example using a favourite classroom character, Drinky Time Squirrel. Following the publication of the first edition of this book, Drinky Time Squirrel received negative attention for his soused sauntering. Due to this unwelcome notoriety, he had cut down his beer drinking to 7 pints a week (x) immediately prior to the Covid-19 pandemic.

Let's see how this decreased intake related to Glasgow's squirrel population beer drinking. The mean squirrel consumption was 10 pints a week (μ) and the standard deviation was 4 pints a week (σ). Let's calculate the z-score:

---

[3]A standard normal distribution is also known as a z distribution, thus the name z-scores.

[4]There are no distribution tables in this book since we can just google them.

$$z = \frac{7-10}{4} = -0.75$$

We next look up the probability in a z-distribution table and find a probability of 0.227 (or 0.773 in a negative z-score table). We interpret this as meaning that *prior to the pandemic, Drinky Time Squirrel drank the same number of pints or more per week than 22.7% of the Glasgow squirrel population*. This can be phrased differently by using the 0.773 probability: *prior to the pandemic, 77.3% of the Glasgow squirrel population drank the same number of pints or more per week than Drinky Time Squirrel*.

This was a big drop in Drinky Time Squirrel's drunkenness – when the first edition was published he was drinking more than 95% of Glasgow squirrels. Drinky Time Squirrel even considered going into rehab to stop drinking completely, but the local rehab facility was run by Firewater Frazzled Fox who, during his drinking days, was an enemy of Drinky Time Squirrel; they always fought over unattended pints on outdoor pub tables. Although time had passed and there was unlikely still to be animosity between them, Drinky Time Squirrel did not want to chance the drama.

When the pandemic hit and pubs closed due to lockdown, the easy access to beer disappeared. Desperate for his tipple, Drinky Time Squirrel broke into a West End pub in a former church (there are a lot of these in Glasgow) and had free rein at the inventory. By the time the pub reopened, Drinky Time Squirrel's beer consumption had skyrocketed to 35 pints a week (*x*); we will not even mention his new found love of gin. Let's see how Drinky Time Squirrel's lockdown consumption compared to the pandemic drinking of the rest of the Glasgow squirrel population.

The mean squirrel pandemic consumption was 15 pints a week (*μ*) and the standard deviation was 6 pints a week (*σ*). Let's calculate the z-score:

$$z = \frac{35-15}{6} = 3.33$$

We next look up the probability in a z-distribution table and find a probability of 0.9996 (or 0.0004 in a negative z-score table). We interpret this as saying that *Drinky Time Squirrel drank the same number of pints or more per week than 99.96% of the Glasgow squirrel population*. This can be phrased differently by using the 0.0004 probability: *only 0.04% of the Glasgow squirrel population drank the same number of pints or more per week than Drinky Time Squirrel*. From this information, we should not expect Drinky Time Squirrel to have much time left.

Let's now look at how we do z-scores in R. We can calculate probability values for different z-scores using the pnorm() function in R. The pnorm() function gives us the cumulative density function for a normal distribution – the cumulative density function gives us the probability of a distribution being equal to or less than some value. We simply include the z-score value and R returns the corresponding probability. First, let's try a z-score value of 1.96. Since our z-score is positive, we know the probability must be above 50%.

```
pnorm(1.96)
[1] 0.9750021
```

We see that the corresponding probability is 0.975 (or 97.5%). This means that if an observation has a z-score of 1.96 it is equal to or greater than 97.5% of the other observations.

How about a z-score of –1.96? Since our z-score is negative, we know the probability must be below 50%.

```
pnorm(-1.96)
[1] 0.0249979
```

We see that the corresponding probability is 0.025 (or, 2.5%). This means that if an observation has a z-score of –1.96 it is equal to or greater than 2.5% of the other observations.

Let's double-check our Drinky Time Squirrel z-scores of –0.75 and 3.33.

```
pnorm(-0.75)
[1] 0.2266274
pnorm(3.33)
[1] 0.9995658
```

We see that both probabilities are the same as we calculated earlier.

Let's now calculate z-scores in R using data. We should really only examine z-scores when our data is roughly normally distributed, since the logic of z-scores assumes a perfect normal distribution. Rarely is 'real-world' data normally distributed and thus we should be cautious when using z-scores. However, there are some real-world data that do approximate normal distributions (e.g., height, IQ). Let's use data on US universities' average student SAT scores from 2019–2020 to perform z-score calculations.[5] The SAT is a common standardised test used in university admissions in the USA. The goal of the test is to provide an assessment metric to directly compare students from all over the USA (where K–12 education is highly devolved) and internationally. For example, if Student 1 has an A average at her high school in Wilmington, North Carolina, and Student 2 has an A average at her high school in Walla Walla, Washington, their SAT scores can be used as a metric to differentiate between the students' records. While research has demonstrated serious social, economic, and cultural biases with the SAT, it continues to be used as an evaluation in university admissions.

The SAT data is in a file named `sat_unis.csv` and thus we'll use the `read_csv()` function to read in the data.

```
sat <- read_csv("sat_unis.csv")
glimpse(sat)
Rows: 1,278
Columns: 2
$ uni     <chr> "Alabama A & M University", "University of Alabama at Birmingh~
$ sat_avg <dbl> 939, 1234, 1319, 946, 1261, 1082, 1300, 1230, 1066, 1076, 1084~
```

---

[5]There is roughly 80% missing data for average SAT score in this data. This is due to a number of reasons including that not all universities require SAT scores and some universities require the ACT (the other main standardised test used in university admissions) instead of the SAT. Therefore, we should assume we are working with a biased dataset.

This file only has two variables – uni for the university names and sat_avg for average SAT scores.

Let's look at the mean and standard deviation for SAT scores. The current minimum score on the SAT is 400 (hence the joke that you get 400 points just for writing your name) and the maximum score is 1600 (considered a 'perfect score').

```
mean(sat$sat_avg)
[1] 1139.942
sd(sat$sat_avg)
[1] 130.1288
```

We see that the mean is 1139.94 and the standard deviation is 130.13.

Let's look at the distribution of sat_avg using a histogram.

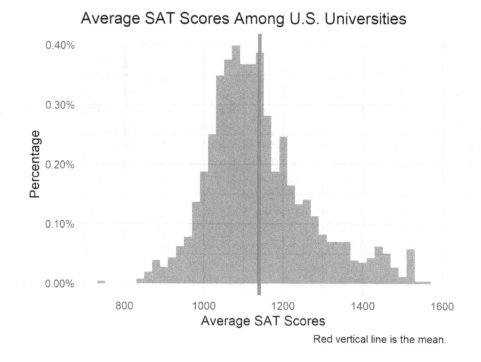

We see that sat_avg is not perfectly normally distributed, but it is a decent approximation for a real-world dataset.

Now let's calculate some z-scores. But before we can do that we need to modify the standard deviation. The sd() function is actually the sample standard deviation (s), and we need the population standard deviation (σ). To do this, we have to convert the sample standard deviation as follows:

$$\sigma = s\sqrt{\frac{N-1}{N}}$$

In R and with our variable `sat_avg`, this conversion looks like this:

```
(pop_sd <- sd(sat$sat_avg)*
    sqrt((length(sat$sat_avg)-1)/(length(sat$sat_avg))))
[1] 130.0779
(pop_mean <- mean(sat$sat_avg))
[1] 1139.942
```

The `length()` function provides the number of observations in the variable `sat_avg`; thus, it tells us how 'long' the variable is. We see that the population standard deviation (with the name `pop_sd`) is roughly the same as the sample standard deviation. We also created a new variable for the population mean, `pop_mean`; this is the same as for the sample mean.

Let's compare a few universities' average SAT scores. First, let's calculate the z-score for a hypothetical university with an average SAT score of 1200, which at least 25 years ago was a minimum target to be a competitive applicant for selective universities.

```
(z <- (1200 - pop_mean)/pop_sd)
[1] 0.4617071
pnorm(z)
[1] 0.6778543
1-pnorm(z)
[1] 0.3221457
```

A university with an average SAT score of 1200 has the same average SAT score or higher than 67.8% of the other universities in the data. Or 32.2% of universities in the data have an average SAT score that is equal to or higher than 1200.

Let's look at where I studied as an undergraduate, SUNY College at Geneseo. We'll use the `filter()` function to find Geneseo's average SAT score.

```
sat %>%
  filter(uni=="SUNY College at Geneseo")
# A tibble: 1 x 2
  uni                      sat_avg
  <chr>                      <dbl>
1 SUNY College at Geneseo     1217
```

We see that Geneseo's average SAT is 1217.

Now let's calculate the z-score.

```
(geneseo <- (1217 - pop_mean)/pop_sd)
[1] 0.592398
pnorm(geneseo)
[1] 0.723208
1-pnorm(geneseo)
[1] 0.276792
```

Geneseo has the same average SAT score or higher than 72.3% of the other universities in the data. Or 27.7% of universities in the data have an average SAT score that is equal to or higher than Geneseo's score. Even though Geneseo's average SAT is only 17 points higher than our hypothetical university, it is nearly 5% higher than other universities in the data.

Now let's look at where I went to graduate school, University of North Carolina (UNC) at Chapel Hill. First, we'll find UNC's average SAT score.

```
sat %>%
  filter(uni=="University of North Carolina at Chapel Hill")
# A tibble: 1 x 2
  uni                                          sat_avg
  <chr>                                          <dbl>
1 University of North Carolina at Chapel Hill     1402
```

We see that UNC's average SAT is 1402. (Thankfully, SAT scores are not used for graduate school admission; but, the GRE is not exactly easier....)

Now let's calculate the *z*-score.

```
(unc <- (1402 - pop_mean)/pop_sd)
[1] 2.014622
pnorm(unc)
[1] 0.9780279
1-pnorm(unc)
[1] 0.02197211
```

UNC has the same average SAT score or higher than 97.8% of the other universities in the data. Or only 2.2% of universities in the data have an average SAT score that is equal to or higher than UNC's score. As you might have surmised simply based on the mean, UNC has one of the highest average SAT scores among US universities.

Finally, let's examine where I currently work, the University of Notre Dame. Again, we first find Notre Dame's average SAT score.

```
sat %>%
  filter(uni=="University of Notre Dame")
# A tibble: 1 x 2
  uni                        sat_avg
  <chr>                        <dbl>
1 University of Notre Dame      1490
```

We see that Notre Dame's average SAT is 1490. (I'm even more thankful that SAT scores are not used in the faculty hiring process!)

Now let's calculate the *z*-score.

```
(nd <- (1490 - pop_mean)/pop_sd)
[1] 2.69114
pnorm(nd)
[1] 0.9964396
1-pnorm(nd)
[1] 0.003560415
```

Notre Dame has the same average SAT score or higher than 99.6% of the other universities in the data. Or only 0.36% of universities in the data have an average SAT score that is equal to or higher than Notre Dame's score. Based on this calculation, we can conclude Notre Dame's average SAT is among the highest in the USA. But is it in the top 10?

As a slight tangent, let's look at which universities have the 10 highest average SAT scores. To sort the data by average SAT, we'll use the desc() function wrapped by the arrange() function.

```
sat %>%
  arrange(desc(sat_avg))
# A tibble: 1,278 x 2
   uni                                    sat_avg
   <chr>                                  <dbl>
 1 California Institute of Technology     1557
 2 Massachusetts Institute of Technology  1547
 3 University of Chicago                  1528
 4 Harvey Mudd College                    1526
 5 Duke University                        1522
 6 Franklin W Olin College of Engineering 1522
 7 Washington University in St Louis      1520
 8 Rice University                        1520
 9 Yale University                        1517
10 Harvard University                     1517
# ... with 1,268 more rows
```

We see that Caltech has the highest average SAT score, followed by MIT, Chicago, and some of the usual suspects. Hence, Notre Dame is not in the top 10.

EXAMPLES

The last section of this chapter applies our knowledge of measures of central tendency and dispersion to understand data on racial segregation in Wayne County, Michigan, and St. Louis, Missouri, in the USA. These examples demonstrate the importance of using central tendency and dispersion statistics in concert for understanding data and variables.

Example I: Racial Segregation in Wayne County, Michigan, USA

Racially segregated housing and communities in the USA are a major problem and area of substantial policy concern. Segregation might have arisen implicitly or explicitly (through discriminatory policies), but the problem is that people of different races tend to live only near people of the same race. This has implications for social, economic, political, and health policies in US cities, states, and the nation as a whole.

Let's use some of the statistics we've learned about in this chapter to get a sense of whether racial segregation might exist in housing in Wayne County, Michigan (which encompasses the city of Detroit) by looking at race by voting precincts from the 2020 US Census. The dataset is called wayne voting precincts.xlsx, and since it is an Excel file, we will use the read_xlsx() function. Let's name the dataset wayne.

```
wayne <- read_xlsx("wayne voting precincts.xlsx")
glimpse(wayne)
Rows: 981
Columns: 3
$ Label     <chr> "Voting District 1632200005125, Wayne County, Michigan", "Vo~
$ white_pct <dbl> 8.450704, 62.903226, 76.329114, 75.844516, 76.531165, 83.632~
$ black_pct <dbl> 87.3239437, 14.2559834, 5.4430380, 3.7945396, 4.7696477, 2.8~
```

Let's first look at the mean and median of the variable white_pct, which is the percentage of white-only residents (excluding mixed-race whites) by voting precinct according to the 2020 US Census.

```
mean(wayne$white_pct)
[1] 38.97423
median(wayne$white_pct)
[1] 27.96221
```

The mean percentage of white residents in voting precincts is roughly 39% and the median is around 28%. This is fairly large drop from the 2010 US Census, when the mean was 45% and the median was around 46%.

Let's now look at the mean and median of black-only residents (excluding mixed-race blacks) with the variable black_pct.

```
mean(wayne$black_pct)
[1] 49.89342
median(wayne$black_pct)
[1] 52.64539
```

The mean percentage of black residents in voting precincts is roughly 50% and the median is around 53%.

Based on these means and medians, we might conclude that Wayne County appears to be a relatively mixed and non-segregated city. However, we do see that the county has become less white since 2010.

But we know better than to stop with the mean and median. Let's also look at the standard deviations.

```
sd(wayne$white_pct)
[1] 35.53676
sd(wayne$black_pct)
[1] 39.53456
```

The standard deviation of percentage white in voting precincts is 35.54% and the standard deviation of percentage black in voting precincts is 39.53%. Relative to the mean values, these are very large standard deviations. It still could be the case that most voting precincts cluster near the mean, but we can get a better understanding of the distribution by plotting the variables.

Here are histograms with the percentage of white- and black-only residents by precinct in Wayne County.

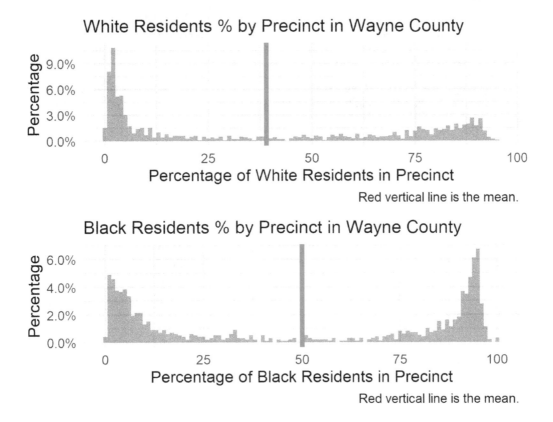

As we suspected, both distributions are U-shaped, with few voting precincts at the mean or median values. The white-only voting precincts distribution has its greatest density on low values, indicating a large proportion of Wayne County voting precincts have no to few white residents. The black-only voting precincts are almost perfectly U-shaped, indicating that precincts either have a small proportion or a large proportion of black residents, and fewer mixed precincts. This explains why the values for the standard deviations are so large. If we just relied on the mean, we would have completed missed that Wayne County is noticeably segregated by race, and in fact one of the most segregated cities in the USA.

Example II: Racial Segregation in St. Louis, Missouri, USA

Let's provide a similar demonstration of the usefulness of combining measures of central tendency and dispersion by looking at race by voting precinct in St. Louis. The dataset is called `stl voting precincts.xlsx`, and since it is an Excel file, we will use the `read_xlsx()` function. Let's name the dataset `stl`.

```
stl <- read_xlsx("stl voting precincts.xlsx")
glimpse(stl)
Rows: 223
Columns: 3
$ Label     <chr> "STL 1-2 Voting District, St. Louis city, Missouri", "STL 1-~
$ white_pct <dbl> 1.0777521, 3.4985423, 1.5497553, 2.3405973, 10.0783875, 0.62~
$ black_pct <dbl> 95.53503, 92.41983, 97.30832, 92.09040, 85.94625, 93.16770, ~
```

Let's first look at the mean and median of the variable `white_pct`, which is the percentage of white-only residents (excluding mixed-race whites) by voting precinct according to the 2020 US Census.

```
mean(stl$white_pct)
[1] 39.65984
median(stl$white_pct)
[1] 41.45078
```

The mean percentage of white residents in voting precincts is roughly 40% and the median is around 41.5%. Like Wayne County, St. Louis had a drop in the white population from the 2010 US Census, when the mean was 47% and the median was around 42.5%.

Let's now look at the mean and median of black-only residents (excluding mixed-race blacks) with the variable `black_pct`.

```
mean(stl$black_pct)
[1] 48.31116
median(stl$black_pct)
[1] 42.00693
```

The mean percentage of black residents in voting precincts is roughly 48% and the median is around 42%.

Even more than Wayne County, if we only used these means and medians we might conclude that St. Louis appears to be a mixed and non-segregated city. Although the city has become less white since 2010, it appears that the average voting precinct's composition is nearly half white and half black.

But let's look at the standard deviations.

```
sd(stl$white_pct)
[1] 31.26898
sd(stl$black_pct)
[1] 35.09159
```

The standard deviation of percentage white in voting precincts is 31.27% and the standard deviation of percentage black in voting precincts is 35.09%. Is it the case that St. Louis has U-shaped distributions like Wayne County? Let's look at histograms to get a better understanding of the distributions in St. Louis.

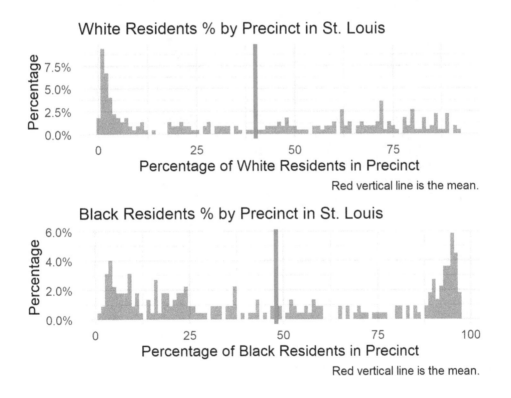

Like Wayne County, we see that the distributions are actually U-shaped with very few voting precincts at the mean or median values.

We can look more closely at the tails of the distribution for black_pct to assess the percentage of voting precincts that have essentially no black residents and all black residents. We could use our eagle eyes (or opera glasses) to figure it out from the histogram, but instead let's subset the data to calculate the percentages. We use the filter() function to find out the number of precincts that have 0–10% black residents and 90–100% black residents.

```
stl %>%
  filter(black_pct <= 10.0)
# A tibble: 44 x 3
   Label                                          white_pct black_pct
   <chr>                                              <dbl>     <dbl>
 1 STL 10-2 Voting District, St. Louis city, Missouri  89.4      1.92
 2 STL 10-3 Voting District, St. Louis city, Missouri  91.3      2.64
 3 STL 10-6 Voting District, St. Louis city, Missouri  82.2      7.74
 4 STL 12-1 Voting District, St. Louis city, Missouri  77.6      5.08
 5 STL 12-2 Voting District, St. Louis city, Missouri  71.5      8.03
 6 STL 12-3 Voting District, St. Louis city, Missouri  71.9      8.49
 7 STL 12-4 Voting District, St. Louis city, Missouri  72.8      4.29
 8 STL 12-5 Voting District, St. Louis city, Missouri  88.9      3.24
 9 STL 12-6 Voting District, St. Louis city, Missouri  79.5      9.17
10 STL 13-4 Voting District, St. Louis city, Missouri  79.9      7.49
# ... with 34 more rows


stl %>%
  filter(black_pct >= 90.0)
# A tibble: 54 x 3
   Label                                         white_pct black_pct
   <chr>                                             <dbl>     <dbl>
 1 STL 1-2 Voting District, St. Louis city, Missouri  1.08     95.5
 2 STL 1-3 Voting District, St. Louis city, Missouri  3.50     92.4
 3 STL 1-4 Voting District, St. Louis city, Missouri  1.55     97.3
 4 STL 1-5 Voting District, St. Louis city, Missouri  2.34     92.1
 5 STL 1-7 Voting District, St. Louis city, Missouri  0.621    93.2
 6 STL 2-5 Voting District, St. Louis city, Missouri  1.88     95.5
 7 STL 3-2 Voting District, St. Louis city, Missouri  1.49     94.8
 8 STL 3-5 Voting District, St. Louis city, Missouri  4.24     92.6
 9 STL 3-7 Voting District, St. Louis city, Missouri  5.63     90.8
10 STL 3-8 Voting District, St. Louis city, Missouri  1.90     93.7
# ... with 44 more rows
```

We see that in roughly 20% ((44 / 223) × 100) of precincts blacks make up 0–10% of residents, while in roughly 24% of precincts ((54/223) × 100) blacks make up 90–100% of the population. Therefore, nearly a majority of the voting precincts in St. Louis are either almost all black or almost no black residents. As before, this explains why the values for the standard deviations are so large. We can conclude that St. Louis and Wayne County appear to have similar levels of racial segregation based on voting precincts.

CONCLUSION

Understanding univariate and descriptive statistics, and how to implement them in R, provides a strong foundation for learning more advanced quantitative methods. Although these statistics are often not the most exciting thing in the world, they can provide valuable insight into data and variables, as demonstrated in the previous section. In the next chapter, we explore ways of visualising data and variables in R.

R Packages Used in This Chapter

- `descr`
- `dplyr` (loaded with `tidyverse`)
- `haven`
- `pillar` (loaded with `tidyverse`)
- `readr` (loaded with `tidyverse`)
- `readxl`
- `tidyverse`

R Functions Used in This Chapter

- `arrange()` - order observations by variable values using `dplyr` package
- `as.factor()` - convert variable to factor
- `as.numeric()` - convert variable to numeric
- `desc()` - sort variable in descending order
- `filter()` - subset data based on variables' values using `dplyr` package
- `freq()` - frequency table from `descr` package
- `glimpse()` - quick view of data using `pillar` package
- `group_by()` - group observations by variables using `dplyr` package
- `is.na()` - check for missing values (NAs) in variables
- `length()` - provide number of observations
- `mean()` - mean
- `median()` - median
- `mutate()` - recode variables using `dplyr` package
- `ordered()` - order values in frequency table from `descr` package
- `pnorm()` - cumulative density function for normal distribution
- `read_csv()` - read in .csv data file using `readr` package
- `read_xlsx()` - read in an Excel data file using `readxl` package
- `round()` - round numeric variables
- `sd()` - standard deviation
- `summarise()` - create new variables based on grouped observations using `dplyr` package
- `sqrt()` - square root
- `table()` - basic frequency table
- `var()` - variance

Additional Resources

Books

- Fox, J. and Weisberg, S. (2018) *An R Companion to Applied Regression*, 3rd edition. Sage.
- Harris, J. K. (2020) *Statistics with R: Solving Problems Using Real-World Data*. Sage.
- Long, J. D. and Teetor, P. (2019) *R Cookbook*, 2nd edition. O'Reilly Media.

Online

- R-bloggers: https://www.r-bloggers.com/
- RStudio Blog: https://www.rstudio.com/blog/

8

DATA VISUALISATION

Chapter contents

The visualisation of data and statistical results has become critical for researchers and students working with social science data. The unifying idea is *how we create a visualisation that clearly conveys a great deal of information – information that is often complicated – in its simplest form*. Often this means displaying data in ways that average citizens can easily understand without having any data analysis background.

Until relatively recently, data visualisation was often ugly and unseemly. Most researchers were reduced to using built-in graphical functions in statistical programs or using Microsoft Excel to display data and results. Increases in computing power and a greater appreciation of data aesthetics (see Tufte 2001; Wickham 2022; Wilke 2019) have led to advancements in data visualisations.

This chapter demonstrates common ways to visualise social science data using the `ggplot2` R package. There are now many other computer programs designed for data display, such as Tableau, but being able to do all the analysis and visualisations with R and RStudio offers a more flexible and efficient means for data visualisations. We will look at bar plots, then different ways to display histograms and box plots, and finally scatterplots. There is usually more code involved when using `ggplot2`, but the visual benefit is well worth the effort. Although the `ggplot2` functions are the focus of this chapter, we will also utilise other packages and functions from `tidyverse` to assist with data and variable manipulation.

By the end of this chapter, you should be able to:

- Understand when you can use different types of plots
- Understand the foundations and basics of `ggplot2`
- Understand how to create and interpret:
  - Bar plots
  - Histograms
  - Smoothed density plots
  - Box plots
  - Scatterplots
- Understand how to include multiple plots in one plot

There are an enormous number of customisations we can do with `ggplot2`, and we will only scratch the surface in this chapter. But once we know the basics and foundations, we can make bespoke changes to fit our own needs and preferences.

GGPLOT2 BASICS

Before we get into the nitty-gritty of producing various types of visualisations, it is necessary to discuss the basics of the `ggplot2` package. The general concept of `ggplot2` is to think of plots as a combination of layers. We start with a layer for our *x*- and *y*-axes, then we add a layer for the type of plot we want, and then we add a layer for the plot labels, etc. To get a basic *x*- and *y*-axis plot layer we use the `ggplot()` function where we leave the parentheses empty.

```
library(ggplot2)
ggplot()
```

We can add another layer to the base plot by simply including the + symbol after the paren-theses, so that each part of the plot is in fact a distinct layer. We specify the type of plot we want by using the geom functions, which simply stands for 'geometric object'. For example, we can use the functions geom_bar() for a bar plot, geom_histogram() for a histogram, etc. There are numerous geoms available and we will use the most relevant ones for our needs; to see all of the options just google 'geom ggplot2'. Next, we use the mapping = argu-ment to specify the *x*- and *y*-axis variables. The specific *x* and *y* variables are always inside the aes() argument, where aes stands for *aesthetics* and is the key code for telling R what is being done in the plot. (Note that we don't always need to specify mapping and aes(), but it is good practice.) In addition to these core plot layers, there are numerous options we can add and use to change the appearance of our plots in ggplot2, such as colours, shading, and labels.

BAR PLOTS

Bar plots are one of the common ways that data is displayed. You have probably come across bar plots in the news and may have already had to create them in primary, secondary school, and/or university. We use bar plots to visually represent nominal- and ordinal-level variables. Bar plots have spaces between the bars which indicate that the variable is not continuous and may or may not be ordered.

We will use data from the 2019 survey about perceptions of voter fraud in England. The name of the data file is VF England.csv, and we will read it in using the read_csv() function.

```
setwd("C:/QSSD/Chapter 8 - Data Visualisation")
getwd()

library(tidyverse)
vf_england <- read_csv("VF England.csv")
```

We will start with a basic bar plot and then build the complexity.

Bar Plots with One Variable

When we are only looking at a single variable to plot using the ggplot() function, we do not specify the *x* and *y* variable, because by default there is only one variable. Let's create an initial bar plot using the variable vfproblem (the belief that voter fraud is a serious problem). Before we do that we need to reorder the values for vfproblem to go from 'Strongly disagree' to 'Strongly agree'. We'll do this with the factor() function and we'll save the reordered version as vfproblem1.

```
vf_england %>%
  count(vfproblem)
# A tibble: 7 x 2
  vfproblem                       n
  <chr>                       <int>
1 Agree                         167
2 Disagree                      245
3 Neither agree nor disagree    670
4 Slightly agree                398
5 Slightly disagree             302
6 Strongly agree                140
7 Strongly disagree             112

vf_england <- vf_england %>%
    mutate(vfproblem1 = factor(vfproblem,
          levels = c("Strongly disagree","Disagree",
                 "Slightly disagree","Neither agree nor disagree",
                 "Slightly agree","Agree","Strongly agree")))

vf_england %>%
  count(vfproblem1)
# A tibble: 7 x 2
  vfproblem1                      n
  <fct>                       <int>
1 Strongly disagree             112
2 Disagree                      245
3 Slightly disagree             302
4 Neither agree nor disagree    670
5 Slightly agree                398
6 Agree                         167
7 Strongly agree                140
```

We will use the geom_bar() function to create the bar plot. We first specify the data we are using in the ggplot() function and then add the geom_bar() function. (When we run the code in the standard RStudio environment, where the plots are in the bottom right-hand window, we will probably see that labels for vfproblem1 overlap one another. We could drag the window to make it larger or click on the Zoom button. If we are creating R Markdown documents, we need to adjust label sizing and alignment based on the rendered document.)

```
ggplot(data = vf_england) +
  geom_bar(mapping = aes(vfproblem1))
```

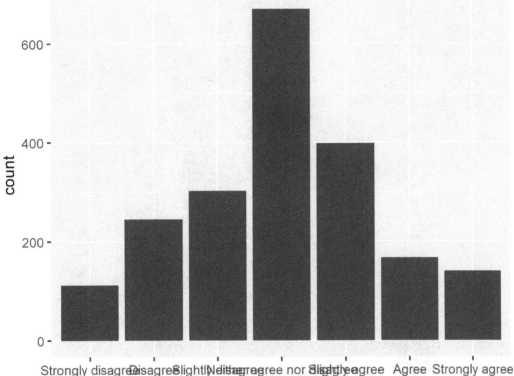

Although this is a pretty bare-bones and ugly plot (e.g., the *x*-axis labels overlap), we are still able to determine that the largest number of respondents said they 'Neither agree nor disagree' that voter fraud is a serious problem in UK elections.

Before we examine cleaning up plots, let's change the colour of the bars – which is often the first thing people want to do when starting to work with ggplot2 – and let's fix the *x*-axis labels so they don't overlap. If we want to change the colour of the bars, we simply include the option fill = in the geom_bar() argument and then whatever colour we want to include. To fix the *x*-axis labels, we'll put them on a 45-degree angle using the scale_x_discrete() function and specifying guide = guide_axis(angle = 45)). Note that we add this as a new layer and not within the geom_bar() argument or as part of the aes() argument.

```
ggplot(data = vf_england) +
  geom_bar(mapping = aes(vfproblem1), fill = "blue") +
  scale_x_discrete(guide = guide_axis(angle = 45))
```

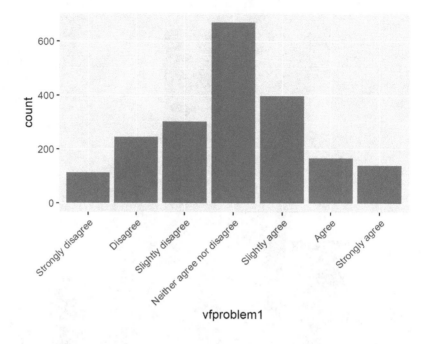

Now the bars are blue and we are able to clearly view the *x*-axis labels.

Bar Plots with Two Variables

Let's now include a second variable into the bar plot. We will plot vfproblem1 and whether respondents voted for the winner (Conservative Party) of the 2017 UK general election or another party (vote2017_dum). Let's first look at vote2017_dum.

```
vf_england %>%
  count(vote2017_dum)
# A tibble: 3 x 2
  vote2017_dum      n
  <chr>         <int>
1 Loser           919
2 Winner          757
3 <NA>            358
```

We see there are two categories ('Loser', those who didn't vote Conservative, and 'Winner', those who did vote Conservative) and a number of missing values (NAs) for vote2017_dum. To add this variable into the bar plot, we specify fill = vote2017_dum within the aes() argument. *However*, by default, the ggplot() function plots missing values as a new category. Hence, we want to get rid of any missing values before plotting. We'll do this with the filter() function prior to the ggplot() specification and connect the code with the pipe operator %>%. In the filter() argument, we specify that we only want non-missing values of vote2017_num. Note that we leave the ggplot() function empty as the piped code above specifies the data being used.

```
vf_england %>%
    filter(!is.na(vote2017_dum)) %>%
ggplot() +
    geom_bar(mapping = aes(vfproblem1, fill = vote2017_dum)) +
    scale_x_discrete(guide = guide_axis(angle = 45))
```

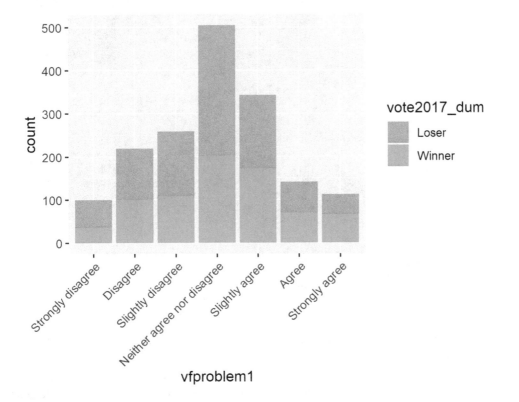

What does the second variable tell us about the belief that voter fraud is a serious problem? Before answering this question, it's important to know that the default option for bar plots and histograms in ggplot2 is that the values are *stacked* and not superimposed. We see that a greater number of respondents who voted for the winning party (again, Conservatives) agree that voter fraud is a serious problem (for all three agree categories) than respondents who voted for another party. The colours here are the default colours in ggplot2, which we are able to change.

Stacked bar plots can be confusing to understand for some people (Wilke 2019). Instead, we might want to de-stack the colours and put them side by side for each *x*-axis category. We can do this by adding the option position = "dodge" to the geom_bar() argument; notice that the code is outside the aes() argument.

```
vf_england %>%
    filter(!is.na(vote2017_dum)) %>%
ggplot() +
    geom_bar(mapping = aes(vfproblem1, fill = vote2017_dum),
             position = "dodge") +
    scale_x_discrete(guide = guide_axis(angle = 45))
```

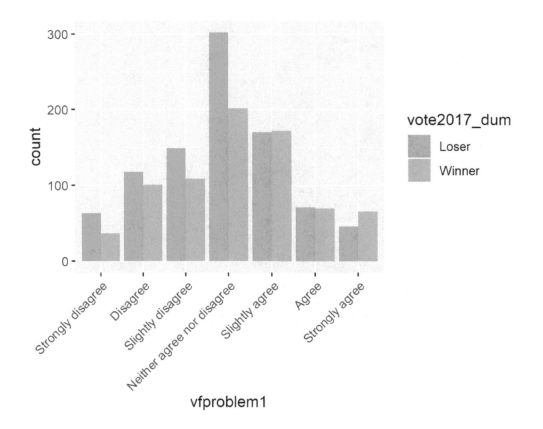

This provides the same information as the previous bar plot, but perhaps in a format that is easier to understand.

For our last example, we'll create a bar plot with all the bells and whistles – one we might want to include a paper. Specifically, let's convert the *y*-axis to percentages instead of counts, add labels, change the overall plot theme, use grey shading for the bars instead of colours, and specify the plot size in our R Markdown code chunk. This is a lot, so let's take it 'bird by bird'.

First, we'll load the `scales` package to provide us the ability to change the *y*-axis to percentages. In the `geom_bar()` function, we specify that `y = ..prop..` to get the proportions and we specify that `group = vote2017_dum` which tells R that all the `vfproblem1` categories for each `vote2017_dum` category add up to 100%. We also need to specify that `stat = "count"` in the `geom_bar()` function. To get the percentages to print on the *y*-axis, instead of the proportions, we need to specify that `labels = percent_format()` in the `scale_y_continuous()` function.

Second, we'll add labels to the plot using the `labs()` function.

Third, we'll use the `theme_minimal()` function, which mainly removes the default grey background of the plot.

Fourth, to get the grey shading for the bars, we'll include the function `scale_fill_grey()`.

Finally, we'll adjust the size of the bar plot in the rendered R Markdown document by including `fig.height=7`, `fig.width=8` in the code chunk header (i.e., the part that starts the code chunk). (This isn't seen in the code output, but changes the size of the plot in the knitted document.)

```
library(scales)

vf_england %>%
  filter(!is.na(vote2017_dum)) %>%
ggplot() +
  geom_bar(mapping = aes(x = vfproblem1, y = ..prop..,
                         group = vote2017_dum, fill = vote2017_dum),
                         stat = "count", position = "dodge") +
  labs(x = "Voter Fraud a Serious Problem",
       title = "Voter Fraud Beliefs & 2017 Vote",
       fill = "2017 Election", y = "Percent") +
  scale_fill_grey() +
  scale_x_discrete(guide = guide_axis(angle = 45)) +
  scale_y_continuous(labels = percent_format()) +
  theme_minimal()
```

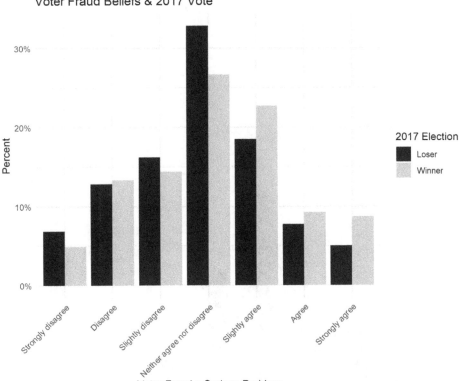

Including the labels and converting the counts to percentages makes it easier to understand the relationship between respondents' voter fraud beliefs and their vote in the 2017 UK general election. Notice that for each voter fraud belief category, the differences between the 'Loser' and 'Winner', though similar, are not identical to our previous bar plot with counts. Why? The reason is that we converted the counts to percentages and the percentages are based on the breakdown of 'Loser' and 'Winner' across the seven values of voter fraud belief. We now clearly see that a higher percentage of 'Winner' voters agree that voter fraud is a serious problem (for all three agree categories) than 'Loser' voters.

If we prefer to use colours, for example for presentations and online documents, we can manually adjust the default ggplot2 colours using the scale_fill_manual() function in the above code. We are able to use colour names (e.g., "blue", "red"), colour palettes (pre-set combinations of colours), as well as hexadecimal colours (e.g., "#0c2340", "#d39f10"). If we want to nerd out, we can use the hexadecimal colours of our university, business, organisation, etc. Below, we repeat the previous bar plot using two of Notre Dame's dominant colours.

```
vf_england %>%
  filter(!is.na(vote2017_dum)) %>%
ggplot() +
  geom_bar(mapping = aes(x = vfproblem1, y = ..prop..,
                         group = vote2017_dum, fill = vote2017_dum),
                         stat = "count", position = "dodge") +
  scale_fill_manual(values = c("#0c2340", "#d39f10")) +
  labs(x = "Voter Fraud a Serious Problem",
       title = "Voter Fraud Beliefs & 2017 Vote",
       fill = "2017 Election", y = "Percent") +
  scale_x_discrete(guide = guide_axis(angle = 45)) +
  scale_y_continuous(labels = percent_format()) +
  theme_minimal()
```

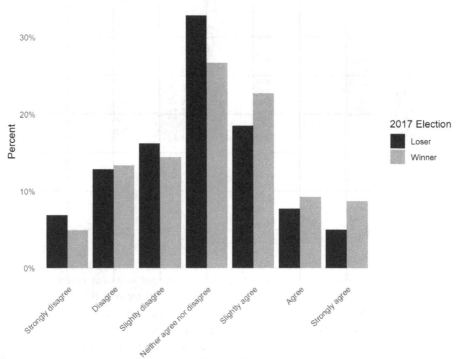

HISTOGRAMS

Histograms are very similar to bar plots, but are used to visualise *interval- and ratio-level variables*. While bar charts have spaces between the bars, histograms do not since interval- and ratio-level variables are generally continuous and there is order to their values. Understanding what histograms are showing us is similar to what we saw and discussed with bar plots.

One key aesthetic choice with histograms is choosing the binwidth. The binwidth specifies how wide we want our bars to be. For example, do we want the bins to include five values of the variable or ten values of the variable? If five values, then our bins will look like [0–4][5–9] [10–14], etc. If ten values, then our bins will look like [0–9][10–19][20–29], etc. Whatever binwidth we choose, all the bars' widths will be the same. The height of the bar is then dependent on the number of observations that fall in that bin. Below we will explore the aesthetic effects of changing the binwidth.

The vf_england dataset only has one variable we can use for histograms: age. Instead, let's use the 2020 Scottish Index of Multiple Deprivation dataset (simd2020.csv). For this section, we'll use the proportion of people in each datazone with psychiatric medication prescriptions (DEPRESS) and whether a datazone is urban or rural (urban). Let's wrangle these variables by setting all the variables to lower case, convert DEPRESS to a percentage, and attach labels to the categories of urban.

```
simd <- read_csv("simd2020.csv", na = "*")

simd <- simd %>%
        rename_with(tolower) %>%
        mutate(pct_depress = depress*100,
               urban_fct = recode(urban, `1` = "Urban", `0` = "Rural"))
```

Let's double-check the values of our new variables pct_depress and urban_fct.

```
summary(simd$pct_depress)
   Min. 1st Qu.  Median    Mean 3rd Qu.    Max.   NA's
   0.00   14.95   18.68   19.07   22.76   47.18      1

simd %>%
  count(urban_fct)
# A tibble: 2 x 2
  urban_fct     n
  <chr>     <int>
1 Rural      2139
2 Urban      4837
```

These recoded variables look correct. Note that pct_depress has a missing value, which we'll need to filter out.

Histograms Using One Variable

We'll first use the `geom_histogram()` function to plot `pct_depress`. We'll set `binwidth = 1` (each bar represents 1%) and filter out the missing value in `pct_depress`, but the rest of the code is similar to what we did with bar plots. For code simplicity, let's not include labels, etc.

```
simd %>%
  filter(!is.na(pct_depress)) %>%
ggplot() +
  geom_histogram(mapping = aes(pct_depress), binwidth = 1)
```

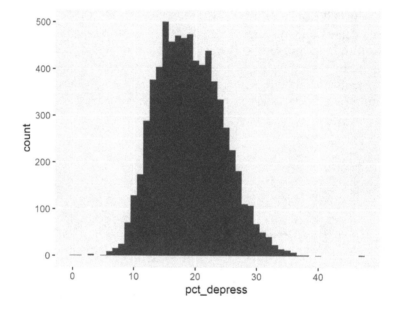

The histogram shows that most Scottish datazones have psychiatric medication prescription rates around 10–30%, but there are some datazones with percentages below 5% or above 35%. The variable also appears somewhat normally distributed. It is uncommon to come across (somewhat) normally distributed variables in the social sciences. When we do, we should consider whether there are any suspicious signals for fabricated data. For example, what is the source of the data? Does it make intuitive sense that the variable appears normally distributed? Here, the data comes from the Scottish government (not exactly a rogue state) and it's reasonable that the data appears somewhat normally distributed.

We can change the binwidth by simply changing the number in the `geom_histogram()` function. Let's change it to `binwidth = 5`.

```
simd %>%
  filter(!is.na(pct_depress)) %>%
ggplot() +
  geom_histogram(mapping = aes(pct_depress), binwidth = 5)
```

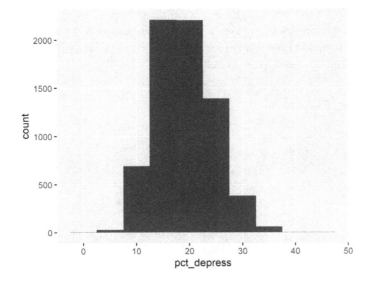

We can also fill the bins with a colour using the option `fill =` in the `geom_histogram()` argument.

```
simd %>%
  filter(!is.na(pct_depress)) %>%
ggplot() +
  geom_histogram(mapping = aes(pct_depress), binwidth = 1, fill = "red")
```

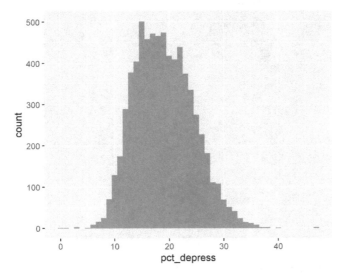

Histograms Using Two Variables

We frequently will want to plot two variables in a histogram. As with the single-variable histogram, we need an interval- or ratio-level variable, but the second variable is often nominal or ordinal.

We'll use `pct_depress` and the `urban_fct` variable as our second variable. Hence, we are looking to see if urban datazones have different percentages of prescribed psychiatric medication than rural datazones. We include `fill = urban_fct` into the `aes()` argument to plot the second variable. Let's also add in some labels to make the histogram clearer. Finally, we'll change the default font size of the plot title to make it slightly smaller, using the `theme()` function. The `theme()` function allows us to customise nearly every aspect of our plot. In the `theme()` function, any adjustments to the text require using the `element_text()` function. We'll specify `plot.title = element_text(size = 12)`.

```
simd %>%
  filter(!is.na(pct_depress)) %>%
ggplot() +
  geom_histogram(mapping = aes(pct_depress, fill = urban_fct),
                 binwidth = 1) +
  labs(x = "Percentage Prescribed Psychiatric Medication",
       y = "Frequency",
       title = "Psychiatric Medication by Urban/Rural Scottish Datazones",
       fill = "Community Type") +
  theme(
    plot.title = element_text(size = 12)
  )
```

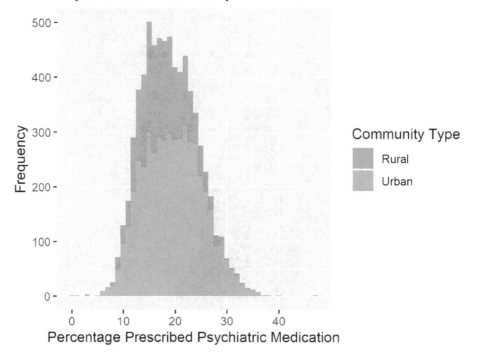

Each bar in the histogram represents the total number of observations, while the colours represent how many observations are rural or urban. As with bar plots, the colours are *stacked* and not superimposed. We can see from this that there are slightly higher prescription percentages in urban areas than in rural areas.

Due to people having difficulty understanding the stacked bars, we may want to avoid using histograms if possible. Instead of histograms, we can use smoothed density plots to convey the same information.

SMOOTHED DENSITY PLOTS

Technically called kernel density plots, smoothed density plots illustrate the smoothed distribution of continuous variables instead of grouping variables into specific bins (as in histograms). Let's again look at `pct_depress` and `urban_fct`. To do so, we just need to change `geom_histogram()` to `geom_density()`, and we remove the `binwidth =` argument because there are now no bars. To make the plot clearer, we can decrease the darkness of the colour shading using the option `alpha =` in the `geom_density()` argument. An `alpha` of 1 is the same as the default point shading, while anything less than 1 is lighter. The smaller the `alpha` value, the lighter the shading. Below we set `alpha = .2`, add labels, and make the plot title smaller.

```
simd %>%
  filter(!is.na(pct_depress)) %>%
ggplot() +
  geom_density(mapping = aes(pct_depress, fill = urban_fct), alpha = .2) +
  labs(x = "Percentage Prescribed Psychiatric Medication",y = "Density",
      title = "Psychiatric Medication by Urban/Rural Scottish Datazones",
      fill = "Community Type") +
  theme(
    plot.title = element_text(size = 12)
  )
```

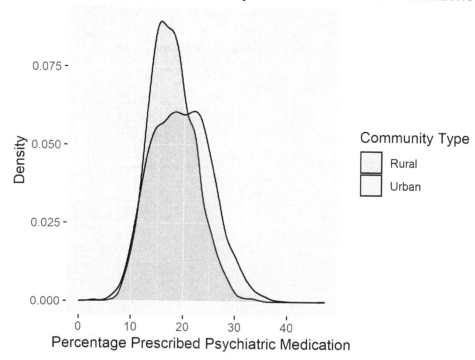

Now we can clearly make out that there are slightly higher prescription percentages in urban datazones than in rural datazones.

A common question users have with smoothed density plots is how to interpret the *y*-axis. By default, the `geom_density()` function scales the values so that the area under the curve adds up to 1 (Wilke 2019). Hence, interpreting the values is not straightforward. To keep things simple, I recommend focusing on the 'big picture' of the distributions and not the specific values. We want to use visualisations to tell stories about the data and our stories are not going to hinge on specific values.

BOX PLOTS

Box plots provide a simple way to visualise the relationship between an *interval/ratio variable* and a *nominal/ordinal variable*. Many researchers prefer using box plots to visualise relationships between two variables because the plots provide five summary statistics – minimum, maximum, median, first quartile or 25% percentile, and third quartile or 75% percentile (the difference between the latter two is known as the inter-quartile range (IQR)).[1]

We'll use the `geom_boxplot()` function and include labels using the `labs()` function and make the plot title smaller.

```
simd %>%
  filter(!is.na(pct_depress)) %>%
ggplot() +
  geom_boxplot(mapping = aes(urban_fct, pct_depress)) +
  labs(x = "Community Type",
       y = "Percentage Prescribed Psychiatric Medication",
       title = "Psychiatric Medication by Urban/Rural Scottish Datazones") +
  theme(
    plot.title = element_text(size = 12)
  )
```

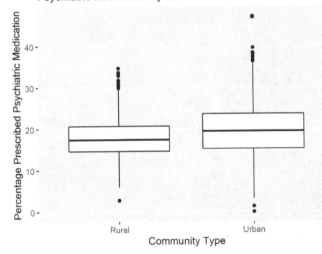

---

[1]Another popular option are violin plots that combine box plots with density plots. I'm not a big fan of violin plots as they often look like mismatched old-timey candlesticks that don't necessarily make the relationships clearer than box plots.

The thick horizontal line is the median and the box represents the values between the first and third quartiles. The lower horizontal line represents −1.5 times the IQR and the upper horizontal line represents +1.5 times the IQR. Any points above or below represent outliers – points that are more than ±1.5 times the IQR. We see that the median psychiatric medication prescription percentage is higher for urban datazones than for rural datazones. We also see that the IQR for urban datazones is wider than for rural datazones. This is something we observed in the smoothed density plot, but the box plot makes it clearer.

SCATTERPLOTS

If we want to visualise the relationship between two *interval- or ratio-level* variables, scatterplots are the preferred visualisation technique. In this section, we will create a series of scatterplots using the simd data.

We will use the percentage of psychiatric medication prescriptions by datazone (pct_depress) as our *y*-axis variable and the percentage of people in a datazone who are employment deprived (pct_employment_deprived) on the *x*-axis. The pct_employment_deprived variable measures the percentage of people in a datazone receiving incapacity benefits, employment and support allowance, or severe disablement allowance – essentially financial support from the government due to being unable to work. If you have been paying attention throughout this chapter, you will know that pct_employment_deprived does not yet exist in the simd data. So, let's create it by multiplying employment_rate by 100 and take a quick peek at its values using the summary() function.

```
simd <- simd %>%
        mutate(pct_employment_deprived = employment_rate*100)

summary(simd$pct_employment_deprived)
   Min. 1st Qu.  Median    Mean 3rd Qu.    Max.    NA's
  0.000   4.000   8.000   9.564  14.000  47.000       3
```

The variable ranges from 0% to 47% and its median equals 8%. Let's pause for a second and digest that last sentence. While the median suggests employment deprivation is fairly low, at least one datazone has zero employment deprivation (i.e., a wealthy datazone) and at least one datazone has almost half of its residents classified as employment deprived. That's a pretty big range.

Scatterplots with Two Variables

The code for creating a scatterplot using ggplot takes the same form as we've used earlier in this chapter. We'll use the geom_point() function to create the scatterplot and specify the *x* and *y* variables in the aes() argument. We'll use the filter() function to remove the missing values for pct_depress and pct_employment_deprived as piped code prior to the ggplot() function.

```
simd %>%
  filter(!is.na(pct_depress) & !is.na(pct_employment_deprived)) %>%
ggplot() +
  geom_point(mapping = aes(x = pct_employment_deprived, y = pct_depress))
```

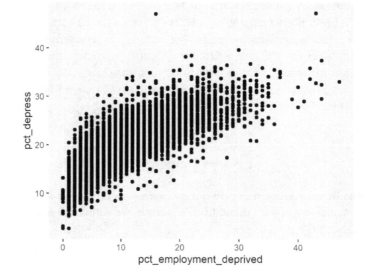

Before we do anything else, let's agree this scatterplot is ugly. Some observations lie on top of each other, creating lines and making it difficult to ascertain how the observations cluster in parts of the plot. This pattern is due to `pct_employment_deprived` being an integer variable (i.e., taking only whole-number values), thus creating optical challenges. To make the points clearer, we can do something called 'jittering' that moves the data points a wee bit so they are not overlapping and can be seen on a plot. The first time I learned about jittering, it sounded to me like cheating. But if we think of data visualisation as a way of communicating information and relationships, slight nudges of data points to gain greater clarity cause no harm. To jitter the observations, we just include `position = "jitter"` into the `geom_point()` argument. (We will continue to include the jitter option for the rest of the scatterplots below.)

Jittering will remove the lines in the scatterplot, and we can also lighten the data points by including `alpha = .1` in the `geom_point()` argument. The combination of these two adjustments will help visualise where the observations cluster. For completeness, let's add in `theme_minimal()`, decrease the title size, and include labels using the `labs()` function.

```
simd %>%
  filter(!is.na(pct_depress) & !is.na(pct_employment_deprived)) %>%
ggplot() +
  geom_point(mapping = aes(x = pct_employment_deprived, y = pct_depress),
             position = "jitter", alpha = .1) +
  labs(x = "Percentage Employment Deprived",
       y = "Percentage Prescribed Psychiatric Medication",
      title = "Prescribed Psychiatric Medication by Employment Deprived") +
  theme_minimal() +
  theme(
    plot.title = element_text(size = 12)
  )
```

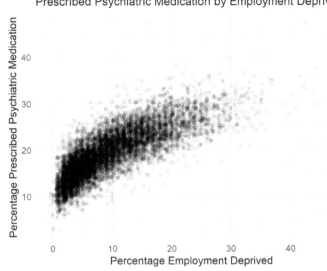

Prescribed Psychiatric Medication by Employment Deprived

We see that the data points are slightly moved and the lighter shading helps reveal a better representation of the relationship between employment deprivation and psychiatric medication prescriptions. As we observed with the ugly plot, there is a positive relationship between employment deprivation and psychiatric medication prescriptions. In other words, datazones with high employment deprivation tend to have higher prescription psychiatric medication than datazones with low employment deprivation. The darker shaded points represent where there are points on top of each other – in other words, points that have the same *x* and *y* values. This illustrates that the bulk of datazones have between 10% and 20% of employment deprivation and psychiatric medication prescriptions.

Scatterplots with Three Variables

We can also include a third variable in scatterplots. The third variable will show up as differences in the points plotted. To show the third variable using colours, we add the colour = option in the aes() argument. Let's add urban_fct as the third variable in our scatterplot, using default colours, and add a subtitle and label for the legend in the labs() function.

```
simd %>%
  filter(!is.na(pct_depress) & !is.na(pct_employment_deprived)) %>%
ggplot() +
  geom_point(mapping = aes(x = pct_employment_deprived, y = pct_depress,
                           colour = urban_fct), position = "jitter",
                           alpha = .1) +
  labs(x = "Percentage Employment Deprived",
       y = "Percentage Prescribed Psychiatric Medication",
       title = "Prescribed Psychiatric Medication by Employment Deprived",
       subtitle = "by Community Type", colour = "Community Type") +
```

```
theme_minimal() +
theme(
  plot.title = element_text(size = 12)
)
```

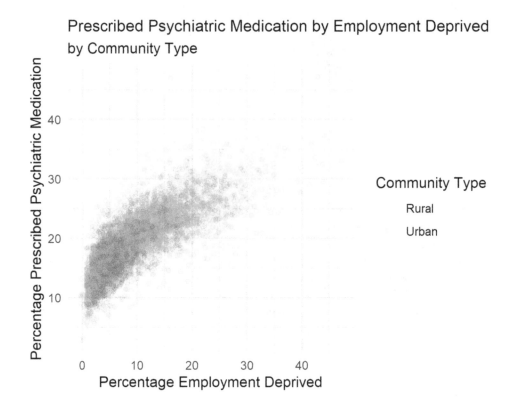

What do we see with urban/rural as the third variable? For the most part, urban and rural data-zones have similar levels of employment deprivation and psychiatric medication prescriptions. However, it appears that datazones with the highest levels of employment deprivation and psychiatric medication prescriptions are all urban.

We can control the colours by using the scale_colour_manual() function and specifying the values as the colours. We need to make sure we specify the same number of colours as categories in our third variable. Each colour we specify links to a specific value in the third variable. For example, the first colour (e.g., blue) will be for the first value of the third variable (e.g., Rural).

```
simd %>%
  filter(!is.na(pct_depress) & !is.na(pct_employment_deprived)) %>%
ggplot() +
  geom_point(mapping = aes(x = pct_employment_deprived, y = pct_depress,
                           colour = urban_fct), position = "jitter",
                           alpha = .1) +
```

```
scale_colour_manual(values = c("blue", "red")) +
labs(x = "Percentage Employment Deprived",
     y = "Percentage Prescribed Psychiatric Medication",
     title = "Prescribed Psychiatric Medication by Employment Deprived",
     subtitle = "by Community Type", colour = "Community Type") +
theme_minimal() +
theme(
  plot.title = element_text(size = 12)
)
```

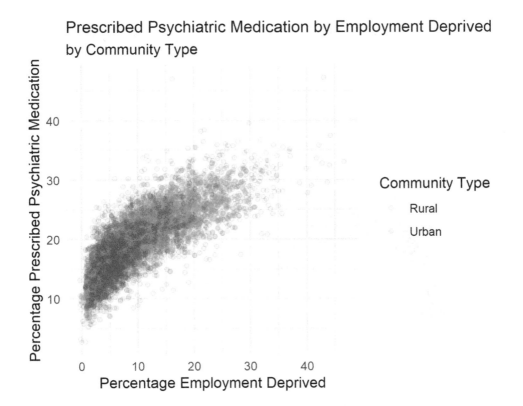

We might choose to represent the third variable using *shapes* instead of colours. This is a good option if we are unable to use colours in our document. To use shapes, we include the option `shape =` into the `aes()` argument instead of the `colour =` option. We also need to replace `colour =` with `shape =` in the `labs()` function.

```
simd %>%
  filter(!is.na(pct_depress) & !is.na(pct_employment_deprived)) %>%
ggplot() +
  geom_point(mapping = aes(x = pct_employment_deprived, y = pct_depress,
                           shape = urban_fct), position = "jitter",
                           alpha = .1) +
```

```
labs(x = "Percentage Employment Deprived",
     y = "Percentage Prescribed Psychiatric Medication",
     title = "Prescribed Psychiatric Medication by Employment Deprived",
     subtitle = "by Community Type", shape = "Community Type") +
theme_minimal() +
theme(
  plot.title = element_text(size = 12)
)
```

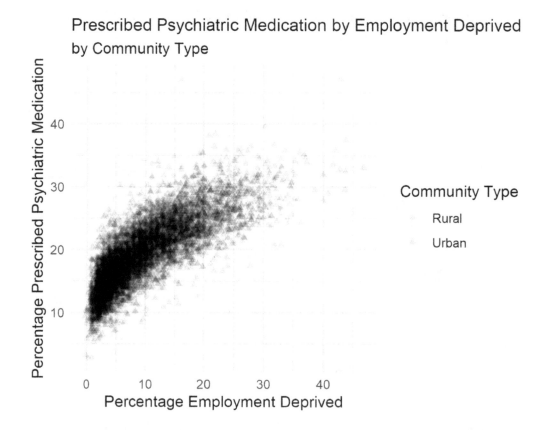

One issue with the shapes option in ggplot is that we are limited to only six types of shape. Thus, using the default settings, our third variable can have at most six categories. We can manually add more than six shapes by using the scale_shape_manual() function to our ggplot() code. However, the developers of ggplot2 argue that using more than six shapes can make it difficult to discern individual shapes in the scatterplot.

Scatterplots with Four Variables

We can include a fourth variable by specifying one variable as different shapes and the other as different colours.

We'll use the variable `university` for our fourth variable, which is the proportion of 17–21-year-olds in a datazone entering university. Let's first take a quick look at `university`.

```
summary(simd$university)
   Min. 1st Qu.  Median    Mean 3rd Qu.    Max.     NA's
0.00000 0.04688 0.07843 0.09188 0.12136 0.81907        2
```

We see that a majority of datazones have a fairly low proportion of 17–21-year-olds entering university as the median is 0.08 and the 3rd quartile is only 0.12. (Note that `university` takes values between 0 and 1 inclusive.)

For our scatterplot, let's create and use a collapsed version of `university` that has three categories, roughly based on the quartile values. To demonstrate the functionality of `tidyverse`, we'll create this variable prior to the `ggplot()` code using the pipe operator. We'll use the `case_when()` function in the `mutate()` function and specify three conditions that are labelled 'Low', 'Medium', and 'High'. Lastly, we'll reorder the category labels using the `factor()` function; if we don't do this the labels will be ordered alphabetically. We also need to add `university` to the `filter()` function to remove missing values. Let's also increase the shading darkness by setting `alpha = .5`.

```
simd %>%
  filter(!is.na(pct_depress) & !is.na(pct_employment_deprived) &
           !is.na(university)) %>%
  mutate(uni_fct = case_when(
    university <= .05 ~ "Low",
    university > .05 & university <= .12 ~ "Medium",
    university > .12 ~ "High")) %>%
  mutate(uni_fct = factor(uni_fct,
                    levels = c("Low","Medium","High"))) %>%
  ggplot() +
  geom_point(mapping = aes(x = pct_employment_deprived, y = pct_depress,
            shape = urban_fct, colour = uni_fct),
            position = "jitter", alpha = .5) +
  labs(x = "Percentage Employment Deprived",
       y = "Percentage Prescribed Psychiatric Medication",
       title = "Prescribed Psychiatric Medication by Employment Deprived",
       subtitle = "by Community Type and University Attendance",
       shape = "Community Type", colour = "University Attendance") +
  theme_minimal() +
  theme(
    plot.title = element_text(size = 12)
  )
```

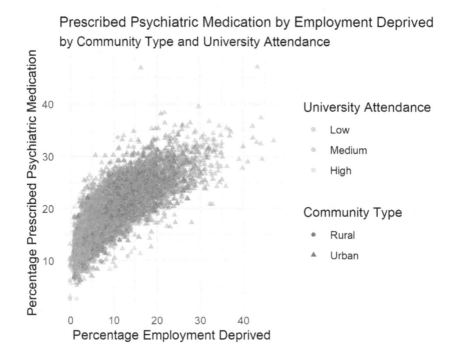

Prescribed Psychiatric Medication by Employment Deprived by Community Type and University Attendance

The cluster of blue observations on the lower left-hand side of the scatterplot illustrates that datazones with low employment deprivation and psychiatric medication prescriptions appear to have a high proportion of young people entering university. With increasing employment deprivation and psychiatric medication prescriptions, there are fewer and fewer blue observations and a gradual shift to mostly red observations (datazones with a low proportion of young people entering university). We further observe that the outliers are urban datazones with a low to medium (the scattering of green observations) proportion of the young people entering university. Overall, this scatterplot adds to understanding of the factors surrounding deprivation in Scotland.

Colour Considerations

We all have our own aesthetic colour preferences when creating data visualisations, and numerous colour combinations are available in ggplot2. However, some people have difficult seeing differences in colours or are colour-blind. This is particularly the case with visualisations, such as maps, that use a number of different colours. One solution to this problem is using brewer colour palettes in ggplot2. The brewer scales are based on the colour palettes from http://colorbrewer2.org developed to allow people to more easily differentiate colours in data visualisations.

Let's do an example using the scale_colour_brewer() function and the palette titled YlOrRd. This palette is colour-blind friendly and can be used for sequential data (e.g., our ordered university attendance variable). We will add this to the end of the code for the previous scatterplot that combines urban_fct as shapes and uni_fct as colours. We'll also set alpha = .75 so that the lightest points are more observable in the plot.

```
simd %>%
  filter(!is.na(pct_depress) & !is.na(pct_employment_deprived) &
         !is.na(university)) %>%
  mutate(uni_fct = case_when(
```

```
    university <= .05 ~ "Low",
    university > .05 & university <= .12 ~ "Medium",
    university > .12 ~ "High")) %>%
  mutate(uni_fct = factor(uni_fct,
                          levels = c("Low","Medium","High"))) %>%
ggplot() +
  geom_point(mapping = aes(x = pct_employment_deprived, y = pct_depress,
             shape = urban_fct, colour = uni_fct),
             position = "jitter", alpha = .5) +
  labs(x = "Percentage Employment Deprived",
       y = "Percentage Prescribed Psychiatric Medication",
       title = "Prescribed Psychiatric Medication by Employment Deprived",
       subtitle = "by Community Type and University Attendance",
       shape = "Community Type", colour = "University Attendance") +
  theme_minimal() +
  theme(
    plot.title = element_text(size = 12)
  ) +
  scale_colour_brewer(palette = "YlOrRd")
```

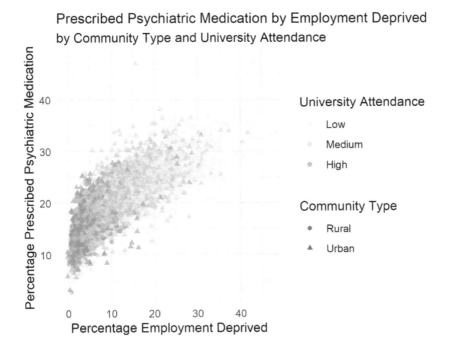

If we aren't necessarily worried about colour-blind friendly visualisations, there are numerous packages with 'theme' colour palettes. As a quick demonstration, let's use a palette based on the film *Grand Budapest Hotel* from the wesanderson package. After loading the wesanderson package, we use the scale_colour_manual() function and specify values = wes_palette ("GrandBudapest1") to get the *Grand Budapest Hotel* palette.

```r
library(wesanderson)

simd %>%
  filter(!is.na(pct_depress) & !is.na(pct_employment_deprived) &
           !is.na(university)) %>%
  mutate(uni_fct = case_when(
    university <= .05 ~ "Low",
    university > .05 & university <= .12 ~ "Medium",
    university > .12 ~ "High")) %>%
  mutate(uni_fct = factor(uni_fct,
                          levels = c("Low","Medium","High"))) %>%
ggplot() +
geom_point(mapping = aes(x = pct_employment_deprived, y = pct_depress,
           shape = urban_fct, colour = uni_fct),
           position = "jitter", alpha = .75) +
  labs(x = "Percentage Employment Deprived",
       y = "Percentage Prescribed Psychiatric Medication",
       title = "Prescribed Psychiatric Medication by Employment Deprived",
       subtitle = "by Community Type and University Attendance",
       shape = "Community Type", colour = "University Attendance") +
  theme_minimal() +
  theme(
    plot.title = element_text(size = 12)
  ) +
  scale_colour_manual(values = wes_palette("GrandBudapest1"))
```

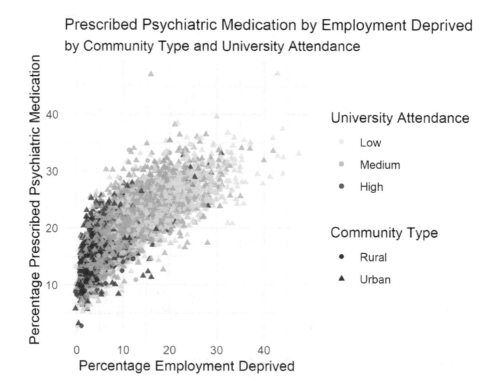

MULTIPLE PLOTS

Often, we want to combine multiple plots into one plot or plot separate aspects of variables. There are a few ways to do this, depending on the type of plot and what we want to achieve in our visualisations. Below we'll look at faceting and combining multiple plots into one plot.

Faceting

Faceting, in the `ggplot2` context, involves creating separate plots for the different values of our variable(s). Ordinarily, this is done with a categorical (nominal- or ordinal-level) variable where each plot consists of a single value from the variable. We can think of faceting as creating subplots for the different categories in our variables.

Let's use faceting to create two separate scatterplots for the two values of `urban_fct`, where `pct_employment_deprived` is on the *x*-axis and `pct_depress` is on the *y*-axis. We do this by adding the `facet_wrap()` function to our code and specifying ~ `urban_fct` in the argument; ~ separates the column and row variables, but here we just use a column variable. Since we are creating separate plots for the values of `urban_fct`, we'll remove `urban_fct` from the `aes()` argument. If we include `urban_fct` in the `aes()` argument all the observations in each plot will be a single colour (e.g., the rural observations will all be red).

```
simd %>%
  filter(!is.na(pct_depress) & !is.na(pct_employment_deprived)) %>%
ggplot() +
  geom_point(mapping = aes(x = pct_employment_deprived, y = pct_depress),
             position = "jitter", alpha = .1) +
  labs(x = "Percentage Employment Deprived",
       y = "Percentage Prescribed Psychiatric Medication",
       title = "Prescribed Psychiatric Medication by Employment Deprived",
       subtitle = "by Community Type", shape = "Community Type") +
  theme_minimal() +
  theme(
    plot.title = element_text(size = 12)
  ) +
  facet_wrap(~ urban_fct)
```

We see there are now two scatterplots: the left-hand side shows the relationship between employment deprivation and psychiatric medication prescriptions for rural datazones and the right-hand side shows the relationship for urban datazones. Both plots show a similar positive relationship between employment deprivation and psychiatric medication prescriptions. This suggests that the type of datazone might not be an important factor in explaining the relationship between these two variables.

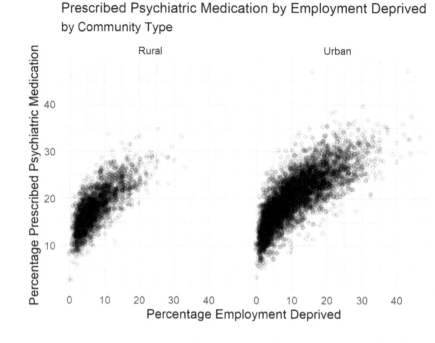

Combining Individual Plots

Sometimes we have individual plots that we want to combine into one plot. The default way to do this in R is using the par() function. However, it can be tricky to get par() to combine plots created using ggplot.

There are a variety of existing R packages we can use to combine multiple plots (e.g., gridExtra, ggpubr). Here, let's use the patchwork package for combining plots. Below, we will create two plots and combine them into a 2 × 1 array by simply separating the plot objects using /. To do so, we need to create and save plots as objects with distinct names. Specifically, we will save the first plot as an object named p1 and the second as an object named p2.[2]

Combining plots often results in smooshed plots and labels. If this occurs, we need to play around with the sizing to get them to look better. If we are using R Markdown to create our document, we could adjust fig.height and fig.width in the code chunk header. We may also adjust the sizing of the axes labels. Let's do this below by decreasing the font sizes of our titles using the theme() function from ggplot. We'll keep theme_minimal(), but we'll decrease the font sizes of our *x*-axis (axis.title.x =), *y*-axis (axis.title.y =), and legend (legend. title =) titles. We'll set all three titles to equal font size 9 (size = 9). Lastly, we'll remove the title and subtitle from each plot, and instead use the plot_annotation() function from patchwork to include an overall title and subtitle to the combined plot.

---

[2]Note that the individual plots aren't printed below because we are just asking R to create an object, not show it.

```
library(patchwork)

p1 <- simd %>%
    filter(!is.na(pct_depress) & !is.na(pct_employment_deprived)) %>%
    ggplot() +
    geom_point(mapping = aes(x = pct_employment_deprived, y = pct_depress,
                             colour = urban_fct), position = "jitter",
                             alpha = .1) +
        labs(x = "Percentage Employment Deprived",
             y = "Percentage Prescribed Psychiatric Medication",
             colour = "Community Type") +
        theme_minimal() +
        theme(
            axis.title.x = element_text(size = 9),
            axis.title.y = element_text(size = 9),
            legend.title = element_text(size = 9)
            )


p2 <- simd %>%
    filter(!is.na(pct_depress) & !is.na(pct_employment_deprived)) %>%
    ggplot() +
    geom_point(mapping = aes(x = pct_employment_deprived, y = pct_depress,
                             colour = urban_fct), position = "jitter",
                             alpha = .1) +
        labs(x = "Percentage Employment Deprived",
             y = "Percentage Prescribed Psychiatric Medication",
             colour = "Community Type") +
        theme_minimal() +
        theme(
            axis.title.x = element_text(size = 9),
            axis.title.y = element_text(size = 9),
            legend.title = element_text(size = 9)
            ) +
        scale_colour_manual(values = c("blue", "red"))

patch <- p1 / p2 +
    plot_annotation(title = "Prescribed Psychiatric Medication by Employment
                    Deprived", subtitle = "by Community Type")

patch
```

The patchwork reference site details all the different possible customisations for combining plots (https://patchwork.data-imaginist.com/).

Prescribed Psychiatric Medication by Employment Deprived

by Community Type

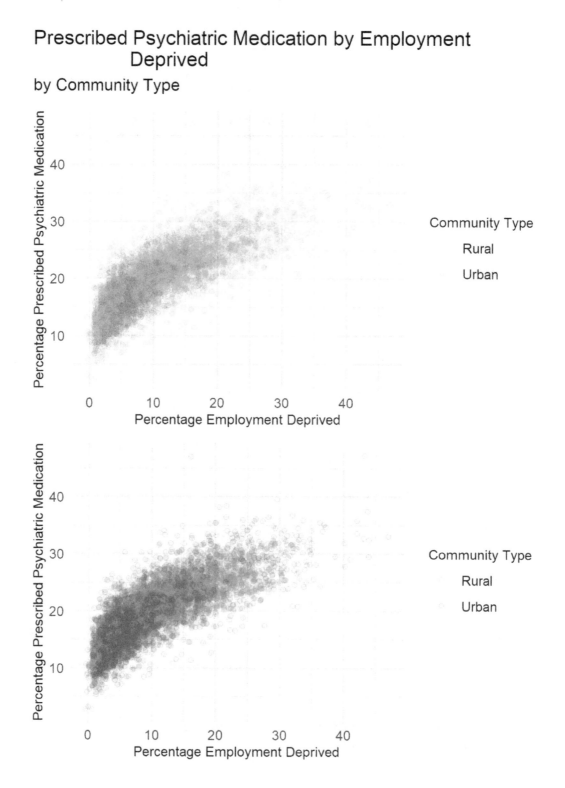

SAVING PLOTS

Unless we are using R Markdown, we need to save our plots in order to include them in our papers and presentations using Word, PowerPoint, LaTeX, etc. To save a plot from the `Plots` window in RStudio, we click on the `Export` button and then choose the file type we want (i.e., PDF or image file). The image file option provides greater functionality for sizing our plots than the PDF option. The plot will then be automatically saved to our working directory. It is important to check the sizing and rendering of our saved plot when using the `Export` option.

Another option is to use the `ggsave()` function from `ggplot2`. By default, the `ggsave()` function saves the most recent plot displayed in the session (e.g., the current plot in the `Plots` window in RStudio). If we save our plots as objects, like we did in our combining plots discussion, we can specify the object in the `ggsave()` function as the plot we want saved using the `plot =` option. We also need to name and specify the format of the file to be saved (e.g., .pdf, .png). We'll probably also need to adjust the sizing of the plot in order for the rendering to be correct. This will probably take a few attempts to get the sizing we prefer.

Below, we'll save the plot object `patch` twice using the `ggsave()` function: once without specifying the plot object (saves the last plot displayed in the `Plots` window) and once with specifying the plot object.

```
ggsave("combined.pdf", height = 7, width = 7)
ggsave("combined1.pdf", plot = patch, height = 7, width = 7)
```

These two plots should now be saved in our working directory folder.

CONCLUSION

Understanding how to visually present data is a critical skill in today's world. There are many techniques and approaches one can use for visualising data – and roughly a billion aesthetic combinations are available. Hopefully, this chapter has provided you a solid foundation of using `ggplot2` in R. We have only touched on what the `ggplot2` package, in concert with the other `tidyverse` packages, is able to offer for data visualisation in R. The type of visualisation you use and need comes down to the type of data, the levels of measurement of your variables, what you are trying to display, and your own personal preferences.

R Packages Used in This Chapter

- `dplyr` (loaded with `tidyverse`)
- `ggplot2` (loaded with `tidyverse`)
- `patchwork`
- `pillar` (loaded with `tidyverse`)
- `readr` (loaded with `tidyverse`)
- `scales`
- `wesanderson`

━━━━━━━━━━ **R Functions Used in This Chapter** ━━━━━━━━━━

- `c()` - concatenate
- `case_when()` - vectorised if statement using `dplyr` package
- `count()` - count the number of unique values of a variable or variables using `dplyr` package
- `element_text()` - control text aspects of `ggplot2` graphs
- `facet_wrap()` - wrap faceting of `ggplot2` graphs
- `factor()` - specify variable as a factor
- `filter()` - subset data based on variables' values using `dplyr` package
- `geom_bar()` - `ggplot2` bar plot
- `geom_boxplot()` - `ggplot2` box plot
- `geom_density()` - `ggplot2` density plot
- `geom_histogram()` - `ggplot2` histogram
- `geom_point()` - `ggplot2` scattered points
- `ggplot()` - base layer for `ggplot2`
- `ggsave()` - save a `ggplot2` object
- `glimpse()` - quick view of data using `pillar` package
- `guide_axis()` - control `ggplot2` axes
- `is.na()` - check for missing values (NAs) in variables
- `labs()` - `ggplot2` labels
- `mutate()` - recode variables using `dplyr` package
- `percent_format()` - add percentages to plot using `scales` package
- `plot_annotation()` - annotate plots using `patchwork` package
- `read_csv()` - read in .csv data file using `readr` package
- `recode()` - recode variable using `dplyr` package
- `rename_with()` - rename variable using a function using `dplyr` package
- `round()` - round numeric variables
- `scale_colour_brewer()` - `ggplot2` colour brewer palettes
- `scale_colour_manual()` - `ggplot2` manually set colours
- `scale_fill_grey()` - `ggplot2` grey shading
- `scale_fill_manual()` - `ggplot2` grey shading
- `scale_x_discrete()` - *x*-axis aesthetics for discrete variables
- `scale_y_continuous()` - *y*-axis aesthetics for continuous variables
- `summary()` - summarise object
- `theme()` - set overall theme of `ggplot2` graph
- `theme_minimal()` - minimal `ggplot2` theme
- `wes_palette()` - colour palettes based on Wes Anderson films

━━━━━━━━━━ **Additional Resources** ━━━━━━━━━━

Books

- Wickham, H. (2022) *ggplot2: Elegant Graphics for Analysis*, 3rd edition. Springer.
- Wickham, H. and Grolemund, G. (2017) *R for Data Science*. O'Reilly Media.

- Wilke, C. O. (2019) *Fundamentals of Data Visualization: A Primer on Making Informative and Compelling Figures*. O'Reilly Media.

Online

- R-bloggers: https://www.r-bloggers.com/
- RStudio Blog: https://www.rstudio.com/blog/
- Tidyverse: https://www.tidyverse.org/

9

HYPOTHESIS TESTING

Chapter contents

When we talk about hypothesis testing, we are referring to whether a relationship or difference we observe through our data analysis is expected to be 'real' or 'likely', or not. Is it the case that a relationship we see in our sample data is expected to actually be the relationship in the population? In a very crude way, hypothesis testing concerns whether we expect a relationship to exist or not. For example, whether a predictor variable 'matters' in explaining an outcome variable. Or whether two groups of individuals are really different or whether they only 'appear' different in our particular data.

We will begin this chapter discussing how to conduct hypothesis testing and the relevant ins and outs. At the end of the chapter we will conduct basic hypothesis testing in R by looking at difference-in-means and nonparametric tests. This chapter builds directly on Chapter 6, where we discussed and worked on creating good empirical hypotheses – hypotheses that could be tested using quantitative data. Whereas in Chapter 6 we merely created hypotheses, this chapter is about building the foundation for testing those hypotheses.

By the end of this chapter, you should be to:

- Understand the basics of statistical inference
- Understand what statistical significance implies
- Understand the basics of hypothesis testing
- Understand how to set up and execute hypothesis tests
- Implement in difference-in-means tests in R
- Implement nonparametric hypothesis testing in R

HYPOTHESIS TESTING

Statistical Inference

Hypothesis testing is a core part of what is known as statistical inference. Statistical inference is concerned with making inferences about a population based on a sample of the population. When working with sample data, we want our results to apply not just to our sample but to the population from which the sample came. We want to be able to generalise our findings from the sample to the population. Using sample data, we derive a statistical estimator (e.g., the sample mean) that we want to be as close as possible to the population parameter (e.g., the population mean). For example, if we are studying the determinants of vote choice in Canada, we do not want our findings to only apply to the sample, but we want to use the findings to say something about determinants of voting for all Canadians.

The problem with data analysis is that we usually do not know what the population looks like. Again, we only have a sample of the population. We have various ways of determining whether what we estimated in the sample is expected to be close to the population parameter, or whether what we find in the sample is expected to be true in the population. The central way of deciding this is through the use of statistical significance testing.

Statistical Significance

Statistical significance testing provides a formal, rigorous procedure for determining whether we expect that a relationship or difference is actually present or whether it could have been observed due to random chance. From a statistical inference standpoint, statistical significance tells us whether or not what we observe in the sample is expected to be 'true' in the population. Crudely, statistical significance tells us whether something is expected to matter or not matter.

So how do we determine whether something is statistically significant? Statistical significance is determined by the probability that something happened by chance or not, or the probability that what we observe in the sample is expected to be true in the population. In deciding statistical significance, we use something called *p*-values. The understanding of *p*-values has evolved away from statements concerning the probability that something is expected to happen by chance or not and towards a more nuanced understanding. The American Statistical Association states that *p*-values should informally be thought of as 'the probability under a specified statistical model that a statistical summary of the data (e.g., the sample mean difference between two compared groups) would be equal to or more extreme than its observed value' (Wasserstein and Lazar 2016).[1]

Every test that includes a test for statistical significance includes what is known as a test statistic which we use, along with other information, to calculate *p*-values; in fact, R does all of this for us. Convention dictates that a relationship or difference is considered *statistically significant* if a *p*-value is less than or equal to 0.05 ($p \leq 0.05$); the phrase '*p*-value' is often used shortened to '*p*'.[2] For our purposes in this book, simply, if a relationship has a *p*-value less than or equal to 0.05 than we'll consider the relationship *statistically significant*; if the *p*-value is greater than 0.05 than we'll consider the relationship *not statistically significant*.

There are in fact several levels of significance that researchers use. Although $p \leq 0.05$ is the standard, researchers also commonly use *p*-values of 0.10, 0.01, and 0.001 (the levels are usually represented by the Greek letter α). Researchers may choose $p \leq 0.10$ when they have a small sample size and choose $p \leq 0.01$ or $p \leq 0.001$ when they want to demonstrate more 'confidence' in the statistical significance tests. We indicate that we are using different levels of significance by including statements such as *significant at the 0.05 level* or *significant at the 0.01 level*. When using different levels of significance in the same analysis, researchers mistakenly assume that if variable *X* is significant at the 0.01 level and variable *Y* is significant at the 0.05 level, then variable X is *more* significant. This comparison makes little sense since the researcher establishes the cut-point for whether something is significant or not, not more significant or less significant. The researcher would be correct to say that the variables are significant at different levels of significance, but not that one is more significant than another. Therefore, we can think of deciding whether a relationship or difference is significant or not as a dichotomous decision, a yes or no decision.

While we can criticise the 0.05 cut-off as arbitrary, there are real-world implications for using specific cut-off values in statistical significance testing. In most quantitative social science, if we get *p*-values above 0.05, then we conclude that what we are looking at is not statistically significant. No one is hurt, no lives are at risk. Now consider that the Federal Drug Administration (FDA) in the USA uses the 0.05 cut-off to determine if a drug has an effect or not in a clinical trial. If a drug has an effect at the 0.05 level of significance, then the FDA concludes it is statistically significantly better than a placebo and approves it for public release and usage. If the drug does *not* have an effect at the 0.05 level, then the FDA concludes the drug is not better than a placebo

---

[1]Statistical significance and *p*-values are a critical element of the difference between frequentism and Bayesianism (see Lambert 2018).

[2]See Field et al. (2011) for a nice, brief discussion of how 0.05 came to be the standard.

and rejects it for public use. What about the situation when $p = 0.06$? For the FDA, it means the drug is not significantly better than a placebo. But it is hard to believe that a drug with a p-value of 0.06 does not have an effect, while a drug with a p-value of 0.05 does have an effect. Here, the FDA's decision means the difference between a patient getting access or not getting access to a new drug. Hopefully, this discussion has laid out the basics of statistical significance and the potential arbitrariness of the 0.05 cut-point.

ALTERNATIVE AND NULL HYPOTHESES

Thus far our discussion has been very generic and abstract. Now let's put hypothesis testing and statistical significance into action by discussing alternative and null hypotheses. An *alternative hypothesis* is simply a hypothesis we create to describe our expectations between two variables – the type of hypothesis that we developed in Chapter 6. An alternative hypothesis is often denoted by H_A.[3] A *null hypothesis* is a hypothesis that states there is no relationship between two given variables – that there is a null effect. We also have null hypotheses that state there is no difference between two groups. A null hypothesis is *not* a hypothesis with a different expectation between two variables from our original alternative hypothesis. A null hypothesis is often denoted by H_0. In determining the statistical significance of a relationship we set our alternative hypothesis against the null hypothesis. If we determine that our relationship is statistically significant (i.e., $p \leq 0.05$), then we reject the null hypothesis that there is no relationship. If the relationship is *not* statistically significant (i.e., $p > 0.05$), then we do *not* reject the null hypothesis. Sometimes, we will see generic alternative and null hypotheses written like this:

- H_A: there is a relationship between x and y
- H_0: there is no relationship between x and y

Let's use an example from Chapter 6 to make this process clearer. We had the hypothesis (which is our alternative hypothesis): *people who have at least a bachelor's degree are more likely to be fully vaccinated against Covid-19 than people who only have a high school diploma.* We want to test whether this relationship is statistically significant or not. We start by deciding on the level of significance, which we'll choose as 0.05. Now we need a null hypothesis. Again, the null hypothesis states there is no relationship. Therefore, our null hypothesis is: *there is no relationship between education level and Covid-19 vaccination status.* For demonstration purposes, let's imagine that we have done the analysis and find that $p = 0.014$. What does that tell us? Since $p \leq 0.05$, we can conclude that the relationship is statistically significant and we can reject the null hypothesis that no relationship exists.[4] Putting words to this statistically significant result, we can say:

> *There is a statistically significant relationship between education level and Covid-19 vaccination status.*

---

[3]Note that an *alternative hypothesis* is different from an *alternative explanation*. We normally use the latter in reference to a *competing hypothesis* for explaining some phenomenon.

[4]We'll skip discussing Type I and Type II errors since keeping them straight is confusing and they do not really affect our analysis. Essentially, Type I and Type II errors get at the idea that if we say a relationship is (*not*) statistically significant, we might be making an error.

We may also phrase the interpretation as:

A person's education level is a statistically significant predictor of their Covid-19 vaccination status.

Since our alternative hypothesis specifically stated the direction of the relationship, we can incorporate additional information into the interpretation:

People who have at least a bachelor's degree are statistically significantly more likely to be fully vaccinated against Covid-19 than people who only have a high school diploma.

Now that we have a basic understanding of statistical significance and how the words 'significant' and 'significantly' are used in interpretations of hypothesis tests, we should avoid using them as synonyms for size and importance when writing and discussing our research. For example, if someone says 'there is a significant difference in the quality of candidates running for a country's presidency and running for local council', we should assume they are implying statistical significance with the word 'significant'. If they aren't referring to statistical significance, then they should use a different word (e.g., large, enormous, etc.). To be unambiguous, we should always pair 'statistical' or 'statistically' with 'significant' and 'significantly'. This will clearly communicate to the reader or listener that we are referring to statistical significance testing and not using a loose term of importance or magnitude.

Steps of Hypothesis Testing

Let's summarise the steps we take in performing hypothesis testing:

- Develop an alternative hypothesis and then the null hypothesis.
- Decide on the statistical test (and thus the test statistic) and the level of significance (usually 0.05).
- Compute the *p*-value (via the test statistic).
- If $p \leq 0.05$, then the relationship is statistically significant and we reject the null. If $p > 0.05$, then the relationship is not statistically significant and we do not reject the null.

Examples of Hypothesis Testing

Let's practise determining and discussing statistical significance with a few examples of hypotheses from Chapter 6. To keep things simple, we will have magically derived *p*-values; in the next section on difference-in-means tests, we will use R to calculate *p*-values.

Example I: Smart People Are *Really* All about Covid-19 Vaccines?

In Chapter 6, we had the following hypothesis:

Parents who have at least a bachelor's degree are more likely to have their children fully vaccinated against Covid-19 compared to parents who only have a high school diploma.

To test whether this hypothesis is statistically significant, we next need to specify the null hypothesis. Ideas? Again, a null hypothesis starts by stating *there is no relationship*. Here, our null hypothesis is:

There is no relationship between a parent's education level and their children's Covid-19 vaccination status.

Now, a little, magical coding unicorn tells us the *p*-value from testing the relationship is *p* = 0.041. What do we conclude? Since this *p*-value is less than or equal to 0.05, we conclude that our alternative hypothesis is statistically significant and we reject our null hypothesis. Let's add the verbal accoutrements to the interpretation:

There is a statistically significant relationship between a parent's education level and their children's Covid-19 vaccination status.

We may also phrase the interpretation as:

A parent's education level has a statistically significant effect on whether their children are fully vaccinated against Covid-19.

We can specify the direction and comparison made in the hypothesis in our interpretation as:

Parents who have at least a bachelor's degree are statistically significantly more likely to have their children fully vaccinated against Covid-19 compared to parents who only have a high school diploma.

Example II: Curing Covid-19 with Political Ideology?

Now let's consider the following hypothesis from Chapter 6:

Politically conservative individuals are more likely to use homeopathic medicine to try to cure Covid-19 infections than politically liberal individuals.

What is the null hypothesis here?

There is no relationship between political ideology and use of homeopathic medicine to try to cure Covid-19 infections.

The magical coding unicorn tells us the *p*-value from testing the relationship is *p* = 0.005. What do we conclude? Since this *p*-value is less than or equal to 0.05, we conclude that our alternative hypothesis is statistically significant and we reject our null hypothesis. Putting this into words, we can say:

There is a statistically significant relationship between individuals' political ideology and use of homeopathic medicine to try to cure Covid-19 infections.

We can also phrase the interpretation as:

An individual's political ideology has a statistically significant effect on whether they use homeopathic medicine to try to cure Covid-19 infections.

Lastly, let's specify the direction and comparison made in the hypothesis in our interpretation as:

Politically conservative individuals are statistically significantly more likely to use homeopathic medicine to try to cure Covid-19 infections than politically liberal individuals.

Example III: Negative Effects of Online Learning?
Let's practise with one more hypothesis from Chapter 6:

States that allowed online learning for secondary education are expected to have lower graduation rates than states that did not allow online learning during the 2020–2021 school year.

What is the null hypothesis here?

There is no relationship between delivery mode of instruction and secondary school graduation rates during the 2020–2021 school year.

We ask the magical coding unicorn for one last test and we learn that $p = 0.54$. What does this tell us? This tells us that there is *not* a statistically significant relationship and we *cannot* reject the null hypothesis. This result does not mean that states that allowed online learning for secondary education had higher graduation rates than states that did not allow online learning. It just means that there is no relationship between delivery mode of instruction and graduation rates. If we wanted to be more explicit about this conclusion, we could state:

There is not a statistically significant relationship between delivery mode of instruction and secondary school graduation rates during the 2020–2021 school year.

When we are conducting statistical significance tests, if a relationship is not significant then we do not interpret any of the associated statistics of the relationship (e.g., coefficients, measures of association, etc.). A non-significant relationship is like *Fight Club* – we don't talk about it. This will come up again and again throughout the rest of the book.

DIFFERENCE-IN-MEANS SIGNIFICANCE TESTS

In this section, we will examine and perform difference-in-means significance tests. Difference-in-means tests provide an easy introduction to performing hypothesis testing in R. In essence, difference-in-means tests look to see if one group (of individuals, bees, dogs) is significantly different from another group (of individuals, bees, dogs).

We have already discussed the basics of these tests with our discussion of the FDA and statistical significance. In the classic medical clinical trial, one group of people are the *treatment* group (i.e., take a new vaccine) and another group of people, who are similar to the first group, are the *control* group (i.e., take a placebo). Then, at the end of the trial, the researchers measure whatever the vaccine is supposed to affect (e.g., becoming infected by a virus) and compare the two groups. If the two groups are statistically significantly different (i.e., $p \leq 0.05$), then the vaccine is considered to be effective. If the two groups are not statistically significantly different (i.e., $p > 0.05$), then the vaccine is considered not effective.

Though there a few different versions of these tests, we will just consider two types: two-sample difference-in-means tests with independent samples and two-sample difference-in-means tests with dependent samples. We use a statistical technique called a *t-test* to assess whether the two groups are significantly different; it is called a *t*-test because it assumes that the sample means follow a Student's *t* distribution. Note that since we are using means, our variable of interest should be at the interval or ratio level (or high ordinal); however, researchers often use difference-in-means tests on ordinal variables with only a few values. How often we use *t*-tests will depend on our research design and, thus, use of *t*-tests is more or less prevalent depending on the discipline. For example, *t*-tests are commonly used to analyse experimental data. Therefore, disciplines and subdisciplines that heavily utilise experimental research designs (e.g., psychology, political psychology) often use *t*-tests. These tests are still used with non-experimental data and research designs, but often they are for exploratory purposes prior to multivariate analyses such as regression modelling.

Two-Sample Difference-in-Means Tests with Independent Samples

This form of the test is essentially what we discussed with the clinical trial above. The idea is that we have observations from sample *x* and observations from sample *y*, and we are testing whether the means ($\bar{x}$) are significantly different. The null hypothesis in this test is that the means of each sample are the same. This is the same as saying there is no difference between the two groups. Let's first specify the null as an equation:

$$\bar{x}_1 = \bar{x}_2$$

If we have no expectation whether one sample mean is larger/smaller than the other, our alternative hypothesis is that the two means are just different. We can write this as:

$$\bar{x}_1 \neq \bar{x}_2$$

To test whether two means are simply different, we use what is a called a *two-tailed t-test*.

If we do have an expectation about the relative size, or direction, of the sample means, our alternative hypotheses would be either

$$\bar{x}_1 > \bar{x}_2$$

or

$$\bar{x}_1 < \bar{x}_2$$

Notice that the inequalities are not ≤ or ≥; including the = would also include the null hypothesis (that they are equal). When we do have an expectation about the relative sizes of the samples means, we use what is called an *one-tailed t-test*.

Let's use variables from the 2020 Scottish Index of Multiple Deprivation data (simd2020.csv) to run our *t*-tests.

```
setwd("C:/QSSD/Chapter 9 - Hypothesis Testing")
getwd()
```

```
library(tidyverse)
simd <- read_csv("simd2020.csv", na = "*")
```

First, let's test whether there is a statistically significant difference between psychiatric medication prescription percentages (DEPRESS) in urban and rural Scottish datazones (urban). Let's first wrangle these variables by setting all the variables to lower case, convert DEPRESS to a percentage, and attach labels to the categories of urban.

```
simd <- simd %>%
        rename_with(tolower) %>%
        mutate(pct_depress = depress*100) %>%
        mutate(urban_fct = recode(urban, `1` = "Urban", `0` = "Rural"))
```

We will use the t.test() function where we first put in our outcome variable (pct_depress), then ~, followed by our grouping variable (urban_fct), and finally which dataset we are using (data = simd). Here, we are not specifying a direction of the relationship, only that they are different.

```
t.test(pct_depress ~ urban_fct, data = simd)

    Welch Two Sample t-test

data:  pct_depress by urban_fct
t = -14.725, df = 5199.7, p-value < 2.2e-16
alternative hypothesis: true difference in means between group Rural
and group Urban is not equal to 0
95 percent confidence interval:
 -2.086990 -1.596565
sample estimates:
mean in group Rural mean in group Urban
           17.78951            19.63129
```

Let's go through the R output we obtain from running the test. After the name of the test, the first line data: tells us which variables are being used in the test. The second line gives us the information about the t-value, degrees of freedom, and the calculated p-value (the p-value is calculated from the t-value and degrees of freedom). We are particularly interested in the p-value. If $p \leq 0.05$, we can conclude that our two groups are statistically significantly different. Here, we see the p-value is indeed less than or equal to 0.05, and we conclude that the groups are statistically significantly different and reject the null that the means are the same. We would interpret this as: *there is a statistically significant difference in the mean psychiatric medication prescription percentage between urban and rural Scottish datazones*. In this test, R actually specifies the alternative hypothesis being tested: true difference in means is not equal to 0, which means $\bar{x}_1 \neq \bar{x}_2$. A final item to point out is that at the bottom of the output, R gives us the means of the two groups; we see that the average percentage of psychiatric medication prescriptions in urban datazones is 19.63 and the average percentage of psychiatric medication prescriptions in rural datazones is 17.79.

We could also use functions from the infer package to conduct *t*-tests.[5] The infer package uses tidyverse-compatible grammar and objects and forces the user to be more conscientious about specifying statistical inference tests. For us, the package probably has more functionality and complexity than we require, but let's take a quick look at one of infer's more straightforward functions – the t_test() function.

After loading the tidymodels package, we'll use the t_test() function to replicate the *t*-test we did above. In the t_test() argument, we first specify the data (simd), the formula for the *t*-test (= pct_depress ~ urban_fct), the order of the grouping variable (the ordering of values of urban_fct), and finally that we want a 'two-sided' test (alternative = "two-sided").

```
library(tidymodels)

t_test(simd,
   formula = pct_depress ~ urban_fct,
   order = c("Rural","Urban"),
   alternative = "two-sided")
# A tibble: 1 x 7
   statistic  t_df  p_value alternative estimate lower_ci upper_ci
       <dbl> <dbl>    <dbl> <chr>          <dbl>    <dbl>    <dbl>
 1     -14.7 5200. 4.12e-48 two.sided      -1.84    -2.09    -1.60
```

The t_test() function produces a tibble with the results, but otherwise the output matches the output from t.test(). For those just starting to learn about *t*-tests, I find the output from the t.test() function is easier to understand than the output from the t_test() function. Specifically, I think by specifying the alternative hypothesis and providing the grouped means, the t.test() output allows a clearer way to understand *t*-tests and check our results. The minimalist t_test() output may become preferable after we have mastered *t*-tests.

Given the results of the first test, we might want to perform a directional test to see if the mean for rural datazones is statistically significantly smaller than the mean for rural datazones. To do this, we add the option alternative = "less" to the t.test() argument; the 'less' implies that the mean of the first group (here, rural) is expected to be smaller than the mean of the second group (here, urban).

```
t.test(pct_depress ~ urban_fct, alternative = "less", data = simd)


    Welch Two Sample t-test

data:  pct_depress by urban_fct
t = -14.725, df = 5199.7, p-value < 2.2e-16
alternative hypothesis: true difference in means between group Rural and
group Urban is less than 0
95 percent confidence interval:
```

---

[5]The infer package is part of the tidymodels package, which is itself part of the world of tidyverse.

```
    -Inf -1.636
 sample estimates:
 mean in group Rural mean in group Urban
           17.78951            19.63129
```

Notice that the alternative hypothesis in the output has changed to: `true difference in means...is less than 0`. Since $p \leq 0.05$, we conclude that *the mean psychiatric medication prescription percentage is statistically significantly smaller for rural datazones than for urban datazones.*

For completeness, let's test whether the mean for rural datazones is statistically significant larger than the mean for urban datazones – which we already know it is not. To do so, we specify `alternative = "greater"` in the `t.test()` argument.

```
t.test(pct_depress ~ urban_fct, alternative = "greater", data = simd)


      Welch Two Sample t-test

data:  pct_depress by urban_fct
t = -14.725, df = 5199.7, p-value = 1
alternative hypothesis: true difference in means between group Rural
and group Urban is greater than 0
95 percent confidence interval:
 -2.047555        Inf
sample estimates:
mean in group Rural mean in group Urban
           17.78951            19.63129
```

As we expected, this test is not statistically significant, as indicated by `p-value = 1`.

One final option to consider is that the `t.test()` function, by default, assumes that the population variances of the two groups are the same – a rather strong assumption. Instead, we can tell the `t.test()` function to carry out the test assuming the population variances are not equal by specifying the option `var.equal = FALSE` in the argument. Let's just do one example of this by performing the non-directional *t*-test.

```
t.test(pct_depress ~ urban_fct, var.equal = FALSE, data = simd)


      Welch Two Sample t-test

data:  pct_depress by urban_fct
t = -14.725, df = 5199.7, p-value < 2.2e-16
alternative hypothesis: true difference in means between group Rural
and group Urban is not equal to 0
95 percent confidence interval:
 -2.086990 -1.596565
sample estimates:
mean in group Rural mean in group Urban
           17.78951            19.63129
```

We see that including the assumption that the population variances are unequal made almost no difference in our results; often it does not make a big difference.

Two-Sample Difference-in-Means Tests with Dependent Samples

This form of the test examines whether there is a difference in two means within the same observations. The classic example of this is an experiment where we have an individual's pre-test measure and the same individual's post-test measure, and we want to see if the two measurements are statistically significantly different. Above, we split Scottish datazones into rural and urban, and compared differences in means. In this section, we will see whether there is a statistically significant difference in the means of the standardised mortality ratio (smr) and the standardised emergency stays in hospital ratio (emerg) in all Scottish datazones. For both of these variables, a value of 100 is the Scottish average for a population with the same gender and age profile. Therefore, a value less (more) than 100 means lower (higher) than the average. Although this test is not the classic pre/post test, it makes sense to do since these are related measures.

We again use the t.test() function to carry out this test. We specify that these are dependent samples by including the option paired = TRUE in the t.test() argument; this alludes to another name for this type of test, the *paired t-test*. First, we will run the test with no directional expectation. Note that we need to use the alternative way of specifying where the variables come from by the use of $ instead of data = simd.

```
t.test(simd$smr, simd$emerg, paired = TRUE)

    Paired t-test

data:   simd$smr and simd$emerg
t = -2.9158, df = 6973, p-value = 0.003559
alternative hypothesis: true difference in means is not equal to 0
95 percent confidence interval:
 -2.2960773 -0.4499259
sample estimates:
mean of the differences
          -1.373002
```

Since $p \leq 0.05$, we can conclude that there is a statistically significant difference between the means of the standardised mortality and standardised emergency stays in hospital ratios. At the bottom of the output, R provides the mean of the differences between the mortality and emergency hospital stays ratios. Since this value is negative, it implies that the mean of standardised mortality is less than the mean of standardised emergency stays in hospital.

Given that, let's run a *t*-test with the alternative hypothesis that the mean of mortality is significantly smaller than the mean of hospital emergency stays. Since mortality is listed first in the argument, we need to specify that alternative = "less".

```
t.test(simd$smr, simd$emerg, alternative = "less", paired = TRUE)

    Paired t-test
```

```
data:   simd$smr and simd$emerg
t = -2.9158, df = 6973, p-value = 0.00178
alternative hypothesis: true difference in means is less than 0
95 percent confidence interval:
        -Inf -0.5983636
sample estimates:
mean of the differences
            -1.373002
```

We see that the mean of mortality is statistically significantly smaller than the mean of hospital emergency stays. To double-check that everything is OK, let's rerun the *t*-test with the expectation in the opposite direction; there should not be a significant difference.

```
t.test(simd$smr,simd$emerg, alternative = "greater", paired = TRUE)


    Paired t-test

data:   simd$smr and simd$emerg
t = -2.9158, df = 6973, p-value = 0.9982
alternative hypothesis: true difference in means is greater than 0
95 percent confidence interval:
 -2.14764       Inf
sample estimates:
mean of the differences
            -1.373002
```

As expected, we see that the mean of mortality is not statistically significantly greater than the mean of hospital emergency stays.

NONPARAMETRIC SIGNIFICANCE TESTS

The main issue with the difference-in-means tests is that we can only use them when our outcome variable is continuous. Further, the tests assume that the sample means follow a Student's *t* distribution, which is similar to a normal distribution. If we cannot satisfy either of those conditions, we should consider other approaches for testing differences between groups. The most common alternative are nonparametric tests. The main difference is that nonparametric tests do not require the assumption of a particular distribution (e.g., a normal distribution). There are a boatload of nonparametric tests available, but let's just concentrate on two: the Wilcoxon rank-sum test for independent samples and the Wilcoxon signed-rank test for dependent samples.

Wilcoxon Rank-Sum Test (Independent Samples)

We can think of the Wilcoxon rank-sum test as the nonparametric version of the *t*-test with independent samples. The Wilcoxon rank-sum test (also known as the Mann–Whitney *U*-test) works by assessing whether two distributions are the same without assuming a normal distribution (thus, nonparametric). Instead of using means, the null hypothesis for this test is commonly that *the medians of each sample are equal*. As with *t*-tests, we can test whether two groups' distributions are simply different (non-directional) or whether one is larger/smaller than the other (directional).

Let's run this test using the same variables we used for the parametric tests. We'll use the `wilcox.test()` function which is specified in a similar manner to the `t.test()` function. We put our outcome variable first (`pct_depress`), followed by `~`, then our grouping variable (`urban_fct`), and lastly we specify the data (`data = simd`). Let's first run the test with the non-directional alternative hypothesis.

```
wilcox.test(pct_depress ~ urban_fct, data = simd)

    Wilcoxon rank sum test with continuity correction

data:  pct_depress by urban_fct
W = 4170616, p-value < 2.2e-16
alternative hypothesis: true location shift is not equal to 0
```

We see that $p \leq 0.05$, which tells us that there is a statistically significant difference between psychiatric medication prescription percentages between urban and rural Scottish datazones. The `alternative hypothesis` statement of `true location shift is not equal to 0` sounds a bit strange. It comes from the fact that the test is comparing two distributions, where the null is that the distributions are equal. This implies that if we plotted the two distributions they would look identical and be superimposed. If they are not equal, it implies that one of the distributions is 'shifted' to the left or right of the other distribution; in other words, not equal to 0. If that still sounds confusing, just think of 'location shift is not equal to 0' as 'groups are not equal'.

Now let's carry out directional alternative hypothesis tests. First, let's test whether the psychiatric medication prescription percentage for rural datazones is significantly less than for urban datazones by specifying `alternative = "less"`.

```
wilcox.test(pct_depress ~ urban_fct, alternative = "less", data = simd)

    Wilcoxon rank sum test with continuity correction

data:  pct_depress by urban_fct
W = 4170616, p-value < 2.2e-16
alternative hypothesis: true location shift is less than 0
```

We see that $p \leq 0.05$ and thus the psychiatric medication prescription percentage for rural datazones is statistically significantly smaller than for urban datazones.

Now, let's test whether rural is significantly greater than urban by including `alternative = "greater"`.

```
wilcox.test(pct_depress ~ urban_fct, alternative = "greater",
    data = simd)
```

```
     Wilcoxon rank sum test with continuity correction

data:  pct_depress by urban_fct
W = 4170616, p-value = 1
alternative hypothesis: true location shift is greater than 0
```

As expected, we see that this alternative hypothesis is not statistically significant.

Wilcoxon Signed-Rank Test (Dependent Samples)

We can think of the Wilcoxon signed-rank test as the nonparametric version of the *t*-test with dependent samples. This test operates in a similar way to the Wilcoxon rank-sum test that we just looked at. Let's assess the difference between the mortality (mortality) and hospital emergency stays (emerg) ratios. To carry out the test, we again use the wilcox.test() function but specify paired = TRUE. We need to use the alternative way of specifying where the variables come from by the use of $ instead of data = simd. For demonstration purposes, we'll just test the non-directional hypothesis version; to run the directional hypothesis version we just need to specify alternative =.

```
wilcox.test(simd$smr, simd$emerg, paired = TRUE)

     Wilcoxon signed rank test with continuity correction

data:  simd$smr and simd$emerg
V = 10256050, p-value < 2.2e-16
alternative hypothesis: true location shift is not equal to 0
```

Since $p \leq 0.05$, we conclude that the distributions for mortality and hospital emergency stays across all Scottish datazones are statistically significantly different.

Although we came to the same conclusions regarding statistical significance when using nonparametric tests as we did with the parametric tests (i.e., difference-in-means tests), it is still useful to carry out nonparametric tests since the assumption of normality is often violated in practice. If our parametric and nonparametric tests agree, we can have more confidence in our results.

CONCLUSION

In this chapter, we discussed hypothesis testing and statistical significance, two important concepts that carry through the rest of the book. You should be comfortable with the concept and steps of hypothesis testing as it is a core part of the classic scientific method. In practice, social science researchers approach hypothesis testing in a less formal manner than we did in this chapter. For example, we typically don't write out hypotheses (unless a journal editor forces us) and null hypotheses. However, understanding the formal steps of hypothesis testing allows us to more effectively communicate our research findings to others.

We only dipped our toe into the fascinating and contentious debate surrounding statistical significance and the use of *p*-values. Our discussion of the topic follows the standard usage by applied quantitative social scientists. I've found that delving into the debate and trying to parse the nuances often confuses students who might be already struggling to learn the foundations, applications, and R programming for the first time. In the next chapters we will address an aspect of the debate – applying the concept of substantive significance alongside statistical significance.

In the next chapter on bivariate analysis, we'll use R to statistically test relationships between two variables – specifically an outcome variable and a predictor variable. The next chapter pulls together all the skills you have learned up to this point, including development of good hypotheses, identifying levels of measurement, wrangling variables, and hypothesis testing.

R Packages Used in This Chapter

- tidymodels
- tidyverse

R Functions Used in This Chapter

- c() - concatenate
- mutate() - recode variables using dplyr package
- read_csv() - read in .csv data file using readr package
- recode() - recode variable using dplyr package
- rename_with() - rename variable using a function using dplyr package
- t.test() - t-test
- t_test() - t-test using tidymodels
- wilcox.test() - nonparametric differences test

Books and Articles

- Field, A., Miles, J. and Field, Z. (2011) *Discovering Statistics Using R*. Sage.
- Fox, J. and Weisberg, S. (2018) *An R Companion to Applied Regression*. Sage.
- Harris, J. K. (2020) *Statistics with R: Solving Problems Using Real-World Data*. Sage.
- Lambert, B. (2018) *A Student's Guide to Bayesian Statistics*. Sage.
- Long, J. D. and Teetor, P. (2019) *R Cookbook*, 2nd edition. O'Reilly Media.
- Wasserstein, R. L., and Lazar, N. A. (2016) 'The ASA's statement on *p*-values: Context, process, and purpose', *American Statistician*, 70: 129–133.

Online

- R-bloggers: https://www.r-bloggers.com/
- RStudio Blog: https://www.rstudio.com/blog/

10

BIVARIATE ANALYSIS

Chapter contents

In this chapter, we will take our first serious look at measuring and testing bivariate relationships. Up until now we have mostly discussed associations and relationships between variables in a general way using intuition and common sense. For example, when we discussed developing and testing hypotheses, we were considering the relationship between two variables, but we did not explore the relationship in a statistical manner.

We will move beyond discussing hypotheses to testing hypotheses using crosstabulations, measures of association, chi-squared analysis, and correlation analysis. This chapter lays the foundation for the next chapter on linear regression modelling.

By the end of this chapter, you should be able to:

- Understand how to display bivariate relationships
- Create and interpret crosstabulations
- Understand when to use and how to interpret measures of association
- Perform and understand chi-squared analysis
- Perform and interpret correlation analysis

ASSOCIATION

What do we mean by association in a statistical context? Typically, we are referring to using a metric or test to characterise the relationship between two variables. The association may be weak or may be strong or even no association (the equivalent of a null hypothesis). While this is true in a general sense, in this chapter we want to start focusing on testing relationships between predictor and outcome variables. When we think of association in this chapter we are implying a relationship between a predictor and an outcome variable. When the predictor variable changes, what happens to the outcome variable? Does the outcome variable increase or decrease or remain the same? This relationship or association is not necessarily causal; and in fact is probably not causal since we are using social science data. However, we are beginning to apply and test theory and hypotheses of how one variable may affect another.

There are many different ways to look at and analyse association. In this chapter, we will consider scatterplots, crosstabulations, and correlation; Chapter 11 involves a fourth way using linear regression. When learning this material for the first time, the trickiest part for students often is understanding *when* different techniques can be used. Frequently, the type of analysis we use comes down to the level of measurement of our variables. Therefore, being able to identify the level of measurement of variables is a critical skill for correctly utilising statistical analysis. Sometimes it will be obvious when you made an error – for instance, using a scatterplot for a nominal variable – and other times you may be none the wiser. Throughout this chapter we will make it clear when we can and cannot use different types of analysis based on our variables.

SCATTERPLOTS

We can use scatterplots as a visual way to determine the association between two variables. Since we looked at scatterplots extensively in Chapter 8, we will not spend much time on them here. However, it is good to keep in mind *when* we can use scatterplots. Do you remember? We can use scatterplots when we have *interval- or ratio-level x* and *y* variables. Aesthetically, we might not want to use scatterplots to determine association. For example, if the data is clumped or spaced out in certain ways, using a scatterplot can be counterproductive. Without adding formal statistical tests, like correlation analysis (which we'll see later in the chapter), scatterplots can only provide a descriptive understanding of association. For example, we can determine if there's a positive or negative or no association between two variables. However, as we observed in Chapter 8, scatterplots can be an effective tool for communicating relationships in data.

If we try to use scatterplots with nominal or ordinal-level variables, the plots will immediately stand out as wrong. As in Chapter 8, we can use bar plots to visually examine nominal- and ordinal-level variables. Researchers also commonly use crosstabulations (usually shortened to crosstabs) to examine the relationship between two nominal- and/or ordinal-level variables.

CROSSTABULATIONS

Crosstabs are a good initial way of analysing quantitative relationships. We have already seen a version of crosstabs when we looked at frequency distributions of individual variables in Chapter 7. Now we are, in essence, looking at the frequency distributions of two variables – one specified as the outcome variable and one as the predictor variable. We only want to use crosstabs with *nominal- and/or ordinal-level* variables. In fact, crosstabs are best with nominal and ordinal variables that only have a few categories. This is because crosstabs are $n \times n$ tables, where n is the number of categories of each variable. Hence, variables with a large number of categories creates a very large table. For example, if both our outcome and predictor variables have seven categories then we will have a table with 49 cells (7×7). Ideally, the variables in our crosstab should have at most seven categories and we should generally keep the number of cells less than 40. This suggestion is for purely aesthetic reasons and if you want to create an enormous table feel free (but no one will want to look at it).

What should we do if we have a variable with many categories and we want to use crosstabs? Depending on the values of the variable, we can collapse some of the categories, provided it makes sense to do so and we do not lose critical information in the variable. For example, let's say we have a variable for income with 10 categories. We could collapse the variable by combining two adjacent categories so we now have five categories. Another example common with agree/disagree Likert-type survey questions is to collapse all the 'agree' and 'disagree' categories together, leaving a three-category variable. For example, researchers will collapse the 'strongly agree', 'agree', and 'somewhat agree' categories into one 'agree' category, do the same for the 'disagree' categories, and leave the middle 'neither agree nor disagree' category as is.

Though it might make our crosstabs more aesthetically appealing, can you identify a potential problem with collapsing categories in this manner? When we collapse categories, we are effectively saying the original categories are equivalent. For the income variable example, depending on the values, collapsing lower values might wash out the difference between people who are above and below the poverty line. By collapsing higher values, we might be equating people with six-figure incomes and billionaires. For the Likert-type variable example, there is probably a large difference between people who 'somewhat agree' and 'strongly agree' with some statement (e.g., whether voter fraud is a serious problem in UK elections). Hence, it is not always the best idea to collapse and combine categories purely for aesthetic purposes.

OK, then, when should we collapse categories? There are two common reasons why researchers will collapse variables – one driven by data and one driven by theory. First, if one or more categories have very few observations it can cause problems with statistical tests. Therefore, we might collapse the category with an adjacent category if it substantively makes sense; we could also just remove those observations from our data. For example, let's imagine the 'strongly agree' category in a Likert-type variable only has two observations while the other categories have observations in the tens or hundreds. We could combine the 'strongly agree' and 'agree' categories, and relabel the category 'strongly agree/agree'. In this example, we would also want to collapse the 'strongly disagree' and 'disagree' categories, and relabel the category 'strongly disagree/disagree'. We want to do this so that the variable is symmetrical. Second, we might have a theoretical reason for collapsing a variable's categories. For example, we might hypothesize that survey respondents who voted for the winning political party will be more accepting of the election results than respondents who voted for a political party that didn't win. To test this hypothesis, we would create a winner/loser dummy variable, where all the parties that didn't win, and thus all the respondents who voted for those parties, would be collapsed into the loser category.

What if we have interval- or ratio-level variables and we want to use crosstabs? In short, *do not* use crosstabs; use something else (e.g., scatterplots, correlation analysis). We could collapse values to create ordinal variables but, as the previous examples demonstrated, we are likely to lose critical information from the data. As a general rule of thumb, we never want to do anything where we lose information (i.e., variation) from our data.

There are a number of ways, via different packages and functions, to do crosstabs in R. However, I have yet to find a crosstab function in R that combines simplicity of code and desired functionality.[1] With that caveat, let's create a couple of crosstabs using the `tabyl()` function from the `janitor` package and variables from the `VF England.csv` dataset. First, we'll set our working directory, load `tidyverse`, and read in `VF England.csv`.

```
setwd("C:/QSSD/Chapter 10 - Bivariate Analysis")
getwd()

library(tidyverse)
vf_england <- read_csv("VF England.csv")
```

Let's look at the relationship between respondents' beliefs that voter fraud is a serious problem in UK elections (`vfproblem`) and their vote in the 2017 UK general election (`vote2017_dum`). If you remember from previous chapters, we need to reorder the values for `vfproblem` to go from 'Strongly disagree' to 'Strongly agree'. We'll again do this with the `factor()` function and `levels =` option, within the `mutate()` function, and we'll save the reordered version as `vfproblem1`. As a reminder about `vote2017_dum`, the 'Winner' category are respondents who voted for the Conservative Party and the 'Loser' category are respondents who voted for a different party.

---

[1] In the first edition of this book, we used the popular `CrossTable()` function from the `descr` package. Although the `CrossTable()` function works well, I found dealing with all the default options quite annoying.

```
vf_england <- vf_england %>%
             mutate(vfproblem1 = factor(vfproblem,
                    levels = c("Strongly disagree","Disagree",
                    "Slightly disagree","Neither agree nor disagree",
                    "Slightly agree","Agree","Strongly agree")))


vf_england %>%
  count(vfproblem1)
# A tibble: 7 x 2
  vfproblem1                    n
  <fct>                      <int>
1 Strongly disagree           112
2 Disagree                    245
3 Slightly disagree           302
4 Neither agree nor disagree  670
5 Slightly agree              398
6 Agree                       167
7 Strongly agree              140


vf_england %>%
  count(vote2017_dum)
# A tibble: 3 x 2
  vote2017_dum     n
  <chr>         <int>
1 Loser          919
2 Winner         757
3 <NA>           358
```

Both of these variables look good – we'll just need to filter out the missing values for vote2017_dum.

Let's do a simple crosstab using the tabyl() function. In crosstabs, the row variable represents our outcome variable and the column variable represents our predictor (or explanatory) variable. After specifying the data (vf_england) and filtering out the missing values for vote2017_dum, we specify our row variable (vfproblem1) and then our column variable (vote2017_dum) in the tabyl() function.

```
library(janitor)


vf_england %>%
  filter(!is.na(vote2017_dum)) %>%
  tabyl(vfproblem1, vote2017_dum)
                  vfproblem1 Loser Winner
           Strongly disagree    63     37
                    Disagree   118    101
           Slightly disagree   149    109
  Neither agree nor disagree   302    202
              Slightly agree   170    172
                       Agree    71     70
              Strongly agree    46     66
```

The output provides the cell frequencies for the different combinations of `vfproblem1` and `vote2017_dum`. What do we see? Well, it's a bit tricky to figure out and put into words. We could use the cell frequencies for interpretations – for instance, there are more respondents who voted for a candidate from a losing party than voted a candidate from the Conservative Party who said 'Strongly disagree' – but using cell frequencies can be confusing.

A better way to make crosstabs easy to understand and interpret is to add column percentages. Why column percentages? As our column variable is our predictor variable, we want to know how each value of `vote2017_dum` relates to our outcome variable `vfproblem1` – here, what percentage of people who voted for a candidate of the losing and winning parties responded 'Strongly disagree', etc. Since our row variable is our outcome variable, we can think of a crosstab as an inverted x–y plot. As x increases, we want to know what happens to y; the difference for crosstabs is that y is pointed downwards instead of upwards as in scatterplots.

To add column percentages and clean up the crosstab, we'll add a series of `adorn_` functions from the `janitor` package. We'll include the `adorn_percentages()` function and specify `"col"` for the column percentages. We'll use the `adorn_pct_formatting(digits = 1)` function to format the percentages to have one decimal place. Lastly, we'll include the cell frequencies in parentheses by including the `adorn_ns()` function (the ns part refers to the number of observations (i.e., Ns)). Although percentages are easier to understand, it is good practice to include cell frequencies for reference purposes. We connect all of these functions using the pipe operator `%>%`.

```
vf_england %>%
  filter(!is.na(vote2017_dum)) %>%
  tabyl(vfproblem1, vote2017_dum) %>%
  adorn_percentages("col") %>%
  adorn_pct_formatting(digits = 1) %>%
  adorn_ns()
                    vfproblem1       Loser        Winner
            Strongly disagree   6.9%   (63)   4.9%    (37)
                     Disagree  12.8%  (118)  13.3%   (101)
             Slightly disagree 16.2%  (149)  14.4%   (109)
 Neither agree nor disagree    32.9%  (302)  26.7%   (202)
               Slightly agree  18.5%  (170)  22.7%   (172)
                        Agree   7.7%   (71)   9.2%    (70)
                Strongly agree   5.0%   (46)   8.7%    (66)
```

The cells include the column percentages and the column frequencies in parentheses. If we add up a column's percentages it will equal 100%. To interpret the results, we need to focus on the column percentages. For example, the first column tells us that 6.9% of respondents who voted for a candidate from a losing party said they 'Strongly disagree' that voter fraud is a serious problem, while 5% said they 'Strongly agree'. Overall, it appears that a greater percentage of respondents who voted for a candidate from a losing party disagreed, at some level, or were neutral on the seriousness of voter fraud as a problem. Meanwhile, a greater percentage of respondents who voted for a candidate from the winning party agreed, at some level, on the seriousness of voter fraud. This suggests that respondents' views on the seriousness of voter fraud in UK elections in 2019 (the time of the survey) are related to their vote choice during the 2017 election.

Let's look at another example of crosstabs. This time we'll use vfproblem1 as our outcome variable and education as our predictor variable. We are now looking to see if there's a relationship between respondents' education level and beliefs about voter fraud. The education variable is not currently labelled and so we'll add labels to make the crosstab clearer. To add the labels, we'll use the recode() function and specify that 1 = Low, 2 = Medium, and 3 = High. We'll wrap the as_factor() function around the recode() function to convert the variable to a factor and maintain the label ordering, and create a new variable called education1. All of this is specified within the mutate() function. Instead of saving education1 as a new variable in our dataset, let's only include the labelling as part of the piping.

```
vf_england %>%
  mutate(education1 = as_factor(recode(education,
        `1` = "Low", `2` = "Medium", `3` = "High"))) %>%
  tabyl(vfproblem1, education1) %>%
  adorn_percentages("col") %>%
  adorn_pct_formatting(digits = 1) %>%
  adorn_ns()
              vfproblem1       Low        Medium        High
       Strongly disagree    4.3%  (25)   6.0%  (53)   6.1%  (34)
                Disagree    9.4%  (55)  11.1%  (99)  16.3%  (91)
        Slightly disagree  11.3%  (66)  14.7% (131)  18.8% (105)
Neither agree nor disagree 39.6% (232)  32.7% (291)  26.3% (147)
          Slightly agree   16.9%  (99)  20.1% (179)  21.5% (120)
                   Agree    9.9%  (58)   8.4%  (75)   6.1%  (34)
          Strongly agree    8.7%  (51)   6.9%  (61)   5.0%  (28)
```

What do we see? For respondents with a low level of education, higher percentages 'Agree' and 'Strongly agree' that voter fraud is a serious problem than respondents with a high level of education. We also see that for respondents with a high level of education, higher percentages 'Strongly disagree', 'Disagree', and 'Slightly disagree' that voter fraud is a serious problem than respondents with a low level of education. This suggests that respondents' education level may have an effect on voter fraud beliefs.

If we stopped here in our examination of whether vote choice and education affect people's beliefs on voter fraud, our analysis would be satisfactory for news stories and the general public. We have only looked at percentages and have a provided an *eyeball* or *superficial* assessment of the data. We have not determined whether or not these relationships are statistically significant or the strength and direction of the relationships. In the next section, we consider chi-squared significance tests before moving on to measures of association.[2]

[2]In the first edition of this book, the discussion of measures of association came before chi-squared tests. These sections are flipped in this edition because if the chi-square test shows a non-significant relationship then we do not calculate measures of association. This logic parallels interpreting linear and generalised linear regression models later in the book.

CHI-SQUARED ANALYSIS

There are a number of ways we could assess statistical significance in bivariate analysis, but we will focus on the canonical chi-squared (χ^2) analysis. Chi-squared analysis, through using a chi-squared test, examines the data on the relationship between two categorical variables and compares it to a hypothetical no relationship. If the data, or relationship, is different enough from the hypothetical no relationship, then the relationship is considered statistically significant. In a crosstab setting, the chi-squared test looks at the crosstab's cell frequencies (called the *observed frequencies*) and then compares them to *expected frequencies* which are calculated by using the margins of the crosstab. The test uses the differences in all the cells to calculate a χ^2 value, then calculates the degrees of freedom (which is simplify the number of rows minus 1 multiplied by the number of columns minus 1). Using the degrees of freedom, the χ^2 value is compared to a critical value for $p \leq 0.05$ in a χ^2 distribution table. If the χ^2 value is equal to or greater than the critical value then the relationship is statistically significant. We could do all this by hand, which is very boring, but instead we will let R do the hard work for us.[3]

We should note that the chi-squared test does *not* tell you what the 'right' relationship is. It merely assesses the statistical significance between two categorical variables. As with all bivariate analyses, it is not taking into account, or controlling, for the influence of any other variables. Additionally, as is common with many statistical significance tests, the chi-squared test is inflated by sample size, which means that with large samples you are more likely to find statistical significance. Finally, the true usefulness of the chi-squared test comes with combining its findings with measures of association and crosstab column percentages. This combination of information allows us to make statistical and substantive sense of bivariate relationships.

We'll use the `chisq.test()` function to perform a chi-squared test between respondents' voter fraud beliefs and vote choice in 2017. Using our `tabyl()` function set-up, we'll remove the `adorn_` functions and add the `chisq.test()` function – again, all connected with the pipe operator `%>%`. We don't need to specify the variables in the `chisq.test()` function as they are being pulled in from the `tabyl()` function.

```
vf_england %>%
  filter(!is.na(vote2017_dum)) %>%
  tabyl(vfproblem1, vote2017_dum) %>%
  chisq.test()


    Pearson's Chi-squared test

data:  .
X-squared = 22.262, df = 6, p-value = 0.001085
```

We see that the χ^2 value is 22.26 with 6 degrees of freedom. Again, we could, if we wanted to, take this information and look up in a χ^2 table whether the relationship is statistically significant, but R also calculates the exact probability. The *p*-value is 0.001. Since $p \leq 0.05$, the relationship is

---

[3]You can find details of the chi-squared test formulas and procedures, by hand, in a plethora of other texts such as Pollock (2015).

statistically significant. Therefore, *there is a statistically significant relationship between respondents' vote choice in the 2017 election and the level of agreement that voter fraud is a serious problem in UK elections.* To make the relationship between predictor and outcome variables clearer, we could rephrase this as *respondents' vote choice in the 2017 election is a statistically significant predictor of their level of agreement that voter fraud is a serious problem in UK elections.*

For our second example, let's run a chi-squared test between respondents' voter fraud beliefs and their level of education. Since we didn't save `education1` as a new variable previously, we need to include the labelling code again (just copy and paste the previous code).

```
vf_england %>%
  mutate(education1 = as_factor(recode(education,
          `1` = "Low", `2` = "Medium", `3` = "High"))) %>%
  tabyl(vfproblem1, education1) %>%
  chisq.test()


    Pearson's Chi-squared test

data:  .
X-squared = 55.12, df = 12, p-value = 1.723e-07
```

What do we find? We see that the χ^2 value is 52.12 with 12 degrees of freedom and that the *p*-value is 1.723×10^{-7} (e-07 simply means to move the decimal point seven places to the left (i.e., 0.0000001723)). Since $p \leq 0.05$, the relationship is statistically significant. Therefore, *there is a statistically significant relationship between respondents' education level and the level of agreement that voter fraud is a serious problem in UK elections.* Again, we can make the relationship between predictor and outcome variables clearer by rephrasing this as *respondents' education level is a statistically significant predictor of their level of agreement that voter fraud is a serious problem in UK elections.*

Using chi-squared analysis, we have determined that both vote choice and education are statistically significant predictors of voter fraud beliefs. In the next section, we calculate measures of association to determine the strength and direction (if possible) of the relationships.

MEASURES OF ASSOCIATION

In addition to cell frequency percentages and statistical significance tests, we would like to have some measure to tell us the strength of the relationship (e.g., weak, moderate, or strong) and the direction of the relationship (i.e., positive or negative). We can use column percentages to get a basic idea of the strength and direction, but we prefer something more concrete.

To do this, we look at measures of association for bivariate relationships. There are a considerable number of measures of association which all provide roughly similar answers, but are only applicable in certain circumstances. All of these measures calculate a value that tells us whether a relationship exists and the strength, but tells us nothing about statistical significance. We should only calculate and discuss measures of association for statistically significant relationships.

We will first consider measures for nominal-level variables and then measures for ordinal-level variables.

Measures of Association with Nominal Variables

When we have one or two nominal-level variables, we can only consider the strength of the relationship and not the direction. Why? Because it makes no sense to discuss increasing or decreasing nominal-level variables. Therefore, we need to consider types of measures of association that do not consider the direction of relationships. There are a number of options, but we will simply focus on one measure: Cramér's *V*. Cramér's *V* is bounded between 0 and 1, and tells us the strength of the relationship when we have at least one nominal variable. For understanding and interpreting the strength of the relationship based on the value of Cramér's *V*, we can use the following rule of thumb (Weisburd and Britt 2007):

- 0 → no association
- Near 0 (0.01–0.3) → weak association
- Around the midpoint (0.31–0.69) → moderate association
- Near 1 (0.7–0.99) → strong association
- 1 → perfect association

With real data, we are unlikely to ever find a measure of association of 0 or 1. Because the above range is a rule of thumb, we usually qualify the strength of the associations by combining terms – such as 'weakly moderate', 'moderately weak', 'moderately strong', etc. This helps us differentiate a value such as 0.31 (which would be 'weakly moderate') from 0.68 (which would be 'moderately strong').

Let's calculate Cramér's *V* for the relationship between respondents' vote choice in 2017 and voter fraud beliefs. We are using Cramér's *V* because vote choice is a nominal-level variable. We'll use the `CramerV()` function from the `DescTools` package, where the *x* variable is first and the *y* variable is second.

```
library(DescTools)

CramerV(vf_england$vote2017_dum, vf_england$vfproblem1)
[1] 0.115251
```

Cramér's *V* is 0.115, which indicates there is a weak relationship or association between respondents' vote choice in 2017 and voter fraud beliefs. Again, though, measures of association for nominal variables do not and cannot tell us about the direction of a relationship.

Measures of Association with Ordinal Variables

All the measures of association for when you have *two* ordinal variables are bounded between –1 and 1, where the sign of the coefficient tells you whether the relationship is positive or negative. Understanding the strength of the relationship for ordinal variables is the same as we talked about with nominal variable measures.

What specific measures of association are available when we have two ordinal variables? Again, there are a plethora of options, but we will focus on two specific measures. The first is called Kendall's tau-B and is used when both variables have the same number of categories.

For example, if the table has the same number of columns and rows (e.g., 2 × 2, 3 × 3, etc.) we can use Kendall's tau-B. The second measure is called Goodman and Kruskal's gamma, which sounds like a type of fungal cream, and can be used regardless of the number of categories of each ordinal variable (e.g., 2 × 2, 2 × 3, 3 × 2). We could just use Goodman and Kruskal's gamma for all tables, but it is worth seeing the commonly used Kendall's tau-B. As mentioned, all the different measures give you roughly the same values and so it is not the end of the world if you choose the 'wrong' one.

Let's calculate the measure of association between respondents' education level and voter fraud beliefs. Education has three categories, while voter fraud beliefs has seven categories. Therefore, we should use Goodman and Kruskal's gamma. We will use the conveniently named function `GoodmanKruskalGamma()` from the `DescTools` package. In the `GoodmanKruskalGamma()` argument the *x* variable (or predictor variable) is listed first and then the *y* variable (or outcome variable). We don't need to label the education values for the test and so we'll just use the `education` variable.

```
GoodmanKruskalGamma(vf_england$education, vf_england$vfproblem1)
[1] -0.1123749
```

We get a measure of association of –0.112 for gamma. We interpret this value as education having a negative and weak association with voter fraud beliefs. This means that as a respondent's education level increases, they have lower agreement that voter fraud is a serious problem in UK elections. We could also say that as a respondent's education level increases, they have higher disagreement that voter fraud is a serious problem in UK elections.

Now, let's do a Kendall's tau-B test on this relationship. Why is this wrong? Because Kendall's tau-B should only be used when a crosstab has the same number of columns and rows. We will use the function `KendallTauB()` from the `DescTools` package for this test.

```
KendallTauB(vf_england$education, vf_england$vfproblem1)
[1] -0.08138494
```

Notice that R did not complain when we ran this test. Statistical programs will often let us do things that we probably should not do; it assumes we know what we are doing. We see a value of –0.081, which is similar to the gamma value, and we interpret the value as indicating a negative and weak association. As mentioned, all of these measures of association usually give us roughly the same answers even though they were designed for different circumstances.

Table 10.1 specifies when we can use the different measures of association we examined in this section.

Table 10.1 Use of different measures of association

Level of measurement	Measure of association
2 nominal variables	Cramér's *V*
2 ordinal variables: equal nos. of categories	Kendall's tau-B, Goodman and Kruskal's gamma
2 ordinal variables: unequal nos. of categories	Goodman and Kruskal's gamma
1 nominal, 1 ordinal variable	Cramér's *V*

CORRELATION

In this last section of the chapter, we will look at correlation analysis. Correlation analysis was originally developed to examine the relationship between predictor and outcome variables at the interval and/or ratio level. Hence, correlation is a measure of association for interval/ratio variables. However, researchers often look at correlations for all types of variables regardless of the level of measurement. We also often look at correlations to assess the relationships between multiple predictors.[4] For our purposes, here, we will stick to examining correlations between interval/ratio-level variables.

Correlation analysis provides a coefficient that tells us, on average, how much two variables (x and y) move together relative to their respective means. We will first look at Pearson's correlation, which provides a correlation coefficient (r) for a linear relationship; thus, it assumes a linear relationship between x and y. Similar to measures of association for ordinal variables, correlation analysis provides the direction and strength of a relationship between two (or more) variables. Because r is standardised to take a value between –1 and 1 ($r \in [-1,1]$), it does not matter how the variables are scaled. For example, r will not be affected whether you use a variable measured in pounds or one measured in thousands of pounds.

We understand the strength and direction of the relationship in a similar manner to our previous measures of association. The sign of r simply tells us whether the relationship is positive or negative.

We can also add qualifiers to the interpretations as we did before with terms like 'weakly moderate', 'moderately strong', etc. When we are using real data, it is very unlikely that we will find correlations of –1, 0, or 1.[5] We can also use r to determine the amount of variance explained in our outcome variable from our predictor variable. To do so, we simply multiply $r \times r$ and we get a value known as R^2 which is called the coefficient of determination.[6] For example, let's assume we are using a person's weekly whisky intake to predictor a person's weekly wine intake, and we find that $r = 0.45$ (indicating a positive, moderate relationship). Hence, we can say that 20.25% ($0.45 \times 0.45 = 0.2025$; $0.2025 \times 100 = 20.25\%$) of a person's weekly wine intake can be explained by their whisky intake.

Before we look at correlations in R, there are a couple of caveats to consider. As you have probably heard sometime in your life, *correlation is not causation*.[7] Correlation really only tells us how two variables 'hang together', and not whether x causes y. This is evident by the fact that the correlation value does not change if we switch variables from x to y or from y to x. In the above example explaining wine intake, *we* decided that whisky intake was the predictor and wine intake was the outcome variable. We could flip it around and it would be the case that 20.25% of a person's weekly whisky intake can be explained by their wine intake.

---

[4]In Chapter 12, we will further examine the use of correlations for predictor variables.

[5]How do we get a correlation of 1 with real data? Correlate a variable with itself.

[6]We will use and discuss R^2 more in Chapter 11.

[7]For your entertainment, there are a number of examples of bizarre correlations you can find at http://www.tylervigen.com/spurious-correlations. This site doesn't appear to have been updated in a while, but it is still fun!

We can also test for statistical significance in correlation analysis. This tells us whether the correlation we observe in our sample data is expected to be true in the population. The main caveat is that even if we find there is a significant correlation, we are only comparing two variables in isolation and not taking into account other factors; more on this in the next chapter. Further, if we have an outcome variable at the interval/ratio level, particularly if we have a predictor variable at the interval/ratio level, we are better off using linear regression (specifically, multiple regression, which we will use in the next chapter) than correlation analysis.

Before we perform correlation analysis, let's take a look at a few scatterplots demonstrating different general types of correlations.

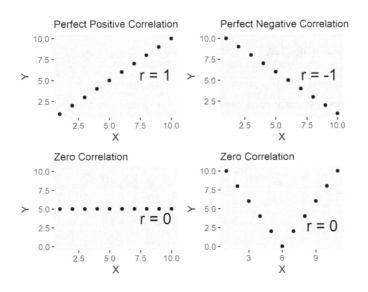

The figure shows four different *extreme* types of correlation. The top left-hand scatterplot demonstrates a perfect positive correlation ($r = 1$), where each increase is x is matched with an equal increase in y. The top right-hand scatterplot shows a perfect negative correlation ($r = –1$), where each increase in x is matched with an equal decrease in y. The bottom two scatterplots show two different scenarios where there is no correlation between x and y ($r = 0$). The bottom left-hand plot shows that when x increases, y remains the same value (here, y can be considered a con-stant). The bottom right-hand plot simply shows a relationship where y is unrelated to changes in x. It is very unlikely that we will run into correlations that look like these when using real data, but they provide a visual sense of correlations.

Next, let's perform a correlation analysis using the 2020 Scottish Index of Multiple Deprivation dataset (simd2020.csv). The base function for correlations in R is simply cor() followed by the y and x variables. We will look at the percentage of psychiatric medication prescriptions (pct_depress) and the percentage of employment deprivation (pct_employment_deprived) in a datazone. As in the previous chapters, we need to create both of these variables from the original `simd2020.csv` dataset. Since both variables have a few missing values, we will include the option `use = "complete.obs"` in the `cor()` argument.

```
simd <- read_csv("simd2020.csv", na = "*")

simd <- simd %>%
          rename_with(tolower) %>%
          mutate(pct_depress = depress*100,
                 pct_employment_deprived = employment_rate*100)

cor(simd$pct_depress, simd$pct_employment_deprived, use = "complete.obs")
[1] 0.8022867
```

We find a correlation of 0.802, which indicates a strong, positive relationship between employment deprivation and psychiatric medication prescriptions percentages in Scottish datazones.

To also test for statistical significance, we can use the `cor.test()` function. As with `cor()`, we put the *y* variable first followed by the *x* variable in the argument. To deal with the missing values, we include the option `na.action = na.rm` in the `cor.test()` argument.

```
cor.test(simd$pct_depress, simd$pct_employment_deprived,
  na.action = na.rm)

    Pearson's product-moment correlation

data:  simd$pct_depress and simd$pct_employment_deprived
t = 112.21, df = 6971, p-value < 2.2e-16
alternative hypothesis: true correlation is not equal to 0
95 percent confidence interval:
 0.7937622 0.8104960
sample estimates:
      cor
0.8022867
```

The output tells us we are using Pearson's correlation followed by information about the significance test. At the bottom of the output is the correlation value – the same as we obtained using the `cor()` function. As before, for assessing statistical significance we only care about whether the *p*-value is less than or equal to 0.05. The output also conveniently tells us the alternative hypothesis and thus the null hypothesis is that the *true correlation is equal to 0*. Since, *p* is below 0.05, we can reject the null and conclude that there is a *statistically significant correlation between datazones' percentage of employment deprivation and psychiatric medication prescription percentage.*

Visualising Correlation

Using the skills we developed in Chapter 8, we can create a data visualisation illustrating the correlation between pct_depress and pct_employment_deprived. Let's replicate the scatterplots we created in Chapter 8 with pct_depress on the *y*-axis and pct_employment_deprived on the *x*-axis. We will globally set pct_depress and pct_employment_deprived by including the mapping = aes() argument in the ggplot() argument. By doing this, we do not need to specify the variables in each geom_ function.

To represent the Pearson's correlation, we'll add a **linear best-fit line** using the geom_smooth() function and specify that method = "lm" (a linear model line) and se = FALSE (don't plot the standard errors).[8] By default, the geom_smooth() generates a solid blue line, but we can customise the line to our preferences (e.g., change the colour, size, etc.).

Let's also add the correlation value to the scatterplot as a text label. The simple way to do this is with the annotate() function from the ggplot2() package. The annotate() function is good for adding brief text to plots. In the annotate() argument, we first specify we are adding "text", which is a short-cut representing a geom_text() layer. Next, we'll include the text we want to add to the plot (label = "r = .802"). Then, we specify where we want the label using (*x,y*) coordinates. The *x* value represents where the label is centred on the *x*-axis and the *y* value represents the height of the label on the, uh, *y*-axis. Below, we'll set the label at x = 35 and y = 15. Finally, we'll increase the default text size (size = 5). We often need to play around with specifications to get the text label where we want.

Lastly, we'll include all the accoutrements that we used in Chapter 8 to dress up the plot.

```
simd %>%
  filter(!is.na(pct_depress) & !is.na(pct_employment_deprived)) %>%
ggplot(mapping = aes(x = pct_employment_deprived, y = pct_depress)) +
  geom_point(position = "jitter", alpha = .1) +
  geom_smooth(method = "lm", se = FALSE) +
  labs(x = "Percentage Employment Deprived",
    y = "Percentage Prescribed Psychiatric Medication",
    title = "Correlation Between Psychiatric Medication &
            Employment Deprivation") +
  theme_minimal() +
  theme(
    plot.title = element_text(size=12)
  ) +
  annotate("text", label = "r = .802", x = 35, y = 15, size = 5)
```

---

[8]We'll explain and discuss best-fit lines in relation to linear regression in Chapter 11.

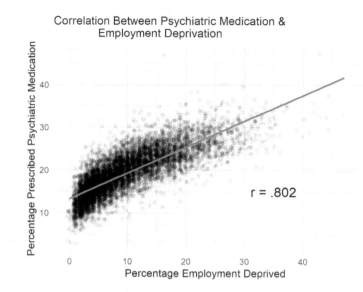

The scatterplot shows a blue line cutting through the data points and our text appears at the bottom right of the scatterplot. Overall, the scatterplot demonstrates there is a positive and strong correlation between the percentage of employment deprivation and the percentage of psychiatric medication prescriptions in Scottish datazones.

Spearman's Correlation Analysis

Although Pearson's correlation is probably the most commonly used correlation measure, many researchers find the linear relationship assumption too restrictive and prefer using less restrictive alternatives. Let's consider one alternative correlation measure: Spearman's correlation. Spearman only considers whether the relationship is increasing or decreasing *monotonically*. So as one variable increases, does the other one increase (positive) or decrease (negative), regardless of the shape of the increase or decrease (i.e., it does not need to be linear)? Additionally, we can use *ordinal-level* variables with Spearman, whereas Pearson technically requires interval- and/or ratio-level variables. Spearman's correlation is also bounded between −1 and 1, and we interpret the strength of the relationship in the same way as before. One notation difference is that instead of denoting the correlation value by *r* it is now denoted by ρ.

To perform the Spearman correlation, we again use the cor.test() function, but now specify that we want Spearman (method = "spearman").

```
cor.test(simd$pct_depress, simd$pct_employment_deprived,
         method = "spearman", use = "complete.obs")
Warning in cor.test.default(simd$pct_depress, simd$pct_employment_
deprived, :
Cannot compute exact p-value with ties


    Spearman's rank correlation rho
```

```
data:   simd$pct_depress and simd$pct_employment_deprived
S = 9621538878, p-value < 2.2e-16
alternative hypothesis: true rho is not equal to 0
sample estimates:
      rho
0.8297305
```

The R output is very similar to the output for Pearson's correlation and we look again for the *p*-value and the correlation, which is at the bottom of the output underneath. We see that Spearman's correlation is 0.830, slightly stronger than Pearson's, and the relationship is statistically significant. (The warning message in the output is essentially telling us that the significance test is not based on the default exact *p*-value and instead it is based on the asymptotic *t* approximation. This is because there are observations in the two variables with the same value (or rank) – a quirk of the Spearman correlation test. Normally, we can ignore this warning and we can suppress it by including `exact = FALSE` in the `cor.test()` argument.)

Correlation Analysis with `tidymodels`

For our purposes performing correlation analysis using the `cor()` and `cor.test()` functions from base R works great. However, we can also perform correlation analysis using functions from the `corrr` package which is part of the `tidymodels` package. After loading the `corrr` package (`library(corrr)`), we use the `select()` function to specify the variables to analyse and then the `correlate()` function. Instead of filtering out the missing values, we'll include the `use = "complete.obs"` option in the `correlate()` function. The default correlation measure is Pearson, but we can specify Spearman if we prefer. As with most `tidymodels` approaches, we'll connect all the functions with the pipe operator `%>%`.

```
library(corrr)

simd %>%
  select(pct_depress, pct_employment_deprived) %>%
  correlate(use = "complete.obs")

Correlation method: 'pearson'
Missing treated using: 'complete.obs'
# A tibble: 2 x 3
  term                     pct_depress pct_employment_deprived
  <chr>                          <dbl>                   <dbl>
1 pct_depress                       NA                   0.802
2 pct_employment_deprived        0.802                      NA
```

The output is a full correlation matrix (actually a `tibble` instead of a matrix) with NA on the diagonal instead of 1. We see that the correlation value, 0.802, is the same value we obtained from the `cor()` and `cor.test()` functions. If we just wanted the lower triangle of the matrix, we can include the `shave()` function with the argument empty.

```
simd %>%
  select(pct_depress, pct_employment_deprived) %>%
  correlate(use = "complete.obs") %>%
  shave()


Correlation method: 'pearson'
Missing treated using: 'complete.obs'
# A tibble: 2 x 3
  term                    pct_depress pct_employment_deprived
  <chr>                         <dbl>                   <dbl>
1 pct_depress                      NA                      NA
2 pct_employment_deprived       0.802                      NA
```

If we only want to perform correlation analysis on two variables, `corrr` is probably overkill. The main usefulness of the `corrr` package is when we want to calculate a correlation matrix for multiple variables and carry out additional analyses and/or data management using other `tidyverse` and `tidymodels` functions.

As a quick demonstration, let's create and visualise a correlation matrix using the `corrr` package. Along with `pct_depress` and `pct_employment_deprived`, let's also correlate the percentage of housing units without broadband (`broadband`) and the percentage of people living in overcrowded housing units (`overcrowded_rate`). We'll create the percentage versions of these two variables using the `mutate()` function, which we'll name as `pct_broadband` and `pct_overcrowded`. Next, we'll use the `select()` function to only include these four variables in the analysis. Lastly, we include the `correlate()` and `shave()` functions as above.

```
simd %>%
  mutate(pct_broadband = broadband*100,
         pct_overcrowded = overcrowded_rate*100) %>%
  select(pct_depress:pct_overcrowded) %>%
  correlate(use = "complete.obs") %>%
  shave()


Correlation method: 'pearson'
Missing treated using: 'complete.obs'
# A tibble: 4 x 5
  term             pct_depress pct_employment_dep~ pct_broadband pct_
overcrowded
  <chr>                  <dbl>               <dbl>         <dbl>    <dbl>
1 pct_depress               NA                  NA            NA       NA
2 pct_employment_~       0.802                  NA            NA       NA
3 pct_broadband         -0.263              -0.244            NA       NA
4 pct_overcrowded        0.370               0.571        -0.277       NA
```

We see that none of the new correlations are as strong as the correlation between `pct_depress` and `pct_employment_deprived`. However, the correlation between `pct_overcrowded` and `pct_employment_deprived` is 0.571, which indicates a positive moderate correlation.

Let's now generate a full matrix correlation plot by adding the `rplot()` function. The default colours in the `rplot()` function struggle to render weak correlations and so we'll change them to dark blue and dark red to make them more visible. We'll also put the *x*-axis labels at a 45-degree angle by adding `scale_x_discrete(guide = guide_axis(angle = 45))` from the `ggplot2` package; this clearly demonstrates how the `corr` package synchronises with the rest of the `tidyverse`.

```
simd %>%
  mutate(pct_broadband = broadband*100,
         pct_overcrowded = overcrowded_rate*100) %>%
  select(pct_depress:pct_overcrowded) %>%
  correlate(use = "complete.obs") %>%
  rplot(colours = c("dark blue","dark red")) +
  scale_x_discrete(guide = guide_axis(angle = 45))
```

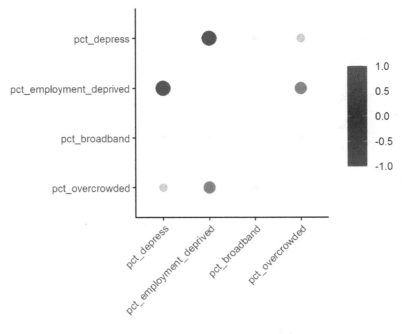

In the correlation plot, we see that the strong correlations are represented by larger and darker shaded circles; for example, the correlation between `pct_depress` and `pct_employment_deprived`. The weaker the correlation, the smaller and lighter shading of the circle.[9]

---

[9]If you are really keen on creating correlation plots, I recommend the `corrplot` package which provides a fairly exhaustive number and variety of customisations.

CONCLUSION

This chapter provided a glimpse of bivariate analysis and how we start statistically testing relationships between variables. Bivariate analysis allows us to determine whether a predictor variable has a statistically significant effect on an outcome variable as well as the strength and, sometimes, direction of the relationship. Going through this chapter, you should have also got the sense that normally *we* determine what are the predictor and outcome variables. In quantitative social science, theory and theory-driven hypotheses still play a major role in determining the analysis.

Bivariate analysis provides a good foundation for testing relationships, but in truth most researchers do not rely on bivariate analysis. The reason, as we will discuss in the next chapter, is that without taking into account the effects of other related predictors, we are less certain that the relationship we observe between a single predictor and outcome variable is correct. To do so, we need to consider types of multivariate analysis, and the linear regression models in the next chapter initiate us into that world.

R Packages Used in This Chapter

- `corrr`
- `DescTools`
- `dplyr` (loaded with `tidyverse`)
- `janitor`
- `readr` (loaded with `tidyverse`)
- `tabyl` (loaded with `janitor`)
- `tidymodels`
- `tidyverse`

R Functions Used in This Chapter

- `adorn_ns()` – add number of observations to `tably` crosstab
- `adorn_pct_formatting()` – format values in `tably` crosstab
- `adorn_percentages()` – add percentages to `tably` crosstab
- `adorn_totals()` – add row and/or column totals to `tably` crosstab
- `annotate()` – add text to `ggplot2` graph
- `as_factor()` – convert variable to factor using `haven` or `forcats` package
- `c()` – concatenate
- `chisq.test()` – chi-square test
- `cor()` – correlation analysis
- `cor.test()` – correlation analysis with significance test
- `correlate()` – correlation analysis using `corrr`
- `count()` – count the number of unique values of a variable or variables using `dplyr` package
- `CramerV()` – Cramér's *V* test

- `factor()` - specify variable as a factor
- `filter()` - subset data based on variables' values using `dplyr` package
- `geom_point()` - ggplot2 scattered points
- `geom_smooth()` - ggplot2 linear and nonlinear lines
- `ggplot()` - base layer for ggplot2
- `GoodmanKruskalGamma()` - Goodman and Kruskal gamma association test
- `is.na()` - checks for missing values (NAs) in variables
- `KendallTauB` - Kendall's tau-B association test
- `labs()` - ggplot2 labels
- `mutate()` - recode variables using `dplyr` package
- `read_csv()` - read in .csv data file using `readr` package
- `recode()` - recode variable using `dplyr` package
- `rename_with()` - rename variable using a function using `dplyr` package
- `rplot()` - plot correlation using `corrr` package
- `scale_x_discrete()` - x-axis aesthetics for discrete variables using `ggplot2` package
- `shave()` - remove lower or upper triangle of correlation matrix using `corrr` package
- `tabyl()` - create a `tably` crosstabulation
- `theme_minimal()` - minimal ggplot2 theme

Additional Resources

Books

- Fox, J. and Weisberg, S. (2018) *An R Companion to Applied Regression*. Sage.
- Harris, J. K. (2020) *Statistics with R: Solving Problems Using Real-World Data*. Sage.
- Long, J. D. and Teetor, P. (2019) *R Cookbook*, 2nd edition. O'Reilly Media.
- Wong, R. S.-K. (2010) *Association Measures*. Sage.

Online

- R-bloggers: https://www.r-bloggers.com/
- Tidymodels: https://www.tidymodels.org/

11

LINEAR REGRESSION AND MODEL BUILDING

Chapter contents

This chapter advances and extends the bivariate analysis from the previous chapter by introducing and examining linear regression. Linear regression is considered the 'backbone' of quantitative social science and multivariate analysis. Understanding how linear regression works provides a grounding and framework for understanding advanced regression methods (see Chapter 13).

We start with the bivariate linear regression model as a means to introduce the concept of ordinary least squares (OLS) estimation. Examining the bivariate model provides a clear and simple way to understand the process of OLS. We also discuss how bivariate regression is subject to issues such as spuriousness and thus we cannot always trust the predicted relationships.

Next we examine multiple regression where we consider several predictors at the same time for explaining our outcome variable. This leads to a discussion of how to build a multiple regression model. The final section of this chapter examines the substance of the multiple regression output. This includes model evaluation, statistical significance testing, substantive variable interpretation, and visualisation of regression results.

By the end of this chapter, you should be able to:

- Identify when you can use linear regression
- Understand the process of OLS
- Understand the difference between bivariate and multiple regression
- Interpret model fit, statistical significance, and coefficients
- Understand concepts behind model building
- Transform predictor variables
- Create visualisations of the linear regression relationships
- Understand substantive significance
- Understand interactions in linear regression

BASICS

In the previous chapter, we reviewed techniques for statistically analysing bivariate relationships between variables with different levels of measurement. An unanswered question was what we can use when our outcome variable is interval or ratio but our predictors are nominal and/or ordinal (we looked at correlation analysis when we have an outcome and predictor at the interval and/or ratio level). The most common technique is linear regression, where we use the OLS procedure to generate estimates of relationships. The benefit of regression is that for an outcome and predictor variable we get the size of the relationship, the direction of the relationship (positive or negative), and the statistical significance all at the same time. More importantly, regression allows us to easily engage in multivariate analysis, where we add in additional predictors to explain an outcome variable. This is called multiple regression and we will explore it later in the chapter. But first, we will explore bivariate regression where we have one outcome variable and one predictor.

Types of Outcome and Predictor Variables

The main requirement for using linear regression is that our outcome variable is at the *interval or ratio level*. That is the *textbook* requirement. In social science, especially outside of fields like economics, we often do not have the luxury of a plethora of interval- and ratio-level variables. Instead, the social sciences are typically 'blessed' with only nominal and ordinal variables. This is particularly true for survey research data.

Therefore, we often follow the rule-of-thumb requirement for linear regression that our outcome variable is at least *ordinal with seven or more categories*. This will make some purists grumpy, but many in QSS suggest that this provides estimates that are 'good enough' for academic research. Analysts in quality publications have even used outcome variables with fewer than seven categories; for example, Carey et al. (2016) use linear regression with a four-value outcome variable (though they check their results with more technically appropriate regression techniques).

Our predictors can be at *any* level of measurement – nominal, ordinal, interval, or ratio. For example, our predictors can be all nominal, or all ratio, or a mix of all types. This is a critical point of emphasis that often confuses students. Every time I teach a regression course, there is at least one student who gets stuck because they believe the predictors all have to be interval or ratio like the outcome variable. Or they think they cannot combine predictors with different levels of measurement. The only difference between the types of predictors is how we interpret the regression results.

BIVARIATE LINEAR REGRESSION

The overall concept here is determining whether our predictor variable (x) has an effect on our outcome variable (y), when our outcome variable is at the interval or ratio level (or when it has seven or more ordered categories). It is exceptionally difficult to determine true *cause and effect* in the social sciences, particularly with secondary data, and therefore we should avoid using terminology like x causes y.[1] Instead, we want to know whether x affects y. Or, more accurately, whether *x is expected to affect y*.

Since we are thinking of the relationship between x and y as a linear relationship, we represent the relationship using the equation for a straight line. At some point in your career as a student – whether at the primary, secondary, or university level – you have most likely come across this equation in some form. It probably looked something like this:

$y = a + bx$

or

$y = mx + c$

where y is the y-axis variable, x is the x-axis variable, a (or c) is the y-intercept (the value of y when $x = 0$), and b (or m) is the slope (the change in the value of y with each one-unit increase in x). You may have forgotten this equation, on purpose or not, but we use the same equation to represent the bivariate linear regression model. The only difference is that we substitute in different symbols to reflect the statistical technique.

---

[1]However, social science researchers have recently made strides using causal inference, which requires specific types of research design. See Hernán and Robins (2023) for more information on causal inference.

Our bivariate regression equation looks like this:

$$y = \alpha + \beta x + \varepsilon$$

where y is our outcome variable (still the y-axis variable), x is our predictor variable (still the x-axis variable), α is our intercept or constant (still the y-intercept), β is our regression coefficient (equivalent to a generic slope), and ε is our error term (which we will talk more about with the OLS process below). Why do we use Greek letters instead of Latin letters for the intercept, coefficient, and error term? In statistics, we use Greek letters to represent population values that we do not know before performing some type of analysis (where we get an estimate of the population) and we use Latin letters to represent values that we do know before doing an analysis. For example, we know the values of our predictor variable (x) and our outcome variable (y), but we need to figure out the values for α, β, and ε through doing a statistical analysis.

Because we are usually working with sample data instead of population data, our regression equation actually should be represented using hats^.[2] Our regression equation when using sample data looks like this:

$$\hat{y} = \hat{\alpha} + \hat{\beta}x + \hat{\varepsilon}$$

where $\hat{y}$ is our *predicted value* of y, $\hat{\alpha}$ is our estimated value of the intercept/constant, $\hat{\beta}$ is our estimated value of the coefficient/slope, and $\hat{\varepsilon}$ is our prediction error. x does not have a party hat because we are using its known values to get estimates of everything else.

So, what's the deal with the predicted value of y ($\hat{y}$)? Remember, we want to estimate the effect of x on y. In other words, given any value of x, what is the estimated or predicted value of y? That is why we talk about the predicted value, $\hat{y}$, and not the actual value of y. To figure this out with linear regression, we use OLS estimation.

Ordinary Least Squares Process

The intuition of OLS is quite simple, even if the mathematics might look slightly scary. What OLS does is figure out (i.e., *estimate*) a line that best describes the linear relationship between our predictor variable x and our outcome variable y. This is known as determining a best-fit line between x and y. The look of the line is based on the values of x and y.

Let's create a visualisation of a best-fit line using a scatterplot from the 2020 Scottish Index of Multiple Deprivation dataset (simd2020.csv). We will use the percentage of psychiatric medication prescriptions (pct_depress) as the y variable and the percentage of employment deprivation (pct_employment_deprived) as the x variable. As in the previous chapters, we need to create both of these variables from the original simd2020.csv dataset. If your spidey senses are tingling it is because we are in fact going to create the same visualisation that we did in Chapter 10 to visualise correlation; the only difference is that we'll drop the text label from the plot.[3] Let's do all the steps in one code chunk!

---

[2]When you see ^ (which I typically refer to as a *party hat*) above symbols and letters, it simply indicates that the values are estimated values.

[3]Since we have previously gone through all the code step by step, it is omitted here.

```
setwd("C:/QSSD/Chapter 11 - Linear Regression & Model Building")
getwd()

library(tidyverse)
simd <- read_csv("simd2020.csv", na = "*")

simd <- simd %>%
        rename_with(tolower) %>%
        mutate(pct_depress = depress*100,
               pct_employment_deprived = employment_rate*100)

simd %>%
  filter(!is.na(pct_depress) & !is.na(pct_employment_deprived)) %>%
ggplot(mapping = aes(x = pct_employment_deprived, y = pct_depress)) +
  geom_point(position = "jitter", alpha = .1) +
  geom_smooth(method = "lm", se = FALSE) +
  labs(x = "Percentage Employment Deprived",
       y = "Percentage Prescribed Psychiatric Medication",
       title = "Prescribed Psychiatric Medication by Employment Deprived") +
  theme_minimal() +
  theme(
    plot.title = element_text(size = 12)
  )
```

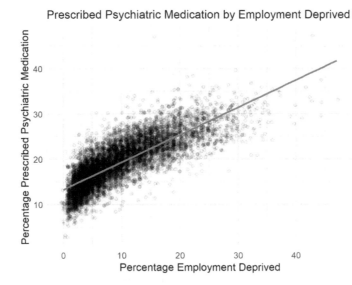

The blue line is our best-fit line using the OLS process. For any given value of x, the corresponding point on the blue line is our predicted value of y ($\hat{y}$). For example, when the percentage of employment deprivation equals 10 ($x = 10$), the predicted percentage of psychiatric medication prescriptions is roughly 19 ($\hat{y} = 19$).

You should notice that not every data point for `pct_employment_deprived` = 10 corresponds to a value of 19 for `pct_depress`. The difference between the predicted value of y ($\hat{y}$) and the observed or actual value of y is our **error** ($\hat{\varepsilon}$ from the regression equation). As an equation, $\hat{\varepsilon} = y - \hat{y}$ for each observation. Therefore, our error term in the regression equation is the sum of all of these errors. When our data points are close to the best-fit line, we will have a smaller error term. When our data points are far from the best-fit line, we will have a larger error term.

Let's use a visualisation to bring home these concepts. Below is a scatterplot showing the relationship between psychiatric medication prescriptions and university attendance for a subset of the `simd` data. The light grey line with a slight downward slope shows the best-fit line between the two variables. The solid circles are the observed or actual values (y) and the open circles on the light grey line are the predicted values ($\hat{y}$). The vertical lines connecting the observed and predicted values represent the *errors*. This is highlighted in red for the second to last observation on the best-fit line.

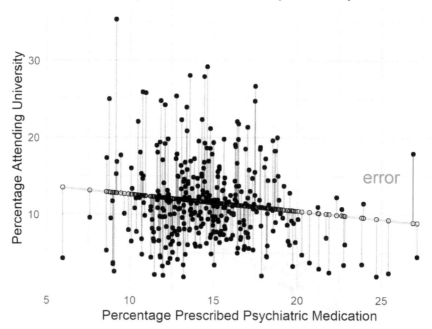

Because any observation may have a positive or negative error, we actually square the error, which has the effect of penalising large errors more than small errors. We can present this summation mathematically as:

$$\hat{\varepsilon}^2 = \sum_{i=1}^{n} \left(y_i - \hat{y} \right)^2$$

where n is the number of observations and i is each observation. This equation is known as the sum of squared residuals (SSR) – residuals is just another name for errors. We can rewrite the above equation to specify the other pieces of the regression equation:

$$\sum_{i=1}^{n} \hat{\varepsilon}^2 = \sum_{i=1}^{n} \left(y_i - \hat{\alpha} - \hat{\beta} x_i \right)^2$$

What OLS does is to find values for $\hat{\alpha}$ and $\hat{\beta}$ that minimise the SSR – in other words, the values of $\hat{\alpha}$ and $\hat{\beta}$ that produce the smallest SSR. Therefore, the OLS estimates are the estimates that give us the least squares of the errors/residuals.[4]

Two final points on the OLS procedure. First, the regression line (best-fit line) will always go through the centre of the data: $(\bar{x}, \bar{y})$. Second, the mean of $\hat{\varepsilon}$ is always 0.[5]

Bivariate Regression Application

Let's now do an example of a bivariate regression. We do not want to spend a lot of time on this because in practice we almost never use bivariate regression; instead we use multiple regression where we include several predictor variables. However, we will examine the default linear regression output in R. We will also consider model evaluation and how to understand the relationship between our outcome and predictor variables.

We'll use the SIMD data again (simd). We will use the percentage of psychiatric medication prescriptions as our outcome variable and the percentage of employment deprivation as our predictor variable. What do you expect the relationship to look like? As we saw in the previous scatterplot, we expect that datazones with higher percentages of employment deprivation will also have higher percentages of psychiatric medication prescriptions.

The standard function for running a linear regression is the lm() function, where 'lm' stands for 'linear model'. We need to put the outcome variable first, then the symbol ~, then the predictor variable, and finally the data we are using. We will create an object, named model.1, to store the regression model information.

```
model.1 <- lm(pct_depress ~ pct_employment_deprived, data = simd)
```

What happened? To actually get the results for a linear regression model we need to ask R to provide a summary of the model, using the conveniently named summary() function and specifying the object (summary(model.1)). We can do this in the line below (or at any time after you run the model) or we can wrap summary() around the original regression code. Let's rerun the model with the summary() function wrapped around the code. Note that, in R, anytime we save an object as the same name of an existing object (e.g., regression model, variable name), it replaces the existing object.

---

[4] We will skip the more mathematical details of OLS estimation since they have been discussed *ad nauseam* in many statistical and econometrics texts (see Greene 2017; Kmenta 1997).

[5] There are a number of assumptions that linear regression and OLS make about the data, variables, and estimates. We will explore these in Chapter 12.

```
summary(model.1 <- lm(pct_depress ~ pct_employment_deprived, data = simd))

Call:
lm(formula = pct_depress ~ pct_employment_deprived, data = simd)

Residuals:
    Min      1Q   Median      3Q      Max
-12.8531  -2.0974  -0.1131  1.9976  23.9995

Coefficients:
                         Estimate Std. Error t value Pr(>|t|)
(Intercept)             13.273687   0.064351   206.3   <2e-16 ***
pct_employment_deprived  0.606264   0.005403   112.2   <2e-16 ***
---
Signif. codes:  0 '***' 0.001 '**' 0.01 '*' 0.05 '.' 0.1 ' ' 1

Residual standard error: 3.203 on 6971 degrees of freedom
  (3 observations deleted due to missingness)
Multiple R-squared:  0.6437,     Adjusted R-squared:  0.6436
F-statistic: 1.259e+04 on 1 and 6971 DF,  p-value: < 2.2e-16
```

Now that we have the output for our simple bivariate regression model, what does it all mean? Let's *Memento* it by starting at the end and working our way backwards to the start.[6]

Model Evaluation

We will start at the bottom of the output with the model evaluation information. Generally, model evaluation information tells us how well our model (the set of predictor variable(s)) does in explaining the outcome variable. Model evaluation information is also frequently referred to as how well your model *fits* the data. There are many ways one can evaluate the fit of regression models, but we will just stick with what R provides us: residual standard error, R^2 and adjusted R^2, and the *F*-statistic.

Residual Standard Error

The residual standard error provides an estimate of how much on average the true outcome variable will deviate from the predicted values (or regression line). If this value is 0, which never happens with real data, it means that all the predicted values equal the actual values of the outcome variable. This metric is similar to but not exactly the same as the more commonly known root mean squared error metric in regression analysis.[7] On its own, the residual standard

---

[6]Feel free to replace *Memento* with a different film that uses reverse chronology. Some candidates include *Pulp Fiction*, *Tenet*, and *Fight Club* (though we usually reserve that reference for things we don't talk about).

[7]The information at the top called Residuals gives the estimated residual values, where we are looking for the median to be around 0 and for the other values to be symmetrical. For our purposes, I do not find the residuals or residual standard error that informative and thus we will ignore them for the rest of the chapter.

error is not that informative. Its usefulness comes from comparing the residual standard errors of different models to determine which fits the data best.

R^2 and Adjusted R^2

R^2 tells us the amount of variance that is explained in our outcome variable by our predictor variable(s); we briefly discussed this in the previous chapter. R^2 ranges from 0 to 1 ($R^2 \in [0,1]$), where $R^2 = 0$ means no variance is explained and $R^2 = 1$ means all the variance is explained; you will probably never see R^2 at these extremes when using real data. Typically, we convert the R^2 value into a percentage, by multiplying the value by 100, for interpretation purposes. The interpretation always follows this standard sentence: *Our model explains x % of the variance in our outcome variable.* In the R output, we see that $R^2 = 0.6437$, so we say that *our model explains 64.37% of the variance in our outcome variable.* We can substitute the generic *outcome variable* with our actual variable: *our model explains 64.37% of the variance in the percentage of psychiatric medication prescriptions in Scottish datazones.* Is that a good amount? Sure, we are explaining more than half of the variance in psychiatric medication prescriptions using just one predictor variable. While higher R^2 values are preferred, there is no specific number or amount you should shoot for. The reason is that different datasets and quantitative relationships are either easier or harder to explain than others; so R^2 values are often relative to what is usually observed for the specific type of analysis and data. For example, R^2 values when using time series data are often quite high because we commonly include the lagged (or previous) value of the outcome variable as one of the predictor variables. Similarly, if we are using survey data, the R^2 values are likely to be low because it is more difficult to explain certain outcome variables.

R^2 and adjusted R^2 provide the same information, but adjusted R^2 takes into account how many predictor variables we have in our model. Why would that matter? R^2 has a quirk that each time we add another predictor variable to our model, the R^2 value will always increase. Therefore, we could add in a ton of predictor variables in order to obtain a high R^2 value. Doing so is ill-advised for a number of reasons, not least of which is that it distracts from the substantive and theoretical approaches of QSS. Adjusted R^2 penalises us if we have predictor variables in our model not contributing to explaining variance in the outcome variable. We interpret the adjusted R^2 value in exactly same way as we did for the R^2 value.[8] In our current model, we see an adjusted R^2 value of 0.6436, which is almost identical to R^2. If we had many predictor variables (which we will below), the R^2 and adjusted R^2 may be further apart if some of the predictors were doing a poor job of explaining the variance in the outcome variable. Therefore, when comparing R^2 and adjusted R^2 we just want to see if they are relatively close or not. Finally, adjusted R^2 is a brute-force statistic that will always be the same value as or lower than R^2. If R^2 is close to 0, you can get a *negative* (!) adjusted R^2 value. Negative adjusted R^2 values obviously make no sense; to be literal, a negative adjusted R^2 implies that our model is so poor at explaining the outcome variable that it is *adding* variance to the outcome variable.

---

[8]There is a debate concerning whether you can or cannot interpret adjusted R^2 as the *percentage of variance explained in the outcome variable*. To quote Shawn Spencer from *Psych*: 'I've heard it both ways'. The scuttlebutt is that you cannot interpret adjusted R^2 with respect to the percentage of explained variance, but the researchers who first developed and applied the statistic did interpret the value as the percentage of variance explained (Ezekiel 1930; Fisher 1924; Tintner 1944; Wendzel 1936).

F-Test

The final piece of model evaluation information we'll consider is the *F-statistic*. The *F*-statistic is the test statistic for the *F-test*, which assesses whether our model is preferred over a model where all the predictor variables' estimates equal 0 (which means they have no effect on the outcome variable). I prefer to think of the *F*-test as telling us whether our model is better than a model with no predictor variables. This is a fairly low bar for our model to meet and it should *always* be the case that the test is significant; if it is not significant it means we have a terrible model. To determine statistical significance using the *F*-statistic information provided by R, we could use the value provided, 1259 with 1 degree of freedom, and check it against an *F*-distribution significance table to see whether our value is equal to or greater than the theoretical critical value for $p = 0.05$, where surely we will die from boredom and/or annoyance. Or we could just look at the provided *p*-value for the *F*-statistic in the R output. As with other significance tests in this book, we simply want to see whether *p* is less than or equal to 0.05. If it is, then our overall model is statistically significant; if it is not, then our overall model is not statistically significant. What about with our current model? We see that $p < 2.2 \times 10^{-16}$ and so, yes, our model is statistically significant, which means that our model is better than a model where all the predictor variables' estimates equal 0 (or, better than a model with no predictor variables).

Plotting Predicted versus Observed Values

In addition to using the model evaluation metric discussed above, researchers sometimes plot the predicted versus observed values of the outcome variable to assess regression models (Kuhn and Silge 2022). This is particularly useful for getting a visual sense of model fit instead of just metrics.

Let's plot the predicted versus observed values of pct_depress using `tidyverse` and `tidymodels` functions. Instead of creating a new tibble, we'll wrangle the data using piping before the ggplot() code. We first filter out missing values for pct_depress and pct_employment_deprived. Then we create a new variable called predicted using the mutate() function. In the mutate() function, we use the predict() function and specify the saved regression model (model.1) to get the predicted values for pct_depress. Although we don't plot pct_employment_deprived, we need to remove its missing values prior to predict() since pct_employment_deprived is the predictor in model.1. If we don't, then we'll get an error saying that we can't combine predicted with the simd data because of a different number of observations.

We'll put the aes() specification in the ggplot() function so we don't need to repeat it. We'll put pct_depress (the observed values) on the *x*-axis and predicted (the predicted values) on the *y*-axis. We'll use the geom_point() function to do a scatterplot where we'll jitter (position = "jitter") and lighten the shading (alpha = 0.5) of the points. Next, we include the geom_abline() function and specify lty = 2 to get a 45-degree diagonal dashed line through our plot starting at (0,0). When the predicted and observe values are exactly the same, the point lies on the 45-degree dashed line. Points below the line are when the observed value is greater than the predicted value (i.e., underpredicted). Points above the line are when the predicted value is greater than the observed value (i.e., overpredicted). In addition to adding labels (labs()) and setting a theme (theme_bw()), we include the coord_obs_pred() function (from the tune package which is loaded with tidymodels) in our code. This function scales the *x*- and *y*-axes to be equal, thus allowing an easier comparison of the observed and predicted values.

```
library(tidymodels)

simd %>%
  filter(!is.na(pct_depress) & !is.na(pct_employment_deprived)) %>%
  mutate(predict = predict(model.1)) %>%
ggplot(mapping = aes(x = pct_depress, y = predict)) +
  geom_point(position = "jitter", alpha = 0.5) +
  geom_abline(lty = 2) +
  coord_obs_pred() +
  labs(x = "Observed % Prescribed Psychiatric Medication",
       y = "Predicted % Prescribed Psychiatric Medication") +
  theme_bw()
```

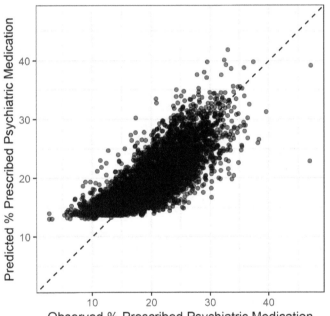

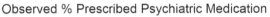

While the great mass of observations are on or near the diagonal line, we see some funky action at the tails. For the lower values, it appears that none of the predicted values are below 13% even though a good number of observed values are under 13%. Also, we see two severely underpredicted values at the right extreme of the x-axis and well below the diagonal line. So, does our model do a good job of fitting the data? It's hard to tell. The model isn't terrible, but it isn't great either. Again, the usefulness of this plot and many model evaluation metrics comes from comparing different models to find the one with the best fit.

Evaluating Predictor Information

Now that we have gone through evaluating the overall model, we can look at the effect of our individual predictor on our outcome variable. This information is in the Coefficients:

section of the R output. *Usually in QSS we are more interested in the predictor information than the model evaluation information.* The reason is that we test our substantive theories and questions using predictors and not using model fit values. For example, we rarely encounter articles discussing model evaluation information (e.g., R^2) as it is ancillary to the effects of our predictors on the outcome variable.[9]

Let's look at the information for our predictor `pct_employment_deprived`. We are first interested assessing whether or not our predictor has a statistically significant effect on our outcome variable. If it does then we want to interpret the coefficient and provide a plain language discussion of the effect. Let's take each of these in turn.

Determining Statistically Significant Predictors

R actually gives us redundant information to figure out whether our variable has a statistically significant effect. First, the *t-value* is simply the coefficient divided by the *standard error*. The standard error (often abbreviated as *s.e.*) for our regression coefficient tells us how closely our estimate of the sample regression line approximates the population regression line. Generally, the smaller the standard error, the better our estimate. The equation for figuring out t is:

$$t = \frac{\beta}{s.e._\beta}$$

We are looking for whether the absolute value of t is equal to or greater than 2 (technically 1.96, assuming a large enough number of observations). If the value is equal to or greater than 2, then our predictor variable has a statistically significant effect on our outcome variable. Why the absolute value of t? The reason is that if our coefficient is negative, then t will be negative (given the equation for t). Hence, we only care about the size of t and not the sign of t. Students sometimes get tripped on this point as they associate a negative t-value with a relationship being 'not good'. Luckily, as we discuss below, the output provides other information to figure out statistical significance. For our variable, we see that the t-value is 112.2, which is well above the 2 threshold. Therefore, `pct_employment_deprived` has a statistically significant effect on `pct_depress`.

R also gives us the p-value to check for statistical significance under the `Pr(>|t|)` heading. As usual, we are looking for whether the probability is equal to or less than 0.05. If it is equal to or less than 0.05 then our predictor variable has a statistically significant effect on our outcome variable. We see that $p \leq 0.05$ and thus our predictor variable is statistically significant.

The final way R provides to check for significance is by the stars (*). R tells us what they mean in the line starting with `Signif. codes:`. Usually, we are only interested in looking for one star, which means that the predictor is significant at the 0.05 level. The reason is that we care whether the predictor is significant (at the 0.05 level) or not; not 'how significant' the predictor is. In our regression output, we see there are three stars and thus our predictor is statistically significant.

Now that we know our variable is significant, we can provide an interpretation of the regression coefficient (the $\hat{\beta}$). Before we do, let's review how we generically interpret regression coefficients. Note that *if our predictor is not statistically significant, then we do not interpret the coefficient.*

---

[9]The exception is articles comparing different statistical modelling approaches by assessing model fits.

How to Interpret Regression Coefficients in General

Let's first cover how to generically interpret regression coefficients based on variables' levels of measurement.

For *ordinal-, interval-, and ratio-level predictors*, we generally interpret regression coefficients the same way we would when interpreting slopes of lines. A generic slope interpretation is:

For a one-unit increase in x, y changes by (the slope).

Except now, we substitute in our x and y variables and the value of our regression coefficient. We also need to specify our unit of analysis and that the regression coefficient effect is *expected*; the effect is *expected* because we are talking about the predicted values of y and not the actual value. For example:

For a one-unit increase in our predictor variable, our outcome variable is expected to change by $\hat{\beta}$.

Depending on the sign of $\hat{\beta}$, we often substitute in *is expected to increase* (for positive coefficients) or *is expected to decrease* (for negative coefficients) for *expected to change*.

Here's a hypothetical example of a regression interpretation:

For a one-unit increase in income, feelings towards Joe Biden are expected to decrease by 10 points.

From this interpretation we know that the predictor variable is income, the outcome variable is feelings towards Joe Biden, and the regression coefficient is –10. Also, note the use of *expected* to signify that the effect is a predicted value. Finally, there are times when it makes sense to include the unit of measurement for the predictor instead of the generic *for a one-unit increase*. For example, if our predictor is income in thousands of dollars, we might start our interpretation with *for a $1000 increase in income*. However, we are *always* correct to use the generic *for a one-unit increase*.

For *dummy* variables it does not make much sense to discuss unit increases when interpreting the regression coefficient. For example, it does not make sense to say *for a one-unit increase in sex*. Regression coefficients for dummy variables tell us the effect of the higher category (i.e., the '1' value) on the outcome variable compared to the lower category (i.e., the '0' value). Therefore, we need to interpret the coefficient value in the same manner. Consider the follow hypothetical example:

Women are expected to rate Joe Biden 10 points higher than (compared to) men.

From this interpretation, we know the predictor variable is sex, where women are the higher category and men are the lower category, feelings towards Joe Biden is the outcome variable, and that the coefficient value is 10.

How to Interpret Regression Coefficients for our Model

Now that we have had our detour through how to generically interpret regression coefficients, let's put it into practice with our regression estimates. The regression coefficient for pct_employment_deprived is 0.61 and we know it's a ratio variable. Therefore, our interpretation is:

> *For a one-unit increase in the percentage of employment deprivation in a datazone, the percentage of psychiatric medication prescriptions is expected to increase by 0.61%.*

Notice that we specified the unit of analysis (*datazone*) and that the effect is *expected*. Since our predictor variable is measured as a percentage, we can substitute *percentage* for the generic *one-unit* interpretation. Our interpretation is now:

> *For a one-point increase in the percentage of employment deprivation in a datazone, the percentage of psychiatric medication prescriptions is expected to increase by 0.61%.*

Our audience might consider this effect to be small or weak. Therefore, we might consider changing the unit of measurement. Since linear regression assumes that a predictor, and thus the coefficient, has a linear effect on the outcome variable, we can easily change the unit of measurement for our current model. Instead of one unit being one percentage point, let's change it so that one-unit is ten percentage points. To do this, we just multiply the coefficient by 10 (0.61 × 10 = 6.1). Now our interpretation is:

> *For a 10-point increase in the percentage of employment deprivation in a datazone, the percentage of psychiatric medication prescriptions is expected to increase by 6.1%.*

Plain Language Discussion

We typically want to also discuss our regression results (and any statistical analysis results) using plain language. The way I think of this is to frame it in terms of how would I explain the statistical results to my parents. There is no specifically correct way to craft the discussion and there are times when we can say more or less about the results, particularly depending on our substantive knowledge of the topic. Here, we might say something like:

> *We find a positive relationship between the percentage of people who are employment deprived and the percentage of psychiatric medication prescriptions in a datazone. In datazones where a large percentage of the population are employment deprived, we expect to find high percentages of psychiatric medication prescriptions. Based on these results, it does appear that being unable to work is related to the use of psychiatric medications.*

Regardless of how we word the explanation, the key is that we *do it*. In QSS it is critical to be able to explain what is going on using plain language in order for a general audience to understand our research. Frequently thinking of our results in plain language also helps us keep the 'big picture' in mind and not the minutiae of the analysis.

How to Interpret Regression Intercepts/Constants

Let's look briefly at the information for the intercept/constant of our regression model ((Intercept) in the output). The Estimate for the intercept tells us the value of *y* when (all) the *x* variables equal 0. Hence, this is the same as interpreting the *y*-intercept in linear algebra. Here, we see the estimate is 13.27, which tells us that when a datazone has 0% of people who are employment deprived, the percentage of psychiatric medication prescriptions is expected to be 13.27%. R provides a statistical significance test for the intercept, but we are not really interested in it.

I find looking at the intercept/constant is really only useful for two things. First, we can use it as a diagnostic tool for our regression model. If the intercept is close to the minimum or maximum of the outcome variable, then it might be difficult for certain predictors to explain variance in the outcome variable. For example, in the current regression model, if our predictor variable actually had a negative effect it could only possibly have a small effect since the intercept is already close to 0 (relative to the range of `pct_depress`). The same thing applies if the outcome variable is near its maximum variable and we have predictor variables with positive coefficients.

Second, we can use the intercept and predictor coefficient to get the expected value of *y* for any given value of *x*. For example, let's say we were interested in the predicted percentage of psychiatric medication prescriptions when 10% of the datazone is employment deprived. To find the value, we simply add the intercept estimate to the predictor estimate and multiply by the value of interest in the predictor variable, which we can do in R.

```
13.27 + (.61*10)
[1] 19.37
```

This tells us that when 10% of a datazone is employment deprived, the predicted percentage of psychiatric medication prescriptions is 19.37%. Unless we are very interested in a specific value of our predictor, calculating these values is inefficient. We are better off using a scatterplot and best-fit line to display the predicted values.

Confidence Intervals

Another way to determine statistical significance for linear regression models is using con- fidence intervals. Confidence intervals provide a lower bound and upper bound for our regression coefficients to where our population regression coefficient may actually be. To use confidence intervals, we need to specify what level of confidence we would like to examine. Commonly, people use 95% confidence levels, but sometimes 90% and 99% confidence levels are used by researchers for how confident they wish to be. As Imai (2017) discusses, a confidence interval tells us the range of values that the true value of the parameter (or population coeffi- cient) is expected to take at different levels of confidence if we were to infinitely repeat the data- generating process. For example, a 95% confidence interval tells us that 95% of the time the true value of the parameter is expected to be in the interval. Generally, the smaller the interval the better our estimate and vice versa.

To test for statistical significance of our predictors we check whether the confidence interval includes 0 or not. *If the confidence interval includes 0, then our variable is not statistically significant.* Why? Because the null hypothesis for a predictor in regression analysis is that $\hat{\beta}_x = 0$. If our con- fidence interval includes 0, then we cannot reject the null hypothesis that our predictor has no effect. We can look at confidence intervals in regression models by using the `confint()` func- tion, where we specify the model and at what confidence level we want the confidence interval. Let's do this for our model (`model.1`) at the 95% confidence level (`level = 0.95`).

```
confint(model.1, level = 0.95)
                            2.5 %      97.5 %
(Intercept)             13.1475390 13.3998355
pct_employment_deprived  0.5956726  0.6168546
```

We check whether the interval (from 2.5% to 97.5%) contains 0 or not. The confidence interval for our predictor, `pct_employment_deprived`, does not contain 0 and thus we can conclude it is statistically significant.[10] In fact, the conclusions we make about what variables are statistically significant by looking at confidence intervals should be the same as we made from looking at the regression output. If they are different then we made a mistake somewhere.

Another situation where researchers commonly use confidence intervals is when plotting relationships between variables. Let's look at the scatterplot from earlier in the chapter with psychiatric medication prescriptions on the *x*-axis and university attendance on the *y*-axis for a subset of the `simd` data. To get the confidence intervals included in the plot, we simply need to change `se = FALSE` in the `geom_smooth()` function to `se = TRUE`; since the default is `se = TRUE`, we could also just not include this option.

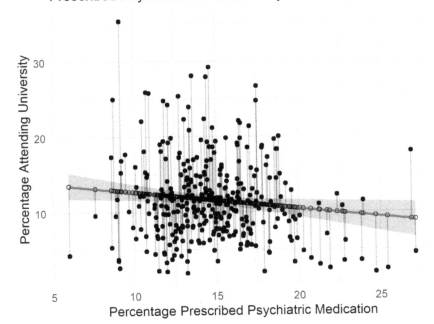

The grey shaded ribbon represents the 95% confidence interval for the best-fit line in blue. The confidence interval in the plot tells us what the actual best-fit line might be. Although we often refer to these as confidence intervals, a more accurate description would be *prediction intervals* as they refer to the predicted effect on *y* and do not directly deal with statistical significance. So, the predicted value of *y* for any given value of *x* might actually be any value within the band. You might notice that the interval is larger at the ends then in the middle. This is due to these values being further away from the mean of the predictor, and thus there is more uncertainty over the predicted value of *y*.

---

[10]We are ignoring the `(Intercept)` confidence interval.

Now that we have learned the basics of linear regression, we can move on to multiple regression and discuss model building.

MULTIPLE REGRESSION AND MODEL BUILDING

Why do we want to use multiple regression? Why can't we just use bivariate regression? There are many reasons, really, but two key reasons revolve around theory and statistical control.

When we are interested in explaining some social phenomenon (our outcome variable), almost never is it the case that one predictor variable can completely or substantially explain the phenomenon. We might think that a specific predictor variable is the most important one, but it is highly unlikely that it is the only variable that matters. We do not expect that unemployment can be explained solely by education attainment. If we are interested in understanding crime rates in different cities, we would not just look at the number of police patrols. Other factors are also likely to matter and if we have measures/variables of those factors, then we should consider them in a statistical model.

A second key reason is that including additional predictor variables in a regression model ensures we are more confident in our results. Each predictor controls for correlation with each other predictor, thus eliminating the potential for spuriousness. Spuriousness (or a *spurious relationship*) is when the observed relationship between two variables, say x and y, is actually explained by a third variable, say z. Here's a classic example of a spurious relationship. We observe that when ice cream sales go up, so does the murder rate. We run a bivariate regression and find that ice cream sales have a positive statistically significant effect on the murder rate. Maybe there's something in the ice cream that makes people more prone to commit murder. Like when Gotham's water supply was dosed with a hallucinogen in *Batman Begins*. What's really going on? In fact, hot weather explains both the rise in ice cream sales and the rise in the murder rate. If we include temperature (hot weather) into a regression model with ice cream sales, we will find the relationship between ice cream sales and the murder rate is not statistically significant. Therefore, we can say that once we control for the temperature, there is no relationship between ice cream sales and murder rates.

Typically, we do not have such clear cases of spuriousness when working with real data. Instead, we may observe statistically significant relationships in bivariate regression models that are not in multiple regression models. The reason is that once we control for additional predictors, our original variable may not really explain our outcome variable. In this case, what should we trust more? Simply, we should trust the results from a multiple regression model more than from a bivariate regression model, realising that if we do not have population data then probably neither is the 'right' model.

How do we control for other variables in a multiple regression model? Usually, we hold the variables that are not being estimated at their mean values. For instance, we estimate the effect of ice cream sales on the murder rate with temperature being kept constant at its mean value. To estimate the effect of temperature on murder rates, we just keep ice cream sales constant at their mean value. For those of you who know some calculus, in multiple regression we actually use partial derivatives to estimate the coefficients (slopes), and thus we technically have partial regression coefficients. Luckily for us, we do not need to do multiple regression by hand – R performs all the estimation for us.

Multiple Regression Equation

If we understand how bivariate linear regression works then understanding multiple regression is relatively easy. Multiple regression is just an extension of bivariate regression where we add in multiple predictors. Since we have multiple predictors we need to subscript the βs and x variables. Our regression equation now looks like this:

$$\hat{y} = \hat{\alpha} + \hat{\beta}_1 x_1 + \hat{\beta}_2 x_2 + \hat{\beta}_3 x_3 + \ldots + \hat{\beta}_k x_k + \hat{\varepsilon}$$

where $\hat{y}$ is our *predicted value* of y, $\hat{\alpha}$ is our estimated value of the intercept/constant, $\hat{\beta}_1$ is our estimated value of the coefficient/slope for predictor 1 (x_1), $\hat{\beta}_2$ is our estimated value of the coefficient/slope for predictor 2 (x_2), $\hat{\beta}_3$ is our estimated value of the coefficient/slope for predictor 3 (x_3), and so on to predictor variable K, and $\hat{\varepsilon}$ is our prediction error. Again, the xs do not have party hats because we are using their known values to get estimates of everything else.

To be more consistent with letters, the multiple regression equation is sometimes written with β_0 instead of α:

$$\hat{y} = \hat{\beta}_0 + \hat{\beta}_1 x_1 + \hat{\beta}_2 x_2 + \hat{\beta}_3 x_3 + \ldots + \hat{\beta}_k x_k + \hat{\varepsilon}$$

Finally, we sometimes come across the multiple regression equation written in matrix form as:

$$\mathbf{Y} = \mathbf{X}\beta + \varepsilon$$

where $\mathbf{Y}$ is a vector of values of the outcome variable, $\mathbf{X}$ is a matrix of values of the predictors, β is a vector of coefficients, and ε is a vector of errors. One of the main reasons why the regression equation is written in matrix form is that it implies we have a bunch of predictors and we do not have to write out the equation listing each predictor (x) and coefficient (β).

OLS and Multiple Regression

The basics of how OLS works are the same for multiple regression as they are for bivariate regression. The main difference is that instead of trying to find a best-fit line, OLS tries to find a best-fit multidimensional plane. This sounds complicated, and it is, but if we just keep in mind how the bivariate version works then we will understand the basics of how it works in multiple regression.

Multiple Regression Application: Explaining Psychiatric Medication Prescriptions in Scottish Datazones

In this application, we will carry on from the bivariate regression application using `pct_depress` as our outcome variable and now include three predictors in one regression. To do so, we simply separate the predictors using + in the R code (just like the multiple regression equation). Otherwise, the code is the same. Along with `pct_employment_deprived`, we will add the predictors `pct_overcrowded` (`overcrowded_rate` in the `simd` data), which is the percentage of people in overcrowded housing in a datazone, and `urban_fct` (urban in the `simd` data), which is a dummy variable for whether the datazone is urban (= 1) or rural (= 0), to our regression model. We need to create `pct_overcrowded` by multiplying `over-crowded_rate` by 100 and we'll create `urban_fct` by adding labels and converting `urban` to a factor variable. Then we'll run our regression model and create an object called `model.2` to save our regression estimates.

```
simd <- simd %>%
          mutate(pct_overcrowded = overcrowded_rate*100,
                 urban_fct = recode(urban, `1` = "Urban", `0` = "Rural"))

summary(model.2 <- lm(pct_depress ~ pct_employment_deprived +
                     pct_overcrowded + urban_fct, data = simd))

Call:
lm(formula = pct_depress ~ pct_employment_deprived + pct_overcrowded +
    urban_fct, data = simd)

Residuals:
    Min      1Q  Median      3Q     Max
-12.1201 -2.0740 -0.1517  1.9603 25.7153

Coefficients:
                        Estimate Std. Error t value Pr(>|t|)
(Intercept)            13.544667   0.080607 168.034  < 2e-16 ***
pct_employment_deprived 0.662875   0.006468 102.481  < 2e-16 ***
pct_overcrowded        -0.097087   0.006101 -15.914  < 2e-16 ***
urban_fctUrban          0.359730   0.086965   4.137 3.57e-05 ***
---
Signif. codes:  0 '***' 0.001 '**' 0.01 '*' 0.05 '.' 0.1 ' ' 1

Residual standard error: 3.147 on 6969 degrees of freedom
  (3 observations deleted due to missingness)
Multiple R-squared:  0.6562,   Adjusted R-squared:  0.656
F-statistic:  4433 on 3 and 6969 DF,  p-value: < 2.2e-16
```

Understanding the output for multiple regression is exactly the same as for bivariate regression. The only difference is that sometimes we need to be conscious we are talking about more than one predictor.

Model Evaluation

To evaluate the overall model, let's look at R^2, adjusted R^2, and the F-test in the output. We see that $R^2 = 0.6562$, which we interpret as saying that *our model explains 65.62% of the variance in the percentage of psychiatric medication prescriptions in Scottish datazones*. This is only slightly more variance explained than in the bivariate regression. This indicates that `pct_employment_deprived` on its own explains a great deal of variance in `pct_depress`. The adjusted R^2 is almost the same value, which is ideally what we want. Again, adjusted R^2 takes into account the number of predictors in our model. When the R^2 and adjusted R^2 values are close it means that we do not have any variables that are not substantially contributing to explaining the variance in the outcome variable. Finally, we see that the p-value for the F-test is below 0.05 and thus our overall model is statistically significant. Again, this means that our model is better than a model where all the predictors equal 0.

Evaluating Predictor Information

Now let's look at the individual predictor results. We see that all three predictors have a statistically significant effect on the percentage of psychiatric medication prescriptions in datazones. We know this because the t-values are all above (the absolute value) 2 and the p-values are all below 0.05. We also see that two predictors have a positive effect and one predictor has a negative effect on psychiatric medication prescriptions. Notice that `pct_employment_deprived` has only a slightly larger coefficient in this model than in the bivariate regression model. Even though these coefficients are similar, we place more confidence in the multiple regression results since we are controlling for other predictor variables.

We can provide an interpretation and plain language discussion for each of our significant predictors. The coefficient interpretation for `pct_employment_deprived` is that *for a one-unit increase in the percentage of employment deprivation in a datazone, the percentage of psychiatric medication prescriptions is expected to increase by 0.663%, while controlling for other variables*. Note this last piece of the interpretation: *while controlling for other variables*. Adding this phrase to the end of a coefficient interpretation tells the reader that we have run a multiple regression and thus the observed effect takes into account the effects of other predictors. Repeating *while controlling for other variables* for each interpretation gets a bit boring and so I advise students to just include it only in the first interpretation; typically published academic work does not include the statement since it is expected that researchers are performing multivariate analysis. Since the coefficient for employment deprivation is roughly the same size as in the bivariate regression, we will not repeat the plain language interpretation.

The coefficient interpretation for `pct_overcrowded` is that *for a one-unit increase in the percentage of people living in overcrowded housing in a datazone, the percentage of psychiatric medication prescriptions is expected to decrease by 0.097%*. How might we discuss this result using plain language? We might say something like *datazones which have higher housing overcrowding tend to have lower percentages of psychiatric medication prescriptions. However, the effect size is small relative to the other predictors. This suggests that overcrowding may have a weaker effect on predicting prescription percentages than the other predictors*. When going through the mechanics of assessing statistical significance and interpreting coefficients, we don't always think about the broader meaning of the results. Including a plain language discussion forces us to think through the implications of the results. Here, does it seem counter-intuitive that the results suggest higher housing overcrowding *reduces* psychiatric medication prescriptions in datazones? Typically areas with overcrowded housing are associated with higher levels of poverty and deprivation, which are both associated with negative mental health. Any thoughts or speculation on what's going on? Perhaps datazones with higher overcrowding might have lower access to mental health resources. Therefore, if we controlled for access to mental health in our regression model, we might find that `pct_overcrowded` is not statistically significant or has a positive coefficient. This is an instance where we might want to do additional data collection and research to more fully understand this result.

We need to provide a dummy variable interpretation for `urban_fct`. The regression coefficient, 0.360 (rounded), tells us the effect of the higher value in the dummy variable on the outcome variable compared to the effect of the lower value in the dummy variable. Here, the higher value is urban datazones and the lower value is rural datazones. The interpretation, then, is that *urban datazones are expected to have a 0.360% higher percentage of psychiatric medication prescriptions than rural datazones*. How would we discuss this using plain language? We might say something like *urban areas appear to have higher percentages of psychiatric medication prescriptions than rural areas. However, the difference is rather small at less than half a per cent. Without additional analysis it is difficult to determine why this is expected to be the case*. This is a similar situation to what we discussed with `pct_overcrowded`, but here we explicitly mention that additional research is needed to parse out the effect. Hence, we are admitting we don't know why urban datazones have percentages than rural datazones and we don't want to speculate. It might be related to increased access to mental health resources, the effect of urban stressors on mental health, or something else.

Determining Substantive Significance

We alluded to the predictors' relative effect sizes in our discussion above. It's one thing for predictors to be *statistically significant*. It's quite another for them to be substantively significant. Substantive significance, in the regression context, refers to whether a predictor's effect (i.e., coefficient) is large enough to have a meaningful impact on an outcome variable (Lewis-Beck et al. 2004). There are theoretical and statistical reasons why we should consider whether or not our statistically significant predictors may be substantively significant. Statistically, we are more likely to find statistically significant predictors when we have large number of observations. This is due to the equation for the standard error of the regression coefficient,

$$s.e._\beta = \sqrt{\frac{1}{N-2}\frac{\sum(y_i - \hat{y}_i)^2}{\sum(x_i - \bar{x})^2}}$$

We see that as the number of observations (N) increases, the standard error will decrease. It is not uncommon for all predictors in a regression model to be statistically significant when we have very large Ns (e.g., 30,000 observations) and thus we need to consider substantive significance.

Theoretically, we may find that our key theoretical predictor is statistically significant, but only has a marginal effect on our outcome variable. And so our key predictor matters (from a statistical significance perspective), but does not really 'matter' (from a substantive significance perspective).

Determining whether or not a predictor is substantively significant can often be a judgement call on our part. We could consider substantive significance by comparing the predictors in our model – which statistically significant predictor has the largest effect on the outcome variable? This allows us to say something like X_1 *has the largest effect on Y in our model*. However, these effects may still be small when we consider absolute substantive significance. For example, let's assume that the effect of X_1 is 0.03% and the effect of X_2 is 0.01%. So, X_1 has a larger effect than X_2, but both are still small in absolute terms.

We could also think about substantive significant relative to what prior research studies have found and our theoretical expectations. For example, a predictor might appear to have a small effect in absolute terms, but it could be much larger than what other researchers have found and/or what we expected to find.

Let's examine how we compare effect sizes of statistically significant predictors. If predictors are on the same scale then we can directly compare their coefficients to determine which one has a larger effect on the outcome variable. For example, in `model.2`, `pct_employment_deprived` and `pct_overcrowded` both are percentages (thus on the same scale) and so we can directly compare their coefficients. Obviously `pct_employment_deprived` has a larger effect on `pct_depress` ($\hat{\beta} = 0.663$) than `pct_overcrowded` ($\hat{\beta} = -0.097$). When predictors are on different scales, we can't directly compare them. For example, we can't compare `urban_fct`'s coefficient with the other two predictors' coefficients.

If we want to directly compare predictors that are on different scales, we can standardise the coefficients. Standardising coefficients involves transforming all the predictors to have a mean of 0 and a standard deviation of 1. There are a number of ways we can do this in R. A simple way is using the `lm.beta()` function from the `lm.beta` package. The `lm.beta()` function automatically standardises coefficients and adds a column to the regression summary output with the standardised coefficients. We just specify our saved regression results (`model.2`) in the `lm.beta()` function.

```
library(lm.beta)

summary(model.2a <- lm.beta(model.2))

Call:
lm(formula = pct_depress ~ pct_employment_deprived + pct_overcrowded +
    urban_fct, data = simd)

Residuals:
     Min       1Q   Median       3Q      Max
-12.1201  -2.0740  -0.1517   1.9603  25.7153

Coefficients:
                         Estimate Standardized Std. Error t value Pr(>|t|)
(Intercept)             13.544667           NA   0.080607 168.034  < 2e-16 ***
pct_employment_deprived  0.662875     0.877202   0.006468 102.481  < 2e-16 ***
pct_overcrowded         -0.097087    -0.141987   0.006101 -15.914  < 2e-16 ***
urban_fctUrban           0.359730     0.030920   0.086965   4.137 3.57e-05 ***
---
Signif. codes:  0 '***' 0.001 '**' 0.01 '*' 0.05 '.' 0.1 ' ' 1

Residual standard error: 3.147 on 6969 degrees of freedom
  (3 observations deleted due to missingness)
Multiple R-squared:  0.6562,    Adjusted R-squared:  0.656
F-statistic:  4433 on 3 and 6969 DF,  p-value: < 2.2e-16
```

We see that next to the `Estimate` column there's a new column named `Standardized` that includes the standardised regression coefficients. Now, we can directly compare coefficient sizes. We see that `urban_fct`'s coefficient is smaller than the other two coefficients. However, standardising a dummy variable is bit weird since it can only take on one of two values (in its original form or in its standardised form). So, comparing `urban_fct` to the other coefficients isn't that useful.

We interpret standardised coefficients as:

> *For a one standard deviation increase in our predictor, our outcome variable is expected to change by $\hat{\beta}$ standard deviations.*

Since understanding changes in standard deviation can be difficult, we might want to avoid interpreting standardised coefficients if possible.

Interactions in Multiple Regression

Researchers often include **interactions** to assess the combined effect of predictors on an outcome variable. The use of interactions is more prevalent in some fields and subfields than others, and for some types of data than others. Generally, we include interactions if we believe that the combined effect of two or more predictors increases our understanding of variation in an outcome variable compared to using only main effects (non-interacted predictors). One word of caution: interactions are notoriously difficult to interpret and so care must be taken when they are included in our model.

We could create new variables for our interactions, but we can also do interactions on the fly in the `lm()` function specification. We simply include * between two predictors, instead of +, and R automatically creates the interaction while maintaining the main effects. This latter approach only works if the current values/levels/labels of our predictors are already coded in the order that we want for the interaction. If we want a different order for one or more of the predictors we are interacting, then it is best practice to create the interaction as a new variable or recode the predictors in our preferred order and then interact the predictors in the `lm()` function.

Let's briefly explore these options by interacting `urban_fct` and `pct_overcrowded`.[11] First, we'll specify `urban_fct*pct_overcrowded` in the `lm()` function and save the results as `model.3`.

```
summary(model.3 <- lm(pct_depress ~ pct_employment_deprived +
                      pct_overcrowded*urban_fct, data = simd))

Call:
lm(formula = pct_depress ~ pct_employment_deprived + pct_overcrowded *
    urban_fct, data = simd)

Residuals:
    Min      1Q  Median      3Q     Max
-11.9792 -2.0601 -0.1493  1.9383 26.0574
Coefficients:
```

---

[11]See the emmeans package for more information on estimating interactions in R.

```
                              Estimate Std. Error t value Pr(>|t|)
(Intercept)                   12.447498  0.129077  96.435  < 2e-16 ***
pct_employment_deprived        0.654083  0.006466 101.154  < 2e-16 ***
pct_overcrowded                0.071305  0.016689   4.273 1.96e-05 ***
urban_fctUrban                 1.729291  0.153105  11.295  < 2e-16 ***
pct_overcrowded:urban_fctUrban -0.182538 0.016860 -10.827  < 2e-16 ***
---
Signif. codes:  0 '***' 0.001 '**' 0.01 '*' 0.05 '.' 0.1 ' ' 1

Residual standard error: 3.121 on 6968 degrees of freedom
  (3 observations deleted due to missingness)
Multiple R-squared:  0.6619,    Adjusted R-squared:  0.6617
F-statistic:  3410 on 4 and 6968 DF,  p-value: < 2.2e-16
```

We see that the interaction has a negative coefficient and is statistically significant. We can interpret the coefficient as saying that *for urban datazones, for a one-unit increase in the percentage of people living in overcrowded housing in a datazone, the percentage of psychiatric medication prescriptions is expected to decrease by 0.183% compared to rural datazones.* Substantively, this result suggests that urban datazones with high percentages of overcrowded housing are expected to have lower percentages of psychiatric medication prescriptions compared to rural datazones.

With interactions, we can't directly interpret the main effects of the predictors (here, urban_fct and pct_overcrowded) without using mathematical gymnastics or specific R packages. Instead, it is common practice to have one model with main effects and then another model with the interaction(s).

Let's imagine that we want the comparison for urban_fct to be rural versus urban, instead of urban versus rural. We can do this by recoding urban_fct using the fct_rev() function from the forcats package (part of tidyverse). The fct_rev() function reverses (or flips) the values of a factor variable. Instead of creating and adding this recoded variable to our dataset, we'll use piping to apply the recoding just for our regression. Since we specify the data (simd) in the pipe, we need to specify that data = . in the lm() function. We'll save the results with the object model.3a and also wrap the summary() function around the code chunk to get the results.

```
summary(model.3a <- simd %>%
        mutate(urban_fct = fct_rev(urban_fct)) %>%
        lm(pct_depress ~ pct_employment_deprived + pct_overcrowded*
                urban_fct, data = .))

Call:
lm(formula = pct_depress ~ pct_employment_deprived + pct_overcrowded *
    urban_fct, data = .)

Residuals:
    Min      1Q  Median      3Q     Max
-11.9792 -2.0601 -0.1493  1.9383 26.0574
Coefficients:
```

```
                             Estimate  Std. Error  t value  Pr(>|t|)
(Intercept)                  14.176790   0.086326   164.22  <2e-16 ***
pct_employment_deprived       0.654083   0.006466   101.15  <2e-16 ***
pct_overcrowded              -0.111233   0.006190   -17.97  <2e-16 ***
urban_fctRural               -1.729291   0.153105   -11.29  <2e-16 ***
pct_overcrowded:urban_fctRural 0.182538  0.016860    10.83  <2e-16 ***
---
Signif. codes:  0 '***' 0.001 '**' 0.01 '*' 0.05 '.' 0.1 ' ' 1

Residual standard error: 3.121 on 6968 degrees of freedom
  (3 observations deleted due to missingness)
Multiple R-squared:  0.6619,    Adjusted R-squared:  0.6617
F-statistic:  3410 on 4 and 6968 DF,  p-value: < 2.2e-16
```

We see that the interaction coefficient is simply the reverse of the previous one. We can interpret the coefficient as saying that *for rural datazones, for a one-unit increase in the percentage of people living in overcrowded housing in a datazone, the percentage of psychiatric medication prescriptions is expected to increase by 0.183% compared to urban datazones.* Using either version of the interaction demonstrates that the effect of overcrowded housing on psychiatric medication prescriptions is different depending on whether it is an urban or rural datazone.

PLOTTING REGRESSION COEFFICIENTS

It is increasingly common to plot regression coefficients instead of using a regression table. There are a variety of ways to do this in R. The GGally package offers several different functions to plot regression coefficients, provides considerable customisations, and allows us also to use ggplot2 functions; thus, providing more functionality than packages like coefplot. We'll use the ggcoef_model() function to plot model.2's coefficients. In the ggcoef_model() function, we first specify the model (model.2), then we add labels for the variables (variable_labels =). We'll also change several of the defaults – we'll not plot the rural category of urban_fct by specifying no_reference_row = "urban_fct", the *p*-values by specifying show_p_values = FALSE, and significance stars by specifying signif_stars = FALSE. Lastly, we'll use the labs() function from ggplot2 to give the plot a title.

```
library(GGally)

ggcoef_model(model.2,
            variable_labels = c(
              pct_employment_deprived = "Employment Deprivation",
              pct_overcrowded = "Overcrowded Housing",
              urban_fct = "Urban/Rural"),
            no_reference_row = "urban_fct",
            show_p_values = FALSE,
            signif_stars = FALSE) +
  labs(title = "Predicting Psychiatric Medication Prescriptions")
```

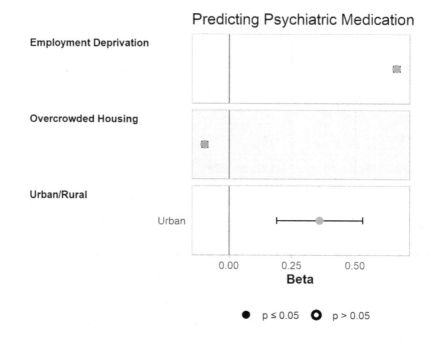

The plot shows the regression coefficient estimates (solid circles) along with the 95% confidence intervals (horizontal lines). By default, the plot includes a vertical line at 0.00. If, for any of the variables, the 95% confidence interval lines cross the 0 dashed line, then the variable is not statistically significant. We see that none of the coefficients intervals cross 0.00, thus they are all statistically significant. The regression coefficient estimates should be identical to the regression results we saw in the earlier `model.2` output and from the `confint()` function.

LINEAR REGRESSION WITH TIDYMODELS

We can also use `tidymodels` to perform linear regression analysis.[12] The `tidymodels` package offers a unified set of functions that can handle a variety of modelling approaches and options. This provides a standard outline or structure of functions where we can more easily specify and swap out different modelling approaches. Hence, we don't need to use different functions from different packages that take different approaches when we want to use different models. However, `tidymodels` is really designed for machine learning approaches to data analysis and for creating `tidy` objects to easily integrate with the rest of the `tidyverse`. For our purposes, particularly when just starting to learn linear regression, `tidymodels` probably provides too much functionality if we are only using linear and

---

[12]See Kuhn and Silge (2022) for an introduction to the `tidymodels` approach.

generalised linear regression. To get a taste, though, let's replicate the analysis for `model.2` using the `tidymodels` package.

First, we use the `linear_reg()` function from the `parsnip` package to specify we are using linear regression. Next, we specify we are using OLS estimation by specifying "lm" in the `set_engine()` function from the `parsnip` package. Then we include our model regression model specification using the `fit()` function. Lastly, we include the `tidy()` function from the `broom` package which automatically creates a tibble with the results in a `tidy` format. We'll connect these four functions with the pipe operator `%>%`. For this demonstration, we will not save the results as an object.

```
linear_reg() %>%
  set_engine("lm") %>%
  fit(pct_depress ~ pct_employment_deprived + pct_overcrowded +
      urban_fct, data=simd) %>%
  tidy()
# A tibble: 4 x 5
  term                      estimate std.error statistic  p.value
  <chr>                        <dbl>     <dbl>     <dbl>     <dbl>
1 (Intercept)                   13.5    0.0806     168.     0
2 pct_employment_deprived      0.663   0.00647     102.     0
3 pct_overcrowded            -0.0971   0.00610    -15.9  4.90e-56
4 urban_fctUrban               0.360    0.0870      4.14 3.57e- 5
```

The results output provides columns for the estimate, standard error, test statistic, and *p*-value. If we double-check these results with `model.2`'s results, we'll see they are the same (as expected). One of the arguments in favour of using `tidymodels` is that we'll use the same functions and the `tidy()` output headers will be the same when using different modelling techniques (e.g., notice that the test statistic is called `statistic` and not something like `t-value` or `z-value`). There are clearly benefits to using the `tidymodels` approach to regression modelling, but it may further steepen learning curves for people just starting out in QSS using R.

CONCLUSION

Understanding when and how to use linear regression provides the foundation for learning more advanced statistical regression techniques (e.g., generalised linear models). As mentioned at the start of the chapter, linear regression is the 'backbone' of QSS and often the first time students are exposed to multivariate analysis. This chapter provides this foundation and how to execute linear regression in R.

What we did not discuss in this chapter is that linear regression in general and OLS in particular make a host of assumptions about the data, variables, and estimates. If these assumptions are not satisfied then our regression results may not be correct. In the next chapter, we discuss the assumptions, how to test for them, and possible corrections.

R Packages Used in This Chapter

- `broom` (loaded with `tidymodels`)
- `dplyr` (loaded with `tidyverse`)
- `forcats` (loaded with `tidyverse`)
- `GGally`
- `ggplot2` (loaded with `tidyverse`)
- `lm.beta`
- `parsnip` (loaded with `tidymodels`)
- `pillar` (loaded with `tidyverse`)
- `tidymodels`
- `tidyverse`
- `tune` (loaded with `tidymodels`)

R Functions Used in This Chapter

- `confint()` - confidence intervals
- `coord_obs_pred()` - scale *x*- and *y*-axes to be equal using `tune` package
- `factor()` - specify variable as a factor
- `fct_rev()` - reverse values of a factor variable using `forcats` package
- `filter()` - subset data based on variables' values using `dplyr` package
- `fit()` - estimate (fit) model using `parsnip` package
- `geom_abline()` - `ggplot2` reference lines
- `geom_point()` - `ggplot2` scattered points
- `geom_smooth()` - `ggplot2` linear and nonlinear lines
- `ggcoef_model()` - plot regression coefficients using `GGally` package
- `ggplot()` - base layer for `ggplot2`
- `is.na()` - check for missing values (NAs) in variables
- `labs()` - `ggplot2` labels
- `linear_reg()` - specify linear regression model using `parsnip` package
- `lm()` - linear regression model
- `lm.beta()` - standardise linear regression coefficients
- `mutate()` - recode variables using `dplyr` package
- `predict()` - calculate predicted values from model
- `read_csv()` - read in .csv data file using `readr` package
- `recode()` - recode variable using `dplyr` package
- `rename_with()` - rename variable using a function using `dplyr` package
- `set_engine()` - specify type of model to fit using `parsnip` package
- `summary()` - summarise object
- `theme_bw()` - black-and-white `ggplot2` theme
- `theme_minimal()` - minimal `ggplot2` theme
- `tidy()` - create `tidy` tibble using `broom` package

===== Additional Resources =====

Books

- Andersen, R. and Armstrong, D. A., II (2022) *Presenting Statistical Results Effectively*. Sage.
- Faraway, J. J. (2014) *Linear Regression in R*, 2nd edition. Chapman and Hall/CRC.
- Fox, J. (2002) *An R and S-Plus Companion to Applied Regression*. Sage.
- Fox, J. and Weisberg, S. (2018) *An R Companion to Applied Regression*. Sage.
- Harris, J. K. (2020) *Statistics with R: Solving Problems Using Real-World Data*. Sage.
- Kleiber, C. and Zeileis, A. (2008) *Applied Econometrics with R*. Springer.
- Kuhn, M. and Silge, J. (2022) *Tidy Modeling with R*. O'Reilly Media.
- Long, J. D. and Teetor, P. (2019) *R Cookbook*, 2nd edition. O'Reilly Media.

Online

- Tidymodels: https://www.tidymodels.org/

12

OLS ASSUMPTIONS AND DIAGNOSTIC TESTING

Chapter contents

Linear regression, and ordinary least squares in particular, make a number of assumptions about the data, variables, and estimates. If we do not satisfy the assumptions then we cannot be certain that our estimates are correct. Certain assumptions matter more than others, and so we will focus on a core set of assumptions and a few ancillary assumptions. In this chapter, we will discuss the assumptions, how to test for violations of assumptions, and examine possible solutions to any violations.

By the end of this chapter, you should be able to:

- Understand BLUE
- Understand the Gauss–Markov theorem
- Understand the consequences of violating assumptions
- Test for violations of assumptions
- Find solutions to violations

OLS ASSUMPTIONS

Best Linear Unbiased Estimator

Our main concern when running a linear regression is that our OLS estimates are BLUE, which stands for best linear unbiased estimator. This means we want estimates that minimise the error variance (best or efficient) and that on average yield the true population parameter (unbiased); and we are using linear regression (so, linear). Having estimates that are BLUE is the best-case scenario for when we are using OLS.

Gauss–Markov Theorem

We want our estimates to be BLUE, but how do we know if they are? The Gauss–Markov theorem, named after the nineteenth-century mathematicians Carl Friedrich Gauss and Andrey Markov, states that if four assumptions hold then the OLS estimates are BLUE. The conditions are:[1]

1   Predictors must be independent of the error term.
2   The correct functional form, which means the conditional mean of the error term, must be 0.
3   Constant variance of errors (known as homoscedasticity).
4   No autocorrelation between errors.

In this section, we will discuss the assumptions, problems that arise from violations, tests for violations, and consider solutions.

Predictors Independent of the Error Term

The first assumption is that predictors must be independent of the error term. When this is the case, we say that we have *exogenous* predictors. When this is not the case, we say we that we have *endogenous* predictors, or that we have an endogeneity problem. Often this

---

[1]See Greene (2017) for a mathematical discussion of these assumptions.

assumption is violated when we have omitted variable bias (OVB), which basically means we have excluded a key predictor (or predictors) from our model. The problem with figuring this out is that there is no test that can tell us *what* variable(s) were excluded to cause this problem. Some suggest using the Ramsey RESET test, discussed below, to test this assumption, but it really does not get at the issue of OVB. The best approach for dealing with potential OVB is to link our statistical model to our theory. Based on our theory, have we included all the relevant predictors for explaining our outcome variable? If we have, then we can theoretically argue that we do not have OVB.[2]

Correct Functional Form

The second assumption is that we have the correct functional form for our model. A correct functional form implies that our predictors have a linear or nonlinear relationship with the outcome variable, and making sure that we are using the correct version of each predictor. If we have the wrong functional form then our estimates will be biased, thus violating the Gauss–Markov theorem. Instead, we might need to include nonlinear versions of predictors (such as squared, logged, or cubed) in a regression. We may have substantive reasons to include nonlinear relationships, such as with age as a predictor, but we also can test for the whether we have the correct functional form.

One test for functional form is to plot the residuals against the fitted values (the predicted values of *y*). If the local mean appears to be around 0 across the fitted values, then we have the correct functional form. A similar test is to plot the residuals against a predictor variable. Again, if the local mean appears to be around 0 as we increase on the predictor's values, then we have the correct functional form. We'll also consider a formal statistical test called the Ramsey RESET test (where RESET stands for 'regression specification error test'). The test works by running an additional regression model which includes nonlinear versions of the predicted values of *y*, usually squared and cubed, as predictors in the original regression model (Ramsey 1969). It then compares whether the new version of the model explains significantly more variance in the outcome variable than our original model. If there is a statistically significant difference between models in explaining variance, we have the incorrect functional form. We can correct for this violation by including nonlinear versions of suspected predictors.

No Heteroscedasticity

The third assumption for the Gauss–Markov theorem to hold is that the errors have constant variance, which is known as homoscedasticity. When the errors do not have constant variance, it is known as heteroscedasticity. When heteroscedasticity is present our estimates are inefficient and, most problematically, our standard errors are biased downwards (are smaller than they should be). Heteroscedasticity is a very common problem when using social science data. Why are we so concerned with our standard errors here? If they are smaller than they should be, we may find statistically significant predictors which in fact are really not, because $t = \beta \,/\, s.e._\beta$. Since whether something is statistically significant or not is thought of as whether something matters or not, we may be drawing the wrong conclusions about our model. In most areas of

---

[2]If we truly believe we might an issue with OVB, we could try an instrumental variables approach (Verbeek 2004), but that is beyond the scope of this book.

social science there are not dramatic consequences from drawing the wrong conclusions from models, but imagine the government instituting some policy because it was shown to matter in an analysis. Or imagine some medical treatment being used because it was shown to have a statistically significant effect, but in fact does not because the model was wrong. Hopefully, you will never make such mistakes in your career, but such examples demonstrate the misuse of statistical significance in the real world.

How do we test for and, if present, correct heteroscedasticity? The first test is to plot the residuals against the fitted values – the same as we did when testing functional form. But instead of looking for a local mean around 0, we are looking to see if there are any patterns in the residuals as we increase on the fitted values. Though there are many different possible patterns the residuals may follow – including a fan and an inverse-fan shape – it only really matters whether there is a pattern or not. If there is a pattern then we probably have heteroscedasticity. If the residuals just look like noise with no obvious pattern, then we probably do not have heteroscedasticity. We shouldn't try too hard to find a pattern – we shouldn't try to find the hidden image in the optical illusion. The pattern should be obvious. If we need to rationalise that a pattern exists, then there probably is no pattern. If we do not trust our pattern recognition abilities, there are also formal statistical tests for heteroscedasticity. The one we will use is called the Breusch–Pagan test for heteroscedasticity. The null hypothesis is that there is constant error variance (homoscedasticity). Hence, if we reject the null then we have heteroscedasticity.

If we have heteroscedasticity, how do we correct for it? The most common solution is to use robust standard errors; some researchers such as Cameron and Trivedi (2005) just assume heteroscedasticity will be present and thus always run their linear models with robust standard errors.

No Autocorrelation between Errors

The fourth assumption for the Gauss–Markov theorem to hold is that there is no autocorrelation between errors. Since we are using cross-sectional data in this book, we do not need to worry about autocorrelation and thus we satisfy the assumption by default. Autocorrelation is, however, an issue for spatial, longitudinal, and time series datasets.

Additional Assumptions of OLS

We also make three additional assumptions when using OLS estimation, though none are part of BLUE. They are not as critical as the assumptions from Gauss–Markov, but they have implications for our regression results.

Normally Distributed Errors

First, we assume that our errors are normally distributed. If our errors are not normally distributed, then we cannot assume that the estimates from our regression apply to the population. Why does that matter? We prefer that the relationships we estimate and observe with our sample data can generally apply to the population; in other words, we want our estimates to be generalisable. For example, we want to be able to say that education level affects unemployment in the whole of Scotland, and not, for instance, only in Glasgow and Edinburgh. Or that American voters' party identification affects their vote in US presidential elections and not, for example, only in Chicago. If we violate the normality assumption it does not necessarily mean our estimates are wrong, just that we are not confident in applying them to statements about the population.

We can test for normality using several different approaches. First, we can look at a histogram of the residuals to see if they appear to approximate a normal distribution (a bell curve distribution). Second, we can look at a quantile–quantile (Q-Q) plot, which compares our residuals to residuals from a theoretical perfect normal distribution. The residuals are compared for each quantile and if they are the same then the point lies on a 45-degree line. Both of these tests are based on our own judgement of whether our residuals appear normally distributed. I prefer to also examine formal statistical tests of normality, and several exist for our purposes in R; we'll use the Anderson–Darling test, because the commonly used Shapiro–Wilk test in R cannot handle data with more than 5000 observations.

What do we do if we violate the normality assumption? One solution is to use logged versions of our variables. Another solution is to use generalised linear models where the normality assumption is relaxed. Although in the next chapter we go over generalised linear models, we only give an introductory treatment. In truth, many researchers just ignore that they violated normality, or don't test for it, because it has no effect on whether estimates are BLUE or not.

No Multicollinearity

Second, we assume there is no multicollinearity between predictors. Multicollinearity is when two or more predictors are functions of one other (possibly latently). When multicollinearity is present then the standard errors will be larger than they should be; though again, multicollinearity does not affect BLUE. It is actually rather uncommon to observe true multicollinearity. Usually if we find it exists we may have put two (or more) versions of the same variable into the regression, either consciously or not. For example, we have included both age by years and age by categories. Some statistical programs will automatically drop variables that exhibit multicollinearity.

There are two ways we usually test for multicollinearity. The first, which is an informal test, is to just do a correlation between our predictor variables. If any variables are correlated at |0.8| or higher, they deserve further attention to check whether they are really measuring the same thing. This does not definitively tell us whether multicollinearity exists or not, but it can give us a sense of potential concerns. The second is a formal test known as the variance inflation factor (VIF) test. The VIF test gives us a measure of how much common variance exists between a predictor and other predictors. The square root of the VIF value tells us how much larger the standard errors are compared to if there were no collinearity. For example, if we have a VIF value of 5, then the standard errors are $\sqrt{5} = 2.24$ as large as they would be without collinearity. R provides a VIF test, and the rule of thumb is that we are looking for any VIF values of 10 or above (Fabozzi et al. 2014). If a predictor has a VIF of 10 or above then it will likely be collinear with other predictors. The most common solution to the problem of multicollinearity is to drop the problematic variable.

No Influential Data Points

The third assumption we make is that we have no influential data points. Influential data points are points that are both outliers and have high leverage on our regression estimates. Outliers are data points that are far away from the other observations. We test for outliers by looking at studentised residuals. The rule of thumb is that any data points that have residuals that are ±2 standard deviations away from 0 are considered outliers (Field et al. 2011; Kabacoff 2022). However, just because a data point is an outlier does not mean it will have an effect on the regression line. Points with leverage have a high predicted value of *y*, though these can be located anywhere, including right in the heart of the observations. To test for leverage we look at hat values, which are the standardised influence of each observation on the predicted value of y. We are concerned when any hat value is equal to or above $2(k + 1)/n$, where k is the number of predictors and n is the number of observations. Any data points that have hat values equal to or greater than this cut-point are considered to have high leverage (Fox 2002).[3] However, just because a data point has leverage does not mean it has a detrimental effect on the regression line. Hence, the points we really care about are those that are both outliers and leverage – the influential data points. We test for influential data points by looking at Cook's distance (often shortened as Cook's d), which measures the effect of each observation on the regression coefficients. There are several different thresholds that are suggested for determining influential data points. The rule of thumb for a large number of observations is that any points that have a Cook's d of 1 or greater are considered to be influential (Lafaye de Micheaux et al. 2013; Ryan 2009). Others have argued that absolute thresholds (e.g., a Cook's d equal to 1) are too restrictive and might miss influential data points (Fox 1991). Instead, the thresholds should vary by the number of observations and predictors. Common alternative thresholds include $4/(n - k - 1)$ (Fox 2002) or $4/(n - k)$ (Bollen and Jackman 1990), where n is the number of observations and k is the number of predictors.

However, points that have a Cook's d greater than or equal to 1, or our calculated threshold, should not be immediately eliminated. Instead, these data points require further investigation to understand why they are influential. There could be a coding error or typo causing the problem. There might be a substantive reason why a data point is influential (e.g., Russia as an observation in a dataset on military spending in eastern Europe; Texas as an observation in a dataset on the prevalence of private prisons in US states). Along with an examination of influential data points' values, researchers also commonly compare regression results with and without the influential data points. If the results are not that different, we may decide not to take a remedial action. The clearest situation for dropping influential data points is when we have a single observation that has a massive effect on the regression. If the dropped point is of substantive interest, we may decide to discuss it as a special case.

Now that we know what assumptions linear regression and OLS make and the basics of how to test for violations and potential fixes, let's perform full diagnostic testing on the multiple regression model from the previous chapter.

MULTIPLE REGRESSION APPLICATION: EXPLAINING PSYCHIATRIC MEDICATION PRESCRIPTIONS IN SCOTTISH DATAZONES

We will rerun the multiple regression model from the previous chapter and then perform diagnostics on the model.

---

[3]Another version of this test says that any point with leverage over 2 or 3 times the average hat value is considered to have high leverage (Kabacoff 2022). The average hat value is the number of parameters estimated in the model divided by the sample size $((k + 1)/n)$. A cut-point twice the average hat value is equivalent to how it is written in the text.

```
setwd("C:/QSSD/Chapter 12 - OLS Assumptions & Diagnostics")
getwd()

library(tidyverse)
simd <- read_csv("simd2020.csv", na="*")

simd <- simd %>%
          rename_with(tolower) %>%
          mutate(pct_depress = depress*100,
                 pct_employment_deprived = employment_rate*100,
                 pct_overcrowded = overcrowded_rate*100,
                 urban_fct = recode(urban, '1' = "Urban", '0' = "Rural"))

summary(model.1 <- lm(pct_depress ~ pct_employment_deprived +
                      pct_overcrowded + urban_fct, data = simd))

Call:
lm(formula = pct_depress ~ pct_employment_deprived + pct_overcrowded +
    urban_fct, data = simd)

Residuals:
    Min       1Q   Median       3Q      Max
-12.1201  -2.0740  -0.1517   1.9603  25.7153

Coefficients:
                          Estimate Std. Error t value Pr(>|t|)
(Intercept)              13.544667   0.080607 168.034  < 2e-16 ***
pct_employment_deprived   0.662875   0.006468 102.481  < 2e-16 ***
pct_overcrowded          -0.097087   0.006101 -15.914  < 2e-16 ***
urban_fctUrban            0.359730   0.086965   4.137 3.57e-05 ***
---
Signif. codes:  0 '***' 0.001 '**' 0.01 '*' 0.05 '.' 0.1 ' ' 1

Residual standard error: 3.147 on 6969 degrees of freedom
  (3 observations deleted due to missingness)
Multiple R-squared:  0.6562,    Adjusted R-squared:  0.656
F-statistic:  4433 on 3 and 6969 DF,  p-value: < 2.2e-16
```

Our diagnostic testing falls into two buckets: plots and formal statistical tests. For diagnostic plots, we could use base R plots, as in the first edition of this book, or run `plot(model.1)`, but let's leverage the `ggplot2` extension package `lindia`.[4] Let's begin our diagnostic testing journey with testing functional form.

---

[4]Another `ggplot2` extension package for linear regression diagnostic plots is `gglm`, as well as the `ggnostic()` function in `GGally`.

Functional Form

Plotting

First, we will plot our model's residuals and fitted values. If we have the correct functional form, the local means will have a value around 0. We'll use the `gg_resfitted()` function, where we specify the saved model (`model.1`) and add `theme_bw()` for aesthetic reasons.

```
library(lindia)

gg_resfitted(model.1) +
  theme_bw()
```

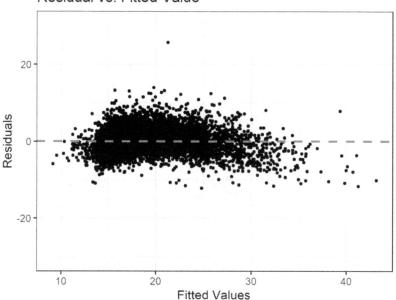

The plot suggests that local means are not 0, particularly for the higher fitted values. Therefore, we have probably violated the assumption.

Ramsey RESET Test

We will use the `resettest()` function from the lmtest package. In the parentheses of the `resettest()` argument, we specify the model name (`model.1`), the `type` of test we want (we want the "fitted" values (the $\hat{y}$)), and what `power` to test (this is equivalent to saying we want $\hat{y}^2$ and $\hat{y}^3$). Again, the test compares the fit of our original model to the fit of a model that includes, here, the squared and cubed versions of the fitted values $\hat{y}$.

```
library(lmtest)

resettest(model.1, power = 2:3, type = "fitted")
```

```
    RESET test

data:  model.1
RESET = 461.63, df1 = 2, df2 = 6967, p-value < 2.2e-16
```

The null hypothesis for this test is that there is no significant difference in the amount of variance explained in the outcome variable. We see that $p \leq 0.05$, we reject the null, and conclude that we do indeed violate the assumption of correct functional form, as suggested by the previous plot.

Possible Solution to Violation

If we made no corrections to violating the functional form assumption, we would conclude our estimates are not BLUE; even if one assumption is violated then BLUE breaks down. Generally, if we can find a solution to a violation, we prefer to use it.

We can get a visual sense of which predictors may not be linearly related to the outcome variable by using a **component-plus-residual plot**. This plots what the linear relationship between outcome and predictors should be compared to the estimated relationship. Any variables' plots that demonstrate nonlinearity may need to be transformed to correct for functional form. To perform this test, we will use the crPlots() function from the car package. We'll also shorten the default y-axis label by specifying ylab = "Comp+Resid" in the function.

```
library(car)

crPlots(model.1, ylab = "Comp+Resid")
```

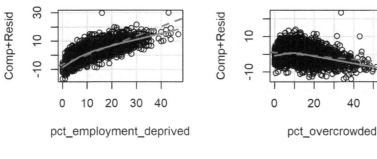

Component + Residual Plots

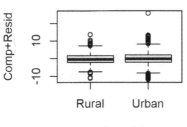

The dashed blue line is what the linear relationship should be, while the solid purple line is the estimated relationship. Both `pct_employment_deprived` and `pct_overcrowded` demonstrate nonlinearity; we will ignore the box plot for `urban_fct` since we do not transform dummy variables.

Our eyeballs have suggested the problematic predictors, but let's use the Box–Tidwell transformation test as a statistical test for identifying problematic predictors. The test assesses whether and how to transform a predictor to improve linearity. We will use the `boxTidwell()` function from the `car` package, where we need to respecify the regression in the argument. Since we do not transform dummy variables, we will leave `urban_fct` out of the test but we'll include it in the specification using `~ urban_fct` (this essentially tells the function to ignore it). One issue with this test is that it will only work if the included predictors only have positive values; that is, we cannot have negative values or zeros. Both `pct_employment_deprived` and `pct_overcrowded` have zeros, and so we will add one (+1) to the values using the `I()` function. Again, the `I()` function allows us to change a variable on the fly instead of creating new versions of the variables.

```
boxTidwell(pct_depress ~ I(pct_employment_deprived + 1) +
           I(pct_overcrowded + 1), ~ urban_fct, data = simd)
                              MLE of lambda Score Statistic (z)  Pr(>|z|)
I(pct_employment_deprived + 1)     0.39435            -24.795 < 2.2e-16 ***
I(pct_overcrowded + 1)             2.03445            -10.089 < 2.2e-16 ***
---
Signif. codes:  0 '***' 0.001 '**' 0.01 '*' 0.05 '.' 0.1 ' ' 1

iterations =  7
```

The output tells us whether we should transform a variable – under the `Pr(>|z|)` heading – and by what value – under `MLE of lambda`. Since $p \leq 0.05$, both `pct_employment_deprived` and `pct_overcrowded` should be transformed. The transformation should be to raise `pct_employment_deprived` to the power 0.39 and `pct_overcrowded` to the power 2.03. As these are non-intuitive values, let's raise `pct_employment_deprived` to the power 0.5 (i.e., take the square root) and square `pct_overcrowded`. Let's rerun the `boxTidwell()` function with these transformations to see if we've solved the problem. Note that we are now making two changes for each predictor using the `I()` function – adding one and the power transformation.

```
boxTidwell(pct_depress ~ I((pct_employment_deprived + 1)^.5) +
           I((pct_overcrowded + 1)^2), ~ urban_fct, data = simd)
                                    MLE of lambda Score Statistic (z)
I((pct_employment_deprived + 1)^0.5)       0.7887            -5.2991
I((pct_overcrowded + 1)^2)                 1.0172            -0.2787
                                    Pr(>|z|)
I((pct_employment_deprived + 1)^0.5) 1.164e-07 ***
I((pct_overcrowded + 1)^2)              0.7805
---
```

```
Signif. codes:  0 '***' 0.001 '**' 0.01 '*' 0.05 '.' 0.1 ' ' 1


iterations =  3
```

We see that squaring `pct_overcrowded` solves its linearity problem (since *p* > 0.05), but that raising `pct_employment_deprived` to the power 0.5 did not (since *p* ≤ 0.05). Let's try the exact suggested value (0.39) from the first Box–Tidwell test for `pct_employment_deprived`.

```
boxTidwell(pct_depress ~ I((pct_employment_deprived + 1)^.39) +
            I((pct_overcrowded + 1)^2), ~ urban_fct, data = simd)
                                        MLE of lambda Score Statistic (z)
I((pct_employment_deprived + 1)^0.39)          1.0111             0.2258
I((pct_overcrowded + 1)^2)                     1.0171            -0.3123
                            Pr(>|z|)
I((pct_employment_deprived + 1)^0.39)   0.8214
I((pct_overcrowded + 1)^2)              0.7548


iterations =  3
```

Yep, that took care of it.

Now, let's include the transformations, using the `I()` function, in a new regression model and save the results as `model.1a`.

```
summary(model.1a <- lm(pct_depress ~ pct_employment_deprived +
                I(pct_employment_deprived^.394) + pct_overcrowded +
                I(pct_overcrowded^2) + urban_fct, data = simd))

Call:
lm(formula = pct_depress ~ pct_employment_deprived + I(pct_employment_
deprived^0.394) +
    pct_overcrowded + I(pct_overcrowded^2) + urban_fct, data = simd)

Residuals:
    Min      1Q  Median      3Q     Max
-12.378  -1.972  -0.156   1.779  26.253


Coefficients:
                                  Estimate Std. Error t value Pr(>|t|)
(Intercept)                      5.7312204  0.2801449  20.458  < 2e-16 ***
pct_employment_deprived          0.1295540  0.0198440   6.529 7.10e-11 ***
I(pct_employment_deprived^0.394) 5.3065534  0.2061331  25.743  < 2e-16 ***
pct_overcrowded                  0.0381722  0.0163254   2.338   0.0194 *
I(pct_overcrowded^2)            -0.0042280  0.0004226 -10.005  < 2e-16 ***
urban_fctUrban                   0.5610599  0.0827880   6.777 1.33e-11 ***
---
```

```
Signif. codes:  0 '***' 0.001 '**' 0.01 '*' 0.05 '.' 0.1 ' ' 1

Residual standard error: 2.938 on 6967 degrees of freedom
  (3 observations deleted due to missingness)
Multiple R-squared:  0.7003,    Adjusted R-squared:  0.7001
F-statistic:  3256 on 5 and 6967 DF,  p-value: < 2.2e-16
```

We see in this new specification of the model that both transformed variables are statistically significant.

Lastly, let's use the `crPlots()` function again to check linearity.

```
crPlots(model.1a, ylab = "Comp+Resid")
```

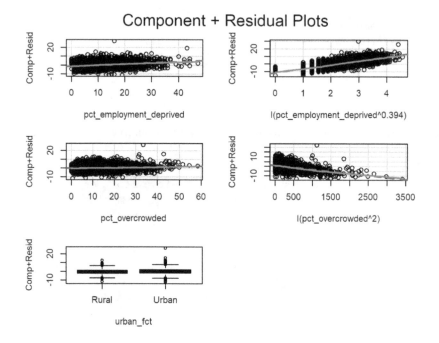

Based on the plots, we see that the transformed versions of `pct_employment_deprived` and `pct_overcrowded` now demonstrate linear relationships with the outcome variable. However, solving one problem can create another for us. How do we interpret the transformed predictors' coefficients? Trying to interpret the transformed predictors based only the coefficients in the output is fairly non-intuitive and difficult. Instead, we can estimate and then plot the effects of the transformed variables using the `ggpredict()` function from the `ggeffects` package.

The `ggeffects` package offers a number of functions that allow easier interpretation of complicated regression model results. For interpreting vanilla linear regression models, `ggeffects` functions are overkill. But when our models include polynomial predictors, interactions, or we are using more complex statistical approaches (e.g., generalised linear models), the `ggeffects` package provides useful functions for understanding regression results.

The `ggpredict()` function estimates predicted values of our outcome variable based on our model. We simply specify our saved model in the argument to get estimated predictions for our predictors.

```
library(ggeffects)

ggpredict(model.1a)
$pct_employment_deprived
# Predicted values of pct_depress

pct_employment_deprived | Predicted |          95% CI
------------------------------------------------------
                     0 |      6.20 | [ 5.60,  6.80]
                     5 |     16.86 | [16.74, 16.98]
                    11 |     21.28 | [21.17, 21.39]
                    17 |     24.61 | [24.48, 24.74]
                    22 |     26.99 | [26.82, 27.16]
                    27 |     29.15 | [28.90, 29.39]
                    33 |     31.52 | [31.17, 31.87]
                    47 |     36.48 | [35.82, 37.14]

Adjusted for:
* pct_overcrowded = 10.94
*         urban_fct = Urban

$pct_overcrowded
# Predicted values of pct_depress

pct_overcrowded | Predicted |         95% CI
---------------------------------------------
          0.00 |     20.45 | [20.18, 20.72]
          3.14 |     20.53 | [20.33, 20.72]
          4.98 |     20.53 | [20.38, 20.69]
          7.04 |     20.51 | [20.38, 20.64]
          9.43 |     20.43 | [20.32, 20.55]
         12.21 |     20.28 | [20.17, 20.40]
         15.43 |     20.03 | [19.91, 20.16]
         58.39 |      8.26 | [ 6.88,  9.65]

Adjusted for:
* pct_employment_deprived =  9.56
*              urban_fct = Urban

$urban_fct
# Predicted values of pct_depress
```

```
urban_fct | Predicted |          95% CI
---------------------------------------------
Rural     |      19.80 | [19.65, 19.95]
Urban     |      20.36 | [20.25, 20.47]

Adjusted for:
* pct_employment_deprived =  9.56
*          pct_overcrowded = 10.94

attr(,"class")
[1] "ggalleffects" "list"
attr(,"model.name")
[1] "model.1a"
```

The output shows the predicted values (and associated 95% confidence intervals) of `pct_depress` for a handful of values of each predictor. Notice that for each predictor, the output also tells us the values that the other predictors are held constant at – the means for `pct_employment_deprived` and `pct_overcrowded`, and the mode for `urban_fct`. For nonlinear predictors, the transformed versions of `pct_employment_deprived` and `pct_overcrowded`, we see that the predicted values aren't linear.

Let's now use the `ggpredict()` function to generate the values for `pct_employment_deprived` and `pct_overcrowded` that we'll plot using `ggplot2`. To keep it simple we'll plot each of the transformed predictors in separate plots. To focus only on a single predictor, we include the option `terms =` in the `ggpredict()` argument. Instead of saving the predictors as an object, let's use the pipe operator to connect `ggpredict()` to the `ggplot2` specification. We've previously used all of these `ggplot2` functions, except for the `geom_ribbon()` function. We'll use the `geom_ribbon()` function to add the estimated 95% confidence intervals for the predicted values to the plot.

Let's start with `pct_employment_deprived`. In the `ggplot(aes())` specification, the `x = x` and `y = predicted` might appear to be generic terms, but they are in fact the names generated by the `ggpredict()` function for the *x*- and *y*-axis, respectively. In the `geom_ribbon(aes())` specification, we set the lower bound of the confidence interval with `ymin = conf.low` and the upper bound with `ymax = conf.high`. We'll also lighten the shading by including `alpha = .25`.

```
ggpredict(model.1a, terms = "pct_employment_deprived") %>%
ggplot(aes(x = x, y = predicted)) +
  geom_line() +
  geom_ribbon(aes(ymin = conf.low, ymax = conf.high), alpha = .25) +
  labs(title = "Transformed Employment Deprived Effect",
       x = "% Employment Deprived",
       y="Predicted % Prescribed Psychiatric Medication") +
  theme_minimal()
```

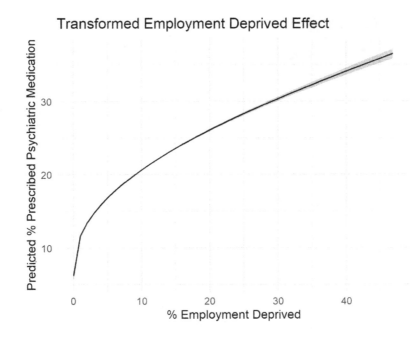

This plot clearly illustrates the nonlinear effect of the transformed `pct_employment_deprived` predictor on `pct_depress`. We see that at the lower percentages of employment deprivation, the predicted percentage of psychiatric medication prescriptions increases rapidly. As the percentage of employment deprivation increases, the predicted percentage of prescriptions continues to increase, but the rate of the increase slows. Notice that the confidence interval gradually widens from around 20% employment deprived. This is due to fewer observations at the higher values of the percentage of employment deprivation contributing to more uncertainty to the predictions.

Let's now plot `pct_overcrowded`. We only need to change the variable name in the `ggpredict()` function and update the labels.

```
ggpredict(model.1a, terms = c("pct_overcrowded")) %>%
ggplot(aes(x = x, y = predicted)) +
  geom_ribbon(aes(ymin = conf.low, ymax = conf.high), alpha = .25) +
  geom_line() +
  labs(title = "Transformed Overcrowded Housing Effect",
       x = "% Overcrowded Housing",
       y = "Predicted % Prescribed Psychiatric Medication") +
  theme_minimal()
```

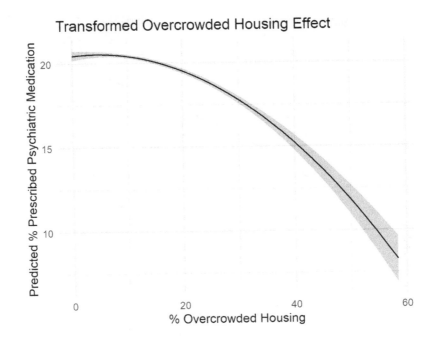

The nonlinear effect of the transformed `pct_overcrowded` predictor on `pct_depress` is clear. As the percentage of overcrowded housing increases, the predicted percentage of psychiatric medication prescriptions is initially flat, and possibly slightly increases, before rapidly decreasing. We see the confidence intervals are wider for lower and higher values of overcrowded housing, particularly for over 40%.

Heteroscedasticity

Plotting

Next, we will test for heteroscedasticity, which is the third assumption of Gauss–Markov. The first test is to plot the residuals and fitted values of our model. This is the same plot as we did for functional form. But instead of examining whether the local means are 0, we are looking to see whether there is any pattern in the residuals. If a pattern exists it implies we may have heteroscedasticity. For sake of consistency, we will use the original model (`model.1`) and not the alternative model (`model.1a`) for testing for heteroscedasticity. Let's rerun the `gg_resfitted()` function and look for a pattern.

```
gg_resfitted(model.1) +
  theme_bw()
```

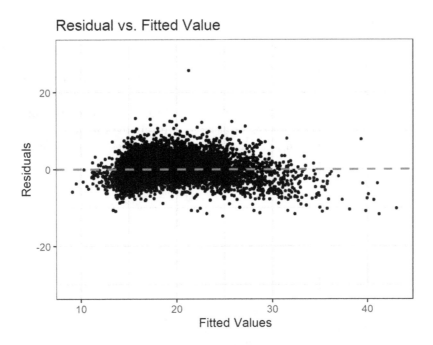

Is there a pattern? Yep. It is not a classic heteroscedastic pattern, but we see some curvature in the residuals and we see the residuals decreasing for higher fitted values. This implies heteroscedasticity may be present.

Breusch-Pagan Test

I usually do not trust myself to only use plots to determine diagnostics, though many researchers prefer to only use diagnostic plots and not formal tests. So, let's use the Breusch–Pagan test for determining whether heteroscedasticity exists. We will use the `bptest()` function from the `lmtest` package. In the argument, we'll specify our model and that we do not want to use studentised residuals (`studentize = FALSE`). The null hypothesis is that *there is constant error variance* (homoscedasticity).

```
bptest(model.1, studentize = FALSE)

    Breusch-Pagan test

data:  model.1
BP = 238.56, df = 3, p-value < 2.2e-16
```

We see that the p-value is below 0.05, thus we reject the null and conclude that we have heteroscedasticity. This means that we violate the third assumption of the Gauss–Markov theorem and therefore our estimates are currently not BLUE.

Correcting Heteroscedasticity with Robust Standard Errors

To correct for heteroscedasticity, we will rerun our regression model with robust standard errors using the `coeftest()` function from the `lmtest` package. In the argument, we'll specify our model (`model.1`) and change the covariance matrix into a heteroscedasticity-consistent one (`vcov = vcovHC`). Although the `coeftest()` function is from the `lmtest` package, we need to load the `sandwich` package to use the `vcovHC` option.[5] The regression coefficients will be the same as before, but the standard errors should be larger. We want to focus on whether the statistical significance results for our predictors change – specifically, whether the predictors that were significant still are significant.

```
library(sandwich)

coeftest(model.1, vcov = vcovHC)

t test of coefficients:

                         Estimate  Std. Error  t value  Pr(>|t|)
(Intercept)             13.5446674  0.0798429 169.6416 < 2.2e-16 ***
pct_employment_deprived  0.6628749  0.0080262  82.5894 < 2.2e-16 ***
pct_overcrowded         -0.0970874  0.0068554 -14.1622 < 2.2e-16 ***
urban_fctUrban           0.3597303  0.0825704   4.3567 1.34e-05 ***
---
Signif. codes:  0 '***' 0.001 '**' 0.01 '*' 0.05 '.' 0.1 ' ' 1
```

We see that all three predictors are still statistically significant when using robust standard errors. Notice that the regression coefficients are the same, but the standard errors are all slightly larger. Correcting for heteroscedasticity in the model gives us greater confidence that the statistical significance results we observed earlier were correct.

If we correct the functional form and use robust standard errors then we conclude that our model satisfies the Gauss–Markov theorem and that our estimates are BLUE. Again, this is an ideal situation, but often it is difficult to achieve. There are times when we try to make the best choices and corrections that are possible, and acknowledge that our OLS estimates might not be BLUE.

Normality

As discussed previously, the normality assumption is not part of BLUE, but it is critical for being able to make inferences about the population from our sample data. If we violate normality and make no corrections, then we cannot be confident that the results we obtain in our sample necessarily apply to the population. We will consider three different tests for normality: histograms, Q-Q plots, and the Anderson–Darling normality test.

---

[5]To the best of the my knowledge, R (still) does not have an easy way to include robust standard errors, unlike other statistical programs like Stata.

Histogram

First, we will plot a histogram of the residuals for `model.1` using the `gg_rehist()` function from the `lindia` package. We are looking for whether the residuals appear normally distributed. With real data, the residuals will never be perfectly normal and so we need to use our own judgement as to how normal they appear.

```
gg_reshist(model.1) +
    theme_bw()
```

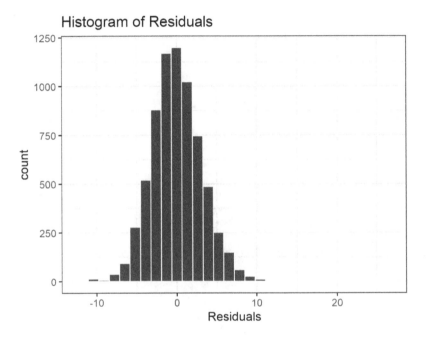

The residuals appear somewhat normally distributed, but the upper tail, in particular, skews the distribution. Given this, we probably violate normality.

Q-Q Plot

Next, we will use a Q-Q plot to examine the normality of the residuals. Q-Q plots illustrate whether our model's residuals are the same as theoretical values for residuals in a perfect normal distribution. Each point represents one quantile. When the residuals are the same, they will lie on a 45-degree diagonal line. We are looking for what proportion, in general, of residuals fall on and off the diagonal. We almost always observe residuals at the tails trailing away from the line and so we want to assess the proportion trailing off. Similar to evaluating the histogram, there is no hard-and-fast rule for determining normality with Q-Q plots and so it is more of a judgement call.

We'll use the `gg_qqplot()` function from the `lindia` package to create our Q-Q plot. We'll also change the default title using the `labs()` function from the `ggplot2` package.

```
gg_qqplot(model.1) +
  labs(title = "Normal Q-Q Plot") +
  theme_bw()
```

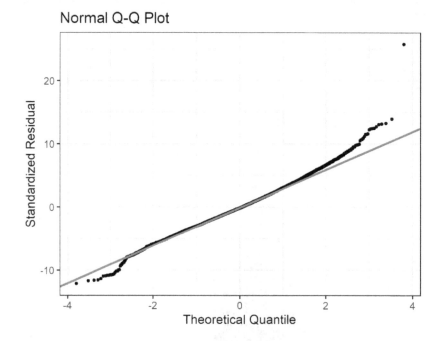

We observe a substantial proportion of residuals off the diagonal line, particularly at the tails. This gives a clearer indication than the histogram that our residuals are not normally distributed.

Anderson-Darling Normality Test

Lastly, we'll perform a formal test for normality. One commonly used normality test is the Shapiro–Wilk normality test (in R, the shapiro.test() function). However, the Shapiro–Wilk test in R can only work if the sample size is between 3 and 5000 observations. The simd dataset has 6,976 observations, and so we need to use an alternative test. There are a number of different alternative tests in R, and we'll use the Anderson–Darling normality test. Using the ad.test() function from the nortest package, we need to specify our model and the residuals (model.1$residuals) in the function's argument. The null hypothesis is that *the residuals are normally distributed*, and so we do not want to reject the null.

```
library(nortest)

ad.test(model.1$residuals)

    Anderson-Darling normality test

data:  model.1$residuals
A = 7.1325, p-value < 2.2e-16
```

We see from the test that $p < 0.05$, we reject the null, and thus we cannot assume our residuals are normally distributed. Since we cannot assume normality of our errors/residuals, we cannot be confident that the results we find from our sample data will apply to the population as a whole. However, again, violating normality has no effect on whether our estimates are BLUE.

Possible Solutions

There are a few possible solutions when we violate the normality assumption. One option is to use a generalised linear model where we can relax the normality assumption. Another option is to transform the outcome variable. Many researchers simply take the logarithm of the outcome variable and rerun the model. In another approach, Kabacoff (2022) suggests using a Box–Cox transformation for figuring out whether and by what value to transform the outcome variable. To do the transformation, we use the `powerTransform()` function from the `car` package. The outcome variable must only have positive values in order to use the `powerTransform()` function with the standard Box–Cox transformation. We've seen that `pct_depress` has one observation with a value of 0, but that observation has a missing value for `pct_employment_deprived` and thus is dropped in `model.1`.

Let's run the `powerTransform()` function, wrapped by `summary()`, for `model.1`.[6]

```
summary(powerTransform(model.1))
bcPower Transformation to Normality
   Est Power Rounded Pwr Wald Lwr Bnd Wald Upr Bnd
Y1    0.9508           1       0.8952       1.0064

Likelihood ratio test that transformation parameter is equal to 0
 (log transformation)
                           LRT df       pval
LR test, lambda = (0) 1151.631  1 < 2.22e-16

Likelihood ratio test that no transformation is needed
                        LRT df      pval
LR test, lambda = (1) 3.003661  1 0.083077
```

There are two important parts of the output. First, the number under the column heading `Est Power` tells us *how* to transform our outcome variable – here, it says that `pct_depress` should be raised to the power 0.9508 (thus, $(pct\_depress)^{0.9508}$). Second, at the bottom, the likelihood-ratio (LR) test for $\lambda = 1$ tells us *whether* we should make the transformation. Here, we see that $p = 0.08$, just above our $p \leq 0.05$ threshold, and thus we should *not* make the transformation. Further, if we were going to transform the outcome variable, the suggested transformation is rounded to 1, which obviously does not change the values. This is a bit of a dilemma. Our testing – histograms, Q-Q plot, and Anderson–Darling test – all showed we violate the normality assumption, but this test suggests we shouldn't transform the outcome variable. *What should we do?*

---

[6]We can use the outcome variable (`simd$pct_depress`) in the `powerTransform()` function instead of `model.1`, but here we are interested in addressing normality in our model's residuals and not normality in the outcome variable. This is a correction to the first edition of this book.

In this case, it turns out that we can't fix non-normality in the residuals by transforming the outcome variable. We could try something like removing outliers to fix non-normality, but we might not want to do that if the outliers are informative and not just random junk (here, they aren't random junk). We also could try a different modelling technique or estimation procedure to deal with non-normality. However, we will pause our investigation as we are approaching a situation where the cure is worse than the disease. Since normality does not affect whether our estimates are BLUE and the central limit theorem suggests normality in large samples, research-ers have suggested not worrying about normality violations (e.g., Knief and Forstmeier 2021; Lumley et al. 2002). In sum, we should probably test for normality and, if we violate the assumption, try to make simple adjustments to remedy the problem. If the solution requires Herculean efforts, we should accept that the violation exists and chalk it up to using real-world social science data.

Multicollinearity

Again, multicollinearity is when one or more of our predictors are functions, in part, of other predictors. When multicollinearity is present, the predictors' standard errors will be larger than they should be, and thus we are less likely to find statistical significance even if it is there.

Correlations

The quick and dirty way of checking for multicollinearity is by examining correlations among our predictor variables. Again, correlations will give us a quick glimpse at potential issues, but they do not definitively tell you whether multicollinearity is present or not.[7] Let's use the `correlate()` function from the `corrr` package to examine correlations between our predictors. We'll use the `select()` function to specify the predictors, then the `correlate()` function with the option `use = "complete.obs"`. Because we can only run correlations on numeric variables in R, we'll use `urban` instead of `urban_fct` in the correlation.

```
library(corrr)

simd %>%
  select(pct_employment_deprived,pct_overcrowded,urban) %>%
  correlate(use = "complete.obs")

Correlation method: 'pearson'
Missing treated using: 'complete.obs'
# A tibble: 3 x 4
  term                    pct_employment_deprived pct_overcrowded urban
  <chr>                                     <dbl>           <dbl> <dbl>
1 pct_employment_deprived                      NA           0.571 0.201
2 pct_overcrowded                           0.571              NA 0.342
3 urban                                      0.20           0.342    NA
```

---

[7]So, don't tell the statistics police that we are using them.

We see that none of the correlations are near |0.8|, thus suggesting we probably do not have a multicollinearity problem.

Variance Inflation Factor Test

The correlations suggested there's no multicollinearity, but it is always best to perform a VIF test. If any of the values are 10 or greater, then the variable is collinear with one or more other predictors. We will use the `vif()` function from the `car` package to run the test.

```
vif(model.1)
pct_employment_deprived        pct_overcrowded            urban_fct
              1.485037               1.613519             1.132491
```

None of the predictors are near 10 and thus we can conclude that we do not have multicollinearity. As previously mentioned, it is rare to have true/actual multicollinearity. It is more likely the case that if we find a high VIF value we have included two versions of the same variable. If we did observe a predictor with a VIF value of 10 or greater, the main solution is to remove the offending variable from our regression model.

Outliers, Leverage, and Influential Data Points

Our final diagnostic tests involve identifying outliers, leverage, and influential data points. First, any data points whose residuals are ±2 standard deviations or more away from 0 are considered outliers. Again, outliers on their own do not necessarily present problems; problems occur when outliers have leverage.

To check for leverage, we need to calculate a cut-point using the expression $2(k+1)/n$, where k is the number of predictors (here, 3) and n is the number of observations in our model (here, 6973). Any observation that has a hat value equal to or greater than the calculated value is considered to have *high leverage* (Fox 2002). For our model:

```
(2*(3+1))/6973
[1] 0.001147282
```

Therefore, any data point that has a hat value equal to or greater than 0.0011 is considered to have high leverage.

Finally, since we have a relatively large number of observations, we'll consider any point that has a Cook's distance greater than 1 to be influential.

Now that we have the relevant diagnostic metrics sorted, let's create plots to examine outliers, data points with leverage, and influential data points using the `influenceIndexPlot()` function from the `car` package. In the `influenceIndexPlot()` function, we need to specify `model.1` and that we want the plots for outliers (`"Studentized"`), leverage (`"hat"`), and influence (`"Cook"`).

```
influenceIndexPlot(model.1,
                   vars = c("Studentized","hat","Cook"))
```

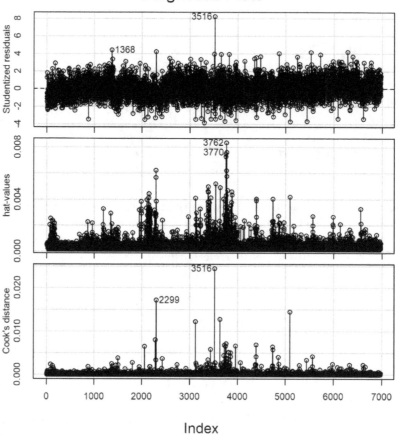

The top plot shows that there a good number of observations that are outliers – residuals that are ±2 standard deviations away from 0. The middle plot shows that there are some points that have high leverage – points whose hat values are equal to or greater than 0.0011. The bottom plot, however, shows that none of the observations are influential. Again, we can have outliers and data points with leverage, but if we do not have any influential data points then we do not need to make any corrections.

We are able to inspect any particular data point to see whether the variables' values indicate why it may be problematic. In the plots, we see that observation 3156 is the largest outlier and has the highest Cook's *d* value. Let's take a look at this observation to see if anything funky stands out about the datazone. We'll use the `select()` function to narrow down the number of variables we are viewing by only including the four variables in `model.1`. We'll use the `slice()` function from the `dplyr` package specify that we only want values for observation 3156.

```
simd %>%
  select(pct_depress,pct_employment_deprived,pct_overcrowded,urban_fct) %>%
  slice(3156)
# A tibble: 1 x 4
```

```
    pct_depress pct_employment_deprived pct_overcrowded urban_fct
          <dbl>                   <dbl>           <dbl> <chr>
  1        17.0                       6            2.20 Rural
```

We see that this observation is a rural datazone with somewhat lower than average percentages of prescribed psychiatric medication (17%) and employment deprivation (6%). Nothing too weird. However, this datazone has a very small percentage of overcrowded housing (2.2%). Let's check how small this value is relative to other datazones using the summary() function.

```
summary(simd$pct_overcrowded)
   Min. 1st Qu.  Median    Mean 3rd Qu.    Max.
  0.000   4.922   9.203  10.951  15.029  58.388
```

We see that the 25% (1st Qu.) value is 4.922, which this datazone is certainly below. We can use the quantile() function to get a finer-grained perspective of the distribution. In the function's argument we'll specify probs = c(.05,.1), which tells R to return the values of pct_overcrowded at the 5% and 10% quantiles.

```
quantile(simd$pct_overcrowded, probs = c(.05,.1))
      5%      10%
1.910639 2.745175
```

So, this datazone's value for pct_overcrowded is between the 5% and 10% quantiles. That's pretty small.

We should also check how this datazone compares to the means of urban datazones and other rural datazones. We'll use the group_by() function to separate urban and rural datazones, and the summarise() function to calculate the means for pct_depress, pct_employment_deprived, and pct_overcrowded.

```
simd %>%
  group_by(urban_fct) %>%
  summarise(mean_depress = mean(pct_depress, na.rm = TRUE),
            mean_employ = mean(pct_employment_deprived, na.rm = TRUE),
            mean_crowd = mean(pct_overcrowded))
# A tibble: 2 x 4
  urban_fct mean_depress mean_employ mean_crowd
  <chr>            <dbl>       <dbl>      <dbl>
1 Rural             17.8        7.41       6.90
2 Urban             19.6       10.5       12.7
```

This shows that the datazone is well below the average of pct_overcrowded among other rural datazones. We could keep going down this rabbit hole of comparisons, but we can reasonably conclude that the pct_overcrowded value is probably the reason for the high Cook's d value.

So, what is the mysterious datazone? Let's add intermediate_zone and council_area to our variables in the select() function to identify the datazone.

```
simd %>%
  select(intermediate_zone,council_area,pct_depress,
         pct_employment_deprived,pct_overcrowded,urban_fct) %>%
  slice(3156)
# A tibble: 1 x 6
  intermediate_zone    council_area pct_depress pct_employment_de~ pct_
overcrowded
  <chr>                <chr>              <dbl>              <dbl>      <dbl>
1 Kennoway and Bonn~   Fife                17.0                  6       2.20
# ... with 1 more variable: urban_fct <chr>
```

We see that this datazone is the Kennoway and Bonnybank area in Fife. Kennoway and Bonnybank are actually two separate small towns combined by the Scottish government for statistical purposes.

In summary, we found that in order for our model's estimates to be BLUE, we had to correct the functional form by using transformed versions of `pct_employment_deprived` and `pct_overcrowded`, and use robust standard errors. We also had to transform our outcome variable to remedy the normality assumption violation. Finally, we found no problems with multicollinearity or influential data points in our model.

CONCLUSION

This chapter has discussed the core and ancillary assumptions of linear regression OLS estimation, including the Gauss–Markov theorem and BLUE, how to test the assumptions, and potential solutions to violations using R. The diagnostic tests and approaches in this chapter are not exhaustive, and you will likely encounter other diagnostic techniques when using linear regression. However, this chapter provides a solid foundation for understanding the intricacies of OLS estimation and applications in R.

If you worked closely through this chapter you have may have found parts of it bewildering. When there are no easy fixes to violations of assumptions or there are easy fixes but they don't work, it can be a fairly frustrating exercise. Sometimes we have to just throw up our hands and accept that we have done the best we can. It is better to know what assumptions may not hold and be aware of the potential implications, than blindly assuming everything is good to go. A smarter approach when we cannot fix violations of OLS assumptions is to utilise different statistical modelling techniques where certain OLS assumptions are relaxed.

Extensions to the linear regression model are commonly called advanced regression or generalised linear models. In the next chapter, we'll introduce and examine such generalised linear models. However, our focus is on regression models for when our outcome variable is categorical (i.e., binary, ordinal, nominal) and not exotic linear regression models.

━━━━━ R Packages Used in This Chapter ━━━━━

- `car`
- `corrr`
- `dplyr` (loaded with `tidyverse`)
- `ggplot2` (loaded with `tidyverse`)
- `ggeffects`
- `lindia`
- `lmtest`
- `nortest`
- `pillar` (loaded with `tidyverse`)
- `sandwich`
- `tidymodels`
- `tidyverse`

━━━━━ R Functions Used in This Chapter ━━━━━

- `ad.test()` – Anderson-Darling normality test using `nortest` package
- `boxTidwell()` – Box-Tidwell test for transforming predictors using `car` package
- `bptest()` – Breusch-Page test for heteroscedasticity using `lmtest` package
- `c()` – concatenate
- `coeftest()` – linear regression with robust standard errors using `lmtest` package
- `correlate()` – correlation analysis using `corrr` package
- `crPlots()` – component-plus-residual plot using `car` package
- `filter()` – subset data based on variables' values using `dplyr` package
- `geom_line()` – ggplot2 line
- `geom_ribbon()` – ggplot2 ribbons plot
- `ggpredict()` – adjusted predictions for regression models
- `gg_qqplot()` – Q-Q plot using `lindia` package
- `gg_reshist()` – histogram of residuals using `lindia` package
- `gg_resfitted()` – residuals by fitted values plot using `lindia` package
- `ggpredict()` – adjusted predictions for regression models
- `group_by()` – group observations by variables using `dplyr` package
- `I()` – transform variable without creating a new variable
- `influenceIndexplot()` – outliers, leverage, and influential data points plot using `car` package
- `is.na()` – checks for missing values (NAs) in variables
- `labs()` – ggplot2 labels
- `lm()` – linear regression
- `mean()` – mean
- `mutate()` – recode variables using `dplyr` package

(Continued)

- `powerTransform()` - Box-Cox test for transforming outcome variable using `car` package
- `quantile()` - calculate sample values corresponding to given probabilities
- `read_csv()` - read in .csv data file using `readr` package
- `rename_with()` - rename variable using a function using `dplyr` package
- `resettest()` - Ramsey RESET test for functional form
- `select()` - subset data based on variables using `dplyr` package
- `slice()` - subset rows using `dplyr` package
- `summarise()` - create new variables based on grouped observations using `dplyr` package
- `summary()` - summarise object
- `theme_bw()` - black-and-white `ggplot2` theme
- `theme_minimal()` - minimal `ggplot2` theme
- `vif()` - variance inflation factor test using `car` package

Additional Resources

Books

- Greene, W. H. (2017) *Econometric Analysis*, 8th edition. Pearson.
- Harris, J. K. (2020) *Statistics with R: Solving Problems Using Real-World Data*. Sage.
- Long, J. D. and Teetor, P. (2019) *R Cookbook*, 2nd edition. O'Reilly Media.

Online

- Tidymodels: https://www.tidymodels.org/

13

GENERALISED LINEAR MODELS

Chapter contents

In this chapter, we'll examine common generalised linear regression models. Our focus is on generalised linear models (GLMs) for categorical outcome variables (i.e., non-continuous outcome variables).[1]

The chapter is designed to provide an introduction to common GLMs and how to run them in R; a complete treatment of GLMs would require its own full-length book. We'll start with a brief discussion of maximum likelihood estimation (MLE), the standard estimation procedure used for GLMs, and then go through binary, ordered, and nominal outcome models. Since this chapter is a concise treatment of GLMs, we will only cover a few critical assumptions, diagnostics, and possible solutions in the models.

In quantitative social science training, GLMs are typically the material covered immediately following linear regression. The reason, as we discussed in Chapters 11 and 12, is that linear regression requires a (near) continuous outcome variable. However, most QSS datasets are bereft of such outcome variables. Although we may not frequently use linear regression in our research, understanding how linear regression works provides the basis for understanding GLMs.

A key difference between linear regression and the GLMs covered in this chapter is that we are now estimating and talking about *probabilities*. We want to know the probability of a specific outcome, given a set of conditions. For example, how does a predictor change the probability of some event occurring?

Trying to understand MLE and GLMs can be tricky for students.[2] Some of the concepts are counter-intuitive, the mathematics involved can be difficult, and interpreting results is not as straightforward as in linear regression. Our goal in this chapter is to learn the intuition behind the different models, how to run the models in R, and how to interpret and communicate the results in plain language. We will keep things simple to make learning GLMs a straightforward task.

By the end of this chapter, you should be able to:

- Understand the intuition and steps of MLE
- Understand and run binary outcome models (logit and probit) in R
- Understand and run ordered outcome models (ordered logit and probit) in R
- Understand and run unordered outcome models (multinomial logit and probit) in R
- Identify statistically significant predictors and perform regression coefficient interpretations
- Create visualisations of regression coefficients

MAXIMUM LIKELIHOOD ESTIMATION

Maximum likelihood estimation (MLE) is simply a procedure to obtain estimates for various statistical techniques. In this chapter, we will use MLE to obtain estimates for our GLMs. Thus, MLE is similar to OLS estimation in what it is trying to achieve.

---

[1]The term 'GLM' can refer to many different regression models that are not a standard linear regression models. Furthermore, depending on the content, GLMs are sometimes called advanced regression models, categorical data analysis, or limited and categorical dependent variable regression.

[2]I definitely struggled when I first learned the material.

Since the mathematics underlying MLE can be daunting, we will instead focus our discussion on the intuition of MLE.[3] In this section we will take a look under the hood – and not try to take all the pieces apart and replace the flux capacitor.

We will briefly discuss the intuition, the analytical procedure, and then how MLE is done in practice with algorithms.

Intuition of MLE

Imagine a variable has a parameter of interest θ (e.g., the mean) that describes a population. We only have a sample of the population (i.e., sample data) and thus we can only obtain estimates of θ, which are denoted by $\hat{\theta}$.

Taking the sample data as given, different values of $\hat{\theta}$ are more likely to have given us the sample that we have. Whichever value of $\hat{\theta}$ is *most likely* to have given us the data is considered the maximum likelihood estimate.

We can phrase this slightly more formally (from Long 1997):

> The maximum likelihood estimate is the value $\hat{\theta}$ that maximizes the likelihood of observing the sample data that we actually observe.

Hence, like reading the regression output in Chapter 11, MLE is like *Memento* – we start at the end and work backwards.

MLE Procedure

Analytically, MLE consists of three steps:

1 We specify the likelihood function, which provides the likelihood of the data.[4] The likelihood function (L) is bounded between 0 and 1 ($L \in [0,1]$). Since likelihood is equivalent to a probability, values closer to 1 are more preferred.
2 We take the natural log (ln) of the likelihood function to obtain the log-likelihood function. This is done because it is easier to calculate derivatives of the log-likelihood function. The log-likelihood function (ℓ) is bounded between minus infinity and 0 ($\ell \in (-\infty, 0]$), where values closer to 0 are more preferred (because ln (1) = 0).
3 We maximise the log-likelihood function. This involves taking the first derivative, setting it equal to zero, and solving for the parameter of interest.[5] The result is the maximum likelihood estimator.

Maximising the likelihood function analytically quickly becomes complicated and intractable. Instead, we (actually R) use numerical algorithms to quickly find the maximum.

---

[3]See Cameron and Trivedi (2005), Long (1997), or pretty much any econometrics textbook for the mathematical details of MLE.

[4]The equation of the likelihood function is derived from the probability distribution (e.g., a normal distribution, a Poisson distribution, etc.).

[5]Don't worry, we are not going to do this by hand.

Numerical Methods for MLE

Intuition

The general idea is as follows:

1. The algorithm starts with an initial guess which is called the starting value; let's name it θ_0. This almost never maximises the log-likelihood function.
2. An adjustment is made to the starting value to see if it maximises the function:

    $$\theta_1 = \theta_0 + \xi_0$$

    where ξ_0 is the adjustment value.
3. Adjustments continue to be made until the log-likelihood function is maximised. Each adjustment is known as an iteration. The general form of this process is given by:

    $$\theta_t = \theta_{t-1} + \xi_{t-1}$$

The most common algorithms are known as hill-climbing algorithms. The basic idea of hill-climbing algorithms is that we keep stepping up the log-likelihood function until the slope switches from positive to negative. When it does, it means we have crossed the maximum. The algorithm keeps making adjustments until the slope is 0. When the slope is 0 that means we have maximised the log-likelihood function.

Visualisation of MLE Algorithm

Let's look at a very simple visualisation of a hill-climbing algorithm.

MLE Algorithm

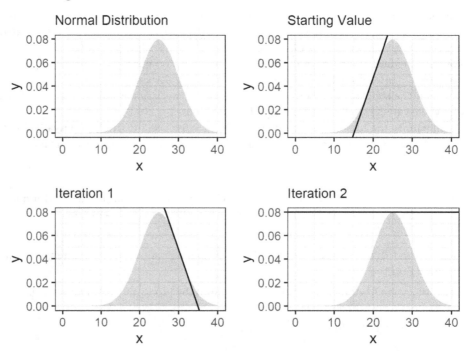

Let's imagine the log-likelihood function is from a normal distribution (top left-hand plot) and we are trying to find the maximum. The algorithm guesses a starting value and sees the slope is positive (top right-hand plot). Since the slope is positive, it means that we have not found the maximum. Next, the algorithm makes an adjustment (an iteration) and sees the slope is now negative (bottom left-hand plot). Since the slope has changed from positive to negative, the algorithm knows that it has passed a maximum (again, where the slope = 0). The algorithm makes another adjustment and sees the slope is zero (bottom right-hand plot). Thus, the algorithm has reached a maximum.

When an algorithm finds (or settles on) a maximum of ℓ, we say it has converged. In practice, the algorithm typically never finds the true (global) maximum. Instead, when each iteration provides no real increase in ℓ, the algorithm stops searching and settles on a value. Although the algorithm starts at a random place, it should converge around the same value each time.[6]

If the algorithm is unable to converge, R will give us some type of warning or error message about non-convergence, non-concavity, or something similar. If R still provides us results when this occurs, we should not trust them. The reason is that R is telling us that it doesn't know the answer, but here is guess; and the guess could be completely wrong. There are a number of possible reasons for non-convergence, including a small number of observations, data-cleaning errors (e.g., a random comma in a value), poor model fit, large scaling differences between variables (e.g., a variable with five values and a variable with a 1000 values), or a complex log-likelihood function (e.g., multinomial probit).

There are many MLE algorithms, but some are more frequently used than others. The default algorithm in the widely used `glm()` function is the *Newton–Raphson algorithm*. This algorithm uses second derivatives – the rate of change – which allows it to take smaller steps as the slope changes decrease. Because the algorithm calculates second derivatives it can be computationally intensive and get stuck on flat parts of the log-likelihood function. A common set of alternative algorithms to Newton–Raphson are known as *quasi-Newton algorithms*. Quasi-Newton algorithms are more efficient because they don't calculate second derivatives. There are a whole gaggle of these algorithms that all use the initials of their authors, including BHHH, BHHH-2, DFP, and BFGS. Typically, we'll only switch to a different algorithm if we have convergence problems or the algorithm takes a very long time to converge.

Our discussion of MLE might have seemed like drinking water from a fire hydrant! If that's the case, we really just need to know that MLE is the way we obtain estimates (i.e., regression coefficients and standard errors) for our GLMs.

Now that we know the basics of how MLE works, let's start our GLM adventure by looking at binary outcome models.

BINARY OUTCOME MODELS

Binary Outcome Variables

As the name implies, binary outcome models are used when we have an outcome variable with only two values and we are interested in predicting whether an outcome occurred. Generically, these variables are defined as:

---

[6]We could set a starting seed so that algorithm begins at the same place each time. However, for non-complex models, this is normally not required.

$$Y = \begin{cases} 0 & \text{if outcome doesn't occur} \\ 1 & \text{if outcome does occur} \end{cases}$$

Can you think of any binary outcome variables? One commonly analysed binary outcome variable is vote choice. For example,

$$Y = \begin{cases} 0 & \text{voted for Trump} \\ 1 & \text{voted for Biden} \end{cases}$$

Another example is whether a fatality occurred during an armed robbery:

$$Y = \begin{cases} 0 & \text{fatality didn't occur} \\ 1 & \text{fatality did occur} \end{cases}$$

Linear Probability Model

Why can't we use OLS linear regression for binary outcome variables? After Chapters 11 and 12, the reasons should be obvious. However, there is a version of linear regression called the linear probability model (LPM). As the name implies, the probability of an event occurring is modelled linearly. People like LPM because the interpretations of the coefficients are the same as we use in linear regression. However, the LPM is not the way to go – *just don't use it.*

There are (at least) four reasons why the LPM ain't cool. First, the errors are not normally distributed. Like the outcome variable, the errors can only take on two values in a binary outcome model. Second, the LPM has built-in heteroscedasticity; thus, the standard errors are biased and the test statistics are incorrect. Third, the LPM can generate non-sensible predictions of y such as negative values and values over 1. Since binary outcome models are used to predict the probability of an event occurring and probability is bounded between 0 and 1, such predicted values are meaningless. Fourth, since the probability is modelled linearly (thus a constant rate of change), the predictors in LPM are likely to have the wrong functional form. Instead, the effect that a predictor has on the probability of an event occurring is more likely to be S-shaped (Long 1997).

Let's look at an example of this last point. Imagine we want to predict the probability of buying a house based on individuals' annual salaries. It is much more likely that as we move from a very low income to a very high income the probability is curvilinear instead of linear. That is, there is probably some threshold salary where the probability of an individual buying a house changes dramatically.

Using the hypothetical probabilities in the plot, let's consider the effect of a $10,000 increase on the probability of buying a house for three individuals with different current salaries: $10,000, $65,000, and $130,000. We see that increasing someone's salary from $10,000 to $20,000 or from $130,000 to $140,000 is unlikely to change their probability of buying a house; it is still not affordable for the former and it is already affordable for the latter. But increasing someone's salary from $65,000 to $75,000 may dramatically change their probability of buying house; the $10,000 increase makes this individual much more likely to buy a house. (This is represented by the blue line in the plot.)

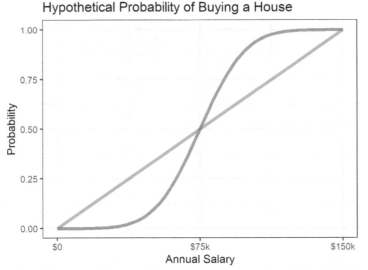

Hypothetical Probability of Buying a House

The red line represents linear probability & the blue line represents curvilinear probability

The LPM, on the other hand, says that a $10,000 salary increase has the same effect on the probability of buying house for each of these three types of individuals. (This is represented by the red line in the plot.) Clearly in this case, assuming a linear probability is wrong. There may be examples where assuming a linear probability is more accurate and intuitive, and using an LPM will not cause the end of the world. However, the models we discuss below provide much greater flexibility and accuracy in estimating the change in probability than the LPM.

Logit and Probit Models

The two dominant regression techniques for analysing binary outcome variables are logit and probit models. Both logit and probit assume symmetrical error distributions,[7] which implies (King 1998):

- The distribution of y is not too skewed
- The greatest probability change occurs in the middle range of the distribution (i.e., on the S-curve)

The main difference between logit and probit is the assumption made about the error distributions. Logit assumes the errors follow a logistic distribution, where $\mu = 0$ and $\sigma^2 = \pi^2 / 3$. Probit assumes the errors follow a normal distribution, where $\mu = 0$ and $\sigma^2 = 1$. Because the normal distribution is well understood, some researchers prefer using probit over logit.

However, whether we use a logit or probit model, the results will almost always be the same. Logit regression coefficients tend to be somewhat larger than probit regression coefficients, but

---

[7]When we cannot assume the errors are symmetrical, we can use models that assume asymmetrical error distributions (e.g., skewed logit and complementary log-log).

the statistical significance tests, the direction of effects, and sizes of the predicted effects will typically be the same using logit or probit regression. How we interpret the coefficients will be slightly different based on using logit or probit (more on this below).

To close the circle with LPM, logit and probit models have nice continuous error distributions, are not heteroscedastic (due to the fixed error variances), never produce inadmissible estimates of the probability (since their lower asymptote is 0 and their upper asymptote is 1), and do not assume a constant change in the probability everywhere along the distribution (they capture a S-shaped relationship) (Long 1997).

Now let's get into the data and run logit and probit models.

Binary Logit and Probit Model Application: Explaining the 2014 Scottish Independence Vote

Data Wrangling

We will use data from the 2014 Scottish Social Attitudes survey in this section. This survey was fielded prior to the 2014 Scottish independence referendum and included a question on respondents' vote intention in the referendum. We will use this variable (RefVoteDum) as the outcome variable in our models.

We'll read in the file 2014 Scottish Social Attitudes.dta using the read_dta() function that is part of the haven package. Let's name this dataset ssa.

```
setwd("C:/QSSD/Chapter 13 - Generalised Linear Models")
getwd()


library(haven)
ssa <- read_dta("2014 Scottish Social Attitudes.dta")
```

For our logit and probit models, we'll use the strength of Scottish identity (ScotID_NoNA), trust in the UK government (GovTrust_NoNa), and age (rage) as our predictors of respondents' expected vote in the referendum. Prior to running our models, we'll wrangle these variables within a single code chunk (since we are pros by this point in the book) as follows:

- Convert RefvoteDum to a factor variable and apply labels (labels are pulled in from the Stata version of the data). We'll name this new variable refvote.
- Rename ScotID_NoNa as scot.
- Flip the four values of GovTrust_NoNa so that they go from 'never trust' to 'always trust', and create a new variable named trust. This is accomplished using three nested functions. First, we'll convert GovTrust_NoNa to a factor variable, then we'll flip the values with the fct_rev() function, and then we'll convert it to a numeric variable. We could do this in three separate lines, but it always best practice to use nested functions if possible – unless it looks too confusing.
- Rename rage as age (the r stands for 'respondent'; though it would be cool if we actually had a variable for *rage*!).

```
library(tidyverse)
ssa <- ssa %>%
        mutate(refvote = as_factor(RefvoteDum, levels = "labels"),
            scot = ScotID_NoNa,
            trust = as.numeric(fct_rev(as_factor(GovTrust_NoNa))),
            age = rage
            )
```

Let's take a quick look at these variables using the summary() function.

```
summary(ssa$refvote)
  0. Vote No 1. Vote Yes          NA's
        680          354           467
summary(ssa$scot)
   Min. 1st Qu.  Median    Mean 3rd Qu.    Max.   NA's
  1.000   5.000   6.000   5.611   7.000   7.000      4
summary(ssa$trust)
   Min. 1st Qu.  Median    Mean 3rd Qu.    Max.   NA's
  1.000   1.000   2.000   1.759   2.000   4.000     30
summary(ssa$age)
   Min. 1st Qu.  Median    Mean 3rd Qu.    Max.
  18.00   38.00   53.00   52.28   66.00   99.00
```

For refvote, only about one-third of respondents planned to vote 'Yes' for Scottish independence; notice the large number of missing values for this variable. The scot variable represents the strength of respondents' Scottish identity, where 1 represents the weakest identity and 7 represents the strongest identity. Based on the median (6.00) and mean (5.61) values, respondents appear to have a fairly strong sense of Scottish identity. The trust variable represents how often respondents trust the UK government (i.e., Westminster) to have the people's best interests in mind. As we might expect, respondents have relatively low levels of trust in the UK government. Lastly, we see that the average age of respondents is roughly 52 years old.

Binary Logit Model

To run logit and probit regression in R, we will use the glm() function, which stands for *generalised linear models*, from the base R stats package. The glm() function allows for a variety of different types of regression models through the family and link function options (use ?glm() to find out what is available).

How we specify the glm() function is very similar to how we specified the lm() function for linear regression. In the glm() function, we first include the outcome variable, followed by ~, then our predictors. The predictors are separated by + (just like in linear regression). To run a logit model, we specify family = binomial and link = "logit"; to run a probit model, we just specify link = "probit". We also need to specify the data we are using: data = ssa. We'll save the regression results as an object (e.g., model.1) using the <- operator and wrap the summary() function around all of it to print the results.

```
summary(model.logit <- glm(refvote ~ scot + trust + age,
                    family = binomial(link = "logit"), data = ssa))

Call:
glm(formula = refvote ~ scot + trust + age, family = binomial(link = "logit"),
    data = ssa)

Deviance Residuals:
    Min       1Q   Median       3Q      Max
-1.5793  -0.9210  -0.6273   1.1487   2.4668

Coefficients:
              Estimate Std. Error z value Pr(>|z|)
(Intercept) -0.690076   0.386779  -1.784   0.0744 .
scot         0.370590   0.050329   7.363 1.79e-13 ***
trust       -0.417777   0.103624  -4.032 5.54e-05 ***
age         -0.026268   0.004145  -6.337 2.34e-10 ***
---
Signif. codes:  0 '***' 0.001 '**' 0.01 '*' 0.05 '.' 0.1 ' ' 1

(Dispersion parameter for binomial family taken to be 1)

    Null deviance: 1310.6  on 1019  degrees of freedom
Residual deviance: 1188.9  on 1016  degrees of freedom
  (481 observations deleted due to missingness)
AIC: 1196.9

Number of Fisher Scoring iterations: 4
```

There are three parts of the output we want to consider – starting from the bottom. We see that the MLE algorithm took four iterations to converge and provide estimates for our model (Number of Fisher Scoring iterations: 4). Is that good or bad? Four iterations is normal for estimating a simple logit regression. We really don't care that much about the number of iterations unless we receive a warning or error message regarding convergence.

The second part to examine is the AIC value, which stands for Akaike information criterion, and here equals 1196.9. The AIC is a fit measure based on the log-likelihood (ℓ) of our model and the number of predictors (k) in our model (AIC = $-2\ell + 2k$).[8] On its own, the AIC is mostly useless. Researchers typically use AIC values to compare the fit of competing

---

[8]A similar, and also commonly used, fit measure is the Bayesian information criterion (BIC), which is given by $-2l + kln n$.

models, such as nested models and models using different estimation techniques. With binary outcomes, we might use the AIC to decide whether a logit model (which assumes a symmetric error distribution) is a better fit to the data than a complementary log-log model (which assumes an asymmetric error distribution).

Third, and most important for our purposes, are the individual predictors' information. We see that all three predictors have a statistically significant effect on respondents' intended referendum vote. We know this because the *z*-values are above (the absolute value) 2, the *p*-values are below 0.05, and they all have stars; again, R is providing us redundant information for determining statistical significance. We also see that one predictor has a positive effect (scot) and two predictors have a negative effect (trust and age) on intended referendum vote. Since logit coefficients are technically *log odds*, they are not intuitive to interpret. We discuss interpretation techniques below, but we can provide a basic idea of the effects based on the variables' values and the direction of the coefficients. For example, the positive coefficient for scot means that as the strength of Scottish identity increases, respondents' are more likely to vote 'Yes' in the referendum. The negative coefficient for trust means that as trust in the UK government increases, respondents' are less likely to vote 'Yes' in the referendum. The negative coefficient for age means that as age increases, respondents' are less likely to vote 'Yes' in the referendum.

We can get a table for the coefficients' confidence intervals using the confint() function, but instead let's create a plot of the logit coefficients and confidence intervals. We'll use the ggcoef_model() function from the GGally package to plot model.logit's coefficients. In the ggcoef_model() function, we first specify the model (model.logit), then we'll add labels for the variables (variable_labels =). We'll also remove several of the defaults: the *p*-values by specifying show_p_values = FALSE and the statistical significance stars by specifying signif_stars = FALSE. Lastly, we'll use the labs() function from ggplot2 to give the plot a title and rename the *x*-axis title as 'Logit Coefficients'.

```
library(GGally)

ggcoef_model(model.logit,
             variable_labels = c(
               scot = "Scottish Identity",
               trust = "Trust in UK Government",
               age = "Age"),
             show_p_values = FALSE,
             signif_stars = FALSE) +
  labs(title = "Predicting the 2014 Scottish Referendum Vote",
       x = "Logit Coefficients") +
  theme(
    plot.title = element_text(size = 12)
  )
```

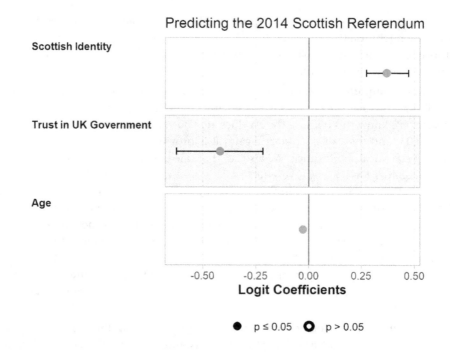

Understanding this plot is the same as for the linear regression coefficient plot in Chapter 11. The plot shows the logit regression coefficient estimates (circles) along with the 95% confidence intervals (horizontal lines). By default, the plot includes a vertical line at 0.00. If, for any of the variables, the 95% confidence interval lines cross the 0 dashed line, then the variable is not statistically significant. We see that none of the coefficients intervals cross 0, and thus they are all statistically significant.

Binary Probit Model

Now let's run a binary probit regression. Remember, the only difference between logit and probit lies in the assumptions made about the errors: logit assumes the errors follow a logistic distribution, while probit assumes the errors follow a normal distribution. To run probit, we simply change the link function to "probit".

```
summary(model.probit <- glm(refvote ~ scot + trust + age,
                            family = binomial(link = "probit"), data = ssa))

Call:
glm(formula = refvote ~ scot + trust + age, family = binomial(link = "probit"),
    data = ssa)

Deviance Residuals:
    Min       1Q    Median       3Q      Max
-1.5647  -0.9284   -0.6325   1.1505   2.5497
```

```
Coefficients:
             Estimate Std. Error z value Pr(>|z|)
(Intercept) -0.356769   0.223520  -1.596     0.11
scot         0.214602   0.028291   7.586 3.31e-14 ***
trust       -0.251992   0.061066  -4.127 3.68e-05 ***
age         -0.015987   0.002471  -6.471 9.76e-11 ***
---
Signif. codes:  0 '***' 0.001 '**' 0.01 '*' 0.05 '.' 0.1 ' ' 1


(Dispersion parameter for binomial family taken to be 1)

    Null deviance: 1310.6  on 1019  degrees of freedom
Residual deviance: 1189.4  on 1016  degrees of freedom
  (481 observations deleted due to missingness)
AIC: 1197.4


Number of Fisher Scoring iterations: 4
```

What do we see? On the whole, the probit results look the same as the logit results. The probit coefficients are smaller than the logit coefficients, but that is simply due to the model assumptions and not to one model being better than the other.

Interpreting Coefficients

We cannot directly interpret logit and probit regression coefficients. Hence, we need to transform the coefficients to allow for sensible interpretations. Two common interpretation techniques are odds ratios and predicted probabilities (Long and Freese 2014). Many researchers prefer using odds ratio interpretations due to a familiarity with odds from gambling. However, odds ratios can *only* be used for logit regression coefficients. Predicted probabilities can be used for both logit and probit regression coefficients, but it can be tricky to provide an overarching understanding of the effects by using predicted probabilities. We discuss and perform both interpretation techniques below.

Odds Ratio

Generally, we can think of the odds ratio as providing the odds of an event occurring compared to the odds of an event not occurring.

To get the odds ratio value, we take the exponential of a logit regression coefficient using the exp() function. If the odds ratio value is above 1, then the odds are 'increasing', 'greater', etc. If the odds ratio value is below 1, then the odds are 'decreasing', 'smaller', etc. An odds ratio value of 1 means 'even odds', which only occurs when $\beta_x = 0$ which is, obviously, never statistically significant.[9] We can also convert the odds to a percentage, which can make the interpretation more intuitive.

---

[9]Note that the implementation of odds for interpreting logit coefficients is slightly different than what is used in gambling.

To get the odds ratio values for all of our predictors at once, we specify `model.logit$coeffi-cients` in the `exp()` function; `coefficients` are one of the items saved in the object `model.logit` (use `names(model.logit)` to see all of them). We'll also include `[-1]` in the `exp()` function to prevent R from printing the intercept.

```
exp(model.logit$coefficients[-1])
      scot      trust        age
 1.4485892  0.6585091  0.9740742
```

Since all of the predictors are statistically significant, we can provide odds ratio interpretations for all of them. The language of odds ratio interpretations is very similar to what we used for linear regression coefficient interpretations. For ordinal, interval, and ratio predictors, we start the interpretation with *for a one-unit increase…*. For dummy variable predictors, we use the same structure of dummy variable interpretations as we did for linear regression. Let's first interpret `scot`:

> *For a one-unit increase in the strength of Scottish identity, the odds of voting 'Yes' increase by a factor of 1.45.*

It is important to include *by a factor of* to indicate that we are using an odds ratio. Now let's interpret `trust` and `age`.

> *For a one-unit increase in trust in the UK government, the odds of voting 'Yes' decrease by a factor of 0.66.*

> *For a one-unit increase in age, the odds of voting 'Yes' decrease by a factor of 0.97.*

Since a 'unit' is meaningful for `age`, we could say *for a one-year increase in age* instead.

Let's now calculate the odds ratio as a percentage. We need to subtract 1 from the code we used above and then multiple by 100.

```
(exp(model.logit$coefficients[-1])-1)*100
      scot      trust         age
 44.858917 -34.149094  -2.592577
```

The interpretations are nearly identical except that we drop *by a factor of* from the sentence. Removing this phrase and discussing effects as the change in a percentage is arguably easier for most people to understand.

> *For a one-unit increase in the strength of Scottish identity, the odds of voting 'Yes' increase by 45%.*

> *For a one-unit increase in trust in the UK government, the odds of voting 'Yes' decrease by 34%.*

> *For a one-year increase in age, the odds of voting 'Yes' decrease by 2.6%.*

This is a good place for us to briefly consider the substantive significance of these effects. If we convert age to ten-year units, instead of one-year units, then all three predictors appear to have a relatively large effect on whether a respondent planned to vote 'Yes' in the referendum. Since the predictors are on different scales, it is somewhat difficult to directly compare the effects, but clearly Scottish identity (which has seven values) has a larger effect on vote choice than the effect of trust in the UK government (which has four values).

Before moving on, we should note that for a one-unit increase in a predictor the maximum decrease in the odds ratio is 100%. This should be obvious – a decrease of 100% implies the event will not occur. However, the maximum increase in the odds ratio for a one-unit increase in a predictor is only bounded by reality. For example, an increase in the odds ratio of 100% is not unusual, but an increase of 10,000% should cause us to take a closer look at our variables and model to make sure there are no errors.

Predicted Probabilities

There are a number of different types of predicted probability interpretations. This includes individual and grouped predicted probabilities, average predicted probabilities, changes in predicted probabilities, and predicted probability plots. The main problem with certain predicted probability calculations is that they can be very specific to certain combinations of predictors' values. Instead, we typically want to tell a broad story of effects when we increase across our predictors' values. Individual probabilities are most useful when there is some specific type of observation that we want to know about. Grouped predicted probabilities are broader, but their usefulness can still be fairly limited. Predicted probability plots probably provide the most generalised interpretation of our regression coefficients. Let's briefly examine individual and grouped predicted probabilities before focusing on creating predicted probability plots.

Individual Predicted Probabilities

Let's get the predicted probability of voting 'Yes' for a respondent who strongly identifies as Scottish (scot=7), thinks that the UK government can never be trusted (trust=1), and is 50 years old (age=50). We could do this by creating a new data frame or tibble with the specific combination of values we want and then running the predict() function. Instead, let's leverage the functionality of the ggpredict() function from the ggeffects package to calculate the individual predicted probabilities.

In the ggpredict() function, we specify our saved model (model.logit), the value for scot (terms = "scot [7]"), and the values for trust and age (condition = c(trust = 1, age = 50)). Notice that we specify the value for scot within quotes, which is a little odd, and use the conditions option for the other values.

```
library(ggeffects)

ggpredict(model.logit, terms = "scot [7]",
          condition = c(trust = 1, age = 50))
# Predicted probabilities of Scotland Independence Vote Referendum Dummy

scot | Predicted |        95% CI
--------------------------------
   7 |      0.54 | [0.49, 0.60]
```

We see the predicted probability is 0.54 (or 54%). Thus the model tells us that *for a 50-year-old individual who strongly identifies as Scottish and thinks the UK government can never be trusted, the predicted probability of voting 'Yes' is 54%.* (Feel free to try different combinations of values.)

Although scot might appear as the variable in the spotlight in the code, if we switch trust (or age) for scot we'll get the same predicted probability. Let's take a look.

```
ggpredict(model.logit, terms = "trust [1]",
          condition = c(scot = 7, age = 50))
# Predicted probabilities of Scotland Independence Vote Referendum Dummy


trust | Predicted |        95% CI
---------------------------------
    1 |      0.54 | [0.49, 0.60]
```

Grouped Predicted Probabilities

Grouped predicted probabilities are often most useful when we have a predictor that's a factor (i.e., a nominal or ordinal variable) and we are interested in the predicted probabilities for each factor level (value). The variables we currently have are all numeric, and so let's compare the predicted probability for a respondent who thinks that the UK government can never be trusted (trust = 1) and can always be trusted (trust = 4), while setting scot and age at their means. We'll do this by using the ggpredict() function, specifying the saved model, and that we want the predicted probabilities for the two values of trust (terms = "trust [1,4]"). We don't need to do anything for scot and age since the ggpredict() function sets them to their means by default.

```
ggpredict(model.logit, terms = "trust [1,4]")
# Predicted probabilities of Scotland Independence Vote Referendum Dummy


trust | Predicted |        95% CI
---------------------------------
    1 |      0.39 | [0.34, 0.44]
    4 |      0.15 | [0.10, 0.23]

Adjusted for:
*  scot =  5.60
*  age = 53.65
```

This shows that *when Scottish identity and age are held at their means, the predicted probability of voting 'Yes' for someone who says you can never trust the UK government is 0.39 (39%) and the predicted probability of voting 'Yes' for someone who says you can always trust the UK government is 0.15 (15%).*

As should be clear, individual and grouped predicted probabilities are interesting, but they offer limited value for obtaining a general understanding of the predictors' effects on our outcome variable. Let's now examine predicted probability plots.

Plotting Predicted Probabilities

Using predicted probability plots is arguably the best way to interpret and communicate the effects of predictors when using GLMs. These plots provide a broader understanding of the curvilinear effects of predictors than we obtain from calculating individual and groups predicted probabilities.

Below, we will create two versions of predicted probability plots using the ggpredict() and ggplot() functions. First, we'll plot a single predictor – scot – while holding our other predictors constant. Second, we'll plot two predictors – scot and trust – while holding age constant.

As we did in Chapter 12, we'll connect the ggpredict() function to our ggplot() code using the pipe operator %>%. We'll use the geom_smooth() function to generate a smoothed predicted probability line for scot. Using the geom_smooth() function creates a more aesthetically appealing curve than we obtain from the geom_line() function. This is due to scot having seven ordered categories and therefore geom_line() draws a series of straight lines connected by each of the seven values. The geom_smooth() function simply smoothes out the choppiness of the curve. We'll use the geom_ribbon() function to plot 95% confidence intervals by setting the lower bound of the confidence interval with ymin = conf.low and the upper bound with ymax = conf.high, and we'll lighten the shading with alpha = .2. Since we are using the geom_ribbon() function to plot the confidence intervals, we'll include the option se = FALSE in the geom_smooth() function to remove the default confidence intervals (which are only based on the bivariate relationship between the x and y variables).

```
ggpredict(model.logit, terms = "scot") %>%
ggplot(mapping = aes(x = x, y = predicted)) +
  geom_smooth(se = FALSE) +
  geom_ribbon(aes(ymin = conf.low, ymax = conf.high), alpha = .2) +
  scale_x_continuous(limits = c(1,7),breaks = c(1:7)) +
  labs(title = "Predicted Probability of Voting 'Yes'",
       x = "Strength of Scottish Identity", y = "Predicted Probability") +
  theme_minimal()
```

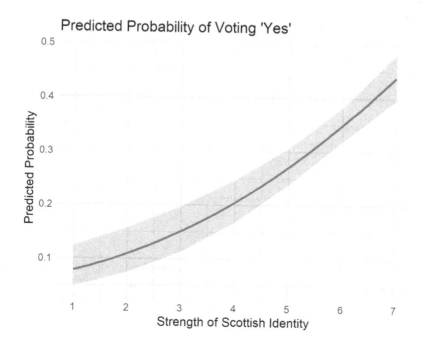

We see that *as the strength of Scottish identity increases, the predicted probability of voting 'Yes' increases. Furthermore, the probability increases more rapidly as we move from moderate to strong Scottish identity.* This predicted probability plot makes the curvilinear relationship between scot and refvote quite clear.

We often want to include the predicted probabilities of two (or more) of our predictors in the same plot; these are akin to plotting interaction effects. We'll create a plot with scot() on the *x*-axis and predicted probability lines for the four values of trust, with age held at its mean. Although we reuse aspects from above, the code is a bit beastly and so we'll go bird by bird:

1   We'll use the ggpredict() function and specify scot and trust in the terms = option. Putting trust second in the specification tells the function to treat trust as the *grouping variable*. This means that each value of scot will have a predicted probability calculated for each value of trust. For example, a predicted probability will be generated for scot = 1 and trust = 1, then for scot = 1 and trust = 2, etc., with the final predicted probability generated for scot = 7 and trust = 4.

2   For our plot, we want individual lines and labels for the four values of trust. To do this, we'll use the mutate() function to convert trust to an ordered factor variable and then use the recode() function to add the labels. We could do this in a separate line of code and save the changes as a new version of trust. Instead, we'll make use of the pipe operator to make changes to trust on the fly prior to using ggplot, thus not altering the original variable.

3   We will put our mapping = aes() specification in the ggplot() function. Doing this tells the function to use the specification for all of the geom_() functions that follow. We also include colour = group and fill = group for the predicted lines and confidence intervals specification; group contains the values for trust.

4   We again use the geom_smooth() function to plot smooth predicted probability lines and the geom_ribbon() function to plot the associated confidence intervals. We also include the option colour = NA in the geom_ribbon() function to get rid of the default outline plotted for the confidence intervals. We don't always have to plot the confidence intervals, but it is best practice to include them if we are able to and they don't muddle the plot's clarity.

5   We'll add labels to the plot with the labs() function. To get the correctly printed labels for the legend, we need to use the guide_legend() function twice within the guides() function – once for the lines (colours =) and once for the confidence intervals (fill =).

6   We'll use the theme_minimal() option and change the default colours by using the built-in viridis colour palette functions. We need to include the viridis functions for both the lines and confidence intervals.

Yes, there are a lot of steps, but the end product is worth it![10]

---

[10]Using the ggpredict() function actually eliminates a truckload of steps and code we would need for manually calculating the predicted probabilities. I apologise to all my former students who were forced to manually calculate predicted probabilities to create these plots.

```
ggpredict(model.logit, terms = c("scot","trust")) %>%
  mutate(group = ordered(as_factor(group)),
         group = recode(group,
                        `1` = "Never",
                        `2` = "Sometimes",
                        `3` = "Usually",
                        `4` = "Always")) %>%
ggplot(mapping=aes(x = x, y = predicted, colour = group, fill = group)) +
  geom_smooth(se = FALSE, size = 1.25) +
  geom_ribbon(aes(ymin = conf.low, ymax = conf.high),
              alpha = .2, colour = NA) +
  scale_x_continuous(limits = c(1,7), breaks = c(1:7)) +
  labs(title = "Predicted Probabilities of Voting 'Yes'",
       x = "Strength of Scottish Identity", y = "Predicted Probability") +
  guides(colour = guide_legend(title = "Govt Trust"),
         fill = guide_legend(title = "Govt Trust")) +
  theme_minimal() +
  scale_fill_viridis_d() +
  scale_colour_viridis_d()
```

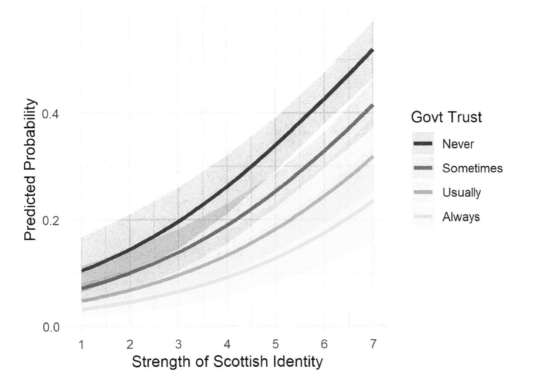

Understanding this plot is slightly more involved than the previous one. Generally, we want to pay attention to two aspects of this plot: first, how the predicted probabilities broadly change as we increase on the x-axis; and second, how the predicted probabilities lines vary relative to one another as we increase on the x-axis. For example, we may interpret and discuss this plot as follows:

For all values of trust, as the strength of Scottish identity increases so does the predicted probability of voting 'Yes' in the referendum. We also see that those who say the UK government can never be trusted have the highest predicted probability of voting 'Yes', while those who say you can always trust the government have the lowest predicted probability of voting 'Yes' across all values of Scottish identity.

ORDERED OUTCOME MODELS

Ordered Outcome Variables

Although modelling binary outcome variables is a nice way to introduce GLMs, depending on our field and research interests, we might not frequently use binary logit and probit regression. Therefore, it's important to examine how to model other types of categorical outcome variables. In this section, we'll work through modelling ordered outcome variables. These are simply ordinal variables that we are using as our outcome variables. We commonly encounter ordered variables in survey data. For example, ubiquitous agree/disagree questions are often analysed using ordered outcome models:

$$Y = \begin{cases} 1 & \text{strongly disagree} \\ 2 & \text{disagree} \\ 3 & \text{neither agree nor disagree} \\ 4 & \text{agree} \\ 5 & \text{strongly agree} \end{cases}$$

Another example are questions like `trust`:

$$Y = \begin{cases} 1 & \text{never} \\ 2 & \text{sometimes} \\ 3 & \text{usually} \\ 4 & \text{always} \end{cases}$$

Below we examine ordered logit and probit models using `trust`, from the `ssa` data, as our outcome variable.

Ordered Logit and Probit Model Application: Explaining Trust in the UK Government

The ordered outcome model is quite similar to the binary outcome model. In fact, we can think of the binary model as a special case of the ordered model. As with binary outcome models, the only difference between logit and probit is the assumption they make about the error distributions (Long 1997; McKelvey and Zavoina 1975).

We can't use the `glm()` function for running ordered outcome models. Instead, we'll use the `polr()` function that is part of the MASS library (the MASS package is installed as part of the base packages with R).[11] The `polr()` function stands for *proportional odds logistic regression*, which is an alternative name given to ordered logit regression (McCullagh 1980). Although the function's name suggests otherwise, we can also use this function to run ordered probit regression by specifying `method = "probit"` instead of `method = "logistic"`; the function's default method is ordered logit.

For our working example, we'll create and use an ordered factor version of `trust` as our outcome variable and include `refvote` as one of our predictors along with `scot` and `age`. Within the `mutate()` function, we'll use the `as_factor()` function to convert `trust` to a factor variable. We'll wrap the `ordered()` function around `as_factor()` to specify it is an ordered factor variable. We'll name this new variable `trust_ordfac`.

We specify `polr()` in almost the exact same way as we did with the `glm()` function. However, instead of specifying `family =` and `link =`, we specify the model with `method =`. Let's first create `trust_ordfac` and then run and save the model as `model.ologit`. (Ignore the red line of `Re-fitting to get Hessian`, if it appears. The Hessian is the observed information matrix which is used to estimate the model.)

```
library(MASS)

ssa <- ssa %>%
  mutate(trust_ordfac = ordered(as_factor(trust)))

summary(model.ologit <- polr(trust_ordfac ~ refvote + scot + age,
                             method = "logistic", data = ssa))
Call:
polr(formula = trust_ordfac ~ refvote + scot + age, data = ssa,
    method = "logistic")

Coefficients:
                        Value Std. Error t value
refvote1. Vote Yes -0.600234    0.133564  -4.494
scot               -0.108029    0.036096  -2.993
age                 0.003963    0.003522   1.125

Intercepts:
     Value   Std. Error t value
1|2 -1.0753  0.2573     -4.1786
2|3  1.3080  0.2588      5.0550
3|4  3.2862  0.3232     10.1662
```

[11]The MASS package will 'mask' the `select()` function from `dplyr`, which means that when MASS is loaded we can't use the `select()` function from `dplyr`. If we want to use the `select()` function from `dplyr`, we need to detach the MASS package.

```
Residual Deviance: 2102.281
AIC: 2114.281
(481 observations deleted due to missingness)
```

The output and its interpretation are very similar to what we saw above with the binary outcome models. However, the output doesn't provide *p*-values or everyone's favourite *s. But we actually don't need the *p*-values or *s to determine the statistical significance of the predictors. We can use the *t*-values, where if the absolute value is roughly 2 (or 1.96 as $N \to \infty$), then the predictor is statistically significant; remember that the *t*-value is just the coefficient divided by the standard error.

Hence, we see that `refvote` and `scot` are statistically significant predictors of trust in the UK government, but `age` is not. The negative coefficient for `refvote` means that respondents who intended to 'Yes' have lower trust in the UK government than respondents who intended to vote 'No'. The negative coefficient for `scot` means that respondents with stronger Scottish identity have lower trust in the UK government.

Let's plot `model.ologit`'s coefficients and confidence intervals using the `ggcoef_model()` function from `GGally`. The one difference in the code from plotting `model.logit` is that we include the option `no_reference_row = "refvote"` to remove the reference category label (`0. Vote No`) from the plot.

```
ggcoef_model(model.ologit,
             variable_labels = c(
               refvote = "Ref Vote",
               scot = "Scottish Identity",
               age = "Age"),
             no_reference_row = "refvote",
             show_p_values = FALSE,
             signif_stars = FALSE) +
  labs(title = "Predicting Trust in Government",
       x = "Ordered Logit Coefficients")
```

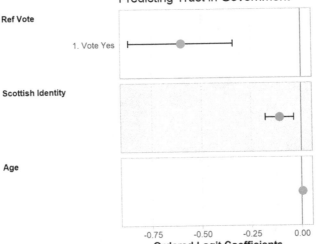

Notice that the plot does not provide us a legend with the closed and open circles. This isn't a big deal since we are relying on the confidence intervals and whether they cross zero to determine statistical significance. We see that the confidence intervals for `refvote` and `scot` do not cross the zero line, while the coefficient for `age` sits right on the zero line (indicating it is not a statistically significant predictor of `trust`).

Ordered Probit Model

To run an ordered probit model, we just specify `method = "probit"` instead of `method = "logistic"` in the `polr()` function.

```
summary(model.oprobit <- polr(trust_ordfac ~ refvote + scot + age,
                              method = "probit", data = ssa))

Re-fitting to get Hessian
Call:
polr(formula = trust_ordfac ~ refvote + scot + age, data = ssa,
    method = "probit")

Coefficients:
                      Value Std. Error t value
refvote1. Vote Yes -0.342419    0.07904  -4.332
scot               -0.062548    0.02104  -2.972
age                 0.003019    0.00205   1.473

Intercepts:
    Value   Std. Error t value
1|2 -0.5988  0.1502    -3.9864
2|3  0.8254  0.1507     5.4768
3|4  1.7642  0.1685    10.4672

Residual Deviance: 2103.028
AIC: 2115.028
(481 observations deleted due to missingness)
```

The results look roughly the same as the ordered logit results.

Testing the Parallel Regression Assumption

Ordered outcome regression models assume the effects of predictors are the same across the values of the outcome variable. This is evident from the fact that the regression output only provides a single coefficient for each predictor, and that the vector β doesn't have an outcome-specific subscript in the ordered outcome regression equation (see Long 1997). This assumption is called the **parallel regression assumption (PRA)** (also known as the **proportional odds assumption**). If the PRA is violated, the estimates of β_x will be inconsistent and thus we can't trust our results. In practice, researchers often don't test the PRA, particularly if the outcome variable is clearly substantively ordered.

We can use the `brant()` function from the `brant` package to test the PRA. The Brant test checks whether the overall model violates the PRA and also, by default, tests individual predictors for PRA violations. The Brant test works by running a series of binary logit regressions on the subsetted ordered outcome categories and comparing the predictors' coefficients (Brant 1990). First it runs a logit regression with the first category against the higher categories of the outcome variable. Then it runs a logit regression with the combined first and second categories against the higher categories of the outcome variable. And so on until it has compared the predictors' coefficients for all the outcome variable's categories minus one. If the PRA holds then a predictor's coefficient should be the same (or close to the same) across each of the binary logit regressions. For `trust`, the first binary logit examines category 1 ('Never') against categories 2, 3, 4 ('Sometimes', 'Usually', 'Always'). Then the binary logit examines categories 1 and 2 ('Never', 'Sometimes') against categories 3 and 4 ('Usually', 'Always'). Lastly, the binary logit examines categories 1, 2, 3 ('Never', 'Sometimes', 'Usually') against category 4 ('Always'). If the coefficients for `refvote`, `scot`, and `age` are (roughly) the same in each of the binary logit regressions then the PRA holds.

We want to first look at the `Omnibus` result, which is for the overall model. If $p \leq 0.05$, then we reject the null of not violating PRA and conclude that we do violate PRA. If we do violate PRA, we can use the individual predictor tests to locate the culprit(s).

```
library(brant)
brant(model.ologit)
---------------------------------------------------------
Test for           X2     df    probability
---------------------------------------------------------
Omnibus            11.14   6     0.08
refvote1. Vote Yes 1.79    2     0.41
scot               1.32    2     0.52
age                8.04    2     0.02
---------------------------------------------------------

H0: Parallel Regression Assumption holds
```

We see that the p-value for the `Omnibus` is above 0.05 and thus our model *does not* violate the PRA. We do observe that `age` violates the PRA, but since the overall model doesn't violate the PRA we don't have to deal with `age`'s violation.[12]

If we do violate the PRA, we can run a generalised ordered logit regression where we relax the PRA for predictors that violate the PRA. This model is technically called a *partial proportional odds*

---

[12]The cause of the violation is possibly that `age` has a nonlinear relationship with `trust` (e.g., squared, logged).

model, where the *partial* implies that the PRA is relaxed for certain predictors. This means that instead of getting a single coefficient for a predictor, we get $J - 1$ coefficients for a predictor, where J is the number of categories in the outcome variable. One option in R to run these models is the `vglm()` function from the VGAM package. We could also use a multinomial logit or probit regression model, but there are additional issues to sort through (see the next section on unordered outcome models).

Interpreting Coefficients

We interpret ordered outcome regression models in a very similar way to binary outcome regression models – using odds ratios and predicted probabilities. The main difference for odds ratios is that we are now talking about cumulative odds, which requires a slight language tweak in our interpretations. We are now also able to examine cumulative predicted probabilities, where we combine the predicted probabilities of different values of our outcome variable.

Odds Ratio

Again, we can only use odds ratios with our ordered logit model. Since we only have a single coefficient for each predictor, the odds ratio value is derived by cumulating over the values in our outcome variable. The odds ratio value now tells us the *generic odds of observing a lower outcome to a higher outcome* for a predictor given our model; that is, the odds will not be specific to a particular category of our outcome variable. For the interpretation, we need to use a generic term to indicate that the value is the cumulative odds across outcomes – for example, 'increased', 'greater', or 'more'. Let's do a few interpretations to get the hang of the interpretations.

The code is the same as we used for calculating odds ratios for binary logit, except that we don't include `[-1]` because the intercepts are not automatically printed. Let's calculate the odds ratio and the odds ratio as a percentage at the same time.

```
exp(model.ologit$coefficients)
refvote1. Vote Yes            scot               age
        0.5486832         0.8976012         1.0039707
(exp(model.ologit$coefficients)-1)*100
refvote1. Vote Yes            scot               age
      -45.1316761       -10.2398833         0.3970667
```

Now, let's provide interpretations for our two significant predictors – `refvote` and `scot`.

Remember that `refvote` is a dummy variable and thus we need to use a dummy variable interpretation structure (i.e., avoiding the phrase *for a one-unit increase*). We interpret the odds ratio values for `refvote` as follows:

> *For those who planned to vote 'Yes' in the referendum, the odds of having more trust in the UK government are smaller by a factor of 0.55 than for those who planned to vote 'No' in the referendum.*

> *For those who planned to vote 'Yes' in the referendum, the odds of having more trust in the UK government are 45% smaller than for those who planned to vote 'No' in the referendum.*

Notice that even though `refvote` has a negative effect on `trust`, we say the 'odds of having *more* trust' and specify there's a negative effect with 'smaller by a factor of 0.55'. The *more trust* phrase is the generic term that clarifies we are talking about cumulative odds. Which generic term we use will be based on what sounds best to us, given the variables.

Since `scot` is an ordinal-level variable, we can use the standard *for a one-unit increase* for the beginning of the interpretation:

> *For a one-unit increase in the strength of Scottish identity, the odds of having more trust in the UK government decrease by a factor of 0.90.*

> *For a one-unit increase in the strength of Scottish identity, the odds of having more trust in the UK government decrease by 10%.*

Predicted Probabilities

We can use the same types of predicted probability interpretations as we did with binary outcome models. Let's quickly do individual and grouped predicted probabilities before focusing on predicted probability plots.

Individual Predicted Probabilities

Let's calculate the predicted probabilities for two different individuals for the four categories of `trust`. We'll consider a respondent who strongly identifies as Scottish (`scot = 7`), is 30 years old (`age = 30`), and planned to vote 'No' (`refvote = 0`), and a respondent with the same values for `scot` and `age` but who planned to vote 'Yes' (`refvote = 1`). Using the `ggpredict()` function, we'll specify our saved model (`model.ologit`), `refvote` to get the two values (`terms = "refvote"`), and the values for `scot` and `age` (`condition = c(scot = 7, age = 30)`).

```
ggpredict(model.ologit, terms = "refvote", condition = c(scot = 7, age = 30))
# Predicted probabilities of trust_ordfac

# Response Level = 1

refvote      | Predicted |       95% CI
----------------------------------------
0. Vote No   |      0.39 | [0.28, 0.51]
1. Vote Yes  |      0.54 | [0.41, 0.66]


# Response Level = 2

refvote      | Predicted |       95% CI
----------------------------------------
0. Vote No   |      0.48 | [0.36, 0.60]
1. Vote Yes  |      0.39 | [0.27, 0.52]


# Response Level = 3
```

```
refvote      | Predicted |      95% CI
----------------------------------------
0. Vote No   |     0.11  | [0.07, 0.16]
1. Vote Yes  |     0.06  | [0.04, 0.10]


# Response Level = 4


refvote      | Predicted |      95% CI
----------------------------------------
0. Vote No   |     0.02  | [0.01, 0.03]
1. Vote Yes  |     0.01  | [0.01, 0.02]
```

Let's interpret the two predicted probabilities for the 'never trust' category (`Response Level = 1` in the output). *For a 30-year-old individual who planned to vote 'No' and has the strongest Scottish identity, the predicted probability of responding that they never trust the UK government is 0.39 or 39%. For a 30-year-old individual who planned to vote 'Yes' and has the strongest Scottish identity, the predicted probability of responding that they never trust the UK government is 0.54 or 54%.* Notice that both values of `refvote` have small differences in the predicted probabilities of responding usually or always trust the UK government. This suggests one (or both) of the other two variables (`scot`, `age`) has a stronger effect on respondents' trust of the UK government than `refvote`.

Cumulative Individual Predicted Probabilities

We might be interested in calculating cumulative individual predicted probabilities. The simple way to do this is to just add together the probabilities we calculated above. Below, we calculate the predicted probability of someone who planned to vote 'Yes', has the strongest Scottish identity, and is 30 years old responding they never trust *or* sometimes trust the UK government.

```
.54 + .39
[1] 0.93
```

We can interpret this as saying that *for a 30-year-old individual who planned to vote 'Yes' and has the strongest Scottish identity, the predicted probability of responding that they never trust or sometimes trust the UK government is 0.93 or 93%.*

Grouped Predicted Probabilities

For demonstration purposes, let's quickly calculate the grouped predicted probabilities for the two values of `refvote` when `scot` and `age` are held at their means. The code is the same except that here we'll drop the `condition` = argument.

```
ggpredict(model.ologit, terms = "refvote")
# Predicted probabilities of trust_ordfac


# Response Level = 1
```

```
refvote      | Predicted |        95% CI
-----------------------------------------
0. Vote No   |     0.34  | [0.24, 0.45]
1. Vote Yes  |     0.48  | [0.35, 0.61]


# Response Level = 2

refvote      | Predicted |        95% CI
-----------------------------------------
0. Vote No   |     0.51  | [0.39, 0.63]
1. Vote Yes  |     0.43  | [0.31, 0.56]


# Response Level = 3

refvote      | Predicted |        95% CI
-----------------------------------------
0. Vote No   |     0.13  | [0.08, 0.19]
1. Vote Yes  |     0.08  | [0.05, 0.13]


# Response Level = 4

refvote      | Predicted |        95% CI
-----------------------------------------
0. Vote No   |     0.02  | [0.02, 0.04]
1. Vote Yes  |     0.01  | [0.01, 0.02]


Adjusted for:
* scot =   5.60
*  age = 53.65
```

Plotting Predicted Probabilities

Let's now create a predicted probability plot for our ordered logit model. In the plot, we'll include scot() on the x-axis and the predicted probability lines will be for the four values of trust_ordfac (our outcome variable).

The code is almost identical to the code for the second binary logit predicted probability plot we created earlier. Here, we only include scot in the terms = option for the ggpredict() function (age is held at its mean and refvote at its mode by default). The predicted probabilities for the four values of trust_ordfac are automatically created and named response.level by ggpredict(). From the second line of the code chunk below, we only need to replace group (from the second binary logit predicted probability plot) with response.level, and change the labels to reflect the variables we are plotting.

```
ggpredict(model.ologit, terms = "scot") %>%
  mutate(response.level = ordered(as_factor(response.level)),
         response.level = recode(response.level,
                   `1` = "Never",
                   `2` = "Sometimes",
```

```
              `3` = "Usually",
              `4` = "Always")) %>%
ggplot(mapping=aes(x = x, y = predicted, colour = response.level,
              fill = response.level)) +
geom_smooth(se = FALSE, size = 1.25) +
geom_ribbon(aes(ymin = conf.low, ymax = conf.high),
              alpha = .2, colour = NA) +
scale_x_continuous(limits = c(1,7),breaks = c(1:7)) +
labs(title = "Predicted Probabilities of Trust in the UK Government",
     x = "Strength of Scottish Identity", y = "Predicted Probability") +
guides(colour = guide_legend(title = "Govt Trust"),
       fill = guide_legend(title = "Govt Trust")) +
theme_minimal() +
scale_fill_viridis_d() +
scale_colour_viridis_d()
```

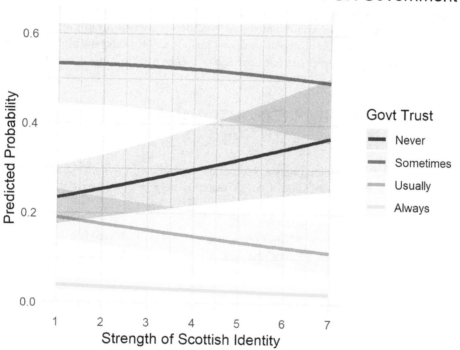

The plotted lines are the predicted probabilities for each value in our outcome variable trust_ordfac across the values of scot. For example, we can interpret the purple line as follows:

As the strength of Scottish identity increases, the predicted probability of respondents never trusting the UK government increases.

This is a different way of understanding the plot than for the second binary logit predicted probability plot. Broadly, we can interpret the plot as follows:

> *We see that as the strength of Scottish identity increases, the predicted probability of never trusting the UK government increases, sometimes trusting the UK government slightly decreases, and both usually and always trusting the UK government decreases. We see that sometimes trusting the UK government has the highest predicted probability and always trusting the UK government has the lowest predicted probability across all values of Scottish identity. The largest change is that as the strength of Scottish identity increases, the predicted probability of never trusting the UK government increases dramatically. So, at the lowest level of Scottish identity, there is roughly a 30% difference between sometimes and never trusting the UK government, while at the highest level of Scottish identity the gap is only around 12%.*

The confidence intervals in the plot are fairly wide, particularly for never and sometimes trusting the UK government. This is really only a problem aesthetically as it might impact the effectiveness of communicating our results. If you remember from earlier in the book, although we refer to these as 'confidence intervals', they are technically 'prediction intervals'. Hence, the wide intervals tell us there's some uncertainty in our predicted effects of scot on the different values of trust. However, our audience might mistakenly interpret the overlapping intervals as suggesting that scot does not have a statistically significant effect on trust. If we are concerned about the possibility of misinterpretation, we could remove the confidence intervals from the plot (i.e., delete the geom_ribbon() function) or leave them in and include a note under the plot specifying that these are prediction intervals (e.g., include caption = <text> in the labs() function).

UNORDERED OUTCOME MODELS

Unordered Outcome Variables

Unordered (nominal) outcome models are sometimes considered the method of last resort for performing cross-sectional regression analysis using a categorical outcome variable. We use them if:

- Our outcome variable has more than two categories and is unordered (i.e., a nominal-level variable with three or more categories)
- It is not clear whether the outcome variable is ordered
- Our ordered outcome model fails the parallel regression assumption and our outcome variable is not clearly ordered

Nominal variables are common in social science datasets, especially in survey data. For example, survey data routinely includes nominal variables for race/ethnicity, religion, geographical region of residence, etc. Depending on our field and specialisation, we may not frequently utilise nominal variables as outcome variables. Sometimes we may want to use a nominal variable as our outcome variable, but some problem hinders our approach. For example, certain categories of our nominal variable may only have a few observations, which will cause estimation problems with unordered outcome models. Or operationalising our theoretical argument requires collapsing the nominal variable down to a binary variable.

One common example of a nominal outcome variable is vote choice among multiple political candidates/parties:

$$Y = \begin{cases} 1 & \text{Conservative Party} \\ 2 & \text{Labour Party} \\ 3 & \text{Scottish Nationalist Party} \end{cases}$$

Another example is employment status:

$$Y = \begin{cases} 1 & \text{employed} \\ 2 & \text{unemployed} \\ 3 & \text{retired} \\ 4 & \text{university student} \end{cases}$$

Below we discuss multinomial logit (MNL) and multinomial probit (MNP) models before moving onto applications using the ssa data.

Multinomial Logit and Probit Models

Unordered outcome models are not the most efficient method (computationally or intuitively), but they may be the 'safest' with respect to the assumptions made. The best way to understand the intuition of these models is to think of them as performing a series of binary outcome regression models simultaneously. Key to these models is that one of the outcome variable's categories is set as the baseline/comparison category. All of our model's estimates are based on comparing against the baseline category. So, each predictor will have a different coefficient for every category of the outcome variable compared to the baseline category. For example, if y has four categories and the first category is the baseline, then we'll have three different coefficients for x: $\hat{\beta}_{2,1}$, $\hat{\beta}_{3,1}$, and $\hat{\beta}_{4,1}$. We normally choose the outcome category with the most observations as our baseline category as it should provide the most consistent estimates. Alternatively, we may choose the baseline category for theoretical reasons (e.g., we are interested in specific comparisons).

Unlike the difference between logit and probit binary and ordered outcome models, there is a critical difference between the MNL and MNP models. The MNL assumes the independence of irrelevant alternatives (IIA), but the MNP does not. The IIA implies that the ratio of the outcome probabilities for two alternatives, j and k, is independent of all other alternatives, say l, in the outcome set. This allows us to assume independent errors across alternatives, which makes estimation much simpler. The problem is that IIA often doesn't hold empirically and we commonly violate it. When this occurs, we can't trust the consistency of our model's estimates (see Long 1997).

To better understand IIA, we'll first consider how IIA applies to a simple decision theory example. Imagine we hold job offers from three different companies – one from Google, one from Apple, and one from Twitter – and we are asked to rank our preference among them. We rank the job offers as Google > Twitter > Apple. Now imagine that the Twitter job offer is taken away and we only have two job offers. If we rank the two remaining job offers as Google > Apple, then we don't violate the IIA since our original preference ordering is maintained. But if we now rank the two remaining job offers as Apple > Google, then we violate the IIA since our original preference ordering breaks down. This should be straightforward to understand: removing (or adding) job offers should not change our ranking among the original job offers.

Now let's consider how this example works when considering the ratio of outcome probabilities. Instead of a simple ranking, let's imagine that the probability of our accepting the Google job offer is 0.5, accepting the Twitter job offer is 0.25, and accepting the Apple job offer is 0.25 (we view the job offers from Twitter and Apple equally). Therefore, the probability ratio of accepting the Google job offer to either of the other job offers is 2 to 1. Now imagine the Twitter job offer is taken away and we are again left with only two job offers. To maintain the probability ratio of 2 to 1 and not violate the IIA, our probability of accepting the Google job offer should now increase to 0.67 and our probability of accepting the Apple job offer should now increase to 0.33. This change in probabilities might make sense, but it might also be the case that removing the Twitter job keeps our probability of accepting the Apple job offer at 0.25. In this case, the IIA is violated.

The MNP model gets around the IIA assumption by allowing the errors to be correlated across outcomes (due to assuming a normal error distribution) (Cameron and Trivedi 2005). Therefore, the MNP is often a better option for performing regression modelling of unordered outcome variables. The trade-off is that the MNP is extremely computationally taxing and very sensitive to the total number of observations and how the observations are distributed across the values of the outcome variable. When using social science data it is not uncommon for the MNP model to fail to converge or to converge but with results that are bizarre and nonsensical. In fact, it wasn't until around 2000 that desktop computers could even attempt to estimate the MNP model.[13] The processing power of desktop computers continues to increase and thus the computational issues that have plagued the MNP model have become less of an obstacle over time. For now, though, realise that the MNP model is likely to cause us convergence and estimation problems. Due to the difficulty in using the MNP model, many researchers often ignore the IIA and use the MNL model for modelling unordered outcome models.

Multinomial Logit and Probit Application: Predicting Partisan Identification

Data Wrangling

For our application, we will use respondents' partisan identification as our outcome variable (Party_Labels in the ssa data) and scot, trust, and age as our predictors. Currently, Party_Labels has six values – three of which have less than 100 respondents. To make our models easier to manage, we will create a new variable where we remove the categories with less than 100 observations (these are respondents who identify with Liberal Democrats, Green Party, and UKIP). We'll do this in two steps within the mutate() function. First, we'll convert Party_Labels to a factor variable (with as_factor()), apply labels (levels = "labels"), and save this as a new variable named pid1. Second, we'll create a subsetted version of pid1 (named pid) where we remove the Liberal Democrat, Green, and UKIP identifiers. We'll use the recode_factor() function to do this, where .default = NA_character_ codes every category not specifically listed as NA (i.e., missing).

```
ssa <- ssa %>%
  mutate(pid1 = as_factor(Party_Labels, levels = "labels"),
         pid = recode_factor(pid1,
```

---

[13]Scott Long's standard-setting 1997 text on GLMs – *Regression Models for Categorical and Limited Dependent Variables* – only includes a single paragraph on the MNP model in which he states that 'the computational burden of computing multidimensional normal integrals makes the model impractical' (pp. 184–185).

```
        "1. Conservative" = "1. Conservative",
        "2. Labour" = "2. Labour",
        "4. SNP" = "3. SNP",
        .default = NA_character_))
```

Let's take a quick look at pid to make sure it is recoded correctly.

```
ssa %>%
  count(pid)
# A tibble: 4 x 2
  pid                 n
  <fct>           <int>
1 1. Conservative   191
2 2. Labour         443
3 3. SNP            363
4 <NA>              504
```

Yep, looks good.

Multinomial Logit Model

There are two functions that are commonly used to run the MNL model in R:

- multinom() from the nnet package – quick and easy, but limited functionality
- mlogit() from the mlogit package – complicated, but expanded functionality

We will use the multinom() function here, but we'll also use the mlogit() function to test the IIA and for running the MNP model later on. The specification of the multinom() function is similar to what we did for the binary and ordered outcome models.

```
library(nnet)
summary(model.mlogit <- multinom(pid ~ scot + trust + age, data = ssa))
# weights:  15 (8 variable)
initial  value 1086.527553
iter  10 value 940.866902
final  value 940.062289
converged
Call:
multinom(formula = pid ~ scot + trust + age, data = ssa)

Coefficients:
           (Intercept)      scot      trust        age
2. Labour    1.8305086 0.2846264 -0.3785999 -0.03105142
3. SNP       0.4632231 0.6678012 -0.6310177 -0.04483630

Std. Errors:
           (Intercept)       scot     trust         age
2. Labour    0.4357686 0.04980245 0.1174766 0.005597068
3. SNP       0.5370312 0.06870762 0.1335313 0.006138524
```

```
Residual Deviance: 1880.125
AIC: 1896.125
```

The output shows the effects of our predictors on identifying with the Labour Party versus the Conservative Party and the SNP versus the Conservative Party; the Conservative Party is our baseline/comparison group. This output doesn't provide significance tests by default, so we need to calculate them ourselves. We will simply divide the coefficients by the standard errors, which gives us z-scores (which are equivalent to t-scores). To get this to work, we need to wrap the summary() function around our model object (model.mlogit). Again, we are looking to see if the absolute value of the z-score is 2 or greater.

```
summary(model.mlogit)$coefficients/summary(model.mlogit)$standard.errors
          (Intercept)      scot      trust       age
2. Labour   4.2006436  5.715109  -3.222769  -5.547801
3. SNP      0.8625628  9.719463  -4.725618  -7.304086
```

We find that all three predictors are statistically significant predictors of both comparisons in the outcome variable. The signs of the coefficients tell us that respondents with stronger Scottish identity are more likely to identify with the Labour Party and the SNP than with the Conservative Party; respondents with higher trust in the UK government are less likely to identify with the Labour Party and the SNP than with the Conservative Party; and older respondents are less likely to identify with the Labour Party and the SNP than with the Conservative Party.

Next, we'll plot the coefficients and confidence intervals. We could use the ggcoef_model() function here, but the function does a poor job of rendering the MNL model. Instead, we'll use the ggcoef_multinom() function from the GGally package for the plot. This function is designed specifically to plot a multinom() object. The specification is the same as we used with the ggcoef_model() function, except that we'll add in the y.level_label = option to get the comparisons to be printed in the plot legend.

```
ggcoef_multinom(model.mlogit,
              variable_labels = c(
                  scot = "Scottish Identity",
                  trust = "Govt Trust",
                  age = "Age"),
              show_p_values = FALSE,
              signif_stars = FALSE,
              y.level_label = c(
                "2. Labour" = "Labour vs. Conservative",
                "3. SNP" = "SNP vs. Conservative"
              )) +
    labs(title = "Predicting Partisan Identification",
        x = "Multinomial Logit Coefficients")
```

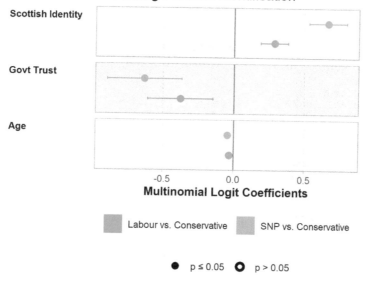

Testing the IIA

Before moving on to the MNP model, let's test the IIA and see whether we *need* to use MNP. The `multinom()` function is the simplest and quickest way to run the MNL in R, but it doesn't have an option to test the IIA. To test the IIA, we'll use the `mlogit()` function from the `mlogit` package. This function allows us to run a regular MNL, MNP, and variations on these models. Since the `mlogit()` function allows variables that are case-specific and alternative-specific (for different types of analysis), the code is more complicated.[14]

We need to first create a new data frame using the `dfidx()` function from the `dfidx package`; the `dfidx()` function is imported by the `mlogit` package and so we don't need to separately load the `dfidx` package. Since we are using case-specific variables, we specify that the type (or shape) of the data is `"wide"`, we don't have any alternative-specific variables (`varying = NULL`), and the variable that identifies the choice made is `pid` ('choice' is the same as 'outcome', just different terminology).

---

[14]Case-specific variables have a single value and row for each column (i.e., variable) in our data. These are the types of variables we use in this book. Alternative-specific variables have a different value and row for each category of the outcome variable for each predictor. The classic example of alternative-specific data is an outcome variable on individuals' choice of mode of transportation (car, bus, train) and predictors that have different values corresponding with the mode of transportation. For example, a predictor on cost would have a different value for each model of transport. We can use multinomial probit or conditional logit regression to model alternative-specific variables. The overwhelming majority of social science data is case-specific.

```
library(mlogit)
iia.data <- dfidx(ssa, shape = "wide", varying = NULL, choice = "pid")
```

To run a 'regular' MNL, we need to specify in the `mlogit()` function that there are no alternative-specific predictors using 0 and then | to separate them from the case-specific predictors.

```
summary(model.mlogit1 <- mlogit(pid ~ 0 | scot + trust + age,
                                data = iia.data))
```

```
Call:
mlogit(formula = pid ~ 0 | scot + trust + age, data = iia.data,
    method = "nr")

Frequencies of alternatives:choice
1. Conservative        2. Labour          3. SNP
        0.19312            0.44590          0.36097

nr method
5 iterations, 0h:0m:0s
g'(-H)^-1g = 0.00125
successive function values within tolerance limits

Coefficients :
                      Estimate Std. Error z-value  Pr(>|z|)
(Intercept):2. Labour  1.8304970  0.4357685  4.2006 2.662e-05 ***
(Intercept):3. SNP     0.4632078  0.5370314  0.8625   0.38839
scot:2. Labour         0.2846238  0.0498024  5.7151 1.097e-08 ***
scot:3. SNP            0.6678004  0.0687077  9.7194 < 2.2e-16 ***
trust:2. Labour       -0.3785983  0.1174765 -3.2228   0.00127 **
trust:3. SNP          -0.6310163  0.1335312 -4.7256 2.294e-06 ***
age:2. Labour         -0.0310511  0.0055971 -5.5477 2.894e-08 ***
age:3. SNP            -0.0448361  0.0061385 -7.3041 2.791e-13 ***
---
Signif. codes:  0 '***' 0.001 '**' 0.01 '*' 0.05 '.' 0.1 ' ' 1

Log-Likelihood: -940.06
McFadden R^2:  0.090872
Likelihood ratio test : chisq = 187.93 (p.value = < 2.22e-16)
```

We see that these results are the same as the results in `model.mlogit`; this makes sense since the `mlogit()` function is actually running the `multinom()` function under the hood. These results are actually easier to understand than results using the `multinom()` function since we are provided the *p*-values.

As a slight detour, we see at the bottom of the output `McFadden R^2: 0.090872`. This is one version of a commonly used model fit measure called **pseudo R^2**. Pseudo R^2 measures were created to replicate R^2 in linear regression since researchers loved the R^2 measure. Yet, we cannot interpret the measure as the amount of variance explained; note that 'pseudo' means 'fake'. The McFadden R^2 is calculated as $1 - \ell_1 / \ell_0$, where ℓ_1 is the log-likelihood of our model and ℓ_0 is the log-likelihood of the null (or empty) model. Pseudo R^2 measures, like the AIC, can be used to compare models, but they are mostly useless on their own. We haven't talked about these measures before now since we probably should avoid using measures that have 'fake' in their name.

To test the IIA, we will use the Hausman–McFadden test (Hausman and McFadden 1984). The intuition of the test is that the estimates we obtain in a restricted model (where we remove one of the outcome variable's values) should be roughly the same as the estimates we obtain in an unrestricted model (our regular model). To do so, we need to run different versions of the model where we remove one of the outcome variable's values. Normally, researchers just remove one outcome and test the difference.

To do the test correctly, we need to have the same reference/baseline/comparison group for the different models. Since the default for both `multinom()` and `mlogit()` is the Conservative Party, we will just make sure it still is by specifying the `reflevel = "1. Conservative"` option in the `mlogit()` function and save the results as x1. Next, we will remove one of the outcome variable values. We'll remove `"3. SNP"`, rerun the model, and save the results as x2.[15] Besides specifying `reflevel`, we also need to specify the other values to include using the `alt.subset()` function. Once we have the different regression model estimates, we test the IIA using the `hmftest()` function.

The test states `alternative hypothesis: IIA is rejected` and thus the null hypothesis is that the IIA is *not* rejected.

```
x1 <- mlogit(pid ~ 0 | scot + trust + age, data = iia.data,
             reflevel = "1. Conservative")

x2 <- mlogit(pid ~ 0 | scot + trust + age, data = iia.data,
             reflevel = "1. Conservative",
             alt.subset = c("1. Conservative", "2. Labour"))

hmftest(x1,x2)

      Hausman-McFadden test

data:  iia.data
chisq = 1.6546, df = 4, p-value = 0.7989
alternative hypothesis: IIA is rejected
```

The test shows that the *p*-value is above 0.05 and thus we cannot reject the null. Therefore, we do not violate the IIA. If we did violate the IIA, then we should use an MNP model.

Multinomial Probit Models

Now let's run an MNP model using the `mlogit()` function. The only difference from above is that we include the option `probit = TRUE` in the specification. Depending on our computer, it may take a couple of minutes for the model to run.

---

[15]By removing SNP identifiers, our outcome variable is now binary. Thus, this is probably not the best demonstration of testing for the IIA.

```
summary(model.mprobit <- mlogit(pid ~ 0 | scot + trust + age,
                                data = iia.data, probit = TRUE))

Call:
mlogit(formula = pid ~ 0 | scot + trust + age, data = iia.data,
    probit = TRUE)

Frequencies of alternatives:choice
1. Conservative      2. Labour        3. SNP
        0.19312          0.44590       0.36097

bfgs method
19 iterations, 0h:0m:28s
g'(-H)^-1g = 2.32E-07
gradient close to zero

Coefficients :
                        Estimate Std. Error z-value  Pr(>|z|)
(Intercept):2. Labour  1.1106386  0.2933960  3.7855 0.0001534 ***
(Intercept):3. SNP     0.7689141  0.8168185  0.9414 0.3465243
scot:2. Labour         0.2052825  0.0575626  3.5662 0.0003621 ***
scot:3. SNP            0.3111148  0.1570300  1.9812 0.0475639 *
trust:2. Labour       -0.2363065  0.0820850 -2.8788 0.0039919 **
trust:3. SNP          -0.3178002  0.1377952 -2.3063 0.0210926 *
age:2. Labour         -0.0186914  0.0038792 -4.8184 1.447e-06 ***
age:3. SNP            -0.0231316  0.0074589 -3.1012 0.0019272 **
2. Labour.3. SNP       0.9796063  0.2469532  3.9668 7.285e-05 ***
3. SNP.3. SNP          0.4666794  0.8726712  0.5348 0.5928081
---
Signif. codes:  0 '***' 0.001 '**' 0.01 '*' 0.05 '.' 0.1 ' ' 1

Log-Likelihood: -941.36
McFadden R^2:  0.089614
Likelihood ratio test : chisq = 185.33 (p.value = < 2.22e-16)
```

Our conclusions about the model are the same as with `model.mlogit1`. This makes sense since we did not violate the IIA.

Interpreting Coefficients

We interpret unordered outcome regression models in a similar way as binary outcome regression models. The main difference is that predictors are not always statistically significant for all of the outcome value comparisons. For odds ratios, we only interpret the comparisons that are statistically significant for each predictor and, again, only when using an MNL model. Because predicted probabilities sum up to 1, the predicted probability for each outcome value is contingent on the predicted probabilities of the other outcome values. Therefore, it's best practice to only interpret predictors that are statistically significant for all comparisons. Below, we'll perform interpretations for our MNL model (`model.mlogit`).

Odds Ratio

The difference from odds ratio interpretations in the binary and ordered logit models is that now we need to add the comparison of the outcome variable values to our interpretations. All three predictors in model.mlogit are statistically significant and so we can interpret all of the coefficients. However, since the structure of the odds ratio interpretation will be the same for each predictor, let's just write out the interpretations for scot. We calculate the odds ratio values the same way as we did previously.

```
exp(coef(model.mlogit))
             (Intercept)      scot      trust        age
2. Labour     6.237058 1.329265 0.6848195 0.9694257
3. SNP        1.589188 1.949945 0.5320501 0.9561540
(exp(coef(model.mlogit))-1)*100
             (Intercept)      scot      trust        age
2. Labour    523.70580 32.92654 -31.51805 -3.057427
3. SNP        58.91878 94.99450 -46.79499 -4.384601
```

For the Labour versus Conservative comparison, we interpret scot as follows:

For a one-unit increase in the strength of Scottish identity, the odds of identifying with the Labour Party compared to the Conservative Party increase by a factor of 1.33.

For a one-unit increase in the strength of Scottish identity, the odds of identifying with the Labour Party compared to the Conservative Party increase by 33%.

For the SNP versus Conservative comparison, we interpret scot as follows:

For a one-unit increase in the strength of Scottish identity, the odds of identifying with the SNP compared to the Conservative Party increase by a factor of 1.95.

For a one-unit increase in the strength of Scottish identity, the odds of identifying with the SNP compared to the Conservative Party increase by 95%.

Interpreting the odds ratio values for trust and age takes the same form as above.

Predicted Probabilities

We can do the same types of predicted probability interpretations as we did with binary and ordered outcome models. Let's first calculate individual and grouped predicted probabilities.

Individual Predicted Probabilities

We'll calculate the predicted probabilities of identifying with the three political parties for two different types of respondents. First, we'll consider a respondent who strongly identifies as Scottish (scot = 7), never trusts the UK government (trust = 1), and is 30 years old (age = 30). We again use the ggpredict() function, where we specify our saved model (model.mlogit), the seventh value for scot (terms = "scot [7]"), and the values for trust and age (condition = c(trust = 1, age = 30)).

```
ggpredict(model.mlogit, terms = "scot [7]",
          condition = c(trust = 1, age = 30))
# Predicted probabilities of pid


scot | Predicted
-----------------
  7 |      0.03
  7 |      0.33
  7 |      0.64
```

Although the output is a bit bare, the order of the three predicted probability values corresponds to the order of the values in our outcome variable pid. We can interpret these as follows:

> *For a 30-year-old individual with the strongest Scottish identity and who never trusts the UK government, the predicted probability of identifying with the Conservative Party is 0.03 (3%), the Labour Party is 0.33 (33%), and the SNP is 0.64 (64%).*

Second, let's look at a respondent who weakly identifies as Scottish (scot = 1), always trusts the UK government (trust = 4), and is 60 years old (age = 60).

```
ggpredict(model.mlogit, terms = "scot [1]",
          condition = c(trust = 4, age = 60))
# Predicted probabilities of pid


scot | Predicted
-----------------
  1 |      0.77
  1 |      0.22
  1 |      0.01
```

We interpret this as follows:

> *For a 60-year old-respondent with the weakest Scottish identity and who always trusts the UK government, the predicted probability of identifying with the Conservative Party is 0.77 (77%), the Labour Party is 0.22 (22%), and the SNP is 0.01 (1%).*

Grouped Predicted Probabilities

Let's calculate the predicted probabilities for each outcome across the seven values of scot, while setting trust and age at their means.

```
ggpredict(model.mlogit, terms = "scot")
# Predicted probabilities of pid


# Response Level = 1. Conservative


scot | Predicted
-----------------
  1 |      0.54
  2 |      0.45
```

```
   3 |        0.37
   4 |        0.29
   5 |        0.21
   7 |        0.10
```

```
# Response Level = 2. Labour
```

```
scot | Predicted
----------------
   1 |        0.42
   2 |        0.47
   3 |        0.51
   4 |        0.53
   5 |        0.52
   7 |        0.42
```

```
# Response Level = 3. SNP
```

```
scot | Predicted
----------------
   1 |        0.05
   2 |        0.08
   3 |        0.12
   4 |        0.19
   5 |        0.27
   7 |        0.48
```

```
Adjusted for:
* trust =  1.80
*   age = 54.21
```

These are the predicted probabilities for each of the outcome values for scot.[16] There is no clear rule for discussing the predicted probabilities, and obviously we don't want to discuss all of them. Instead, there might be a value and/or category that is of particular interest to us. Take note of how the values change as scot increases – this underlies the lines in the predicted probability plot we create next.

Plotting Predicted Probabilities

Lastly, we'll look at how to plot predicted probabilities using ggpredict() and ggplot() for unordered outcome models. In the plot, we'll include scot on the *x*-axis and the predicted probability lines will be for the three values of pid (our outcome variable). We will hold trust and age at their means.

The code is very similar to what we used previously for creating predicted probability plots, and actually simpler than what we used to plot our ordered logit model. The predicted probabilities for the three values of pid are automatically created and named response.level by

---

[16]We see that the predicted probabilities for scot = 6 are not included in the output. This is a quirk of how the ggpredict() function prints results and does not imply that scot = 6 has been removed or is missing from the calculations.

`ggpredict()`. Unfortunately, the confidence intervals are not automatically generated by the `ggpredict()` function and thus they will not be plotted with the `geom_ribbon()` function; therefore, we don't include `fill =` in the `ggplot()` specification. We could calculate the confidence intervals manually, but that's a lot of work to add something that might make the plot confusing to understand. The only other change is that we'll update the labels to reflect the variables we are plotting.

```
ggpredict(model.mlogit, terms = "scot") %>%
ggplot(mapping = aes(x = x, y = predicted, colour = response.level)) +
  geom_smooth(se = FALSE, size = 1.25) +
  scale_x_continuous(limits = c(1,7), breaks = c(1:7)) +
  labs(title = "Predicted Probabilities of Partisan Identification",
      x = "Strength of Scottish Identity", y = "Predicted Probability") +
  guides(colour = guide_legend(title = "PID")) +
  theme_minimal() +
  scale_fill_viridis_d() +
  scale_colour_viridis_d()
```

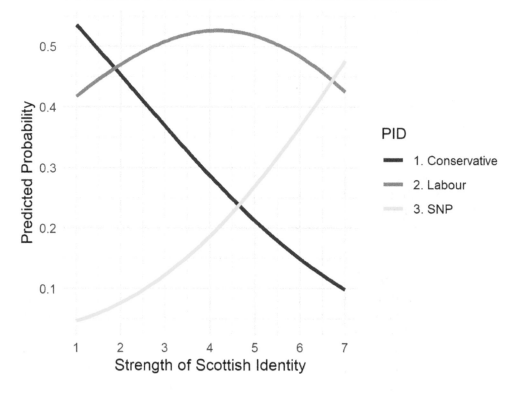

The plotted lines are the predicted probabilities for each value in our outcome variable pid across the values of scot. Clearly, there's a lot of movement going on here! We should discuss this plot in a similar fashion to the previous predicted probability plots. For example:

> *We see that as the strength of Scottish identity increases, the predicted probability of respondents' identifying with the Conservative Party decreases, identifying with the Labour Party increases then decreases, and identifying with the SNP increases. We see the predicted probability of identifying with Labour starts below Conservative when* scot = 1, *increases up to the middle categories of Scottish identity, starts decreasing for the higher values of Scottish identity, and is surpassed by the SNP at* scot = 7. *We can conclude that respondents who moderately identity as Scottish are most likely to identify with the Labour Party.*

Let's make this plot a little more interesting by adding a second predictor, trust. The code we'll use is nearly identical to the code for the second binary logit predicted probability plot we previously created. In addition to not plotting the confidence intervals and changing the labels, we'll split the plot into three subplots for each category of the outcome variable using the facet_grid() function. In the function, we'll specify response.level ~. to only plot the three outcome variable categories saved as response.level. We also let the scales of the y-axis vary between the subplots based on the predicted probabilities (scales = "free"); the alternative is to fix them to be equal. To make the subplots clearly distinctive, we'll use theme_bw() instead of theme_minimal().

```r
ggpredict(model.mlogit, terms = c("scot","trust")) %>%
  mutate(group = ordered(as_factor(group)),
         group = recode(group,
                        `1` = "Never",
                        `2` = "Sometimes",
                        `3` = "Usually",
                        `4` = "Always")) %>%
ggplot(mapping = aes(x = x, y = predicted, colour = group, fill = group)) +
  geom_smooth(se = FALSE, size = 1.25) +
  scale_x_continuous(limits = c(1,7), breaks = c(1:7)) +
  labs(title = "Predicted Probabilities of Partisan Identification",
       x = "Strength of Scottish Identity", y = "Predicted Probability") +
  guides(colour = guide_legend(title = "Govt Trust"),
         fill = guide_legend(title = "Govt Trust")) +
  theme_bw() +
  scale_fill_viridis_d() +
  scale_colour_viridis_d() +
  facet_grid(response.level ~., scales = "free")
```

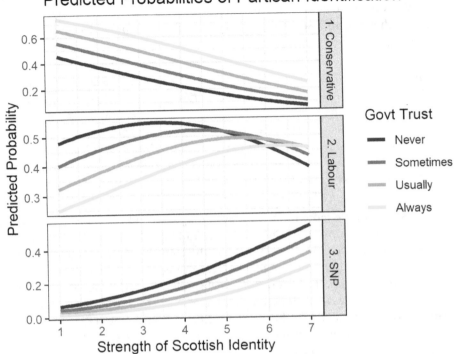

Each line is the predicted probability of identifying with the specific political party for a certain level of trust as the strength of Scottish identity increases. For example, in the top plot, the purple line is the predicted probability of respondents identifying with the Conservative Party who 'never trust' the British government as Scottish identity increases. For each plot, the probabilities of each different line add up to 1.

We want to interpret the overall plot and subplots by what happens as we increase on the x-axis and the differences in the trust lines. Let's have a go at interpreting the top plot (1. Conservative):

> *The predicted probability of identifying with the Conservative Party decreases as the strength of Scottish identity increases for all levels of trust. Respondents who always trust the UK government are the most likely to identify with the Conservative Party across all values of Scottish identity, followed by those who usually trust, etc.*

We might discuss the Labour plot (2. Labour) as follows:

> *We see that respondents with weak Scottish identity and who never trust the UK government are the most likely to identify with Labour. However, at the moderate strength of Scottish identity, the predicted probability begins to decrease to where, at the strongest identity, respondents who never trust the UK government have the lowest probability of identifying with the Labour Party. Generally, the overall plot reflects the predicted probability changes we observed in the first MNL model plot, but conditioned on respondents' trust in the UK government.*

The SNP plot (3. SNP) is essentially the inverse of the Conservative plot. Hence, we might interpret it as follows:

> *The predicted probability of identifying with the SNP increases as the strength of Scottish identity increases for all levels of trust. Respondents who never trust the UK government are the most likely to identify with the SNP across all values of Scottish identity, followed by those who sometimes trust, etc.*

We now have tools to analyse binary, ordered, and unordered outcome models in R. In the next section, we briefly discuss survey weighting.

SURVEY WEIGHTING

We have used survey data for the binary, ordered, and nominal outcome models in this chapter, as well as throughout this book. What we have not discussed or implemented is survey weighting. The general idea of survey weighting is that we need to adjust our sample data to make it more reflective of the population from which it is drawn (Heeringa et al. 2017). If we don't then our estimates may be biased and lead us to the wrong conclusions. As a simple example, let's imagine that we have national survey data on Brazilians' views on gender roles and norms in Brazilian society. Inspecting the data, we observe that 20% of the respondents are from the state of Amazonas, even though Amazonas only makes up around 2% of the Brazilian population. If we don't weight the sample our estimates will clearly be biased and unrepresentative of Brazilians' views. In this simple example, we would likely want to weight the sample to reflect the actual distribution of the Brazilian population.

Whether and how to create survey weights comes down to sample designs and data collection procedures (Groves et al. 2009), the specific details of which are beyond the scope of this book. Generally, survey weights are created and used to account for unequal probabilities of being selected for a survey (e.g., in a stratified multistage design), non-responses, sample totals that are not reflective of the population (as in the Brazil example), and purposeful selection bias in the sample (Groves et al. 2009; Heeringa et al. 2017). The last reason is when researchers oversample a subgroup in a national or subnational survey in order to have a large enough sample size to conduct statistical analysis; this often referred to as a 'boosted' sample. This is commonly done for studying minority groups (e.g., racial/ethnic minorities) within a national or subnational context. For example, if survey researchers were interested in Native Americans' political beliefs in a national survey, they would need to oversample Native Americans relative to the US population in order to ensure an adequate number of Native American respondents to conduct analysis. If the researchers wanted to combine the boosted Native American sample with the rest of the survey respondents, they would need to create and use survey weights to reflect the oversampling.

As secondary survey data users, we typically do not have to create survey weights. Instead, the survey weights are normally already in the dataset and details on how they were created and how to use them are part of the codebook. We may find that the weights need to be recalculated for some reason, but rarely are we starting from scratch.

Although we should use weights when working with survey data, I have deliberately avoided them throughout the book in an attempt to keep the content more straightforward. Correctly implementing survey weights can sometimes be tricky and can befuddle people starting to learn

R and QSS. In my own experience, survey weights often have a marginal impact, if any at all, on results. Hence, I tend to view survey weights like a security blanket that provides protection against critiques of our modelling choices and results. However, if your field or your research is heavily reliant on survey data than you should read up on how to using weights and to implement them in R.[17] The most basic way to include survey weights in our models is by specifying the option `weights = <weights variable>` in a R function, assuming the weighting option is available in the function.

CONCLUSION

This chapter offers an introduction to and applications of GLMs using social science data. Although only an introduction, we have squeezed in about 8 weeks of coursework into a single chapter. This chapter hopefully has provided you with an understanding of what comes after linear regression modelling and a solid foundation for expanding your QSS skill set.

▬▬▬ R Packages Used in This Chapter ▬▬▬

- `brant`
- `dplyr` (loaded with `tidyverse`)
- `forcats` (loaded with `tidyverse`)
- `GGally`
- `ggeffects`
- `ggplot2` (loaded with `tidyverse`)
- `haven`
- `MASS`
- `mlogit`
- `nnet`
- `pillar` (loaded with `tidyverse`)
- `tidymodels`
- `tidyverse`

▬▬▬ R Functions Used in this Chapter ▬▬▬

- `as_factor()` - convert variable to factor using `haven` or `forcats` package
- `as.numeric()` - convert variable to numeric
- `brant()` - Brant test for parallel regression assumption using `brant` package
- `c()` - concatenate
- `coef()` - extract regression coefficients
- `count()` - count the number of unique values of a variable or variables using `dplyr` package
- `dfidx()` - set new data frame for the `mlogit()` function
- `exp()` - compute exponential value
- `facet_grid()` - lay out `ggplot2` plots in a grid

---

[17]The additional resources section at the end of the chapter includes suggestions for further learning.

- `factor()` - specify variable as a factor
- `fct_rev()` - reverse values of a factor variable using `forcats` package
- `geom_point()` - ggplot2 scattered points
- `geom_ribbon()` - ggplot2 ribbons plot
- `geom_smooth()` - ggplot2 linear and nonlinear lines
- `ggcoef_model()` - regression coefficient plot
- `ggcoef_multinom()` - multinomial logit regression coefficient plot using `GGally` package
- `ggplot()` - base layer for ggplot2
- `ggpredict()` - adjusted predictions for regression models using `ggeffects` package
- `glm()` - generalised linear model
- `guide_legend()` - legend aesthetics using `ggplot2` package
- `guides()` - axes and legend aesthetics using `ggplot2` package
- `hmftest()` - Hausman-McFadden test using `mlogit` package
- `labs()` - ggplot2 labels
- `mlogit()` - multinomial logit and probit models using `mlogit` package
- `multinom()` - multinomial logit model using `nnet` package
- `mutate()` - recode variables using `dplyr` package
- `ordered()` - order a factor variable
- `polr()` - ordered logit and probit models using `MASS` package
- `read_dta()` - read in .dta data file using `haven` package
- `recode()` - recode variable using `dplyr` package
- `recode_factor()` - recode factor variable using `forcats` package
- `scale_colour_viridis_d()` - viridis colour scale for discrete variables using `ggplot2` package
- `scale_fill_viridis_d()` - viridis fill scale for discrete variables using `ggplot2` package
- `scale_x_continuous()` - x-axis aesthetics for continuous variables using `ggplot2` package
- `summary()` - summarise object
- `theme_bw()` - black-and-white ggplot2 theme
- `theme_minimal()` - minimal ggplot2 theme

Additional Resources

Books and Articles

- Andersen, R. and Armstrong, D. A., II (2022) *Presenting Statistical Results Effectively*. Sage.
- Faraway, J. J. (2016) *Extending the Linear Model with R*. 2nd edition. CRC.
- Fox, J. and Weisberg, S. (2018) *An R Companion to Applied Regression*. Sage.
- Gelman, A. (2007) 'Struggles with survey weighting and regression modeling'. *Statistical Science*, 22(2): 153-164.
- Gelman, A. and Hill, J. (2007) *Data Analysis Using Regression and Multilevel/Hierarchical Models*. Cambridge University Press.
- Groves, R. M., Fowler, F. J. Jr., Couper, M. P. Lepkowski, J. M., Singer, E. and Tourangeau, R. (2009) *Survey Methodology*, 2nd edition. Wiley.
- Heeringa, S. G., West, B. T. and Berglund, P. A. (2017) *Applied Survey Data Analysis*, 2nd edition. Chapman and Hall/CRC.
- Liu, X. (2022) *Categorical Data Analysis and Multilevel Modeling Using R*. Sage.
- Long, J. S. (1997) *Regression Models for Categorical and Limited Dependent Variables*. Sage.

14

COUNT MODELS

Chapter contents

Social scientists love to count things. For instance, researchers might count the number of wars and deaths in a given year, the number of news articles on presidential candidates in US papers during an election, or the number of arrests at protests. While in certain circumstances one could use OLS linear regression, typically we cannot as count variables are discrete in nature. If we use OLS linear regression for a count outcome variable, our estimates will be biased, inconsistent, and inefficient (King 1988; Hilbe 2014).

In this chapter, we examine regression models for analysing count outcome variables for when the event is counted for a fixed period of time.[1] Count regression models are classified as generalised linear models and typically use maximum likelihood estimation to obtain results. Although there are similarities with the GLMs covered in Chapter 13, count data and count regression models are different enough to warrant a separate discussion.

We will focus our discussion on the widely used Poisson regression model (PRM) and negative binomial regression model (NBRM). A large number of variations of these standard models exist, including zero-inflated and zero-truncated models, as well as more exotic count models that make different distributional assumptions about the data (e.g., the Poisson inverse Gaussian regression model). In practice, we often do not need to utilise extensions and variations of standard count models. However, we will discuss how to test for and deal with excess zeros in our count data using zero-inflated and hurdle versions of the PRM and NBRM in this chapter.[2]

By the end of this chapter, you should be able to:

- Determine the optimal count model
- Understand and run standard count models (Poisson and negative binomial) in R
- Understand and run zero-inflated and hurdle count models (zero-inflated and hurdle Poisson and negative binomial) in R
- Identify statistically significant predictors and perform regression coefficient interpretations
- Create visualisations of regression coefficients

OVERVIEW OF POISSON AND NEGATIVE BINOMIAL REGRESSION MODELS

The Poisson regression model assumes that the count data follow a Poisson distribution. In fact, many count models use the Poisson distribution as a starting point. The key property of the Poisson distribution is the assumption that the *variance equals the mean* in the count outcome variable – this is known as equidispersion. The PRM, since it is directly based on the Poisson distribution, also assumes equidisperson. However, it is rarely the case that the variance equals the mean in count variables. Instead, it much more common for the variance to be larger than the mean – this is known as overdispersion.

---

[1]Therefore, we are using cross-sectional analysis. For analysing counts over time, we would use time series count models.

[2]See Cameron and Trivedi (2013) and Hilbe (2014) for more information on non-canonical count regression models.

Why do we care about overdispersion? When overdispersion is present, the standard errors will be biased downwards and thus the *z*-values will be inflated (Cameron and Trivedi 2013). Hence, we are more likely to find that certain predictors are statistically significant when they actually are not. Obviously, this presents a problem. We will test for overdispersion with a likelihood-ratio test as well as comparing models' AIC values.

In my experience, the PRM is almost always the *wrong model* to use due to the ubiquity of overdispersion. We can make some corrections for overdispersion and still use a PRM (Hardin and Hilbe 2012; Hilbe 2014), but often the simplest practical solution is to use a negative binomial regression model. The NBRM includes an extra parameter that accounts for overdispersion, often denoted by α or θ. If overdispersion is not present, the NBRM is equivalent to the PRM (Hilbe 2014); thus, the PRM is nested in the NBRM.

EXAMINING THE DATA

In this chapter, we will use data on the impact of promoting academic research on Twitter (Klar et al. 2020). Klar et al. (2020) assessed whether scholars could increase the number citations of their academic articles using self-promotion on Twitter. Further, they wanted to know whether and what systematic differences might exist between scholars on the impact of self-promotion. For example, are there gender differences in whether promoting research on Twitter has an impact on citations?

We'll use the `read_csv()` function to read in the dataset `citations_twitter.csv` and name it `citations`.[3] The data measured the number of citations in 2019 of all articles in six prominent political science and communication journals published during 2016.

```
setwd("C:/QSSD/Chapter 14 - Count Models")
getwd()
[1] "C:/QSSD/Chapter 14 - Count Models"
library(tidyverse)

citations <- read_csv("citations_twitter.csv")
glimpse(citations)
Rows: 308
Columns: 7
$ articlecites   <dbl> 8, 0, 13, 1, 2, 14, 1, 10, 6, 3, 13, 12, 3, 3,
14, 7, ~
$ womanleadauthor <dbl> 0, 1, 1, 1, 0, 1, 0, 1, 0, 0, 0, 1, 0, 0, 1, 0,
0, 0, ~
$ womanauthor    <dbl> 1, 1, 1, 1, 0, 1, 1, 1, 0, 0, 0, 1, 0, 0, 1, 0,
0, 0, ~
$ tweet_dum      <dbl> 1, 1, 1, 0, 0, 1, 0, 1, 1, 0, 1, 1, 0, 0, 1, 1,
0, 1, ~
$ fullprof       <dbl> 1, 0, 0, 0, 1, 0, 1, 1, 0, 0, 0, 1, 0, 1, 0, 0,
1, 1, ~
```

---

[3]This is a cleaned-up, smaller version of Klar et al.'s original data.

```
$ retweets      <dbl> 2, 0, 2, NA, NA, 0, NA, 35, 0, NA, 3, 5, NA, NA,
0, 1,~
$ totfav        <dbl> 6, 0, 7, NA, NA, 1, NA, 64, 1, NA, 8, 5, NA, NA,
1, 2,~
```

We'll use `articlecites` as our outcome variable and three predictors – `tweet_dum`, `womanleadauthor`, and `fullprof` – in our model. The three predictors are all dummy variables: whether an article had any tweets (`tweet_dum`), whether a woman was the lead author (`womanleadauthor`), and whether at least one of the authors was a full professor (`fullprof`).

As discussed throughout this book, we should always examine our data and variables prior to performing analysis. This is particularly important when working with count data. Our initial examination allows us to diagnose potential problems the data might present and whether certain models might be more appropriate than the PRM or NBRM. For example, if we see a ton of zeros, we might want to consider whether a zero-inflated count model fits the data better than the PRM or NBRM. Or if the distribution has a large peak at lower count values and a very long tail, we might want to consider count models with different distributional assumptions (e.g., the Poisson inverse Gaussian model). Let's look at the descriptive statistics and a smoothed density plot for `articlecites`.

```
summary(citations$articlecites)
   Min. 1st Qu.  Median    Mean 3rd Qu.    Max.    NA's
  0.000   0.000   2.000   3.052   4.000  21.000       1
var(citations$articlecites, na.rm=TRUE)
[1] 13.33061
```

The number of article citations has a median of 2 and mean of 3, suggesting that at least a few articles have a relatively high number of citations, pulling the distribution to the right. The variance of 13.33 suggests we probably have a problem with overdispersion.

We also see that the first quartile (`1st Qu.`) of `articlecites` consists of articles that received 0 citations. This doesn't necessarily imply we have an excess of zeros. But it does suggest we should test whether a hurdle or zero-inflated model is a better choice.[4]

We also want to examine the overall distribution of `articlecites` as it may suggest alternative count models to test for fitting our data. We'll use a smoothed density distribution to plot the distribution. To create a colour-filled density plot when using only one variable, we need to specify `fill = <"colour">` in the `geom_density()` argument; this is a small tweak from what we did in Chapter 8. We'll specify `fill = "steelblue"` and lighten the shading with `alpha = .5`.[5] As `articlecites` has one missing value, we'll filter it out prior to the `ggplot()` function.

---

[4]The large number of zeros also doesn't mean that these articles are necessarily of poor quality. Instead, it is probably reflective of the fact that academic publishing can take several years from inception to appearing in print. Therefore, the articles with 0 citations in this dataset (measured in 2019) may not have 0 if we remeasured citations in 2022.

[5]Note that 'bluesteel' will not work here. In an ideal world, it would work and it would render Ben Stiller's face from *Zoolander* on the plot.

```
citations %>%
   filter(!is.na(articlecites)) %>%
ggplot() +
   geom_density(mapping = aes(articlecites), fill = "steelblue", alpha = .5) +
   labs(x = "Number of Citations") +
   theme_minimal()
```

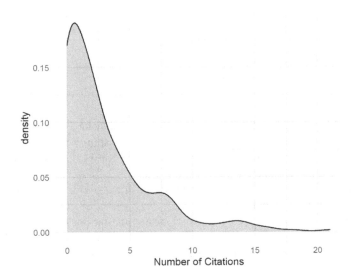

We should informally examine three aspects of count distribution plots.[6] First, the proportion of observations with low counts – observations with counts of 0, 1, 2, 3, etc. – relative to the median and mean values. This tells us about the 'typical case' and informs us about possible problems with excess zeros. Second, the proportion of observations with very high counts – the size of the right tail of the distribution – relative to the median and mean. We want to assess the length of the right tail and the proportion of observations along the right tail. For example, if there is only one observation with a very high count, we would treat the observation as an outlier and remove it from our data. But if there are multiple observations with very high counts, we might consider an alternative count model to the PRM or NBRM (e.g., the Poisson inverse Gaussian model). Third, whether there are multiple modes ('humps' of observations) along the distribution. Most count distributions have a mass of observations at the lower values and a tail of observations with higher values. However, it is possible that there are multiple values of the distribution with masses of observations. In this situation, we may consider using certain model specifications (e.g., clustered standard errors), predictors, and/or alternative count models.

In this plot, we see that most articles have a small number of citations and a few articles have a relatively high number of citations. This is a very typical count distribution. There are only a few observations in the right tail, but none appear extreme enough to worry about as outliers or to consider a different count model.

---

[6]This is a quick look for suggestive information about the count distribution.

The descriptive statistics and density plot suggest we may have overdispersion and an excess zero problem in our outcome variable `articlecites`. Therefore, we will test for both of these possible issues.

Unlike the other regression models we have covered in this book, modelling count data involves progressively testing and comparing a series of different models to decide on the model that appears to best fit the data. This does not mean we engage in data mining to find the best model (e.g., *p*-hacking to include only statistically significant predictors). Instead, we go through logical steps to determine the best model for our count data. Commonly, we take the following steps:

1   Run a PRM and test for overdispersion.
2   Run an NBRM.
3   Based on the overdispersion test and model fit statistics, decide whether the PRM or NBRM is preferred.
4   Using the model preferred in step 3, assess whether there may be a problem with excess zeros.
5   If there is evidence of an excess zero problem, run a corresponding hurdle count model and/or a zero-inflated count model. For example, if the NBRM is preferred in step 3, we would run a hurdle and/or zero-inflated NBRM.
6   Based on model fit statistics and the Vuong test (if using a zero-inflated count model), decide on the preferred model.
7   Interpret the regression coefficients and create data visualisations using the preferred model.

In the rest of this chapter, we will walk through each of these steps.

POISSON REGRESSION MODEL

We'll run a PRM using the `glm()` function from the `stats` package. We need to specify `family = "poisson"`, but the rest of the code takes the same form as the previous regression models we have run in this book. We'll save the results as `model.prm`.

```
summary(model.prm <- glm(articlecites ~ tweet_dum + womanleadauthor +
                         fullprof, family = "poisson", data = citations))

Call:
glm(formula = articlecites ~ tweet_dum + womanleadauthor + fullprof,
    family = "poisson", data = citations)

Deviance Residuals:
    Min      1Q   Median      3Q      Max
-3.5230  -2.0522  -0.8497  0.8469   7.5360

Coefficients:
                Estimate Std. Error z value Pr(>|z|)
(Intercept)      0.74463    0.05667  13.140  < 2e-16 ***
tweet_dum        0.84126    0.06609  12.729  < 2e-16 ***
```

```
womanleadauthor  0.05350    0.06728   0.795  0.42652
fullprof                    0.18607    0.06619   2.811  0.00494 **
---
Signif. codes:  0 '***' 0.001 '**' 0.01 '*' 0.05 '.' 0.1 ' ' 1

(Dispersion parameter for poisson family taken to be 1)

    Null deviance: 1181.0  on 305  degrees of freedom
Residual deviance: 1017.9  on 302  degrees of freedom
  (2 observations deleted due to missingness)
AIC: 1701.2

Number of Fisher Scoring iterations: 5
```

We see that `tweet_dum` and `fullprof` are statistically significant, but not `womanleadauthor`, and both have a positive coefficient. This means that tweeting about an article and having at least one full professor as an author both increase the expected number of citations.

Before we can trust the PRM results, we need to test for whether there is overdispersion – or, more specifically, test whether there is enough overdispersion present to cause problems with our estimates. We'll use the `dispersiontest()` function from the AER package. This test compares the null hypothesis of no overdispersion (i.e., equidispersion) with the alternative of overdispersion (and/or the less commonly observed underdispersion).[7]

```
library(AER)
dispersiontest(model.prm)

      Overdispersion test

data:  model.prm
z = 4.6433, p-value = 1.714e-06
alternative hypothesis: true dispersion is greater than 1
sample estimates:
dispersion
  3.616107
```

The part `alternative hypothesis: true dispersion is greater than 1` corresponds to the variance being greater than the conditional mean (overdispersion). Hence, the null hypothesis is that the true dispersion is equal to 1 (equidispersion).[8] To the surprise of no one, the p-value is less than 0.05, we reject the null, and conclude that our PRM is overdispersed. Therefore, we

---

[7]By default the `dispersiontest()` tests for overdispersion. To test for underdispersion, we include the option `alternative = "less"`.

[8]If we want the test formulated using the estimated dispersion parameter α, we can include the option `trafo =`.

can't trust the PRM results and we should use negative binomial regression (or, more generally, a different count model than PRM).

NEGATIVE BINOMIAL REGRESSION MODEL

To run a negative binomial model, we use the `glm.nb()` function from the MASS package. The specification takes the same form as our previous models, but we don't need to include `family =` or `method =` since the function is only for the NBRM.

```
library(MASS)

summary(model.nbrm <- glm.nb(articlecites ~ tweet_dum + womanleadauthor +
                        fullprof, data=citations))

Call:
glm.nb(formula = articlecites ~ tweet_dum + womanleadauthor +
    fullprof, data = citations, init.theta = 1.097281755, link = log)

Deviance Residuals:
    Min      1Q   Median      3Q      Max
-2.0402  -1.5328  -0.4058   0.3874   3.2615

Coefficients:
                Estimate Std. Error z value Pr(>|z|)
(Intercept)      0.74365    0.10388   7.159 8.13e-13 ***
tweet_dum        0.84316    0.14326   5.885 3.97e-09 ***
womanleadauthor  0.04831    0.13419   0.360   0.719
fullprof         0.19177    0.13277   1.444   0.149
---
Signif. codes:  0 '***' 0.001 '**' 0.01 '*' 0.05 '.' 0.1 ' ' 1

(Dispersion parameter for Negative Binomial(1.0973) family taken to be 1)

    Null deviance: 381.90  on 305  degrees of freedom
Residual deviance: 341.81  on 302  degrees of freedom
  (2 observations deleted due to missingness)
AIC: 1359.5

Number of Fisher Scoring iterations: 1

             Theta:  1.097
         Std. Err.:  0.139

  2 x log-likelihood:  -1349.518
```

We see that only `tweet_dum` is a statistically significant predictor of the number of article citations; `fullprof` is no longer statistically significant. Again, overdispersion inflates the z-values and, when present, we commonly observe a difference in statistically significant predictors between the PRM and NBRM.

To be doubly sure of our model choice, let's do a likelihood-ratio test and compare AIC values between our PRM and NBRM. These tests allow us to assess which model provides a better fit to the data.

Let's first look at the log-likelihood values of our PRM and NBRM using the `logLik()` function.

```
logLik(model.nbrm)
'log Lik.' -674.759 (df=5)
logLik(model.prm)
'log Lik.' -846.6187 (df=4)
```

We see that our NBRM has a much larger log-likelihood (closer to 0), indicating a better fit to the data. But, let's do a proper likelihood-ratio test using the `lrtest()` function from the `lmtest` package; the `lmtest` package is automatically imported by the `AER` package. In the function, we specify `model.prm` and then `model.nbrm` as the PRM is nested in the NBRM through the dispersion parameter estimated by the NBRM.

```
lrtest(model.prm, model.nbrm)
Likelihood ratio test

Model 1: articlecites ~ tweet_dum + womanleadauthor + fullprof
Model 2: articlecites ~ tweet_dum + womanleadauthor + fullprof
  #Df  LogLik Df  Chisq Pr(>Chisq)
1   4 -846.62
2   5 -674.76  1 343.72  < 2.2e-16 ***
---
Signif. codes:  0 '***' 0.001 '**' 0.01 '*' 0.05 '.' 0.1 ' ' 1
```

The output provides the log-likelihood values (`LogLik`), the difference in degrees of freedom (`Df`), the calculated chi-square value (`Chisq`), and the corresponding p-value (`PR(>Chisq)`). We see that $p \leq 0.05$ and thus we conclude that our NBRM is preferred over our PRM according to the likelihood-ratio test.

Now let's compare the AIC values. The model with the smaller AIC value is considered to fit the data better and thus is preferred.

```
c(model.prm$aic, model.nbrm$aic)
[1] 1701.237 1359.518
```

The first number is the AIC for our PRM and the second number is the AIC for our NBRM. Our NBRM's AIC value is much smaller than our PRM's AIC value and thus is the preferred model.

We actually don't need to check the AIC values here as it constitutes a redundant test when using the likelihood-ratio test. If you remember from Chapter 13, the AIC is calculated using the log-likelihood and number of parameters of a model (AIC $= -2\ell + 2k$). Therefore, if the likelihood-ratio test tells us there is a statistically significant difference between the PRM and NBRM, then we will also find a relatively large difference between the PRM's and NBRM's AIC values. However, examining AIC values is good practice for when we can't use a formal statistical test (e.g., the likelihood-ratio test) to compare models.

These series of tests make clear that our negative binomial regression model is preferred to our Poisson regression model.[9] Often deciding between modelling techniques winds up making little difference to our substantive conclusions (e.g., binary logit versus binary probit models). Here, however, we see that if we relied on the results from our PRM, we would have made the wrong conclusions about what explains the number of article citations.

DO WE HAVE AN EXCESS ZERO PROBLEM?

An abundance of zeros is a common problem in count data. Therefore, testing for the presence of 'too many zeros' (Hilbe 2014) is commonly the next step researchers take after deciding between the PRM and NBRM.

Although the PRM and NBRM assume that there will be some zero counts in the data, based on the underlying distribution, neither model does well at predicting zeros when there are a large number of zeros in the data. This is because both models assume that each observation has a non-zero probability of not being zero (Long and Freese 2014). If our count variable has an excess of zeros we should consider alternative models to the PRM and NBRM. The two most frequently used options are zero-inflated models and hurdle models.

Before we discuss these models further, let's figure out whether we *need* to use them in the first place. Earlier we saw that around 25% of the values in our outcome variable `articlecites` are zeros – a relative large proportion. However, the number of zeros in our outcome variable (the *observed zeros*) is not the sole determinant for whether we have an excess zero problem. The better determinant is comparing the number of observed zeros to the number of predicted zeros estimated by our models. If the number of zeros predicted by the PRM and/or NBRM is close to the number of observed zeros, then we don't need to use a hurdle or zero-inflated count model.

---

[9]There are additional ways that researchers compare PRM and NBRM, as well as other types of count models. One common technique is plotting the observed counts against the predicted counts for each of the models. The model whose predicted counts are closest to the observed counts is considered the preferred model (see Hilbe 2014; Long and Freese 2014). While these plots can be great fun, in practice they are often a lot of work to wind up with the same conclusions as our other tests.

We can easily compare predicted and observed zeros using the `check_zeroinflation()` function from the `performance` package.[10] For each model, the function tells us the number of observed and predicted zeros, their ratio (predicted/observed), and an assessment of whether our model is underfitting (or overfitting) the number of zeros. By default, if the ratio is below 0.95 (underfitting), the function recommends trying a zero-inflated count model.[11] We simply need to include the name of our saved model object in the `check_zeroinflation()` function. Since we've determined that our NBRM is preferred over our PRM, we'll only compare the predicted and observed values for our NBRM.

```
library(performance)

check_zeroinflation(model.nbrm)
# Check for zero-inflation

   Observed zeros: 81
  Predicted zeros: 78
            Ratio: 0.96
Model seems ok, ratio of observed and predicted zeros is within the
   tolerance range.
```

We see that the number of observed zeros is 81, the number of predicted zeros is 78, and thus their ratio is 0.96 (78/81 = 0.963). The output tells us that the `Model seems ok`, which means we don't have an excess zero problem with NBRM. Although the function's text doesn't seem like a ringing endorsement, having correctly predicted 96.3% of the zeros is pretty good! Therefore, we don't need to try a hurdle or zero-inflated negative binomial count model.

In keeping with the steps outlined earlier for determining the count model that best fits our data, we will next plot the coefficients and perform interpretations for our NBRM. Since excess zeros are ubiquitous in count data, we'll revisit zero-inflated and hurdle count models in the last section of this chapter.

PLOTTING AND INTERPRETING COEFFICIENTS

Plotting Coefficients

Let's plot coefficients and confidence intervals for `model.nbrm` using the `ggcoef_model()` function from the `GGally` package. One difference in the code from our previous use of `ggcoef_model()` is that we set the option `no_reference_row = broom.helpers::all_dichotomous()`.

---

[10]The `performance` package includes a number of different functions for model comparisons and diagnostic testing.

[11]We can change this cut-point by using the `tolerance =` option.

This option tells the `ggcoef_model()` function that all of the predictors are binary (i.e., dichotomous) by using the `all_dichotomous()` function from the `broom.helpers` package. Using the specification `broom.helpers::` calls the `all_dichotomous()` function without explicitly loading the `broom.helpers` package.

```
library(GGally)
ggcoef_model(model.nbrm,
             variable_labels = c(
                tweet_dum = "Tweeted Article",
                womanleadauthor = "Woman Lead Author",
                fullprof = "Full Professor"),
             no_reference_row = broom.helpers::all_dichotomous(),
             show_p_values = FALSE,
             signif_stars = FALSE) +
   labs(title = "Predicting Article Citations",
        x = "Negative Binomial Regression Coefficients")
```

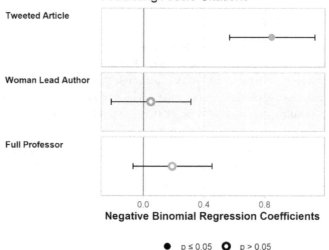

This coefficient plot is interpreted in the same way as the others we have seen throughout the book.

Interpreting Coefficients

Using the `model.nbrm` results, we'll use **predicted counts** to interpret the `tweet_dum` coefficient (since it's the only significant predictor) in two ways.[12] First, we'll calculate predicted counts

---

[12]**Expected counts** are another common way to interpret count model coefficients. Expected counts are calculated and interpreted like odds ratios. We won't look at them here because they are not good for understanding and communicating baseline counts and relative differences in counts.

for the two values of `tweet_dum` – in a similar manner to how we calculated individual predicted probabilities in Chapter 13. Second, we'll plot predicted counts – in a similar manner to how we created predicted probability plots in Chapter 13.

Calculating Predicted Counts

We'll use the `ggpredict()` function from the `ggeffects` package to calculate the predicted counts for `tweet_dum`.

```
library(ggeffects)

ggpredict(model.nbrm, terms = "tweet_dum")
# Predicted counts of articlecites

tweet_dum | Predicted |         95% CI
-------------------------------------------
       0 |      2.30 | [1.98, 2.67]
       1 |      5.34 | [4.21, 6.78]

Adjusted for:
* womanleadauthor = 0.36
*         fullprof = 0.37
```

We see that the predicted number of citations for tweeted articles is 5.34, while the predicted number of citations for non-tweeted articles is 2.30. Hence, articles that receive at least one tweet are expected to receive three more citations than articles that receive zero tweets.

Notice that the `ggpredict()` output shows the predicted counts are based on `womanleadauthor` and `fullprof` held at their means. This is done automatically by the `ggpredict()` function because these variables are classified as numeric, even though they should be factors. Instead, we may want to calculate predicted counts for when `womanleadauthor` and `fullprof` are held at their modal values. We can simply including the `condition =` option and set the two predictors at their modes (both have modes of 0).

```
ggpredict(model.nbrm, terms = "tweet_dum",
          condition = c(womanleadauthor = 0, fullprof = 0))
# Predicted counts of articlecites

tweet_dum | Predicted |         95% CI
-------------------------------------------
       0 |      2.10 | [1.72, 2.58]
       1 |      4.89 | [3.69, 6.47]
```

Now we see that the predicted number of citations for tweeted articles is 4.89, while the predicted number of citations for non-tweeted articles is 2.10. Hence, articles that receive at least one tweet are expected to receive almost three more citations than articles that receive zero tweets. Changing to modal values slightly narrowed the difference in the predicted number of citations between tweeted and non-tweeted articles, but our substantive conclusion remains the same.

Plotting Predicted Counts

Let's now plot the predicted counts for `tweet_dum` when `womanleadauthor` and `fullprof` are set at their modes. Since we only have dummy variables, we are unable to create a cool-looking curvilinear plot like we did for predicted probabilities in Chapter 13. Instead, we'll plot the predicted count and the 95% confidence (prediction) interval for each value of `tweet_dum`.

We'll connect the `ggpredict()` function to our `ggplot()` code using the pipe operator `%>%`. We include the main `aes()` argument in the `ggplot()` function and convert x to a factor using the `as_factor()` function. Converting x to a factor is needed to get the labels for `tweet_dum` to print on the x-axis. We'll use the `geom_pointrange()` function from the `ggplot2` package to generate a plot with a dot for the predicted count and vertical lines for the 95% confidence intervals. In the `geom_pointrange(aes())` specification, we set the lower bound of the confidence interval with `ymin = conf.low` and the upper bound with `ymax = conf.high`. The `tweet_dum` variable does not have labels attached to the values. Since we want labels on these values, we can simply specify them in the `scale_x_discrete()` function using the `labels =` option. Lastly, we'll add plot labels and use `theme_minimal()`.

```
ggpredict(model.nbrm, terms = "tweet_dum",
          condition = c(womanleadauthor = 0, fullprof = 0)) %>%
ggplot(aes(x = as_factor(x), y = predicted)) +
  geom_pointrange(aes(ymin = conf.low, ymax = conf.high)) +
  scale_x_discrete(labels = c("No Tweet","Tweet")) +
  labs(title = "Predicted Number of Article Citations",
       x = "Whether Article was Tweeted", y = "Predicted Citations") +
  theme_minimal()
```

Predicted Number of Article Citations

This plot provides a simple visualisation of the predicted counts for `tweet_dum`. If we had ordinal, interval, or ratio variable in our model, we could create a predicted count plot similar to the predicted probability plots we created earlier in the previous chapter.

Since overdispersion is almost always present in count data, we rarely use the PRM over the NBRM in practice. However, we should always start with the PRM and test for overdispersion in order to better understand our data and justify the use of NBRM.

In the next section, we turn to zero-inflated and hurdle count models.

ZERO-INFLATED AND HURDLE COUNT MODELS

To motivate our discussion of zero-inflated and hurdle count models, let's compare the number of predicted zeros and the number of observed zeros for our PRM using the `check_zeroinflation()` function.

```
check_zeroinflation(model.prm)
# Check for zero-inflation

  Observed zeros: 81
 Predicted zeros: 24
           Ratio: 0.30
Model is underfitting zeros (probable zero-inflation).
```

Unlike our NBRM, we see that our PRM does a terrible job of predicting the number of zeros in `arti-clecites`; the model only correctly predicts 30% of the observed zeros. Let's imagine we couldn't use the NBRM for some reason – a travesty – or imagine that we found a similar result for our NBRM. To deal with this excess zero problem, we can try using a zero-inflated or hurdle count model.

The basic idea of zero-inflated and hurdle models is that if we can model the probability of an observation being a positive count (rather than being zero), we'll get better estimates in our count models. The two models differ in how they approach this problem.

Hurdle models use two separate steps to model the count data (Hilbe 2014). First, a binary outcome model (e.g., logit, probit) is used to estimate the probability of an observation being a positive count (rather than a zero). Second, only positive counts ($y > 0$) are included in the count model (e.g., PRM, NBRM). When our count data only have positive counts, we use what are known as zero-truncated count models.[13] Therefore, hurdle models treat the excess zero problem using two separate steps that don't directly inform each other's estimates.[14] The most common hurdle count models use logit or probit for the outcome model and zero-truncated Poisson or zero-truncated negative binomial for the count model.

Zero-inflated models also use two steps, but the steps are not treated as separate and zeros are not kept out of the count model. Zero-inflated models assume there are two types of zeros – either an

---

[13]Outside of the hurdle model context, it is uncommon to have social science count data with no zeros in the outcome variable. Zero-truncated count models are primarily used with count data where in order for an observation to be included in the data it must have a positive count. The classic example is data on the length of patients' hospital stays. For a patient to be included in the data, they must have stayed at least 1 day (or whatever the unit of measurement might be).

[14]Hurdle models can also be used when there are too few zeros (Long and Freese 2014).

observation is always zero (for some reason) or an observation is zero because whatever is being counted didn't occur (but that the observation is not always zero). A classic example for motivating zero-inflated count models is with data on the number of publications of early-career biochemists (Long 1997; Long and Freese 2014). Some biochemists might have zero publications because their employer does not allow them to publish their work (e.g., biochemists working for certain government agencies). Other biochemists might have zero publications because they have yet to have an article accepted for publication. Zero-inflated models attempt to estimate these two types of zeros and incorporate the information into the count model's estimations.

Zero-inflated models use a binary outcome model (e.g., logit, probit) to model the probability of an observation always being zero (or not always being zero). Then a count model (e.g., PRM, NBRM) is used for observations that are not estimated to always be zero. Since these two estimation steps are combined, zero-inflated count models are considered to be *mixture models* (Hilbe 2014). The two most common zero-inflated count models are the zero-inflated Poisson (ZIP) regression model and the zero-inflated negative binomial (ZINB) regression model.

Practically speaking, it is often unclear whether we should use a hurdle or a zero-inflated model for dealing with excess zeros. Hilbe (2014) recommends that zero-inflated models should only be used when a researcher has a theory for why there are an excess zeros and why there are two types of zeros in the data. This is a rather limiting recommendation as often count data do not have clear systematic reasons for excess zeros. If this is not the case, then we should consider a hurdle model (Hilbe 2014). Statistically, we can compare AIC (or BIC) values to decide whether a hurdle or a zero-inflated model provides the best fit to the data. We may also find that our specific discipline tends to use one of the models more frequently than the other model. For example, I've found that political scientists use zero-inflated models considerably more than hurdle models.

Zero-Inflated Count Models

We'll start by running zero-inflated count models. One the main challenges we face with estimating a zero-inflated model is correctly specifying the inflation model (i.e., the binary outcome model). The most common option is to use the same predictors in the inflation model and the count model. However, if we have a small N this can cause estimation problems since we are estimating our predictors twice. We'll know there is an estimation problem if we obtain nonsensible results in the inflation model. Another option is to only include predictors that clearly affect whether an observation is always zero. The problem is that it is often unclear whether such a variable exists in our data. For example, none of the variables in the `citations` data appear to be a determining factor for whether an article will always have zero citations. By contrast, the hurdle model doesn't have this problem since the binary outcome and count models are estimated separately.

Let's first run a ZIP model using the `zeroinfl()` function from the `pscl` package. We'll include `tweet_dum`, `womanleadauthor`, and `fullprof` as predictors in both the inflation and count models parts of ZIP. In the `zeroinfl()` function, we first specify our outcome variable (`articlecites`), then ~, and then the count model predictors (`tweet_dum + womanleadauthor + fullprof`). We include | to separate the count model and inflation model. After the | we specify the inflation model predictors (`| tweet_dum + womanleadauthor + fullprof`). The default model options in `zeroinfl()` are the PRM and logit, but we can change them using the `dist =` and `link =` options. We also need to include the name of the data (`data = citations`). We'll save the results as `model.zip`.

```
library(pscl)


summary(model.zip <- zeroinfl(articlecites ~ tweet_dum + womanleadauthor +
                              fullprof | tweet_dum + womanleadauthor +
                              fullprof, data=citations))

Call:
zeroinfl(formula = articlecites ~ tweet_dum + womanleadauthor + fullprof |
    tweet_dum + womanleadauthor + fullprof, data = citations)

Pearson residuals:
   Min     1Q Median     3Q     Max
-1.9563 -1.0219 -0.5331  0.6567  9.0897

Count model coefficients (poisson with log link):
                Estimate Std. Error z value Pr(>|z|)
(Intercept)      1.12894    0.05949  18.977  <2e-16 ***
tweet_dum        0.63862    0.06864   9.304  <2e-16 ***
womanleadauthor  0.01703    0.07034   0.242   0.809
fullprof         0.08268    0.06910   1.197   0.231

Zero-inflation model coefficients (binomial with logit link):
                Estimate Std. Error z value Pr(>|z|)
(Intercept)     -0.73559    0.21511  -3.420 0.000627 ***
tweet_dum       -1.07682    0.39613  -2.718 0.006561 **
womanleadauthor -0.09214    0.30488  -0.302 0.762480
fullprof        -0.47637    0.31311  -1.521 0.128160
---
Signif. codes:  0 '***' 0.001 '**' 0.01 '*' 0.05 '.' 0.1 ' ' 1

Number of iterations in BFGS optimization: 13
Log-likelihood: -762.6 on 8 Df
```

The ZIP results are split into two sections. The top section is the PRM results (Count model coefficients) and the bottom section is the logit model results (Zero-inflation model coefficients). The zero-inflation model is estimating the probability of always being a zero. Here, this is the probability of an article never receiving a citation. In the logit model, we see that tweet_dum is the only statistical significant predictor. Its negative coefficient means that articles that have received at least one tweet have a *lower* probability of *never* receiving a citation.

In the PRM results, we see that tweet_dum is the only statistically significant predictor of the number of expected citations and it has a positive coefficient. Remember from earlier that both tweet_dum and fullprof were statistically significant in the standard PRM, and that the NBRM demonstrated that fullprof actually did not have a statistically significant effect. Therefore, it appears that our ZIP model does a better job modelling the counts than our PRM. But, let's run a **Vuong test** to assess whether the ZIP is better than the PRM.

The Vuong test is a likelihood-ratio test where the null hypothesis is that both models (i.e., PRM and ZIP) are equally close to the actual model and the alternative hypothesis is that one model is closer (Vuong 1989). The Vuong test calculates a test statistic with critical values, based on an asymptotically normal distribution, for deciding between models. When the value of the Vuong test statistic is greater than 1.96, the first specified model is preferred and the null is rejected. When the value is less than –1.96, the second specified model is preferred and the null is rejected. When the value is between –1.96 and 1.96, the two models are indistinguishable and the null is not rejected (Vuong 1989).[15]

We can use the vuong() function from the pscl package to run the Vuong test. In the function, we'll first specify model.prm and then model.zip.

```
vuong(model.prm, model.zip)
Vuong Non-Nested Hypothesis Test-Statistic:
(test-statistic is asymptotically distributed N(0,1) under the
null that the models are indistinguishible)
--------------------------------------------------------------
              Vuong z-statistic              H_A     p-value
Raw                 -4.641829 model2 > model1 1.7267e-06
AIC-corrected       -4.420969 model2 > model1 4.9130e-06
BIC-corrected       -4.009774 model2 > model1 3.0388e-05
```

In the output, the first row (Raw) is the standard Vuong test, while the next two rows are AIC and BIC corrections to the standard Vuong test. These corrections exist because the standard Vuong test is biased in favour of the zero-inflated model (Desmarais and Harden 2013; Hilbe 2014). The Vuong z-statistic column is the test statistic value, the H_A column suggests which model is preferred based on the test statistic value, and the last column is the test's *p*-value. All three rows conclude that the ZIP is preferred over the PRM. Specifically, the test statistic is less than –1.96 (so, the second model is preferred) and $p \leq 0.05$ for each row. A word of caution: the information in the column H_A can be deceiving as it may report a favoured model even if the test statistic is between –1.96 and 1.96, and $p > 0.05$.

Hurdle Count Models

Let's now compare our ZIP model with a hurdle model that uses a PRM. We could perform the hurdle model as separate regressions with the glm() function and then combine the results to calculate the log-likelihood, AIC, and BIC. Instead we'll use the hurdle() function from the pscl package, which presents the results together and is roughly equivalent to running separate models.

```
summary(model.hp <- hurdle(articlecites ~ tweet_dum + womanleadauthor +
                     fullprof | tweet_dum + womanleadauthor +
                     fullprof, data=citations))

Call:
hurdle(formula = articlecites ~ tweet_dum + womanleadauthor + fullprof |
    tweet_dum + womanleadauthor + fullprof, data = citations)
```

---

[15]The critical values are larger with small *N*s (e.g., 2 instead of 1.96).

```
Pearson residuals:
    Min      1Q  Median      3Q      Max
-1.9521 -1.0224 -0.5333  0.6569  9.0865


Count model coefficients (truncated poisson with log link):
                 Estimate Std. Error z value Pr(>|z|)
(Intercept)       1.12832    0.05979  18.871  <2e-16 ***
tweet_dum         0.63842    0.06861   9.305  <2e-16 ***
womanleadauthor   0.01810    0.07025   0.258   0.797
fullprof          0.08351    0.06902   1.210   0.226
Zero hurdle model coefficients (binomial with logit link):
                 Estimate Std. Error z value Pr(>|z|)
(Intercept)       0.59998    0.19791   3.032  0.00243 **
tweet_dum         1.19767    0.38395   3.119  0.00181 **
womanleadauthor   0.08827    0.27822   0.317  0.75104
fullprof          0.46509    0.28386   1.638  0.10133
---
Signif. codes:  0 '***' 0.001 '**' 0.01 '*' 0.05 '.' 0.1 ' ' 1


Number of iterations in BFGS optimization: 11
Log-likelihood: -762.6 on 8 Df
```

The hurdle model output appears very similar to the ZIP output, but there are some key differences to note. First, the bottom section of results (Zero hurdle model coefficients) uses an outcome variable that equals 1 for articlecites $\geq$ 1 and 0 for articlecites = 0. Hence, the logit model in the hurdle model is estimating the probability of having at least one citation. We see that tweet_dum is the only statistically significant predictor. The positive coefficient indicates that articles that have received at least one tweet have a higher probability of receiving at least one citation. Although tweet_dum has different coefficient signs in the ZIP and hurdle models, we arrive at the same conclusion about its effect – articles with at least one tweet have a lower probability of never receiving at least one citation (or a higher probability of receiving at least one citation).

Second, the top section of results (Count model coefficients) uses a truncated PRM for the case when articlecites $\geq$ 1. Therefore, the PRM is based only on observations with at least one citation. We see that tweet_dum is the only statistically significant predictor of the number of expected citations and has a positive coefficient.

Comparing Zero-Inflated, Hurdle, and Standard Count Models

We can use AIC values to decide between the ZIP and hurdle models. Since the AIC is not saved by the zeroinfl() function, we'll use the AIC() function from the base stats package to obtain the AICs.[16] We simply include the model name in the AIC() function.

---

[16]Use names(<object name>) to check the saved objects.

```
AIC(model.zip)
[1] 1541.101
AIC(model.hp)
[1] 1541.113
```

We see that the AIC values for ZIP (AIC = 1541.10) and the hurdle (AIC = 1541.11) models are essentially the same. Therefore, we are unable to determine whether one model is preferred over the other.

For completeness, let's compare these AIC values to the AIC for our PRM model.

```
model.prm$aic
[1] 1701.237
```

As we would expect given the Vuong test results, the PRM's AIC is much worse than either of the other two models.

How do the ZIP and hurdle models compare to the NBRM? Let's recheck the AIC value for our NBRM.

```
model.nbrm$aic
[1] 1359.518
```

Our NBRM's AIC value is much smaller than the AIC values for the ZIP and hurdle models. This suggests that the NBRM fits the data better than either of the other two models.

If we wanted or needed to run a ZINB or hurdle negative binomial model, we simply include the option dist = "negbin" in the zeroinfl() or hurdle() functions. In our current example, we don't need to run a ZINB or hurdle model. The main reason is that nothing has suggested the need for trying a ZINB or hurdle negative binomial model. Specifically, our NBRM does a good job of correctly predicting the number of observed zeros and doesn't need assistance from a zero-inflated version. In our case, if we run a ZINB model, we'll find bizarre coefficients and standard errors in the inflation equation.

Interpreting Zero-Inflated and Hurdle Count Models

Although we have decided that our NBRM is the best model choice, let's briefly discuss how to interpret zero-inflated and hurdle model coefficients.

We can use the same interpretation techniques that we used with GLMs (in Chapter 13) and the NBRM. The main difference is that we need to word the interpretations to reflect the two parts of the models.

We'll first look at our ZIP results. We'll use the ggpredict() function from the ggeffects package to calculate the predicted counts for tweet_dum. In the function, we'll include the option type = "zero_inflated" to indicate that the predicted counts are conditioned on the inflation equation.[17]

---

[17]For simplicity, we will hold womanleadauthor and fullprof at their means.

```
ggpredict(model.zip, terms = "tweet_dum", type = "zero_inflated")
# Predicted counts of articlecites

tweet_dum | Predicted |         95% CI
-------------------------------------
        0 |      2.31 | [2.00, 2.62]
        1 |      5.37 | [4.65, 6.08]

Adjusted for:
* womanleadauthor = 0.36
*          fullprof = 0.37
```

For the interpretation, we should include some text to indicate that these predicted counts are from a zero-inflated count model (Long and Freese 2014). For example, *for articles that are not expected to always have zero citations, the predicted number of citations for tweeted articles is 5.37, while the predicted number of citations for non-tweeted articles is 2.31.* The beginning of the interpretation indicates the predicted counts are conditioned on the set of observations that are not expected to always be zero.

We can also use the ggpredict() function for calculating predicted probabilities for the inflation model. Generically, these are the predicted probabilities of always being a zero. In the ggpredict() function, we specify the option type = "zi_prob".

```
ggpredict(model.zip, terms = "tweet_dum", type = "zi_prob")
# Predicted zero-inflation probabilities of articlecites

tweet_dum | Predicted |         95% CI
-------------------------------------
        0 |      0.28 | [0.26, 0.30]
        1 |      0.12 | [0.11, 0.13]

Adjusted for:
* womanleadauthor = 0.36
*          fullprof = 0.37
```

The interpretation for tweet_dum = 0 is that *for non-tweeted articles, the predicted probability of always having 0 citations is 0.28 (28%).* For tweet_dum = 1, the interpretation is that *for tweeted articles, the predicted probability of always having 0 citations is 0.12 (12%).*

We can calculate the odds ratio for tweet_dum in the inflation model by manually including the coefficient in the exp() function.

```
exp(-1.08)
[1] 0.3395955
(exp(-1.08)-1)*100
[1] -66.04045
```

What this means is that, *for tweeted articles, the odds of always having 0 citations is smaller by a factor of 0.34 than non-tweeted articles*. Or, *for tweeted articles, the odds of always having 0 citations is 66% smaller than non-tweeted articles*.

The interpretations for the hurdle model take a similar, but not identical, form. Specifically, we need to clarify that the predicted counts are from the truncated Poisson model (where `articlecites > 0`).

```
ggpredict(model.hp, terms = "tweet_dum")
# Predicted counts of articlecites

tweet_dum | Predicted |       95% CI
-------------------------------------
       0 |      3.21 | [2.93, 3.52]
       1 |      6.08 | [5.50, 6.71]


Adjusted for:
* womanleadauthor = 0.36
*         fullprof = 0.37
```

Our interpretation is that, *for articles with at least 1 citation, the predicted number of citations for tweeted articles is 6.08, while the predicted number of citations for non-tweeted articles is 3.21*. The beginning of the interpretation indicates that the predicted counts are conditioned on the set of observations that have at least one citation.

Specifying the option `type = "zi_prob"` in the `ggpredict()` function provides the predicted probabilities for the logit model part of the hurdle model. These are the predicted probabilities of having a positive value (or *not* always being a zero).

```
ggpredict(model.hp, terms = "tweet_dum", type = "zi_prob")
# Predicted zero-inflation probabilities of articlecites

tweet_dum | Predicted |       95% CI
-------------------------------------
       0 |      0.72 | [0.70, 0.74]
       1 |      0.88 | [0.87, 0.89]


Adjusted for:
* womanleadauthor = 0.36
*         fullprof = 0.37
```

The interpretation for `tweet_dum = 0` is that, *for non-tweeted articles, the predicted probability of having at least 1 citation is 0.72 (72%)*. For `tweet_dum = 1`, the interpretation is that, *for tweeted articles, the predicted probability of having at least 1 citation is 0.88 (88%)*. Notice that these predicted probabilities are the complement of the predicted probabilities from the inflation model of our ZIP model; they add up to 1.

We can calculate the odds ratio for `tweet_dum` in the same way as previously.

```
exp(1.19)
[1] 3.287081
(exp(1.19)-1)*100
[1] 228.7081
```

What this means is that, *for tweeted articles, the odds of having at least 1 citation is greater by a factor of 3.29 than for non-tweeted articles. Or, for tweeted articles, the odds of having at least 1 citation are 228.71% greater than non-tweeted articles.*

CONCLUSION

In this chapter, we have examined standard count models, diagnosed common problems, and discussed alternative count models. The material we covered encompasses most of the basics and techniques that quantitative social scientists use for count regression modelling. As mentioned earlier, we rarely should use the standard Poisson regression model due to the ubiquitous over-dispersion in count data. Even though there are many variations and alternative count models, we often will find that the negative binomial regression model provides the best fit to our data.

R Packages Used in This Chapter

- AER
- dplyr (loaded with tidyverse)
- GGally
- ggeffects
- ggplot2 (loaded with tidyverse)
- MASS
- performance
- pillar (loaded with tidyverse)
- pscl
- tidyverse

R Functions Used in This Chapter

- AIC() - calculate model's AIC value
- as_factor() - convert variable to factor using haven or forcats package
- c() - concatenate
- check_zeroinflation() - compare predicted and observed zeros for count models using the performance package
- dispersiontest() - over-/underdispersion test for Poisson GLM using AER package
- exp() - compute exponential value

(Continued)

- `filter()` - subset data based on variables' values using `dplyr` package
- `geom_density()` - ggplot2 density plot
- `geom_point()` - ggplot2 scattered points
- `geom_pointrange()` - ggplot2 point range plot
- `ggcoef_model()` - regression coefficient plot
- `ggplot()` - base layer for ggplot2
- `ggpredict()` - adjusted predictions for regression models using `ggeffects` package
- `glimpse()` - quick view of data using `pillar` package
- `glm()` - generalised linear model
- `glm.nb()` - negative binomial model using `MASS` package
- `hurdle()` - hurdle count regression model using `pscl` package
- `is.na()` - checks for missing values (NAs) in variables
- `labs()` - ggplot2 labels
- `logLik()` - extract log-likelihood from GLM
- `lrtest()` - likelihood-ratio test using the `lmtest` package
- `read_csv()` - read in .csv data file using `readr` package
- `scale_x_discrete()` - x-axis aesthetics for discrete variables using `ggplot2` package
- `summary()` - summarise object
- `theme_minimal()` - minimal ggplot2 theme
- `var()` - variance
- `vuong()` - Vuong test for zero-inflation using `pscl` package
- `zeroinfl()` - zero-inflated count regression model using `pscl` package

===== Additional Resources =====

Books

- Cameron, A. C. and Trivedi, P. K. (2013). *Regression Analysis of Count Data*, 2nd edition. Cambridge University Press.
- Faraway, J. J. (2016) *Extending the Linear Model with R*, 2nd edition. CRC.
- Hilbe, J. M. (2014) *Modeling Count Data*. Cambridge University Press.
- Long, J. S. (1997) *Regression Models for Categorical and Limited Dependent Variables*. Sage.

15

PUTTING IT ALL TOGETHER

Chapter contents

In this final chapter, we will take (almost) everything that we learned throughout the course of this book and analyse a research question from start to finish. Usually in QSS the steps and process from starting to finishing a research project are not as straightforward as they appear in this chapter. Normally, there are starts and stops, side adventures, data that do not work, methods that do not work, and results that may make no sense. The main piece of a research project that we are excluding from this chapter is building a substantively strong theory and providing a supporting literature review; these are simply outside the scope of this book.

In this chapter, we examine two empirical questions. First, what explains Kenyans' level of satisfaction with their current political system? Second, what explains Kenyans' feelings towards having a dictator in charge of the country? Kenya is one of the most successful democracies in Africa, but corruption is pervasive throughout government and questions have been raised about the integrity of recent elections (Freedom House 2021).

To do so, we will use data from the 2021 Kenyan module of Wave 7 of the World Values Survey (WVS).[1] The WVS has been conducted since the early 1980s, time-staggered across countries around the world, and is one of the best-known international social science surveys (Haerpfer et al. 2022).

By the end of this chapter, you should be able to:

- Carry out all aspects of a QSS research project in R (again, without the theory and literature review aspects)
- Feel confident that you can do the above with any QSS dataset

FINDING THE DATA

Our first task is to find and download the 2021 Kenyan WVS data.[2] On the WVS homepage's left-hand-side menu (https://www.worldvaluessurvey.org/wvs.jsp) click on *Data and Documentation*, then *Data Download* on the next left-side menu, and then *Wave 7 (2017-2022)* on the next left-hand-side menu. This gets us to the WVS Wave 7 main page. Now on the right-side menu, find and click the *Kenya 2021* option. This takes us to the Kenyan module page of the WVS. On this page, there is all the documentation and various data formats (e.g., .xlsx, .dta) for the Kenya survey.

We can simply download the data and files without needing to register.[3] Let's download the Excel version (`WVS Wave 7 Kenya Excel v3.0`) – though feel free to download one of the other formats if preferred. We also want to download the codebook file and perhaps the other documentation as well. Finally, we want to make sure that we know where we saved the data (e.g., external hard drive). This might sound silly, but often we quickly download files without thinking where we saved them. Ideally, we put them in a folder that is obvious – such as `Chapter 15 - Putting it Altogether`.

---

[1]https://www.worldvaluessurvey.org/WVSDocumentationWV7.jsp

[2]Instead of a nice and clean dataset, like the ones we have used thus far, in this chapter we will deal with a big, dirty dataset.

[3]There is a simple request to cite the data if it's used.

READING IN AND EXAMINING THE DATA

We need to first set our working directory to the folder where the 2021 Kenya WVS data is saved, load the `tidyverse` and `readxl` packages, read in the data (I've saved it as `kenya_wvs.xlsx`) using the `read_xlsx()` function, and name it `kenya`.

The raw `kenya_wvs.xlsx` file's column names are versions of the questions, which makes them very long and ugly when they are read in. To save ourselves from inevitable typos, let's use the `name.repair` option in the `read_xlsx()` function to shorten the names. The built-in `name.repair` options (e.g., `"unique"`) don't solve our column name problem and so instead we'll use the `str_sub()` function from the `stringr` package to shorten the names. In the function, we first specify the character vector `.x` to reference back to the data we are loading. Then we specify characters' positions to create the substring – we want the substring to start at the first character (`start = 1`) and end at the seventh character (`start = 7`) of the column names. This will shorten all of the column names to their first seven characters (letters, numbers, symbols, etc.). Why the first seven characters? From glancing through the column names and testing a few combinations, seven appears to be the smallest number of characters required to produce identifiable column names for our variables of interest.

However, by shortening the column names, we create a new problem of having some duplicate named columns. Since none of the duplicate names are the actual survey questions we are interested in analysing (which all start with the letter Q), there is an easy solution. We will specify `starts_with("Q")` within the `select()` function to only keep the survey questions, which will also remove all of the duplicate columns. Let's utilise the functionality of `tidyverse` by adding the `select()` function specification to the `read_xlsx()` function via the pipe operator `%>%`.[4]

```
setwd("C:/QSSD/Chapter 15 - Putting it Altogether")
getwd()
[1] "C:/QSSD/Chapter 15 - Putting it Altogether"
library(tidyverse)
library(readxl)

kenya <- read_xlsx("kenya_wvs.xlsx", .name_repair =
                    ~ str_sub(.x, start = 1, end = 7)) %>%
             select(starts_with("Q"))
```

The data should appear in the `Environment` window in the RStudio interface under the `Data` heading. Our dataset `kenya` should have 1266 observations and 339 variables.[5] We can check out the data with the `glimpse()` function if we would like.

It is best practice to use the codebook at the same time as we are first exploring a dataset. We might browse the codebook or search for certain keywords in the codebook to locate variables of interest, and then we can check the data to see if the variables will work for us. Without cross-referencing the codebook, it is often very difficult to understand the data and variables.

---

[4]We could also read in the `kenya_wvs.xlsx` file and then subset the data with the `select()` function.

[5]The original `kenya_wvs.xlsx` file has 488 variables. Thus, we removed 149 variables using the `select()` function.

FINDING AND RECODING VARIABLES

As mentioned at the beginning of this chapter, we'll examine two outcome variables: Kenyans' satisfaction with their current political system (which we will name `polsyst_satis`) and their support for authoritarian regimes (`strong_leader`).

Next, we need to identify a set of explanatory variables for our models. We each probably have different ideas for variables that may or not matter for explaining our outcome variables. We are further constrained by what variables are in the data and the distribution of the variables' values. On the latter point, some potential explanatory variables' values might not substantially vary and thus would likely produce null effects as predictors in our models, even if they are theoretically important. For our models in this chapter, we'll use predictors for political ideology (`ideology`), social welfare as government versus individual responsibility (`responsibility`), confidence in the national government (`confidence`), satisfaction with household financial situation (`hhfin_satis`), age (`age`), sex (`sex`), and education (`edu`). We'll treat age, sex, and education as control variables in our models.

Instead of examining each variable, recoding, and then examining each variable again, I've saved us some time and trees by previously identifying what needs to be recoded. Let's do all of the recoding in one big chunk and then take a look at each variable. Our recoding steps are:

1   Rename all of the original variable names using the `rename()` function from the `dplyr` package. We need to pay close attention to the exact shortened original variable names, otherwise the `rename()` function will not work. For example, some variables' names include one end letter and some include two end letters.

2   In the `kenya` data, variables' missing values are represented by negative numbers (e.g., –1). These are 'don't know', 'no answer', etc., responses. We need to recode the negative numbers to NAs. We could do this separately for each variable, but instead we'll leverage the functionality of the `dplyr` package to recode all of the variables at the same time. Within the `mutate()` function, we'll use the `across()` function that allows us to apply a recoding task to multiple columns (i.e., variables) at once. Generally, we have to specify two parts in the `across()` function. First, we specify the columns we are recoding. We'll use the `everything()` function, which literally means we want to recode all the columns in the data (we could have just specified the nine variables we renamed). Second, we specify the recoding function. For simplicity, we'll use the `replace()` function from base R to recode the negative values to NAs. The `recode()` function has three parts to specify: the data we are using (`.`, which is a place-filler referring to the previous specification of all columns), what we are replacing (`.x < 0`, where `.x` is a generic reference to all of the columns), and then what we are replacing with (`NA`).

3   We'll flip the values of `confidence` and `strong_leader`, so that higher values of `confidence` mean greater confidence and higher values of `strong_leader` imply greater support. To do this, we'll use three nested functions like we did in Chapter 13 when we recoded trust in the UK government. First, we'll convert the variable to a factor with the `as_factor()` function, then we'll flip the values with the `fct_rev()` function from the `forcats` package, and lastly we'll convert it to a numeric variable with the `as.numeric()` function.

4   We'll use the `select()` function from `dplyr` to only keep the nine variables we will work with in this chapter. We'll save all of our recoding as a new tibble named `kenya_subset`.

```
kenya_subset <- kenya %>%
  rename(polsyst_satis = `Q252: S`,
         strong_leader = `Q235: P`,
         ideology = `Q240: L`,
         responsibility= `Q108: G`,
         confidence = `Q71: Co`,
         hhfin_satis = `Q50: Sa`,
         age = `Q262: A`,
         sex = `Q260: S`,
         edu = `Q275R: `
         ) %>%
  mutate(across(everything(), ~replace(., .x < 0, NA))) %>%
  mutate(confidence = as.numeric(fct_rev(as_factor(confidence))),
         strong_leader = as.numeric(fct_rev(as_factor(strong_leader)))
         ) %>%
  select(polsyst_satis,strong_leader,ideology,responsibility,confidence,
         hhfin_satis,age,sex,edu)

glimpse(kenya_subset)
Rows: 1,266
Columns: 9
$ polsyst_satis <dbl> 10, 4, 5, 2, 4, 7, 8, 2, 5, 4, 1, NA, 10, 5, 3,
1, 8, 1~
$ strong_leader <dbl> 3, 1, 1, 1, 1, 2, 3, 2, 4, 2, 1, NA, 4, 1, 2, 4,
4, 4, ~
$ ideology      <dbl> 7, 7, 1, 5, NA, 5, 5, 6, NA, 3, 2, 1, 2, 7, 4,
3, 4, 3,~
$ responsibility <dbl> 10, 3, 1, 1, 2, 1, 1, 5, 10, 1, 10, 10, 2, 4, 8,
1, 1, ~
$ confidence    <dbl> 1, 2, 3, 4, 1, 4, 2, 1, 1, 1, 4, NA, NA, 4, 1,
1, 1, 3,~
$ hhfin_satis   <dbl> 10, 5, 1, 6, 5, 3, 3, 6, 5, 3, 9, 1, 9, 10, 4,
1, 1, 1,~
$ age           <dbl> 63, 24, 26, 29, 37, 45, 21, 50, 26, 28, 30, 38,
40, 24,~
$ sex           <dbl> 1, 1, 1, 2, 1, 1, 1, 2, 1, 1, 2, 2, 1, 1, 2, 1,
1, 2, 2~
$ edu           <dbl> 2, 3, 3, 3, 2, 2, 2, 3, 1, 3, 1, 2, 1, 2, 3, 3,
1, 2, 2~
```

EXAMINING VARIABLES

Outcome Variables

Particularly when examining outcome variables, we want to make sure that there is decent variation across the values. If the variable is heavily skewed or similarly distributed, it may be very difficult for our analysis (e.g., regression) to explain any of the variation that does exist. Let's first take a look at `polsyst_satis` using the `count()` function. The variable measures respondents' satisfaction with the current political system in Kenya and the values range from 1 (= 'not at all satisfied') to 10 (= 'completely satisfied').

```
kenya_subset %>%
  count(polsyst_satis)
# A tibble: 11 x 2
   polsyst_satis      n
           <dbl> <int>
1              1    271
2              2     73
3              3    117
4              4    113
5              5    159
6              6    173
7              7    136
8              8    101
9              9     32
10            10     77
11            NA     14
```

Here, `polsyst_satis` does demonstrate variation, with the modal category equal to 1 and most observations clustering in the middle categories. Let's now calculate the mean, median, and standard deviation for `polsyst_satis`. We need to include the `na.rm = TRUE` option in the `mean()`, `median()`, and `sd()` functions due to the variable's NAs.

```
mean(kenya_subset$polsyst_satis, na.rm = TRUE)
[1] 4.689297
median(kenya_subset$polsyst_satis, na.rm = TRUE)
[1] 5
sd(kenya_subset$polsyst_satis, na.rm = TRUE)
[1] 2.758047
```

We see the mean is 4.69, the median is 5, and the standard deviation is 2.76. These descriptives confirm our quick assessment from the frequency distribution that most of the action is in the middle categories.

Given the composition of `polsyst_satis` what regression analysis technique, among those covered in this book, should we use? Since we consider `polsyst_satis` a 'high' ordinal variable, we will use OLS linear regression.

Now let's look at `strong_leader`. This variable measures respondents' support for authoritarian regimes. Although the survey question used doesn't precisely state 'dictator' – the question's key phrase is 'having a strong leader who does not have to bother with parliament and elections' – that is the implied political system (or at least some version of authoritarianism). There are four ordinal values for `strong_leader`: 1 = 'very bad', 2 = 'fairly bad', 3 = 'fairly good', and 4 = 'very good'.

```
kenya_subset %>%
  count(strong_leader)
# A tibble: 5 x 2
  strong_leader     n
          <dbl> <int>
1             1   249
2             2   294
3             3   370
4             4   321
5            NA    32
```

The responses are somewhat equally distributed between the four values of strong_leader. The values don't currently have category labels – we'll include them later on when necessary.

Now let's look at some descriptives. Since the variable only has four ordered categories, technically we can only look at the mode and median, though in practice we might also calculate the mean and standard deviation.

```
median(kenya_subset$strong_leader, na.rm = TRUE)
[1] 3
```

From the frequency distribution we know the mode is 3 (= 'fairly good') and we see the median is also 3. Consider this for a minute – the modal and median response is that it would be 'fairly good' if Kenya had an authoritarian regime.

We will use strong_leader as one of the predictors of polsyst_satis in our first analysis, but in the second analysis we will use it as our outcome variable. Given the composition of strong_leader, what regression analysis technique, among those covered in this book, should we use? Since strong_leader is an ordinal variable with four values, we will use ordered logit regression.

Next, we examine our explanatory variables.

Predictors

Although less critical than for outcome variables, we need to examine the distributions and descriptive statistics of our predictors to assess variation. Let's start with ideology, whose values range from 1 (= 'Left'; e.g., very liberal, etc.) to 10 (= 'Right'; e.g., very conservative, etc.). We can examine the mode, median, mean, and standard deviation.

```
kenya_subset %>%
  count(ideology)
# A tibble: 11 x 2
   ideology     n
      <dbl> <int>
1         1   153
2         2    39
```

```
 3          3    59
 4          4   105
 5          5   247
 6          6   158
 7          7   133
 8          8    91
 9          9    47
10         10   132
11         NA   102
median(kenya_subset$ideology, na.rm = TRUE)
[1] 5
mean(kenya_subset$ideology, na.rm = TRUE)
[1] 5.50945
sd(kenya_subset$ideology, na.rm = TRUE)
[1] 2.687332
```

The modal category is 5, and a large proportion of responses are clustered at the ends and in the middle of `ideology`. Hence, most respondents consider themselves ideologically moderate, but large proportions are at the extreme ends. We see the median is 5, the mean is 5.51, and the standard deviation is 2.69. Clearly the 'average' respondent is a moderate.

The `responsibility` predictor measures respondents' views on government and individual responsibility. Using a ten-value scale, one extreme is the view that the government should take more responsibility to make sure that everyone in provided for (1 = 'More Government's Responsibility'). The other extreme is the view that individuals should do more to take responsibility for themselves (10 = 'More Individual's Responsibility').

```
kenya_subset %>%
  count(responsibility)
# A tibble: 11 x 2
   responsibility       n
            <dbl> <int>
 1              1   316
 2              2   120
 3              3   120
 4              4    94
 5              5   152
 6              6    92
 7              7    77
 8              8    54
 9              9    39
10             10   192
11             NA    10
median(kenya_subset$responsibility, na.rm = TRUE)
[1] 4
mean(kenya_subset$responsibility, na.rm = TRUE)
[1] 4.654459
sd(kenya_subset$responsibility, na.rm = TRUE)
[1] 3.202344
```

We see decent variation of responses even with more observations towards the lower value of the scale (i.e., more government responsibility). The mode is 1, the median is 4, the mean is 4.65, and the standard deviation is 3.20. This suggests that although the average response is a balance of responsibility, the weight of opinion is shifted towards believing that the government should be doing more to make sure that everyone is provided for. The use of 'more' in the end values' labels might have affected responses away from the middle of the response scale. For example, if the response ends were less nuanced (e.g., removing 'the government should take more responsibility' and replace it with 'it is the government's responsibility') we may observe a greater number of respondents taking more moderate positions.

The `confidence` variable measures respondents' level of confidence in the national government. The values range from 1 (= 'None at all') to 4 (= 'A great deal'); remember that we flipped the original variables' values to get this ordering. Since `confidence` is an ordinal variable with four values, we can only look at the mode and median.

```
kenya_subset %>%
   count(confidence)
# A tibble: 5 x 2
   confidence      n
        <dbl> <int>
1           1    262
2           2    415
3           3    336
4           4    231
5          NA     22
median(kenya_subset$confidence, na.rm = TRUE)
[1] 2
```

Most observations are in the middle categories, with the mode and median both equal to 2, but there are large proportions at the ends. This suggests that confidence in the national government is somewhat balanced, with slightly more respondents expressing lower confidence.

The variable `hhfin_satis` asks respondents how satisfied they are with their household financial situation. The values range from 1 (= 'Dissatisfied') to 10 (= 'Satisfied'), thus we can look at the mode, median, mean, and standard deviation.

```
kenya_subset %>%
   count(hhfin_satis)
# A tibble: 11 x 2
   hhfin_satis      n
         <dbl> <int>
1            1    206
2            2     74
3            3    119
4            4    166
5            5    211
6            6    148
7            7    100
8            8     98
```

```
  9              9    38
 10             10   100
 11            NA     6
median(kenya_subset$hhfin_satis, na.rm = TRUE)
[1] 5
mean(kenya_subset$hhfin_satis, na.rm = TRUE)
[1] 4.87619
sd(kenya_subset$hhfin_satis, na.rm = TRUE)
[1] 2.691835
```

As we might expect, more people responded 'dissatisfied' than 'satisfied' with their financial situation. However, we see the observations cluster in the middle categories, which is supported by the mean (4.88) and median (5) values.

Lastly, let's quickly look at the three other explanatory variables we are including as controls: age, sex, and edu. For age, we'll skip the frequency distribution and mode, and just look at the median, mean, and standard deviation.

```
median(kenya_subset$age, na.rm = TRUE)
[1] 28
mean(kenya_subset$age, na.rm = TRUE)
[1] 30.74027
sd(kenya_subset$age, na.rm = TRUE)
[1] 10.06521
```

The age of respondents is fairly young, with a mean of 30.74 and median of 28. If we did a histogram we'd see that the vast majority of respondents are under 40.

We can only look at the mode for sex. The 1 category is men and the 2 category is women.

```
kenya_subset %>%
  count(sex)
# A tibble: 3 x 2
    sex       n
  <dbl> <int>
1     1    637
2     2    622
3    NA      7
```

There are almost exactly equal numbers of men and women respondents.

The edu variable is a collapsed three-category version of, obviously, respondents' education. The values are 1 (= 'lower'), 2 (= 'middle'), and 3 (= 'higher'). Let's look at the mode and median.

```
kenya_subset %>%
  count(edu)
```

```
# A tibble: 4 x 2
     edu     n
   <dbl> <int>
1      1   394
2      2   556
3      3   310
4     NA     6
median(kenya_subset$edu, na.rm = TRUE)
[1] 2
```

We see that the mode and median are both the middle category.

HYPOTHESES

Although we are not developing and writing up a substantive theory and engaging in a literature review, let's develop a set of testable hypotheses for our explanatory variables. If you remember, we can create good empirical hypotheses regardless of whether they make intuitive sense or not. Yet, it is better if our hypotheses do make intuitive sense. Crafting intuitive hypotheses is easier and more straightforward when we have solid substantive knowledge of the research area and data.

For each outcome variable, we have eight predictors, and thus we would create eight hypotheses and eight corresponding null hypotheses. However, writing out 16 hypotheses and null hypotheses is a bit laborious and mind-numbing. To keep it fresh, let's not write out hypotheses for our control variables (age, sex, and education) and let's just write out one generic null hypothesis for each outcome variable (two null hypotheses in total). We'll use the hypothesis numbering convention (e.g., H_1) to provide clarity to our hypothesis testing.[6]

First, we'll craft hypotheses for the outcome variable `polsyst_satis`, starting with the generic null hypothesis.

H_{01}: There is no relationship between `predictor`[7] and level of satisfaction with the political system.

Now, let's write out alternative hypotheses for our five predictors ($H_1,..., H_5$):

H_1: As support for an authoritarian regime increases, respondents are expected to have less satisfaction with the current political system.

H_2: As political ideology increases, respondents are expected to have more satisfaction with the current political system.

---

[6]Numbering hypotheses is a common convention when we first learn hypothesis testing. However, in practice, many researchers do not number their hypotheses unless it is part of a journal's or book publisher's formatting requirements, or their own personal preference.

[7]Substitute in the predictor name.

H_3: As belief in individual responsibility increases, respondents are expected to have more satisfaction with the current political system.

H_4: As confidence in the national government increases, respondents are expected to have more satisfaction with the current political system.

H_5: As satisfaction with household finances increases, respondents are expected to have more satisfaction with the current political system.

Next, let's state hypotheses for the outcome variable `strong_leader`, starting with the generic null hypothesis.

H_{02}: There is no relationship between `predictor` and support for an authoritarian regime.

Now, let's write out hypotheses for our five predictors (H_6,..., H_{10}):

H_6: As satisfaction with the current political system increases, respondents are expected to have lower support for an authoritarian regime.

H_7: As political ideology increases, respondents are expected to have higher support for an authoritarian regime.

H_8: As belief in individual responsibility increases, respondents are expected to have lower support for an authoritarian regime.

H_9: As confidence in the national government increases, respondents are expected to have lower support for an authoritarian regime.

H_{10}: As satisfaction with household finances increases, respondents are expected to have higher support for an authoritarian regime.

When we conduct our statistical analysis, we may find these hypotheses are all wrong and that's OK. If we discover one or more of our hypotheses to be incorrect, we should consider whether or not they were derived correctly based on theory and existing literature. Maybe previous research has shown that a predictor is statistically significant only under certain conditions. Or that the direction of the effect (i.e., positive, negative) varies depending on circumstances. We shouldn't engage in data mining, but we might also consider other theoretical important explanatory variables or different control variables.

VISUALISING RELATIONSHIPS

In this section, we will create two data visualisations to gain insight into the relationships between our outcome variable `polsyst_satis` and our predictors `strong_leader` and `confidence`; we'll look at data visualisations with `strong_leader` as the outcome variable later on.

Plotting the ten values of `polsyst_satis` and a predictor could be a bit tricky. We can't use histograms, density plots, or standard scatterplots. Since `strong_leader` and `confidence` both only have four values, we can create an aesthetically appealing bar plot using dodged bars; if `strong_leader` or `confidence` had more than four values, a bar plot might not work as everything would be too squished. We'll first plot `polsyst_satis` and `strong_leader`, and then `polsyst_satis` and `confidence`.

To create the bar plots, we'll redeploy the code we used in Chapter 8. The only part of the code that we haven't seen before is the use of the `scale_x_continuous()` function to provide labels at the lowest and highest values on the *x*-axis. In this function, we specify `breaks = c(1,10)` to set the labels' locations (at *x* = 1 and *x* = 10) and then provide the labels with `labels = c("Not At All Satisfied","Completely Satisfied")`.[8]

```
library(scales)

kenya_subset %>%
  filter(!is.na(polsyst_satis) & !is.na(strong_leader)) %>%
  mutate(strong_leader = as_factor(strong_leader),
         strong_leader = recode(strong_leader,
           `1` = "Very Bad",
           `2` = "Fairly Bad",
           `3` = "Fairly Good",
           `4` = "Very Good")) %>%
ggplot() +
  geom_bar(mapping = aes(x = polsyst_satis, y = ..prop..,
                         group = strong_leader, fill = strong_leader),
                         stat = "count", position = "dodge") +
  labs(title = "Satisfaction with Current Political System",
       subtitle = "by Authoritarian Regime Support",
       x = "Satisfaction with Current Political System",
       fill = "Auth. Regime", y = "Percent") +
  scale_x_continuous(breaks = c(1,10),
     labels = c("Not At All Satisfied","Completely Satisfied"),
     guide = guide_axis(angle = 45)) +
  scale_y_continuous(labels = percent_format()) +
  theme_minimal() +
  scale_fill_viridis_d()
```

---

[8]Alternatively, we could label the values using the `mutate()` function prior to the `ggplot` code.

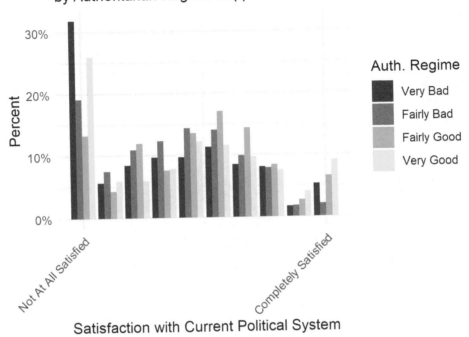

Satisfaction with Current Political System

Let's focus on the ends of the plot. Among respondents who thought an authoritarian regime would be 'very bad', roughly 32% said they were 'not at all satisfied' with the current political system. Without examining support for alternative political systems, we don't know whether these respondents prefer a different system or just think the current democratic system needs to be reformed. Among respondents who thought an authoritarian regime would be 'very good', roughly 26% said they were 'not at all satisfied' with the current political system. We might conclude these respondents prefer an authoritarian regime over the current democratic system, but, again, to be more certain we would need to compare their responses for different political systems.

What about respondents who said they were 'completely satisfied' with the current political system? We see about 5% of 'very bad' respondents and 9% of 'very good' respondents said they were 'completely satisfied' with the current political system. If we thought that respondents who said an authoritarian regime would be 'very good' are turning away from democracy, we wouldn't expect to find as high a percentage who are 'completely satisfied'. This leads to our next question.

Are there any trends in the response percentages across the two variables? We see that 'fairly bad' and 'fairly good' respondents tend to cluster in the middle categories of satisfaction, but no clear trends stand out. This suggests that `strong_leader` might not be a strong predictor of `polsyst_satis`.

To visualise the relationship between `polsyst_satis` and `confidence` will use the same code as above, and change a few of the labels for `confidence`.

```
kenya_subset %>%
  filter(!is.na(polsyst_satis) & !is.na(confidence)) %>%
  mutate(confidence = as_factor(confidence),
         confidence = recode(confidence,
           `1` = "None At All",
           `2` = "Not Very Much",
           `3` = "Quite A Lot",
           `4` = "A Great Deal")) %>%
ggplot() +
  geom_bar(mapping = aes(x = polsyst_satis, y = ..prop..,
                         group = confidence, fill = confidence),
                         stat = "count", position = "dodge") +
  labs(title = "Satisfaction with Current Political System",
       subtitle = "by Confidence in Govt",
       x = "Satisfaction with Current Political System",
       fill = "Govt Confidence", y="Percent") +
  scale_x_continuous(breaks = c(1,10),
    labels = c("Not At All Satisfied","Completely Satisfied"),
    guide = guide_axis(angle = 45)) +
  scale_y_continuous(labels = percent_format()) +
  theme_minimal() +
  scale_fill_viridis_d()
```

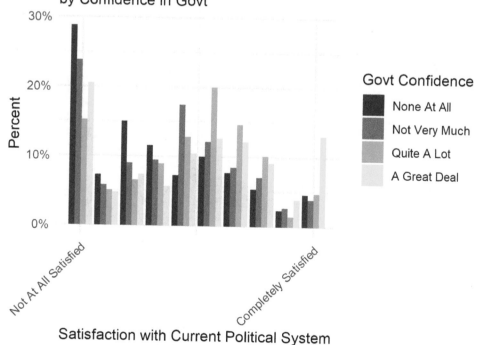

What do see here? We find a high percentage of respondents for all confidence levels say they were 'not at all satisfied' with the current political system, as in the previous plot. Respondents with the least confidence in the national government had the highest percentage of saying they were 'not at all satisfied'. We also see that among those with a 'great deal' of confidence in the national government, roughly 21% said they were 'not at all satisfied' but 13% said they were 'completely satisfied'.

What about trends? We observe fewer respondents at the lowest two confidence levels ('none at all', 'not very much') as satisfaction with the current political system increases. If we ignore, for the moment, the percentage at the lowest satisfaction level, we find an increasing percentage of respondents at the highest confidence level ('a great deal') as satisfaction with the current political system increases. Hence, there appears to be a trend in responses when comparing these two variables. This suggests that confidence, unlike strong_leader, might be strong predictor of polsyst_satis.

However, our tentative conclusions are simply based on imperfect bar plots. We could next use bivariate analysis (e.g., chi-square analysis and measures of association) to investigate these, and the other variables, relationships, but we might leave ourselves open to observing spurious relationships. Instead, let's cut to the real action and use multiple linear regression to analyse our outcome variable and predictors.

EXPLAINING SATISFACTION WITH THE CURRENT KENYAN POLITICAL SYSTEM

Following Chapters 11 and 12, we'll run a linear regression model with polsyst_satis as our outcome variable and include all eight predictors. We'll follow this up by running diagnostic tests to assess any violations of the assumptions of OLS.

Let's save our regression results as model.1 and plot the coefficients and confidence intervals using the ggcoef_model() function from the GGally package.

```
summary(model.1 <- lm(polsyst_satis ~ strong_leader + ideology +
                responsibility + confidence + hhfin_satis +
                age + sex + edu, data = kenya_subset))

Call:
lm(formula = polsyst_satis ~ strong_leader + ideology + responsibility +
    confidence + hhfin_satis + age + sex + edu, data = kenya_subset)

Residuals:
    Min      1Q  Median      3Q     Max
-6.0845 -2.0363  0.0233  1.8007  7.7190

Coefficients:
              Estimate Std. Error t value Pr(>|t|)
(Intercept)   2.275222   0.568895   3.999 6.78e-05 ***
strong_leader 0.109107   0.075175   1.451 0.146963
```

```
ideology         0.182193   0.029537    6.168 9.70e-10 ***
responsibility   0.068301   0.024462    2.792 0.005327 **
confidence       0.328087   0.079003    4.153 3.54e-05 ***
hhfin_satis      0.158142   0.029853    5.297 1.42e-07 ***
age              0.001475   0.007968    0.185 0.853182
sex             -0.029371   0.158667   -0.185 0.853175
edu             -0.408374   0.108092   -3.778 0.000167 ***
---
Signif. codes:  0 '***' 0.001 '**' 0.01 '*' 0.05 '.' 0.1 ' ' 1

Residual standard error: 2.599 on 1096 degrees of freedom
  (161 observations deleted due to missingness)
Multiple R-squared:  0.1148,    Adjusted R-squared:  0.1083
F-statistic: 17.76 on 8 and 1096 DF,  p-value: < 2.2e-16
```

```
library(GGally)
ggcoef_model(model.1,
            show_p_values = FALSE,
            signif_stars = FALSE) +
  labs(title = "Predicting Current Political System Satisfaction") +
  theme(
    plot.title = element_text(size = 12)
  )
```

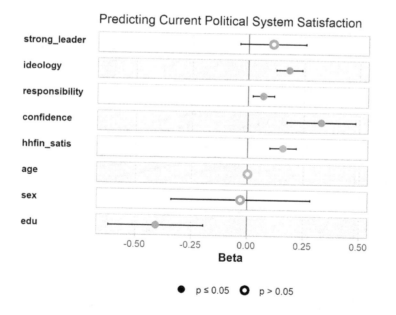

We see that the overall model is statistically significant (from the F-test) and R^2 is 0.1148, indicating that our model explains 11.48% of the variance in satisfaction with the current political system; the adjusted R^2 is only slightly lower. All of the predictors are statistically significant except for `strong_leader` (which was suggested by the bar plot), `age`, and `sex`. For the statistically significant predictors, `ideology`, `responsibility`, `confidence`, and `hhfin_satis` have positive coefficients. This implies that as respondents become more conservative, think individuals should take more responsibility, have higher confidence in the national government, or have greater satisfaction with their household financial situation, they are expected to have higher satisfaction with the current political system. Education (`edu`) has a negative coefficient, indicating that as respondents' education level increases, they are expected to have lower satisfaction with the current political system.

Before we engage in additional interpretation and substantive discussions, we need to carry out diagnostics to assess any violations of the assumptions of OLS. We will follow the same sequence of diagnostics that we used in Chapter 12.

Diagnostics

Functional Form

Our first test for functional form violations is to plot the model's residuals and fitted values. If the residuals appear to have local means of 0, then we conclude that our model does have the correct functional form.

```
library(lindia)

gg_resfitted(model.1) +
   theme_bw()
```

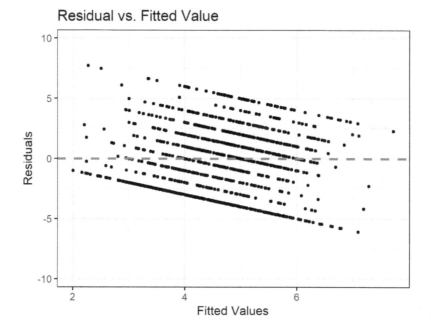

At a quick glance, this plot suggests the residuals do not have local means of 0 and thus we may have violated functional form. However, the pattern makes this somewhat difficult to decipher and so let's also run a Ramsey RESET test.

```
library(lmtest)

resettest(model.1, power = 2:3, type = "fitted")

    RESET test

data:  model.1
RESET = 1.617, df1 = 2, df2 = 1094, p-value = 0.199
```

Since $p > 0.05$, we do not violate functional form. As I do not trust my eyes to suss out the residuals' local means, I would lean towards the conclusion of the Ramsey RESET test. Therefore, we will not pursue any corrections to the functional form.

Heteroscedasticity

We know from the previous plot that heteroscedasticity is definitely present, but let's double-check by conducting the formal Breusch–Pagan test.

```
bptest(model.1, studentize = FALSE)

    Breusch-Pagan test

data:  model.1
BP = 17.348, df = 8, p-value = 0.02668
```

Since $p \leq 0.05$, we reject the null of constant error variance and conclude that we have heteroscedasticity. To deal with heteroscedasticity, we will rerun our model with robust standard errors using the `coeftest()` function with the `vcovHC` option from the `sandwich` package.

```
library(sandwich)

coeftest(model.1, vcov = vcovHC)

t test of coefficients:

                Estimate Std. Error t value  Pr(>|t|)
(Intercept)    2.2752222  0.5822546  3.9076 9.893e-05 ***
strong_leader  0.1091070  0.0785912  1.3883 0.1653324
ideology       0.1821931  0.0341661  5.3326 1.176e-07 ***
responsibility 0.0683013  0.0272525  2.5062 0.0123463 *
confidence     0.3280870  0.0847350  3.8719 0.0001144 ***
hhfin_satis    0.1581422  0.0347257  4.5540 5.852e-06 ***
age            0.0014748  0.0082825  0.1781 0.8587064
sex           -0.0293713  0.1602538 -0.1833 0.8546121
edu           -0.4083739  0.1080864 -3.7782 0.0001665 ***
---
Signif. codes:  0 '***' 0.001 '**' 0.01 '*' 0.05 '.' 0.1 ' ' 1
```

Are any of the predictors' significance tests different now? Nope – the same predictors are statistically significant when using robust standard errors. Correcting for heteroscedasticity in the model gives us greater confidence that the statistical significance results we observed earlier were correct.

Normality

Next, we will check whether our model's errors are normally distributed. Again, normality is not part of the Gauss–Markov theorem, but if we violate normality we have less confidence that our results using sample data can apply to the population. First, we will create a histogram of the residuals.

```
gg_reshist(model.1) +
   theme_bw()
```

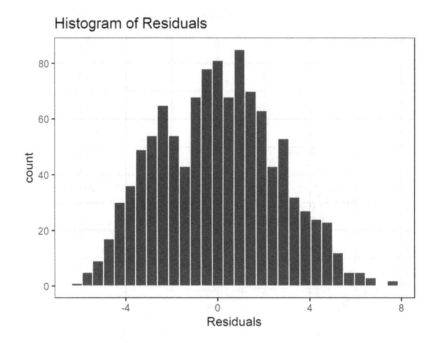

The residuals are not terribly off from a normal distribution, but they are probably far enough off to violate the assumption. Next, we will look at a Q-Q plot.

When our model's residuals are the same as residuals from a theoretical perfect normal distribution, each point (for each quintile) will lie on the 45-degree line. The further away the points are from the line, the less confidence we have that our residuals are normally distributed.

```
gg_qqplot(model.1) +
   labs(title = "Normal Q-Q Plot") +
   theme_bw()
```

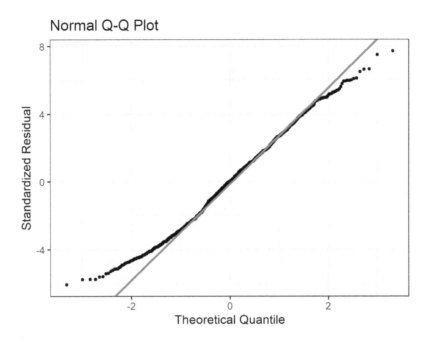

Although a good proportion of points are on or near the 45-degree line, the lower tail has a sizable number of points off the line, which suggests our model's residuals might not be normally distributed.

As a final test, let's conduct the formal Shapiro–Wilk normality test. This test was briefly mentioned in Chapter 12, but we were unable to use it with the `simd` data since the maximum number of observations allowed by the test is 5000. To run this test, we use the `shapiro.test()` function and specify `model.1$residuals`.

```
shapiro.test(model.1$residuals)

        Shapiro-Wilk normality test

data:   model.1$residuals
W = 0.99241, p-value = 1.888e-05
```

We find that the *p*-value is below 0.05 and thus we reject the null that our residuals are normally distributed. Since we violate normality, we cannot be confident that the model's results apply to the population. Specifically, we cannot confidently conclude that the predictors we found to matter for explaining satisfaction with the current political system using sample data also matter for the Kenyan population.

Let's run the Box–Cox transformation test to assess if and how to transform our outcome variable to correct for non-normality.

```
library(car)
summary(powerTransform(model.1))
bcPower Transformation to Normality
```

```
        Est Power Rounded Pwr Wald Lwr Bnd Wald Upr Bnd
Y1      0.5935         0.59       0.5049           0.682

Likelihood ratio test that transformation parameter is equal to 0
 (log transformation)
                              LRT df         pval
LR test, lambda = (0) 175.3832  1 < 2.22e-16

Likelihood ratio test that no transformation is needed
                              LRT df         pval
LR test, lambda = (1) 78.52651  1 < 2.22e-16
```

The likelihood-ratio (LR) test for $\lambda = 1$ indicates that we should transform the outcome variable (since $p \leq 0.05$). The suggested transformation is that `polsyst_satis` should be raised to the power 0.59. Since this is a non-intuitive transformation, we could instead try raising `polsyst_satis` to the power .5 (the equivalent of taking the square root). Let's do that and rerun the `powerTransform()` function.

```
summary(model.1a <- lm(I(polsyst_satis^.50) ~ strong_leader + ideology +
                        responsibility + confidence + hhfin_satis + age +
                        sex + edu, data = kenya_subset))

Call:
lm(formula = I(polsyst_satis^0.5) ~ strong_leader + ideology +
    responsibility + confidence + hhfin_satis + age + sex + edu,
    data = kenya_subset)

Residuals:
    Min      1Q  Median      3Q     Max
-1.6524 -0.5197  0.1119  0.4809  1.7162

Coefficients:
                 Estimate Std. Error t value Pr(>|t|)
(Intercept)     1.4548909  0.1443145  10.081  < 2e-16 ***
strong_leader   0.0237968  0.0190701   1.248 0.212348
ideology        0.0470127  0.0074929   6.274 5.05e-10 ***
responsibility  0.0166620  0.0062054   2.685 0.007361 **
confidence      0.0772984  0.0200411   3.857 0.000121 ***
hhfin_satis     0.0411593  0.0075730   5.435 6.75e-08 ***
age             0.0003512  0.0020212   0.174 0.862083
sex            -0.0147136  0.0402499  -0.366 0.714767
edu            -0.0968551  0.0274202  -3.532 0.000429 ***
---
Signif. codes:  0 '***' 0.001 '**' 0.01 '*' 0.05 '.' 0.1 ' ' 1

Residual standard error: 0.6594 on 1096 degrees of freedom
  (161 observations deleted due to missingness)
```

```
Multiple R-squared:  0.1114,    Adjusted R-squared:  0.1049
F-statistic: 17.17 on 8 and 1096 DF,  p-value: < 2.2e-16
```

```
summary(powerTransform(model.1a))
bcPower Transformation to Normality
   Est Power Rounded Pwr Wald Lwr Bnd Wald Upr Bnd
Y1    1.1869          1.19       1.0099          1.364
```

```
Likelihood ratio test that transformation parameter is equal to 0
 (log transformation)
                              LRT df       pval
LR test, lambda = (0) 175.3832  1 < 2.22e-16
```

```
Likelihood ratio test that no transformation is needed
                         LRT df       pval
LR test, lambda = (1) 4.303821  1 0.038027
```

The test still shows that we should transform the outcome variable. Let's try the suggested value of 0.59 from the first test.

```
summary(model.1a <- lm(I(polsyst_satis^.59) ~ strong_leader + ideology +
                       responsibility + confidence + hhfin_satis + age +
                       sex + edu, data = kenya_subset))

Call:
lm(formula = I(polsyst_satis^0.59) ~ strong_leader + ideology +
   responsibility + confidence + hhfin_satis + age + sex + edu,
   data = kenya_subset)

Residuals:
    Min      1Q  Median      3Q     Max
-2.1631 -0.6935  0.1223  0.6289  2.3298

Coefficients:
                Estimate Std. Error t value Pr(>|t|)
(Intercept)    1.5696167  0.1908827   8.223 5.57e-16 ***
strong_leader  0.0324398  0.0252237   1.286 0.198686
ideology       0.0621686  0.0099107   6.273 5.09e-10 ***
responsibility 0.0222442  0.0082078   2.710 0.006831 **
confidence     0.1039844  0.0265080   3.923 9.30e-05 ***
hhfin_satis    0.0543094  0.0100167   5.422 7.25e-08 ***
age            0.0004704  0.0026734   0.176 0.860346
sex           -0.0176991  0.0532379  -0.332 0.739611
edu           -0.1299792  0.0362683  -3.584 0.000353 ***
---
Signif. codes:  0 '***' 0.001 '**' 0.01 '*' 0.05 '.' 0.1 ' ' 1

Residual standard error: 0.8721 on 1096 degrees of freedom
```

```
(161 observations deleted due to missingness)
Multiple R-squared:  0.1125,    Adjusted R-squared:  0.106
F-statistic: 17.36 on 8 and 1096 DF,  p-value: < 2.2e-16
```

```
summary(powerTransform(model.1a))
bcPower Transformation to Normality
   Est Power Rounded Pwr Wald Lwr Bnd Wald Upr Bnd
Y1   1.0059          1      0.8558       1.1559


Likelihood ratio test that transformation parameter is equal to 0
 (log transformation)
                          LRT df       pval
LR test, lambda = (0) 175.3832  1 < 2.22e-16


Likelihood ratio test that no transformation is needed
                        LRT df      pval
LR test, lambda = (1) 0.00588056  1 0.93887
```

Terrific! The test shows there are no further transformations to be made to the outcome variable. The problem? How do we interpret these values? Since violating the normality assumption does not affect whether our estimates are BLUE, let's continue on our journey using the non-transformed version of `polsyst_satis`.

Multicollinearity

Next, we will test for multicollinearity in our model. Again, it is fairly rare to find actual multicollinearity, but testing for it is quick and easy, and it is good to know that we have no collinearity issues.

First, we will examine the correlations among the predictors as a quick and dirty test.[9] To clean up the correlation matrix, we'll include the `fashion()` function with the `correlate()` function from the `corrr` package and specify `decimals = 3`.

```
library(corrr)

kenya_subset %>%
  select(!polsyst_satis) %>%
  correlate(use = "complete.obs") %>%
  shave() %>%
  fashion(decimals = 3)


Correlation method: 'pearson'
Missing treated using: 'complete.obs'
```

---

[9]The `select()` function from the `dplyr` package does not work when the MASS package is loaded. Although we have not directly loaded the MASS package, the package is imported by the `lindia` package. Therefore, we need to detach both the `lindia` and MASS packages to get the `select()` function to work.

```
   term         strong_leader ideology responsibility confidence hhfin_satis age sex edu
1 strong_leader
2 ideology             .058
3 responsibility      -.032   .064
4 confidence           .119   .066      -.029
5 hhfin_satis          .114   .088       .073       .121
6 age                  .046  -.003      -.057       .037   -.040
7 sex                  .001   .068       .008       .011    .011     -.069
8 edu                 -.150  -.050       .091      -.145   -.001     -.125    -.119
```

We see all of the predictors are weakly correlated with one another, suggesting we probably don't have multicollinearity.

Now, let's carry out the formal variance inflation factor (VIF) test for multicollinearity.

```
vif(model.1)
  strong_leader        ideology responsibility     confidence    hhfin_satis
       1.048371        1.023057       1.021368       1.049072       1.041316
            age             sex            edu
       1.029926        1.027537       1.084253
```

Since none of the VIF values are near 10, we conclude that there is no multicollinearity in our model.

Outliers, Leverage, and Influential Data Points

Our final diagnostic tests involve looking for outliers, leverage, and influential data points. Again, we really only care whether there are any influential data points since they are outliers with leverage. As a reminder, we consider points whose residuals are ±2 standard deviations from 0 to be outliers. To assess points with high leverage, we need to calculate the cut-point for high leverage using the formula $2(k + 1)/n$. For our model, the calculation is:

```
(2*(8+1))/1105
[1] 0.01628959
```

Thus any data point with a hat value equal to or greater than 0.016 is consider to have high leverage. To assess the presence of influential data points, we check whether any point has a Cook's *d* value greater than 1.

Let's now check for outliers, points with high leverage, and influential data points.

```
influenceIndexPlot(model.1,
                   vars = c("Studentized","hat","Cook"))
```

Diagnostic Plots

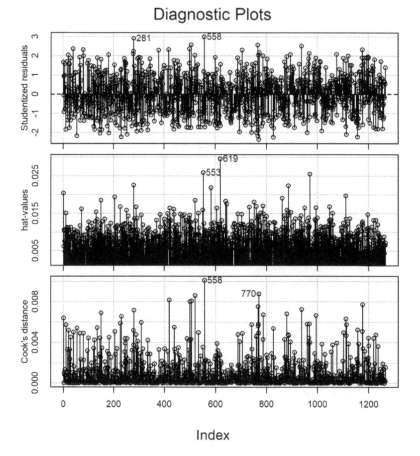

Index

We see that there a number of outliers – but nothing severe – and a handful of points with leverage. However, none of the points have a high Cook's *d* value, indicating that there are no influential data points. Thus, we do not need to make any corrections to our data or model.

Even though we do not have any influential data points, it can be instructive, and fun, to examine certain points with higher Cook's *d* values. Let's take a look at observation 558, which is one of the points identified in our Cook's *d* plot.

```
kenya_subset %>%
  slice(c(558))
# A tibble: 1 x 9
  polsyst_satis strong_leader ideology responsibility confidence hhfin_
satis
        <dbl>         <dbl>    <dbl>          <dbl>      <dbl>    <dbl>
1          10             1        1              1          1        1
# ... with 3 more variables: age <dbl>, sex <dbl>, edu <dbl>
```

This respondent is a 24-year-old woman with a moderate amount of education who places herself at the leftmost ideological position. She is completely satisfied with the political system, thinks an authoritarian regime would be very bad, thinks the government should do more to make sure everyone is provided for, has no confidence in the national government, and is dissatisfied with her household financial situation. This respondent might stand out because she has the lowest value on five predictors and the highest value for the outcome variable. But substantively there is nothing quirky.

Let's remove the observation and rerun our results.

```
test <- kenya_subset %>%
  slice(-c(558))
```

```
summary(model.1b <-lm(polsyst_satis ~ strong_leader + ideology +
        responsibility + confidence + hhfin_satis + age + sex + edu,
        data = test))
```

```
Call:
lm(formula = polsyst_satis ~ strong_leader + ideology + responsibility +
    confidence + hhfin_satis + age + sex + edu, data = test)

Residuals:
    Min      1Q  Median      3Q     Max
-6.1230 -2.0106  0.0259  1.7975  7.5399

Coefficients:
                Estimate Std. Error t value Pr(>|t|)
(Intercept)     2.188514   0.567575   3.856 0.000122 ***
strong_leader   0.117202   0.074952   1.564 0.118180
ideology        0.186070   0.029459   6.316 3.89e-10 ***
responsibility  0.070633   0.024386   2.896 0.003849 **
confidence      0.335878   0.078760   4.265 2.18e-05 ***
hhfin_satis     0.160772   0.029758   5.403 8.05e-08 ***
age             0.001922   0.007940   0.242 0.808814
sex            -0.045039   0.158179  -0.285 0.775903
edu            -0.406434   0.107703  -3.774 0.000169 ***
---
Signif. codes:  0 '***' 0.001 '**' 0.01 '*' 0.05 '.' 0.1 ' ' 1

Residual standard error: 2.59 on 1095 degrees of freedom
  (161 observations deleted due to missingness)
Multiple R-squared:  0.119, Adjusted R-squared:  0.1125
F-statistic: 18.48 on 8 and 1095 DF,  p-value: < 2.2e-16
coeftest(model.1b, vcov = vcovHC)
```

```
t test of coefficients:

                Estimate Std. Error t value  Pr(>|t|)
(Intercept)    2.1885142  0.5776284  3.7888 0.0001596 ***
strong_leader  0.1172015  0.0782487  1.4978 0.1344716
ideology       0.1860699  0.0340017  5.4724 5.503e-08 ***
```

```
responsibility  0.0706326  0.0271687   2.5998 0.0094540 **
confidence      0.3358783  0.0844347   3.9780 7.408e-05 ***
hhfin_satis     0.1607716  0.0346452   4.6405 3.895e-06 ***
age             0.0019216  0.0082749   0.2322 0.8164088
sex            -0.0450388  0.1596509  -0.2821 0.7779141
edu            -0.4064337  0.1080878  -3.7602 0.0001787 ***
---
Signif. codes:  0 '***' 0.001 '**' 0.01 '*' 0.05 '.' 0.1 ' ' 1
```

We see that the same predictors are statistically significant and the coefficients are essentially the same. The R^2 and adjusted R^2 values have slightly improved, which indicates that our model is fitting the data a wee bit better without this observation, though not enough to justify removing the observation.

Interpretations and Discussion of Model

Now that we have performed diagnostics on our model, identified certain problems, and examined potential solutions, we are ready to engage in coefficient interpretations and discussion of the results; we already discussed model evaluation. We can use the results with or without robust standard errors since the same predictors are statistically significant and the coefficients are the same.

Let's refresh our memories about `model.1` using the `tidy()` function from `tidymodels`. This function prints the regression results without the model evaluation information.

```
library(tidymodels)
tidy(model.1)
# A tibble: 9 x 5
  term            estimate std.error statistic  p.value
  <chr>              <dbl>     <dbl>     <dbl>    <dbl>
1 (Intercept)      2.28      0.569      4.00   6.78e- 5
2 strong_leader    0.109     0.0752     1.45   1.47e- 1
3 ideology         0.182     0.0295     6.17   9.70e-10
4 responsibility   0.0683    0.0245     2.79   5.33e- 3
5 confidence       0.328     0.0790     4.15   3.54e- 5
6 hhfin_satis      0.158     0.0299     5.30   1.42e- 7
7 age              0.00147   0.00797    0.185  8.53e- 1
8 sex             -0.0294    0.159     -0.185  8.53e- 1
9 edu             -0.408     0.108     -3.78   1.67e- 4
```

Again, we find that `ideology`, `responsibility`, `confidence`, and `hhfin_satis` are statistically significant and have a positive effect on `polsyst_satis`, while `edu` has statistically significant and negative effect on `polsyst_satis`. The other predictors are not statistically significant.

How do these results correspond with our five hypotheses from earlier in the chapter? Hypothesis 1 (for `strong_leader`) is not correct, but the rest of our hypotheses have statistical merit in terms of both statistical significance and the expected direction of the effect. Let's go through each significant predictor, including education, and give a coefficient interpretation and brief discussion.[10]

First, *for a one-unit increase in political ideology, respondents' satisfaction with the current political system is expected to increase by 0.182 (units)*. Thus, conservative respondents are expected to be more satisfied with the current political system in Kenya than liberal respondents. Conservatives tend to favour the status quo more than liberals and thus may report greater satisfaction with the current political system as it is what's known and predictable.

Second, *for a one-unit increase towards more of a belief in individual responsibility, respondents' satisfaction with the current political system is expected to increase by 0.068 (units)*. This means that respondents who believe that individuals should take more responsibility for providing for themselves are expected to have higher satisfaction with the current political system in Kenya than respondents who think the government should be doing more. Although Kenya has a higher quality of life than many African countries, the Kenyan government still struggles, for numerous reasons, to ensure everyone is taken care of. In truth, one could argue that every government in the world struggles with this. People who believe that individuals should be responsible for their own welfare may not want the government to provide social welfare (e.g., libertarians) and thus may be more satisfied with a government that does not offer services for those in poverty.

Third, *for a one-unit increase in confidence in the national government, respondents' satisfaction with the current political system is expected to increase by 0.328 (units)*. Intuitively, this makes sense. Respondents with greater confidence in the government are expected to exhibit greater satisfaction with the current political system. It would be weird if this wasn't the case.

Fourth, *for a one-unit increase in satisfaction with household finances, respondents' satisfaction with the current political system is expected to increase by 0.158 (units)*. This result has a similar status-quo flavour to the result for ideology. Essentially, people who are financially satisfied, typically wealthier individuals who are more economically secure, tend to prefer the status quo as 'things are good for them'. Hence, they exhibit greater satisfaction with the current political system that allows them to keep their economic status.

Lastly, *for a one-unit increase in education level, respondents' satisfaction with the current political system is expected to decrease by 0.408 (units)*. We are using the collapsed three-category version of respondents' education level, and so a one-unit increase is a fairly large step in the level of education. This result makes sense since educated individuals may have a better understanding of the government's problems and failings, and how Kenyan democracy compares to democracies in other countries.

Let's now extend our analysis and examine what factors explain levels of support for an authoritarian regime in Kenya.

---

[10]With the massive caveat that I don't have substantive expertise in Kenyan politics or society, and thus I'm unable to provide much insight in the discussion.

EXPLAINING LEVELS OF SUPPORT FOR AUTHORITARIAN REGIMES IN KENYA

We have already laid the groundwork for performing ordered logit regression to explain respondents' levels of support for authoritarian regimes. Before we hop off to run the analysis, let's create a visualisation to provide an initial understanding of the relationship between our outcome variable `strong_leader` and our predictor `confidence`; we previously visualised the relationship between `strong_leader` and `polsyst_satis`, though with the variable roles flipped.

Prior to our code, we need to detach the `car` package as its `recode()` function conflicts with the `recode()` function from `dplyr`. We can detach `car` simply by unchecking the box next to `car` in the `Packages` window in RStudio or by running the following code:

```r
detach("package:car", unload = TRUE)


kenya_subset %>%
  filter(!is.na(strong_leader) & !is.na(confidence)) %>%
  mutate(confidence = as_factor(confidence),
         confidence = recode(confidence,
            `1` = "None At All",
            `2` = "Not Very Much",
            `3` = "Quite A Lot",
            `4` = "A Great Deal"),
         strong_leader = recode(strong_leader,
            `1` = "Very Bad",
            `2` = "Fairly Bad",
            `3` = "Fairly Good",
            `4` = "Very Good")) %>%
ggplot() +
  geom_bar(mapping = aes(x = strong_leader, y = ..prop..,
                         group = confidence, fill = confidence),
                         stat = "count", position = "dodge") +
  labs(title = "Support for Authoritarian Regime",
       subtitle = "by Confidence in National Government",
       x = "Authoritarian Regime",
       fill = "Govt Confidence", y="Percent") +
  scale_x_discrete(guide = guide_axis(angle = 45)) +
  scale_y_continuous(labels = percent_format()) +
  theme_minimal() +
  scale_fill_viridis_d()
```

Support for Authoritarian Regime
by Confidence in National Government

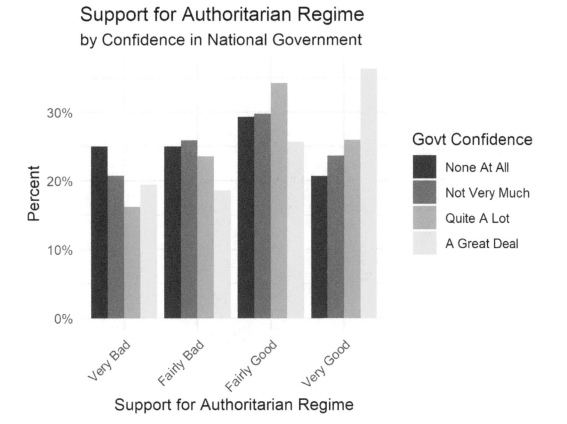

We don't find a great deal of variation in support for an authoritarian regime between different levels of confidence in the national government. The most striking result is that among respondents who have 'a great deal' of confidence in the national government, roughly 36% said an authoritarian regime would be 'very good' for Kenya. This is a bit odd. It is possible that these respondents are considering the national government in a more abstract way and thus they think that an authoritarian regime, which by definition centralises power typically in the national government, would be a good thing for the country.

Now let's have a go at the ordered logit regression model. Following the approach used in Chapter 13, we'll use the same predictors as previously, as well as `polsyst_satis`, to analyse our outcome variable `strong_leader`. We need to first load the MASS package and create an ordered factor version of `strong_leader` to use in the `polr()` function. Let's name this ordered version `strldr_ordfac`. Let's save our regression results as `model.2` and plot the coefficients and confidence intervals using the `ggcoef_model()` function from the GGally package.

```
library(MASS)

kenya_subset <- kenya_subset %>%
  mutate(strldr_ordfac = ordered(as_factor(strong_leader)))

summary(model.2 <- polr(strldr_ordfac ~ polsyst_satis + ideology +
                  responsibility + confidence + hhfin_satis +
                  age + sex + edu, method = "logistic",
                  data = kenya_subset))
Call:
polr(formula = strldr_ordfac ~ polsyst_satis + ideology + responsibility +
    confidence + hhfin_satis + age + sex + edu, data = kenya_subset,
    method = "logistic")

Coefficients:
                    Value Std. Error t value
polsyst_satis    0.036409   0.021426  1.6993
ideology         0.020010   0.021467  0.9321
responsibility  -0.020150   0.017609 -1.1443
confidence       0.147223   0.055628  2.6465
hhfin_satis      0.066368   0.021417  3.0989
age              0.005539   0.005525  1.0024
sex             -0.056420   0.110189 -0.5120
edu             -0.301883   0.075515 -3.9977


Intercepts:
     Value    Std. Error t value
1|2 -1.0735   0.3887     -2.7620
2|3  0.1130   0.3874      0.2917
3|4  1.5116   0.3900      3.8759


Residual Deviance: 2979.306
AIC: 3001.306
(161 observations deleted due to missingness)

ggcoef_model(model.2,
              show_p_values = FALSE,
              signif_stars = FALSE) +
  labs(title = "Predicting Support for a Strong Leader",
       x = "Ordered Logit Coefficients")
```

Again, the output doesn't provide *p*-values or *s, but we can use the *t*-values to determine which predictors are statistically significant. We see that confidence, hhfin_satis, and edu are statistically significant predictors of support for an authoritarian regime. Additionally, polsyst_satis is statistically significant at the 0.10 probability level, but let's only focus on the predictors statistically significant at the 0.05 probability level.

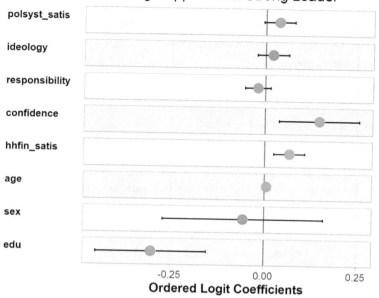

Predicting Support for a Strong Leader

Ordered Logit Coefficients

Both `confidence` and `hhfin_satis` have positive coefficients, which means as respondents have greater confidence in the national government or have greater satisfaction with their household financial situation, they are expected to be more supportive of an authoritarian regime. Education (`edu`) has a negative coefficient, indicating that as respondents' education level increases, they are expected to be less supportive of an authoritarian regime.

Before we provide interpretations of the coefficients and a substantive discussion, we will test the parallel regression assumption (PRA) using the `brant()` function from the `brant` package.

```
library(brant)
brant(model.2)
```

Test for	X2	df	probability
Omnibus	42.36	16	0
polsyst_satis	11.21	2	0
ideology	3.73	2	0.15
responsibility	2.28	2	0.32
confidence	6.64	2	0.04
hhfin_satis	6.46	2	0.04
age	0	2	1
sex	4.18	2	0.12
edu	2.7	2	0.26

H0: Parallel Regression Assumption holds

This is where the 'party foul' music comes in. Since the *p*-value for `Omnibus` is below 0.05, our model fails the PRA. Violating the PRA means that the coefficient estimates are inconsistent and thus we can't trust our results. We see that the culprits for the malfeasance are `polsyst_satis`, `confidence`, and `hhfin_satis`. What should we do?

We have three possible options.

1   We can use multinomial logit regression instead of ordered logit regression. However, our outcome variable `strldr_ordfac` is clearly ordered and thus multinomial logit regression is probably not the best option (McFadden 1974).
2   We can use generalised ordered logit regression. This approach relaxes the PRA for predictors that violated the PRA in the ordered logit regression.
3   We can ignore that we violated PRA. Not the most satisfying option, but, again, researchers commonly do this for outcome variables that are clearly ordered.

For the sake of simplicity, let's choose option 3 and move forward to interpretations.

Interpreting Coefficients

As we saw in Chapter 13, we can't directly interpret ordered logit coefficients as we do in linear regression. Below we'll use the odds ratio as a percentage and create predicted probability plots for the statistically significant predictors.

Odds Ratio

```
(exp(model.2$coefficients)-1)*100
   polsyst_satis       ideology responsibility       confidence      hhfin_satis
       3.7080153      2.0211241     -1.9948696       15.8611837        6.8619622
             age            sex            edu
       0.5553977     -5.4857777    -26.0575783
```

First, *for a one-unit increase in confidence in the national government, the odds of respondents' having more support for an authoritarian regime are expected to increase by 15.86%.* As speculated in the earlier bar plot discussion, these respondents are possibly associating the national government with a government that centralises and consolidates power like an authoritarian regime. But this is just conjecture.

Second, *for a one-unit increase in satisfaction with household finances, the odds of respondents having more support for an authoritarian regime are expected to increase by 6.86%.* Although an authoritarian regime would represent a change in the political system's status quo, wealthier individuals may prefer a government that is unlikely to change due to the 'whims' of an election. However, the exact nature of the authoritarian regime would probably impact the level of support granted by the wealthy. For example, a regime that nationalises and centrally controls industry might not find support from wealthy business people.

Third, *for a one-unit increase in education level, the odds of respondents having more support for an authoritarian regime are expected to decrease by 26.06%*. Educated individuals, particularly those with college degrees, are normally not big fans of authoritarian regimes – at least right-wing versions of authoritarian regimes. It is more likely that educated individuals would be most in favour of democratic systems with free and fair elections, and protected civil rights and liberties.

Plotting Predicted Probabilities

Let's create a predicted probability plot for each of our statistically significant predictors using ggpredict() and ggplot(). We will need to make a few tweaks to the code we used in Chapter 13 to produce good-looking plots for confidence and edu. Specifically, in Chapter 13, we used the geom_smooth() function instead of the geom_line() function in order to create smooth predicted probability lines for the outcome variable categories. However, if we use geom_smooth() here to plot confidence and edu, we get a bunch of warnings and plots with weird squiggly lines; this appears to be due to the smaller number of categories for these two variables since geom_smooth() works fine for hhfin_satis. Hence, we'll use geom_line() for confidence and edu, and accept the sharp turns in the lines, and use geom_smooth() for hhfin_satis and enjoy the smoother lines.

First, we'll plot the predicted probabilities for confidence and strong_leader.

```
library(ggeffects)

ggpredict(model.2, terms = "confidence") %>%
  mutate(response.level = ordered(as_factor(response.level)),
         response.level = recode(response.level,
                          `1` = "Very Bad",
                          `2` = "Fairly Bad",
                          `3` = "Fairly Good",
                          `4` = "Very Good")) %>%
ggplot(mapping = aes(x = x, y = predicted, colour = response.level)) +
  geom_line(size = 1.25) +
  scale_x_continuous(limits = c(1,4), breaks = c(1:4)) +
  labs(title = "Predicted Probabilities of Authoritarian Regime Support",
       x = "Confidence in the National Government",
       y = "Predicted Probability") +
  guides(colour = guide_legend(title = "Auth. Regime")) +
  theme_minimal() +
  theme(
    plot.title = element_text(size = 12)
  ) +
  scale_colour_viridis_d()
```

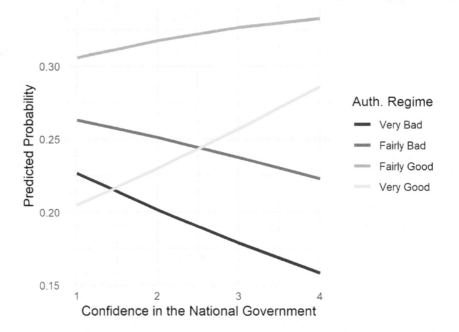

Predicted Probabilities of Authoritarian Regime Support

We see that as confidence in the national government increases, the predicted probability of responding that an authoritarian regime would be 'fairly good' or 'very good' increases, while the predicted probability of responding that an authoritarian regime would be 'fairly bad' or 'very bad' decreases.

Next, we'll plot the predicted probabilities for `hhfin_satis` and `strong_leader`.

```
ggpredict(model.2, terms = "hhfin_satis") %>%
  mutate(response.level = ordered(as_factor(response.level)),
         response.level = recode(response.level,
               `1` = "Very Bad",
               `2` = "Fairly Bad",
               `3` = "Fairly Good",
               `4` = "Very Good")) %>%
ggplot(mapping = aes(x = x, y = predicted, colour = response.level)) +
  geom_smooth(se = FALSE, size = 1.25) +
  scale_x_continuous(limits = c(1,10), breaks = c(1:10)) +
  labs(title = "Predicted Probabilities of Authoritarian Regime Support",
       x = "Household Financial Satisfaction",
       y = "Predicted Probability") +
  guides(colour = guide_legend(title = "Auth. Regime")) +
  theme_minimal() +
  theme(
    plot.title = element_text(size = 12)
  ) +
  scale_colour_viridis_d()
```

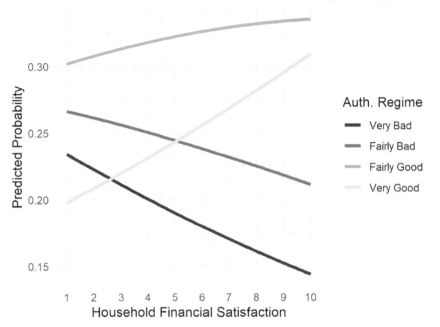

Predicted Probabilities of Authoritarian Regime Support

We observe a similar pattern of changes in predicted probabilities for respondents' level of satisfaction with their household financial situation to that for confidence in the national government. Specifically, as satisfaction with respondents' household financial situation increases, the predicted probability of responding that an authoritarian regime would be 'fairly good' or 'very good' increases, while the predicted probability of responding that an authoritarian regime would be 'fairly bad' or 'very bad' decreases. Further, the predicted probability of 'very good' has a fairly steep increase as we move from the lowest to highest value on household financial satisfaction.

Lastly, we'll plot the predicted probabilities for edu and strong_leader.

```r
ggpredict(model.2, terms = "edu") %>%
  mutate(response.level = ordered(as_factor(response.level)),
         response.level = recode(response.level,
                `1` = "Very Bad",
                `2` = "Fairly Bad",
                `3` = "Fairly Good",
                `4` = "Very Good")) %>%
ggplot(mapping = aes(x = x, y = predicted, colour = response.level)) +
  geom_line(size = 1.25) +
  scale_x_continuous(limits = c(1,3), breaks = c(1:3)) +
  labs(title = "Predicted Probabilities of Authoritarian Regime Support",
       x = "Education Level", y = "Predicted Probability") +
  guides(colour = guide_legend(title = "Auth. Regime")) +
  theme_minimal() +
  theme(
```

```
    plot.title = element_text(size = 12)
) +
scale_colour_viridis_d()
```

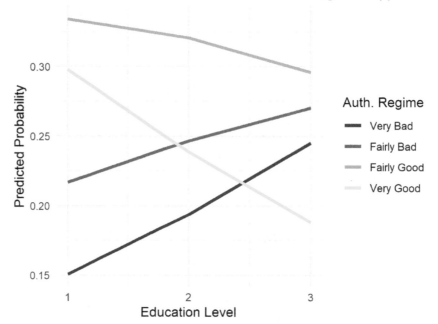

The predicted probability lines in this plot diverge from the previous plots, reflecting education's negative coefficient. We see that as education level increases the predicted probability of responding that an authoritarian regime would be 'fairly good' or 'very good' decreases, while the predicted probability of responding that an authoritarian regime would be 'fairly bad' or 'very bad' increases. (Notice the ugly bends in the lines when education equals 2. Again, this is due to using the geom_line() function.)

CONCLUSION

Through this moderately long and, hopefully, only moderately winding chapter, we have gone through many of the steps a quantitative social scientist takes when tackling a new research project.[11] This chapter has allowed us to practise the skills we learned in the previous 14 chapters and see how we link the different techniques to examine and understand a dataset and statistical models. Hopefully, having gone through this book and this chapter in particular, you are more confident in successfully carrying out your own QSS research project in R.

---

[11]This chapter would still be deficient if we tried to turn it into a journal article.

▬▬▬ R Packages Used in This Chapter ▬▬▬

- `brant`
- `car`
- `corrr`
- `dplyr` (loaded with `tidyverse`)
- `forcats` (loaded with `tidyverse`)
- `GGally`
- `ggeffects`
- `ggplot2` (loaded with `tidyverse`)
- `lindia`
- `lmtest`
- `MASS`
- `pillar` (loaded with `tidyverse`)
- `readxl`
- `sandwich`
- `scales`
- `tidymodels`
- `tidyselect` (loaded with `tidyverse`)
- `tidyverse`

▬▬▬ R Functions Used in This Chapter ▬▬▬

- `across()` - apply a function to multiple columns using `dplyr` package
- `as_factor()` - convert variable to factor using `haven` or `forcats` package
- `as.numeric()` - convert variable to numeric
- `bptest()` - Breusch–Pagan test for heteroscedasticity using `lmtest` package
- `brant()` - Brant test for parallel regression assumption using `brant` package
- `c()` - concatenate
- `coeftest()` - linear regression with robust standard errors using `lmtest` package
- `correlate()` - correlation analysis using `corrr` package
- `count()` - count the number of unique values of a variable or variables using `dplyr` package
- `everything()` - select all variables using `tidyselect` package
- `exp()` - compute exponential value
- `fct_rev()` - reverse values of a factor variable using `forcats` package
- `filter()` - subset data based on variables' values using `dplyr` package
- `geom_bar()` - ggplot2 bar plot
- `geom_line()` - ggplot2 line
- `geom_smooth()` - ggplot2 linear and nonlinear lines
- `gg_qqplot()` - Q-Q plot using `lindia` package
- `gg_resfitted()` - residuals by fitted values plot using `lindia` package
- `gg_reshist()` - histogram of residuals using `lindia` package
- `ggcoef_model()` - regression coefficient plot using `GGally` package
- `ggplot()` - base layer for `ggplot2`
- `ggpredict()` - adjusted predictions for regression models using `ggeffects` package

(Continued)

- `glimpse()` - quick view of data using `pillar` package
- `guide_axis()` - axis aesthetics using `ggplot2` package
- `guide_legend()` - legend aesthetics using `ggplot2` package
- `guides()` - axes and legend aesthetics using `ggplot2` package
- `I()` - transform variable without creating a new variable
- `influenceIndexPlot()` - outliers, leverage, influential data points plot using `car` package
- `is.na()` - check for missing values (NAs) in variables
- `labs()` - ggplot2 labels
- `lm()` - linear regression model
- `mean()` - mean
- `median()` - median
- `mutate()` - recode variables using `dplyr` package
- `ordered()` - order a factor variable
- `percent_format()` - add percentages to plot using `scales` package
- `polr()` - ordered logit and probit models using `MASS` package
- `powerTransform()` - Box-Cox test for transforming outcome variable using `car` package
- `read_xlsx()` - read in an Excel data file using `readxl` package
- `recode()` - recode variable using `dplyr` package
- `rename()` - rename variables using `dplyr` package
- `resettest()` - Ramsey RESET test for functional form using `lmtest` package
- `replace()` - replace existing values with new values
- `scale_colour_viridis_d()` - viridis colour scale for discrete variables using `ggplot2` package
- `scale_x_continuous()` - *x*-axis aesthetics for continuous variables
- `scale_x_discrete()` - *x*-axis aesthetics for discrete variables
- `scale_y_continuous()` - *y*-axis aesthetics for continuous variables
- `sd()` - standard deviation
- `select()` - subset data based on variables using `dplyr` package
- `shapiro.test()` - Shapiro-Wilk normality test
- `shave()` - remove lower or upper triangle of correlation matrix using `corrr` package
- `slice()` - subset rows using `dplyr` package
- `summary()` - summarise object
- `theme_bw()` - black-and-white `ggplot2` theme
- `theme_minimal()` - minimal `ggplot2` theme
- `tidy()` - creates tidy tibble using `broom` package
- `vif()` - variance inflation factor test using `car` package

REFERENCES

Andersen, Robert, and David A. Armstrong II. (2022) *Presenting Statistical Results Effectively.* London: Sage.

Bollen, Kenneth A., and Jackman, Robert W. (1990) 'Regression diagnostics: An expository treatment of outliers and influential cases', in Fox, John, and Long, J. Scott (eds.), *Modern Methods of Data Analysis.* pp. 275–291. Newbury Park, CA: Sage.

Brant, R. (1990) 'Assessing proportionality in the proportional odds model for ordinal logistic regression', *Biometrics, 46*: 1171–1178.

Cameron, A. Colin and Trivedi, Pravin K. (2005) *Microeconometrics: Methods and Applications.* Cambridge: Cambridge University Press.

Cameron, A. Colin and Trivedi, Pravin K. (2013) *Regression Analysis of Count Data*, 2nd edition. Cambridge: Cambridge University Press.

Carey, John M., Nyhan, Brendan, Valentino, Benjamin and Liu, Mingnan (2016) 'An inflated view of the facts? How preferences and predispositions shape conspiracy beliefs about the Deflategate scandal', *Research & Politics, 3*(3).

Desmarais, Bruce A. and Harden, Jeffrey J. (2013) 'Testing for zero inflation in count models: Bias correction for the Vuong test', Stata Journal, 13(4): 810–835.

Ezekiel, Mordecai (1930) 'The sampling variability of linear and curvilinear regressions: A first approximation to the reliability of the results secured by the graphic "successive approximation" method', *Annals of Mathematic Statistics, 1*: 275–315.

Fabozzi, Frank J., Focardi, Sergio M., Rachev, Svetlozar T. and Arshanapalli, Bala G. (2014) *The Basics of Financial Econometrics.* Hoboken, NJ: John Wiley & Sons.

Faraway, Julian J. (2014) *Linear Models with R*, 2nd edition. Boca Raton, FL: Chapman & Hall/CRC.

Faraway, Julian J. (2016) *Extending the Linear Model with R*, 2nd edition. Boca Raton, FL: CRC.

Field, Andy, Miles, Jeremy and Field, Zoë (2011) *Discovering Statistics Using R.* London: Sage.

Fisher, Ronald A. (1924) 'The influence of rainfall on the yield of wheat at Rothamsted', *Philosophical Transactions of the Royal Society of London, Series B, 213*: 89–142.

Fogarty, Brian J., Curtis, Jessica, Gouzien, Patricia Frances, Kimball, David C. and Vorst, Eric C. (2015) 'News attention to voter fraud in the 2008 and 2012 US elections', *Research & Politics, 2*(2). http:// rap.sagepub.com/content/sprap/2/2/2053168015587156.full.pdf

Fox, John (2002) *An R and S-Plus Companion to Applied Regression.* Thousand Oaks, CA: Sage.

Fox, John (1991) *Regression Diagnostics.* Thousand Oaks, CA: Sage.

Fox, John and Weisberg, Sanford. (2018) *An R Companion to Applied Regression*, 3rd edition. Thousand Oaks, CA: Sage.

Freedom House (2021) 'Kenya', *Freedom in the World 2021.* https://freedomhouse.org/country/kenya/freedom-world/2021

Gandrud, Christopher (2020) *Reproducible Research with R and RStudio.* Boca Raton, FL: Chapman and Hall/CRC.

Gayle, Vernon and Lambert, Paul S. (2017) 'The workflow: A practical guide to producing accurate, efficient, transparent and reproducible social survey data analysis' National Centre for Research Methods, Working Paper 1/17.

Gelman, Andrew (2007) 'Struggles with survey weighting and regression modeling', *Statistical Science, 22*: 153–164.

Gelman, Andrew and Hill, Jennifer (2007) *Data Analysis Using Regression and Multilevel/Hierarchial Models*. Cambridge: Cambridge University Press.

Greene, William H. (2017) *Econometric Analysis*, 8th edition. New York: Pearson.

Groves, Robert M., Fowler, Jr., Floyd J., Couper, Mick P., Lepkowski, James M., Singer, Eleanor and Tourangeau, Roger (2009) *Survey Methodology*, 2nd edition. New York: Wiley.

Haerpfer, C., Inglehart, R., Moreno, A., Welzel, C., Kizilova, K., Diez-Medrano J., M. Lagos, P. Norris, E. Ponarin & B. Puranen (eds.). 2022. World Values Survey: Round Seven – Country-Pooled Datafile Version 4.0. Madrid, Spain & Vienna, Austria: JD Systems Institute & WVSA Secretariat. doi:10.14281/18241.18.

Hardin, James W., and Joseph M. Hilbe (2012) *Generalized Linear Models and Extensions*, 3rd edition. College Station, TX: Stata Press.

Harris, Jenine K. (2020) *Statistics with R: Solving Problems Using Real-World Data*. Thousand Oaks, CA: Sage Publications.

Hausman, Jerry, and McFadden, Daniel. (1984) 'Specification tests for the multinomial logit models', *Econometrica, 52*: 1219–1240.

Heeringa, Steven G., West, Brady T. and Berglund, Patricia A. (2017) *Applied Survey Data Analysis*, 2nd edition. Boca Raton, FL: Chapman and Hall/CRC.

Hernán, Miguel A., and Robins, James M. (2023) *Causal Inference: What If*. Boca Raton, FL: Chapman and Hall/CRC.

Hilbe, Joseph M. (2014) *Modeling Count Data*. Cambridge: Cambridge University Press.

Imai, Kosuke (2017) *A First Course in Quantitative Social Science*. Princeton, NJ: Princeton University Press.

Ismay, Chester and Kim, Albert Y. (2019) *Statistical Inference via Data Science*. Boca Raton, FL: Chapman and Hall/CRC.

Kabacoff, Roger I. (2022) *R in Action*, 3rd edition. Shelter Island, NY: Manning Publications.

Karol, David. and Miguel, Edward. (2007) 'The electoral cost of war: Iraq casualties and the 2004 U.S. presidential election', *Journal of Politics, 69*: 633–648.

Kearney, Michael W. (2019) 'rtweet: Collecting and analyzing Twitter data', *Journal of Open Source Software, 42*: 18–29.

King, Gary (1988) 'Statistical models for political science event counts: Bias in conventional procedures and evidence for the exponential Poisson regression model', *American Journal of Political Science, 32*: 838–863.

King, Gary, Keohane, Robert O. and Verba, Sidney (1994) *Designing Social Inquiry*. Princeton, NJ: Princeton University Press.

Klar, Samara, Krupnikov, Yanna, Ryan, John Barry, Searles, Kathleen, Shmargad, Yotam (2020) 'Using social media to promote academic research: Identifying the benefits of Twitter for sharing academic work', *PLoS ONE, 15*: e0229446. https://doi.org/10.1371/journal.pone.0229446.

Kleiber, Christian and Zeileis, Achim (2008) *Applied Econometrics Using R*. New York: Springer.

Knief, Ulrich, and Forstmeier, Wolfgang (2021) 'Violating the normality assumption may be the lesser of two evils', *Behavior Research Methods, 15*: 2576–2590.

Kuhn, Max, and Silge, Julia (2022) *Tidy Modeling with R*. Sebastopol, CA: O'Reilly Media.

Kmenta, Jan (1997) *Elements of Econometrics*, 2nd edition. Ann Arbor: University of Michigan Press.

Lafaye de Micheaux, Pierre, Drouilhet, Rémy and Liquet, Benoît (2013) *The R Software*. New York: Springer.

Lambert, Ben (2018) *A Student's Guide to Bayesian Statistics*. London: Sage.

Levitt, Steven D. and Dubner, Stephen J. (2006) *Freakonomics: A Rogue Economist Explores the Hidden Side of Everything*. London: Penguin.

Lewis-Beck, Michael S., Bryman, Alan and Liao, Tim Futing (2004) 'Substantive significance', *The SAGE Encyclopedia of Social Science Research Methods*. 1099-1100. Thousand Oaks, CA: Sage.

Long, J. Scott and Freese, Jeremy (2014) *Regression Models for Categorical Dependent Variables Using Stata*, 3rd edition, College Station, TX: Stata Press.

Liu, Xing (2022) *Categorical Data Analysis and Multilevel Modeling Using R*. Thousand Oaks, CA: Sage.

Long, J. Scott (1997) *Regression Models for Categorical and Limited Dependent Variables*. Thousand Oaks, CA: Sage.

Long, J.D., and Teetor, Paul (2019) *R Cookbook*, 2nd edition. Sebastopol, CA: O'Reilly Media.

Lumley, Thomas, Dieh, Paula, Emerson, Scott and Chen, Lu (2002) 'The importance of the normality assumption in large public health data sets', *Annual Review of Public Health, 23*: 151–169.

Lynch, Scott M. (2013) *Using Statistics in Social Research*. New York: Springer.

McCullagh, Peter (1980) 'Regression models for ordinal data', *Journal of the Royal Statistical Society: Series B, 42*: 109–127.

McFadden, Daniel (1974) 'Conditional Logit Analysis of Qualitative Choice Behavior', Institute for Urban and Regional Development, University of California.

McKelvey, Richard D. and Zavoina, William (1975) 'A statistical model for the analysis of ordinal level dependent variables', *The Journal of Mathematical Sociology, 4*: 103–120.

Pollock, Philip H., III (2015) *The Essentials of Political Analysis*. Washington, DC: CQ Press.

Ramsey, James B. (1969) 'Tests for specification errors in classical linear least squares regression analysis', *Journal of the Royal Statistical Society, Series B, 31*(2): 350–371.

Ryan, Thomas P. (2009) *Modern Regression Methods*, 2nd edition. Hoboken, NJ: Wiley.

Kuhn, Max and Silge, Julia (2022) *Tidy Modeling with R*. O'Reilly Media.

Tintner, Gerhard (1944) 'An application of the variate difference method to multiple regression', *Econometrica, 12*: 97–113.

Tufte, Edward R. (2001) *The Visual Display of Quantitative Information*. Cheshire, CT: Graphics Press.

Verbeek, Marno (2004) *A Guide to Modern Econometrics*, 2nd edition. Chichester: John Wiley & Sons.

Vuong, Quang H. (1989) 'Likelihood ratio tests for model selection and non-nested hypotheses', *Econometrica, 57*: 307–333.

Walker, Kyle (2022) *Analyzing US Census Data: Methods, Maps, and Models in R*. Boca Raton, FL: Chapman and Hall/CRC.

Wasserstein, Ronald L. and Lazar, Nicole A. (2016) 'The ASA's statement on p-values: Context, process, and purpose', *American Statistician, 70*: 129–133.

Weisburd, David and Britt, Chester (2007) *Statistics in Criminal Justice*. New York: Springer.

Wendzel, Julius T. (1936) 'The mill demand for wool and inter-textile competition', *Review of Economics and Statistics, 18*: 172–182.

Wickham, Hadley (2022) *ggplot2: Elegant Graphics for Analysis*, 3rd edition. New York: Springer.

Wickham, Hadley and Grolemund, Garrett (2017) *R for Data Science*. Sebastopol, CA: O'Reilly.

Wickham, Hadley, Mara Averick, Jennifer Bryan, Winston Chang, Lucy McGowan, Romain François, Garrett Grolemund, et al. (2019) 'Welcome to the Tidyverse', *Journal of Open Source Software 4*: 1686. https://doi.org/10.21105/joss.01686.

Wilke, Claus O. (2019) *Fundamentals of Data Visualization: A Primer on Making Informative and Compelling Figures*. Sebastopol, CA: O'Reilly Media.

Wong, Raymond Sin-Kwok (2010) *Association Measures*. London: Sage. (Little Green Book on Sage Research Methods website.)

INDEX

Printed in the USA
CPSIA information can be obtained
at www.ICGtesting.com
JSHW061732291123
52807JS00002B/5

9 781529 790450